CW00733161

'Dr El-Agraa's book represents a gold o[ ]
economics that combines elements of
economy, statistical analysis, and institu
particular theme running throughout the
than overt, involving the economic pros and cons or the various political compromises that have inevitably been made in the creation of
the Union, and in particular in the roles to be played by the individual
members. It also takes this further by considering the possible paths
forward within an ever-changing internal and external environment.
Over the years the former European Coal and Steel Community has
transmogrified into the world's largest economic unit, involving over
500 million people, and the author provides explanations for this, and
for why it has largely been encouraged by outsiders. But it also sets this
creation within larger economic changes that have seen the end of the
Soviet Union and the rise of new mega-economic superpowers such as
China, and more general trends in globalization. Thus he places the
appropriate joint emphasis on internal economic integration within
the EU, and the broader, global economic integration process that have
been taking place. The book is an important addition to the study of the
political economy of market structures and institutional challenges that
underlie the ultimate outcomes. Europe is the central theme, but the
analysis offered here has much broader connotations'.

— Professor Kenneth Button, *School of Policy, Government and*
International Affairs George Mason University

'There is no shortage of books on the EU, but Ali El-Agraa's new text offers
an up-to-date assessment from an economic perspective of the contribution and progress of the EU and where it is going. With a comprehensive
coverage of the wide ranges of EU policies, it offers an excellent starting
point for those who want to get their mind round the problems'.

— Professor David Geoffrey Mayes,
The University of Auckland

'This book provides a good and comprehensive overview for the general
reader interested to learn more about the EU and how it works. It effectively debunks some of the common misunderstandings and downright
misinformation about what the EU is and does'.

— Professor Iain Beggs, *European Institute,*
London School of Economics and Political Science

'El-Agraa offers a lucid insight into the past, present and future of the European Union (EU). He discusses many of the difficulties that the EU is faced with today. A veteran textbook writer, he has once again produced an outstanding book, fully up to date, written in a clear and accessible style — a must-read for anyone who wishes to understand the ins and outs of European integration'.

— Professor Amy Verdun,
University of Victoria, Canada

The European Union Illuminated

Its Nature, Importance and Future

Ali M. El-Agraa
Emeritus Professor of International Economic Integration,
Fukuoka University, Japan

First published 2015 by
PALGRAVE MACMILLAN

Palgrave Macmillan in the UK is an imprint of Macmillan Publishers Limited, registered in England, company number 785998, of Houndmills, Basingstoke, Hampshire RG21 6XS.

Palgrave Macmillan in the US is a division of St Martin's Press LLC, 175 Fifth Avenue, New York, NY 10010.

Palgrave Macmillan is the global academic imprint of the above companies and has companies and representatives throughout the world.

Palgrave® and Macmillan® are registered trademarks in the United States, the United Kingdom, Europe and other countries.

ISBN: 978–1–137–53363–0 hardback
ISBN: 978–1–137–53364–7 paperback

This book is printed on paper suitable for recycling and made from fully managed and sustained forest sources. Logging, pulping and manufacturing processes are expected to conform to the environmental regulations of the country of origin.

A catalogue record for this book is available from the British Library.

Library of Congress Cataloging-in-Publication Data
El-Agraa, A. M.
  The European Union illuminated : its nature, importance and future / Ali El-Agraa.
    pages cm
  Includes bibliographical references and index.
  ISBN 978–1–137–53363–0 (hardcover : alk. paper) –
  ISBN 978–1–137–53364–7 (pbk. : alk. paper)
    1. European Union. 2. European Union countries – Economic policy. 3. European Union countries – Foreign economic relations. 4. European Union countries – Politics and government. I. Title.
HC241.2.E4253 2015
337.1'42—dc23   2015012632

Contents

List of Illustrations

Boxes

Figures

Acknowledgements

In writing this book I had the privilege of relying on the help and support of several distinguished scholars with whom I have been collaborating in research over many decades. I would like to thank Emeritus Professor Harvey Armstrong of the University of Sheffield (UK) and Ian Barnes of the University of Lincoln (UK), and Professor Kenneth Button of George Mason University (USA), Ulrich Koester of the University of Kiel (Germany), Stephen Martin of Purdue University (USA) and Wolf Sauter of Groningen University (the Netherlands) – now with the Ministry of Finance (the Netherlands) – for thoroughly checking the sections on the EU policies in Chapter 4 that fall under their expertise and for offering comments and valuable suggestions. My special thanks go to Professor David Mayes of the University of Auckland (New Zealand) for his collaboration on Chapter 6 on the EU's European Monetary Union (EMU); he contributed a joint chapter with me on the development of the EMU and a full chapter on its operation in my book *The European Union: Economics and Policies*, the 9th edition of which was published in 2011 by Cambridge University Press. But he has done much more than that for this book by thoroughly checking a number of chapters and offering further helpful comments and suggestions. He and I have been collaborating since the early 1970s and have been close friends ever since.

I would like to acknowledge, but without in any way implicating, Brian Ardy of London South Bank University (UK), who jointly authored with me three full chapters on the European Single Market (SEM), the EU general budget and social policies in the above book. Here, I have updated simpler versions of the SEM and social policy chapters as sections of Chapter 4 on the EU policies, and the EU budget as Chapter 5.

I am also deeply indebted to Dr Martin Westlake, Visiting Fellow, the European Institute, the London School of Economics and Political Science (UK) and former Secretary General of the European Economic and Social Committee, for his most thorough checking and extensive comments and suggestions on Chapter 3. I am also grateful to Professor Amy Verdun of the University of Victoria, Canada, and co-editor of the *Journal of Common Market Studies*, for her helpful comments on the Introduction and Appendix.

And I am equally grateful to Alain Lamassoure, a distinguished French politician and a member of the European Parliament, chairing the EP's Committee on Budgets, for reading chapter 2 and suggesting a valuable addition.

I owe a special debt to the staff of the London offices of the European Union and the European Parliament, especially to Jeffrey Lamb for promptly responding to my questions and for supplying me with the maps, data, charts and figures that I requested. And I am deeply indebted to Mr Petre Dumitru of the EU Budget directorate general for providing me with a specially designed figure for EU revenues.

Finally, I wish to acknowledge the enthusiasm for the book by Rachel Sangester (Publisher, Economics) and Laura Pacey (Assistant Editor) of Palgrave Macmillan and for their excellent editorial work. And I extend my greatest appreciation to Vidhya Jayaprakash and her entire team for their excellent production.

Without the care, understanding and support of Diana, my wife, it would not have been possible for me to write this or any of my other books. Diana and I are fortunate to have our son, Mark, and daughter, Frances, working in the City in London and living not far from us, so constantly entertaining us, making life easier for research and writing; we are grateful to both of them.

About the Author

Ali M. El-Agraa, a British citizen, is Emeritus Professor of International Economic Integration at Fukuoka University in Japan. His main research interest is international economics, with most of his research concentrated on international economic integration. During his career, Ali has acted as General Consultant for the Anglo-Japanese Economic Institute, Senior International Consultant for the United Nations and Member of the Committee of the International Economics Study Group, sponsored by the UK Economic and Social Research Council. He has held visiting professorships at the University of York, the International University of Japan, Fudan University in Shanghai and Vanderbilt University after Sangyo. He was also Adjunct Professor of EU Studies at Kyushu National University, Seinan Gakuin University and Kyushu Sangyo University (all in Japan), and has taught several intensive graduate courses at the Japan International Development Institute sponsored by the World Bank in Tokyo, and Chulalongkorn University, in Bangkok, Thailand. Ali was with the University of Leeds during 1971–92 where he was a senior lecturer and a member of both University's Council and Senate as well as University Advisor to Overseas Students.

List of Abbreviations

AAU	Arab-African Union
ACC	Arab Cooperation Council
ACM	Arab Common Market
ACP	African, Caribbean and Pacific Countries Party to the Lomé Convention (now the Contonou Agreement)
AEC	African Economic Community
AL	Arab League
ALADI	Associação Latino-Americana de Integração (Association for Latin American Integration)
AMU	Arab Maghreb Union
ANZCERTA	Australia and New Zealand Closer Economic Relations and Trade Agreement (also CER)
ASEAN	Association of South-East Asian Nations
AU	African Union
BENELUX	Belgium, the Netherlands and Luxembourg Economic Union
BU	Benin Union
CAA	Civil Aviation Authority
CACM	Central American Common Market
CAEU	Council for Arab Economic Unity
CAP	Common Agricultural Policy
CARICOM	Caribbean Community
CARIFTA	Caribbean Free Trade Association
CCP	Common Commercial Policy
CCT	Common Customs Tariff
CEP	Common Energy Policy
CEPGL	Communauté Économique des Pays des Grand Lacs (Economic Community of the Countries of the Great Lakes)
CER	Closer Economic Relations
CET	Common External Tariff
CFP	Common Fisheries Policy
CFSP	Common Foreign and Security Policy
CIS	Commonwealth of Independent States
CM	Common Market
CMEA	Council for Mutual Economic Assistance

COMECON	*see* CMEA
COMESA	Common Market for Eastern and Southern Africa
COREPER	Comité des représentants permanents (Committee of Permanent Representatives)
CTP	Common Transport Policy
CU	Customs Union
DDR	Deutsche Demokratische Republik (German Democratic Republic, now part of Germany)
DG	Directorate General
EAC	East African Community
EAGGF	European Agricultural Guidance and Guarantee Fund
EBA	European Banking Authority
EBRD	European Bank for Reconstruction and Development
EC	European Community
ECB	European Central Bank
ECCAS	Economic Community of Central African States
ECHR	European Court of Human Rights
ECJ	European Court of Justice
ECMT	European Conference of Ministers of Transport
ECOFIN	Economic and Financial Affairs Council
ECOWAS	Economic Community of West African States
ECSC	European Coal and Steel Community
ECU	European Currency Unit
EDC	European Defence Community
EDF	European Development Fund
EEA	European Economic Area
EEC	European Economic Community
EEZ	Exclusive Economic Zone
EFSF	European Financial Stability Facility
EFTA	European Free Trade Association
EIB	European Investment Bank
EIF	European Investment Fund
EIOPA	European Insurance and Occupational Pensions Authority
EMCF	European Monetary Cooperation Fund
EMF	European Monetary Fund
EMI	European Monetary Institute
EMS	European Monetary System
EMU	European Monetary Union, or Economic and Monetary Union
EP	European Parliament

EPC	European Political Cooperation
Erasmus	European Community Action Scheme for the Mobility of University Students
ERDF	European Regional Development Fund
ERM	Exchange-Rate Mechanism
ESCB	European System of Central Banks
ESF	European Social Fund
ESM	European Social Model
ESMA	European Securities Market Authority
ESRB	European Systemic Risk Board
ETUC	European Trade Union Confederation
EU	European Union
EUA	European Unit of Account
Euratom	European Atomic Energy Community
EUROSTAT	Statistical Office of the EC/EU
FCO	Foreign and Commonwealth Office
FEER	Fundamental Equilibrium Exchange Rate
FEOGA (see EAGGF)	Fonds Européen d'Orientation et de Garantie Agricole (European Agricultural Guidance and Guarantee Fund)
FIFG	Financial Instrument for Fisheries Guidance
FSAP	Financial Services Action Plan
FSU	Former Soviet Union
FTA	Free Trade Area
GATS	General Agreement on Trade in Services
GATT	General Agreement on Tariffs and Trade (UN)
GCC	Gulf Cooperation Council
GDP	Gross Domestic Product
GFCM	General Fisheries Council for the Mediterranean
GNI	Gross National Income
GNP	Gross National Product
GSP	Generalized System of Preferences
IAEA	International Atomic Energy Agency (UN)
IATA	International Air Transport Association
IBRD	International Bank for Reconstruction and Development (World Bank) (UN)
IEA	International Energy Agency (OECD)
IEM	Internal Energy Market
IGAD	Intergovernmental Authority on Development
IGC	Intergovernmental Conference
IIT	Intra-Industry Trade

ILO	International Labour Organization
IMF	International Monetary Fund (UN)
LAFTA	Latin American Free Trade Area
LDC	Less-Developed Country
M&A	Mergers and Acquisitions
MEP	Member of the European Parliament
MERCOSUR	Mercado Común del Sur (Southern Cone Common Market)
MFA	Multifibre Arrangement (arrangement regarding international trade in textiles)
MFN	Most-Favoured Nation
MFP	Multi-Annual Framework Programme
MNE	Multinational Enterprise
MRU	Mano River Union
NAFTA	North Atlantic Free Trade Agreement (New Zealand Australia Free Trade Area)
NAIRU	Non-Accelerating Inflation Rate of Unemployment
NATO	North Atlantic Treaty Organization
NCB	National Central Bank
NEAFC	North-East Atlantic Fisheries Commission
NTB	Non-Tariff Barrier
OAPEC	Organization of Arab Petroleum Exporting Countries
OAU	Organization for African Unity
ODA	Overseas Development Aid
OECD	Organization for Economic Cooperation and Development
OEEC	Organization for European Economic Cooperation
OMC	Open Method Cooperation
OPEC	Organization of Petroleum Exporting Countries
PAFTAD	Pacific Trade and Development Conference
PBEC	Pacific Basin Economic Council
PECC	Pacific Economic Cooperation Conference
PPP	Polluter Pays Principle and Purchasing Power Parity
PTA	Preferential Trade Area
PTC	Pacific Telecommunications Conference
QMV	Qualified Majority Voting
R&TD	Research and Technological Development
RCD	Regional Cooperation for Development
RIA	Regional Impact Assessment
RTA	Regional Trade Agreement
RTD	Research and Technological Development

SACU	Southern African Customs Union
SADC	Southern African Development Community
SAP	Social Action Programme
SDR	Special Drawing Rights
SDS	Sustainable Development Strategy
SEA	Single European Act
SEDOC	Interstate Notification of Job Vacancies
SEM	Single European Market
SIAC	Special Immigration Appeals Court
SMEs	Small- and Medium-Sized Enterprises
TAC	Total Allowable Catch
TACIS	Technical Aid to the Commonwealth of Independent States
TARIC	Integrated Tariff of the European Union
TENs	Trans-European Networks
TEU	Treaty on European Union
TRIPs	Trade-Related Aspects of Intellectual Property Rights
TUC	Trades Union Congress
UDEAC	Union Douanière et Économique de l'Afrique Centrale (The Central African Customs and Economic Union)
UEMOA	West African Economic and Monetary Union
UN	United Nations
UNCTAD	United Nations Conference on Trade and Development
UNECA	United Nations Economic Commission for Africa
UTR	Unilateral Tariff Reduction
VAT	Value-Added Tax
WEU	Western European Union
WTO	World Trade Organization

Introduction

The European Union (EU) is going through hard times. Some would even go so far as to claim that it is in the midst of a serious survival crisis. What are the reasons for such concerns? And to what extent are they justified? This book aims to analyse, discuss and illuminate such questions.

The EU was badly hit by the 2008 global financial crisis and its aftermath, so much so that in 2014 it was still in the process of weathering the storm, or rather the hurricane, with muted prospects for the immediate future. Indeed, a number of the Member States have yet to return to their 2008 pre-crisis gross national income (GNI) levels measured using the World Bank's *Atlas Method*: Croatia, Greece, Hungary, Ireland, Italy, Luxembourg, the Netherlands, Portugal, Slovenia, Spain and the UK. Furthermore, despite 11 out of 28 EU Member States being a substantial number, almost all of the rest have only just managed to pass the threshold. As Table I.1 shows, this observation is more or less repeated using Purchasing Power Parity (PPP) GNI comparisons. Because the financial crisis wreaked so much havoc and many analysts and observers have blamed the euro for contributing to it, the appendix to this book is devoted to what was the real culprit: a combination of macro-imbalances and financial market developments and innovations. Because the euro was not the primary cause, this concern should not distract from the main message here, but the topic of the causes of the financial is necessary since it is referred to in several chapters of the book, especially in Chapter 6 on the EU's Economic and Monetary Union (EMU).

The Member States that have suffered greatly since the financial crisis blame Germany,[1] the richest and most populous EU Member State, for their misery, due to its running huge trade surpluses with them.[2] They also accuse it, together with the other larger Member States, of not offering sufficient gratuitous bailouts to help ease their pain. Moreover, they are angry, again especially with Germany, for bullying them into submission,[3] due to the larger states' insistence that they cannot be bailed out unless they adopt appropriate austerity measures to attain sustainable fiscal positions and restore growth, and play by the rules of the EU game. In this regard, Greece stands out due to its having 'creatively' dealt with its national accounting in order to pass the criteria for joining the single currency,[4] for offering its people unrealistic and unaffordable pensions as well as earlier retirement, when life expectancy is on the rise, and for continuing persistently to deny that Greece is a culprit. All this has led to popular revolt and violent strikes, creating a culture of blame and shame. This has sown the seeds for uncertainty that threatens the cohesiveness of the club and encourages scepticism over the EU venture itself and what it stands for.

There has also been growing apprehension regarding whether the euro itself, and the EMU of which it is the jewel in the crown, can survive. That is because some Member States, and groups thereof, attribute the deep recession since 2008 to the consequences of the Eurozone membership ('Eurozone', being the general term, is used throughout this book or interchangeably with the EU jargon 'euro area'). Hence, they mourn the death of their previous national currencies for depriving them of the ability to conduct their own monetary and exchange rate policies to cater for their own unique economic problems. This they cannot do in the EMU because the European Central Bank (ECB) sets policy for the entire Eurozone. And, by definition, a one-for-all policy will not suit the particular needs of every single Eurozone Member State, unless all of them have precisely the same economic problems (being 'symmetric' in the economic jargon), which they have not. Others argue that the EMU would fare better provided some Member States exit the Eurozone, hence the popular term 'Grexit' for the case of Greece. But exiting was never considered an option when the euro was established in 1999. In fact there is not a EU treaty clause about leaving the euro, although, as shown in Chapter 2, there is such a clause in the Lisbon Treaty for those wishing to leave the EU. Indeed, if exiting were to become a reality, then those inside the Eurozone would have to take action to ensure that the EMU does not collapse altogether, and this would necessitate getting rid of the EMU's foundational failings, which are fully set out in Chapter 6: the lack of a common fiscal policy and a common banking union. But doing so would transform the Eurozone into more or less a single nation. Such further integration would leave those EU Member States outside the Eurozone regressing into second-tier nations, or even lower. This enhances the apprehension over the EMU as well as the EU itself.

Table I.1 EU Member States' population and GNI, 2008 and 2013

		GNI (WB Atlas Method)		GNI (PPP)	
	Population	2013	2008	2013	2008
Austria	8.50	411.7	390.1	371.3	330.9
Belgium	11.20	506.1	483.8	451.0	402.2
Bulgaria	7.30	51.1	43.4	110.4	100.8
Croatia	4.30	56.7	61.2	86.6	87.2
Cyprus	1.10	22.8	21.9	25.5	23.6
Czech Republic	10.50	190.0	186.0	268.7	257.2
Denmark	5.60	343.1	324.3	249.5	222.3
Estonia	1.30	23.0	20.1	32.1	28.1
Finland	5.40	256.3	254.9	209.3	203.2
France	66.00	2,789.7	2,699.8	2,481.2	2,229.8
Germany	80.60	3,716.8	3,487.3	3,590.7	3,083.4
Greece	11.00	248.6	304.3	282.7	321.8
Hungary	9.90	123.1	129.4	207.6	192.0
Ireland	4.60	179.4	223.1	161.0	164.2
Italy	59.80	2,058.2	2,139.8	2,040.0	1,974.9
Latvia	2.00	28.6	27.2	43.5	40.6
Lithuania	3.00	41.3	40.3	69.0	64.0
Luxembourg	0.50	38.1	40.9	31.7	32.6
Malta	0.40	8.3	7.7	11.3	10.0
Netherlands	16.80	797.2	802.8	726.0	690.8
Poland	38.50	499.5	452.4	859.1	670.7
Portugal	10.50	216.2	228.9	265.2	255.4
Romania	20.00	180.9	174.3	360.6	313.8
Slovakia	5.40	93.0	85.9	134.8	117.2
Slovenia	2.10	47.0	48.9	57.0	57.1
Spain	46.70	1,361.1	1,451.1	1,485.7	1,470.1
Sweden	9.60	567.3	483.0	428.4	378.0
UK	64.10	2,506.9	2,842.3	2,292.2	2,293.5
Total	506.70	16,444.2	17,455.1	17,332.1	16,015.4

Source: Selected from the World Bank's World Development Indictors (2014).

Moreover, many people and governments, especially in Germany, the Netherlands and the UK, are unhappy with the increasing number of immigrant workers coming to them from the new Member States. Two UK political parties (the Conservative Party and the UK Independent Party, UKIP); the Dutch Party for Freedom, led by the outspoken Geert Wilders; and the French National Front Party, headed by the equally vehement Marine Le Pen, stand out in this respect. This is in spite of the fact that most EU immigrants come to perform the jobs that the local population shuns or for which it does not have the expertise.[5] And, for instance in the case of the UK, more than 2 million British citizens have not only found it desirable to comfortably and happily settle down or work in other Member States, due to EU membership, but also to be welcomed there with open arms. Demands for restrictions on the rights of movement run against the major 'pillar' of EU integration discussed in Chapter 6: the Single European Market (SEM). Hence, naturally, the other Member States, especially those in Eastern Europe, from where most of the 'unwanted' immigrant workers originate, deeply resent this, and so too do the British, and their ilk, residing in the rest of the EU. Such resentment is aggravated when it is perceived that the UK has no qualms regarding the number of mostly rich, by profession rather than wealth, French citizens residing in the UK; it is now popular to state that the 600,000 French living in London make London the sixth-largest French city. Such demands and concerns undermine the EU.

Furthermore, the UK's Conservative Party wants to change the EU treaties in such a way that it can pick and choose what suits its purposes.[6] It also wants to opt out of the European Court of Human Rights (ECHR), although the ECHR is not in the EU lexicon, that is, it is not enshrined in EU treaties. Since the Conservative Party has promised a referendum in 2017 to decide whether the UK will exit the EU, if it is elected to rule in 2015 and the changes in the EU that it seeks have not been accommodated, such a referendum is highly likely to take place. This is because the other major UK political party, the Labour Party, may have to match this commitment if it is to stand a chance of being elected to govern in 2015. This is in spite of the fact that the leader of the Labour Party, Ed Miliband, declared (in March 2014 and reiterated in late May after the European Parliament elections between the twenty-second and the twenty-fifth, as well as later on) that he would only hold a referendum in the event that Britain has to transfer fresh powers to Brussels. The UKIP's political agenda has as its main aim to take the UK out of the EU. Although it is a small party, it is increasing in popularity with the EU-sceptic British voter, gaining 25 per cent of the vote for the European Parliament (EP) in 2014 and winning two by-elections in England. And the Liberal Democratic Party, now part of the coalition government, although fully committed to EU membership, did very badly in the 2014 EP elections and lost its £500 deposit on seven by-elections since the 2010 general election, after securing less than 5 per cent of the vote, so many analysts believe that it is set to do likewise in the UK general election, and hence cannot be a force with which to reckon. Of course, the EU will survive in the absence of the UK, as it did before the UK joined, but that would go against the EU's aspiration of encompassing the whole of Europe and even to go beyond it (for example, Turkey is a candidate for membership). As argued below, the departure of the UK would also diminish the EU globally since it is one of its largest Member States in terms of both population and GNI. These are unwelcome prospects for the EU.

Additionally, Spain has persistently refused to recognize Kosovo as a nation since its declaration of independence on 17 February 2008. This is because Kosovo declared its independence unilaterally, an act which Serbia does not accept due to its being adamant that Kosovo is an integral part of Serbia. Spain's refusal is due to its realization that in recognizing Kosovo as a unilaterally independent nation, it would be setting a precedent that would lead to its own disintegration. This is because Catalonia would be encouraged to follow in the footsteps of Kosovo. What this amounts to is that the right of every European nation to apply for EU membership, the basic precept of the EU discussed in Chapter 2, would be threatened since Spain is not likely to endorse EU membership for a country it does not recognize. The admission of new member states requires unanimity. This enhances apprehension about the EU's future.

Within this last context, one is right to ask about the implications of the Spain-Kosovo stalemate for those promoting the independence of Scotland. Of course, had Scotland decided to go its own way on 18 September 2014,[7] this would have greatly impacted the UK itself, but not necessarily for economic reasons: Scotland accounts for only 8.3 per cent of the UK's population and 8.1 per cent of UK's GNI. What is important is that the break-up would have undermined the over three-century 'unity' (by the Act of Union in 1707)[8] that has served the UK so well both internally and externally. The internal, such as the stability of having one currency, is too obvious to dwell on. The external would vitally have included whether the UK would continue to be one of the most influential EU Member States. At present, the UK, with a population of 63 million, has roughly the same population as that of France (66 million) and Italy (61 million), both about 20 million short of Germany's (82 million), but without Scotland, it would have been reduced to a halfway house between them and Spain (46 million). Since the EU needs a diversified 'leadership', a diminished UK would have left France and Germany at the helm, with Italy (61 million) a close third. Of course, France and Germany have arguably done an excellent job in guiding the EU since the establishment of the European Coal and Steel Community in 1951, when the EU had only 'the original' six Member States. But today with 28 Member Nations and more to come, surely, the number of those at the helm needs to be increased in order to carry the EU forward: more ideas can be produced than from a mere two leading members! One of the salient points, however, is that, had Scotland decided to go independent, this would have been as a result of the people living in Scotland having so decided as agreed by the UK government. Thus, Scottish independence would not have raised the same problem for Spain, since independence would not have been a 'unilateral' Scottish declaration as was the case with Kosovo. In short, Spain would have had no reason to stop an independent Scotland from joining the EU. However, if the UK were to decide to withdraw from EU membership in 2017, then Scottish independence should be most welcomed by all those who believe in the importance of the EU. But one should not lose sight of the second salient point: Scotland's decision to stay in the UK enhances the prospects for a 'yes' vote in case of a referendum on the UK's EU membership, thus ensuring that the UK stays a major player in the EU.

Then there is the constant complaint about Brussels dictating the rules and telling everyone what and what not to do, the so-called Brussels diktat. Although, as we shall see in Chapter 3, this is a misconception, it nevertheless undermines the integrity of the EU amongst many of its citizens and adds to the apprehension.

There is more along these lines, but for the sake of brevity it is vital to consider some external EU factors. These come mainly from the major developments in the Far East, especially in China and India, and from across the EU's eastern border with Russia.

The emergence of China, with about one-sixth of the world's population (1.354 million), as the second-largest global economy after the US (certainly the first by the time this book is published), would of course be most welcomed by all those who believe that US hegemony in this respect has not been very good for the world. This welcome would also be extended to India if it manages to catch up with China, since its population (1.27 billion) is not that far off China's. Of course, in terms of income per head, both China and India are still very poor nations (China, $5,720; India, $1,580; EU average, $33,510; US, $52,340), so perhaps most people would be happy if and when they manage to elevate themselves to the status of 'rich' nations. Japan, although it has lost its number two position in the league of GNI, and is now standing third after China, is still a force with which to be reckoned, especially since it is a rich and technologically advanced nation. And there are several countries in its neighbourhood that have caught up (Singapore) or are gradually catching up with the advanced world, including South Korea and Indonesia, not to mention neighbouring Australia and New Zealand. Thus, the (extended) East is becoming the focus of attention in terms of market access, competition, the finding of resources overseas for further development (China is doing so all over the world), and foreign direct investment (FDI). In this sense, the developments in the East offer both a challenge (competition for markets and resources) as well as an opportunity (new markets and FDI) for the EU. Obviously, it is in the interest of the EU Member States to realize the 'opportunity', but as will be discussed in Chapter 7, they would achieve this more readily by acting together, since each acting alone is not likely to be so successful. Yet, this is precisely how the Member States have been behaving.

Closer to home is the case of Russia. It has been exercising its position as the major provider of natural gas to the EU in politically unacceptable ways. This is not in reference to Russia holding the EU Member States to ransom by threatening to shut down the pipelines carrying natural gas to the EU via Ukraine whenever Russia is unhappy about a political issue[9] between the two. Such action would cut both ways: Russia's economy is largely driven by the income from energy sales to the EU. What is of major concern, however, is how Russia is behaving towards countries like Ukraine. In Ukraine, there is support, some would claim overwhelming support, for closeness to the EU (as the Kiev November 2013 protests and the results of the 27 October 2014 parliamentary elections have shown), including future membership. In order to dissuade the Ukraine government from acceding to this popular sentiment towards the EU, Russia's president, Vladimir Putin, has declared that Russia would come to the rescue of the financially troubled neighbour by providing it with $15 billion in loans and a steep discount on natural gas prices. This is a sharp rebuff to the EU for offering a far less generous deal, and is aimed at encouraging Ukraine's sentiments in its favour. But, Putin's main objective is that Ukraine would join his customs union with Belarus and Kazakhstan to develop it into a political and trading bloc to be known as the Eurasian Union, a counterpart to the EU. What is of the essence, however, is that if Russia succeeded in enticing Ukraine and bordering countries away from the EU, then the EU's aspiration for a club of the whole of Europe, however geographically loosely defined, would be undermined. Russia's annexation of the Crimea in March 2014 reinforces the EU's concern in this regard and so does its support for the pro-Russian fighters in Eastern Ukraine.

All this necessitates the publication of a basic book on the nature and importance of the EU that offers an insight for those interested in the workings of this politico-economic unit. The 'nature', because some of the mentioned accusations regarding the EU are completely false, indicating that the general public is still not conversant with what the EU stands for or how it operates. It is vital that EU citizens be aware of the nature of the EU, especially at a time when some major political parties are promising to offer referendums on EU membership and others are canvassing hard against staying in the fold. And, it is equally vital to know why the EU is important for its Member States and its citizens, as well as globally. Therefore, this book begins by looking at the EU within the international context of global economic integration in Chapter 1. This is followed in Chapter 2 by a narration of the journey taken by the Member States to reach the present EU. Then, to dispel the accusations that Brussels is dictating the rules, Chapter 3 explains how the EU reaches decisions. Chapters 4 and 5, respectively and briefly, deal with the vast number of EU policies and how they are financed. Chapter 6 is devoted to the EU's pride, if not complete joy, the EMU, with its single currency. Chapter 7 spells out why the EU is important both for its Member States and globally. And the final chapter is devoted to where the EU is heading in the future.

1
The EU within Regional Integration Worldwide

1.1 Introduction

The European Union (EU) is a voluntary association whose membership is open to all European nations, provided they have democratically elected governments. At the beginning of 2014, it comprised 28 such nations and it has been getting much closer to encompassing the whole of Europe. Moreover, the EU has decided that Europe's traditional geographical designation should not be sacrosanct, and so has extended the right to negotiate membership to Turkey.

As an association of independent nations, the EU falls under the general umbrella of what is termed 'regional integration', precisely 'international economic integration' (IEI). This is because IEI is concerned with the creation of 'clubs' between some nations, to the exclusion of others, and clubs, by their very nature, discriminate against the non-members, the non-participants. Hence, the United Nations (UN), established in 1945 to promote cooperation between all governments, does not constitute IEI since its membership is open to all countries. Nor does the World Trade Organization (WTO), since its membership is for all nations that meet its conditions. Nor does the Organization for Economic Cooperation and Development (OECD), since, as a club of the richest countries in the world, it is open to all such nations and is therefore non-discriminatory. Nor does the Organization for Petroleum Exporting Countries (OPEC), founded in 1960 with a truly international membership, with the aim of protecting the main interest of its member nations, petroleum.[1] Nor does the Organization for Arab Petroleum Exporting Countries (OAPEC), established in January 1968.[2] All such organizations are for intergovernmental cooperation rather than IEI; therefore, except where appropriate, they will not be mentioned in this book.

IEI is in contradiction to 'multilateralism', under which all nations are treated equally, extending agreed 'arrangements' between them to the entire world. The WTO is the body entrusted to deal with IEI, but the WTO is based on the principle of 'non-discrimination'; hence, any analysis of the nature and importance of the EU would be vacuous if it did not commence with a treatment of the EU within the context of IEI and what the WTO has to say about IEI.

Thus the first aim of this chapter is to provide a precise definition of IEI since what it means to those specializing in trade theory is very different from what one would expect on purely linguistic grounds. The second aim is to examine how IEI fits within the WTO guiding principles because there is a contradiction between its commitment to non-discrimination and IEI. The third aim is to briefly describe the various schemes of IEI that have actually been adopted worldwide and to set the EU within their broader picture. The fourth aim is to consider why most countries seek IEI, that is, to examine what economic and other benefits become possible as a consequence of IEI. The chapter ends by raising pertinent EU questions.

1.2   What is IEI?

IEI is one aspect of 'international economics' that has been growing in importance for about seven decades. The term itself has quite a short history; indeed, there is no single instance of its use prior to 1942.[3] Since then, the term has been used at various times to refer to practically any area of international economic relations. By 1950, however, the term had been given a specific definition by international trade specialists to denote *a state of affairs or a process that involves the amalgamation of some separate economies into larger free trading regions* (author emphasis). It is in this more limited sense that the term is used today. It should be noted that IEI is also referred to as 'regional integration', 'regional trading agreements' (RTAs), 'preferential trading agreements' (PTAs) and 'trading blocs'. And one should hasten to add that IEI should not be confused with globalization, which is concerned with simply the increasing economic interdependence between nations.

More specifically, there are two basic elements to IEI. The first is the discriminatory removal of all trade impediments between at least two participating nations, discriminatory because such removal is not extended to the non-participating nations, the 'outside world'. The second is concerned with the establishment of certain elements of cooperation and coordination between the member nations. The latter depends entirely on the actual form that IEI takes. Different forms of IEI can be envisaged (see Table 1.1 for a schematic presentation) and many have actually been implemented

1. Free trade areas (FTAs), in which the member nations eliminate tariffs among themselves but retain their freedom to determine their own policies vis-à-vis the outside world, the non-participants. Recently, the trend has been to extend this treatment to investment.
2. Customs unions (CUs), which are very similar to FTAs except that member nations must conduct and pursue common external commercial relations – for instance, they must adopt common external tariffs (CETs) on imports from the non-participants.
3. Common markets (CMs), which are CUs that also allow for free factor mobility across the frontiers of the member nations, that is, capital, labour, technology and enterprises should move unhindered between them, and services should be provided likewise.
4. Complete economic unions, or economic unions (EconUs), are CMs that also incorporate the complete unification of monetary and fiscal policies, that is, the member nations must introduce a central authority to exercise control over these matters so that they effectively become regions of the same nation.

Of course, the member nations may opt for a complete political union (PU), that is, become literally one nation, with the central authority needed in complete economic unions being paralleled by a common parliament and other institutions needed to guarantee the sovereignty of one state. But this would take IEI beyond the purely economic. Nevertheless, IEI has to be borne in mind since it has implications not just for the EU, and not simply because of the unification of the two Germanys in 1990, but also for other parts of the world, such as the pursuit of the unification of the Korean Peninsula. Also, one should naturally be interested in its economic consequences (see below). More generally, one should stress that each of these forms of IEI can be introduced in its own right; hence, they should not be confused with stages in a process which eventually leads to either complete economic or political union.

As a digression, it should also be noted that there could be sectoral integration, as distinct from general across-the-board IEI, in particular areas of the economy, as was the case with the European Coal and Steel Community (ECSC, see Chapter 2), created in 1951, and which is fully explained in Chapter 2. But sectoral integration is considered to be only

Table 1.1   Schematic presentation of economic integration schemes

Scheme	Free intrascheme trade	Common commercial policy (CCP)	Free factor mobility	Common monetary and fiscal policy
Free trade area (FTA)	Yes	No	No	No
Customs union (CU)	Yes	Yes	No	No
Common market (CM)	Yes	Yes	Yes	No
Economic union (EconU)	Yes	Yes	Yes	Yes

a form of cooperation because it is inconsistent with the accepted definition of IEI and also because it may contravene the rules of the General Agreement on Tariffs and Trade (GATT), which in 1995 began to be run by the WTO (see below). Sectoral integration may also occur within any of the mentioned schemes, as is the case with the EU's Common Agricultural Policy (CAP, see Chapter 4), but then it is nothing more than a 'policy'.

It has been claimed that IEI can be negative or positive.[4] Negative IEI refers to the simple act of the removal of impediments on trade between the member nations. Positive integration relates to the modification of existing instruments and institutions and, more importantly, to the creation of new ones so as to enable the market of the integrated area to function properly and effectively and also to promote other broader policy aims of the scheme. Hence, at the risk of oversimplification, according to this classification, it can be claimed that FTAs require only negative integration, while the remaining types need positive integration. This is because, as a minimum, they need the positive act of adopting common external trade, which entails long negotiations and compromises, and investment relations. However, in reality this distinction is over-simplistic not only because practically all existing types of IEI have found it essential to introduce some elements of positive integration but also because theoretical considerations indicate that no scheme of IEI is viable without certain elements of positive integration. For example, even the ECSC deemed it necessary to establish new institutions to tackle its specified tasks (see below and Chapter 2).

1.3   IEI and WTO rules

Given that IEI is a concern of the WTO, a few words on the organization and what it has to say about IEI are in order. Note that the WTO is the successor of the GATT. The GATT was signed in 1947 after the failure to create the International Trade Organization (ITO)[5] and became effective in 1948. Its aim was the 'substantial reduction of tariffs and other trade barriers and the elimination of preferences, on a reciprocal and mutually advantageous basis' (GATT preamble). Under the Marrakech Agreement of 15 April 1994, it was replaced by the WTO on 1 January 1995, which deals with broader issues. Therefore, one need not refer to the GATT, unless there are compelling reasons for doing so.

The general aim of the WTO is, as mentioned, to supervise and liberalize trade and investment worldwide. It does so by regulating the trade between the member nations and freeing restrictions on capital movements. Note that not all countries are members, due to strict conditions for joining. In January 2014, the WTO had 159 members. The WTO also provides a framework for the negotiation and formalization of trade agreements between the members. And, vitally, it acts as a dispute resolution platform for problems arising amongst the members and for ensuring that they adhere to WTO agreements.

To liberalize world trade, the WTO conducts what is called 'Rounds of Negotiations'. The first such Round was held in Geneva in April 1947 and lasted for seven months. The latest round is the ninth and it started in November 2001, but is yet to be concluded. Table 1.2 provides a brief summary of the Rounds, their outcomes or achievements and the number of countries taking part.

There are four basic WTO principles: (a) trade liberalization on a most-favoured-nation (MFN) basis (the lowest tariff applicable to one member must be extended to all members); (b) non-discrimination; (c) transparency of instruments used to restrict trade (now called tariffication) to enable informed negotiations on their reduction or complete elimination; and (d) the promotion of growth and stability of the world economy. More generally, these principles are reduced to three: nondiscrimination, transparency and reciprocity.

Given that nondiscrimination is a basic principle of the WTO, it is natural to ask why IEI is tolerated by the organization. The GATT's Article XXIV[6] allows the formation of IEI schemes on the understanding that (a) they may not pursue policies which increase the level of protection beyond that which existed prior to their formation, (b) tariffs and other trade restrictions (with some exceptions) are removed on substantially (increasingly interpreted to mean at least 90 per cent) all the trade among the member nations and (c) they get established within a reasonable period of time, understood to be within a decade. Due to this article's importance, Box 1.1 provides the full text of item 5 of Article XXIV. The drafters of Article XXIV believed that the combination of these conditions would lead to benefits for the countries partici-pating in IEI, while, at the same time, not impacting adversely on the non-participants.

Box 1.1   GATT's Article XXIV.5

Accordingly, the provisions of this Agreement shall not prevent, as between the territories of contracting parties, the formation of a customs union or of a free-trade area or the adoption of an interim agreement necessary for the formation of a customs union or of a free-trade area; provided that:

(a) with respect to a customs union, or an interim agreement leading to the formation of a customs union, the duties and other regulations of commerce imposed at the institution of any such union or interim agree-ment in respect of trade with contracting parties not parties to such union or agreement shall not on the whole be higher or more restrictive than the general incidence of the duties and regulations of commerce applicable in the constituent territories prior to the formation of such union or the adoption of such interim agreement, as the case may be;

(b) with respect to a free-trade area, or an interim agreement leading to the formation of a free-trade area, the duties and other regulations of commerce maintained in each of the constituent territories and appli-cable at the formation of such free-trade area or the adoption of such interim agreement to the trade of contracting parties not included in such area or not parties to such agreement shall not be higher or more restric-tive than the corresponding duties and other regulations of commerce existing in the same constituent territories prior to the formation of the free-trade area, or interim agreement, as the case may be; and

(c) any interim agreement referred to in sub-paragraphs (a) and (b) shall include a plan and schedule for the formation of such a customs union or of such a free-trade area within a reasonable length of time.

Source: GATT (1986).

There are more serious arguments suggesting that Article XXIV is in direct contradiction of the spirit of the WTO.[7] However, it can be argued that if nations decide to treat one another as if they are part of a single economy, nothing can be done to prevent them from doing so, and that IEI schemes, particularly the EU at the time of its formation in 1957, can have a strong impulse towards liberalization. In the EU case, the setting of CETs by 1969 (see appendix to Chapter 2) happened to coincide with the GATT's Kennedy Round of tariff reductions (by about 35 per cent) in 1967. However, experience suggests that IEI can be associated with protec-tionism, for example, the EU's CAP, which would not have been possible in the absence of the EU. But the point about the WTO not being able to deter countries from pursuing IEI has general validity: the WTO ulti-mately is dependent upon the member states' respecting its rules.

Table 1.2 GATT/WTO rounds of negotiations

Name of round	Round starting date	Round duration	Number of participating countries	Topics covered	Outcome
Geneva	April 194	7 months	23	Tariffs	The signing of the GATT agreement; 45,000 tariff concessions impacting on $10 billion of trade
Annery	April 1949	5 months	13	Tariffs	About 5,000 tariff concessions exchanged between participants
Torquay	September 1950	8 months	38	Tariffs	Exchanged about 8,700 tariff concessions, cutting the 1948 tariff levels by 25%
Geneva II	January 1956	5 months	26	Tariffs; admission of Japan	Tariff reductions worth $2.5 billion
Dillon	September 1960	11 months	26	Tariffs	Tariff concessions worth $4.9 billion
Kennedy	May 1964	37 months	62	Tariffs; Anti-dumping	Tariff concessions worth $40 billion
Tokyo	September 1973	74 months	102	Tariffs; non-tariff measures; framework' agreements	Tariff reductions worth in excess of $300 billion
Uruguay	September 1986	87 months	123	Tariffs; non-tariff measures; rules; services; intellectual property; dispute settlement; textiles; agriculture; creation of WTO; etc.	WTO creation; extending the range of trade negotiations, resulting in 40% in tariff reductions and agricultural subsidies; agreement to allow full access for textiles and clothing from developing nations; an extension of intellectual propery rights
Doha	November 2001	still in progress	159	Tariffs; non-tariff measures; agriculture; labour standards; environment; competition; investment; transparency; patents; etc.	The round is yet to be concluded, but a Bali Package was signed on 7 December 2013 which is expected to facilitate the conclusion of the Round

Source: Compiled from various GATT and WTO publications.

Of course, these considerations are more complicated than is suggested here, particularly since there are those who would argue that nothing could be more discriminatory than for a group of nations to remove all impediments (import quotas and non-tariff-trade barriers, NTBs) on their mutual trade and investment, while *at the same time* maintaining the initial levels against outsiders.[8] But it is difficult to find 'clubs' which extend equal privileges to non-subscribers, although the Asia Pacific Economic Cooperation (APEC) forum (see Section 1.4.3) aspires to 'open regionalism', one interpretation of which is the extending of the removals of restrictions on trade and investment to all countries, not just member nations. This point lies behind the concern with whether IEI hinders or enhances the prospects for the free multilateral reductions in trade and investment barriers that the WTO is supposed to promote. Moreover, as we shall see below in Section 1.5, IEI schemes may lead to resource reallocation effects that are economically undesirable. However, to deny nations the right to form such associations, particularly when the main driving force may be political rather than economic, as was the case with the ECSC, would have been a major setback for the world community. Hence, much as Article XXIV raises serious problems regarding how it fits in with the general spirit of the WTO – and many proposals have been put forward for its reform – its adoption also reflects deep understanding of the future development of the world economy.

1.4   IEI worldwide

Since the end of the Second World War various forms of IEI (see Map 1.1) have been proposed and numerous schemes have actually been implemented.[9] Even though some of these were subsequently discontinued or completely reformulated, the number adopted during the decade commencing 1957 was so great as to prompt the description of that period as the 'age of IEI'.[10] Since 1964, however, there has been an unprecedented proliferation of IEI schemes, so the depiction is more apt for the post-1964 era: by mid-2013, 575 RTAs were notified to the WTO, of which 379 are in force. The following subsections provide a brief summary of all these schemes by continent, naturally ending with Europe, given that it is the focus of this book.

1.4.1   IEI in Africa

Africa has numerous schemes of IEI (Map 1.1). Indeed, practically every single African country belongs to more than one scheme. And if one included integration during colonial times, then Africa would claim

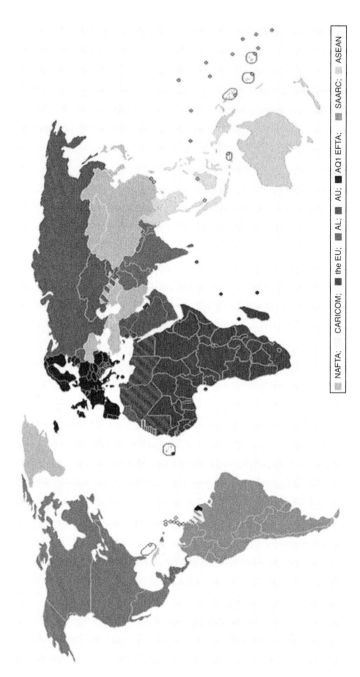

| NAFTA; | CARICOM; | the EU; | AL; | AU; | AQ1 EFTA; | SAARC; | ASEAN |

Map 1.1 Economic Integration Worldwide

Source: To be found on the internet at 'map of regional integration schemes'.

to have the oldest two schemes in the world. The first is the Southern African Customs Union (SACU, created in 1910, which is dominated by South Africa, with all members except for Botswana being part of a Rand-based common monetary area). The second is the East African Community (EAC, established by the British in 1919 for their own colonial administrative ease). But it should be stressed that IEI is confined to countries that adopt it voluntarily, in other words, not being imposed on them by colonialists or empire builders.

In West Africa, the West African Economic and Monetary Union (UEMOA; its French acronym) and the Mano River Union (MRU) coexist with the Economic Community of West African States (ECOWAS) with considerable membership overlap. A similar situation exists in Central Africa with the Economic Community of Central African States (ECCAS), the Central African Economic and Monetary Community (CEMAC; its French acronym) and the Economic Community of the Countries of the Great Lakes (CEPGL). In Eastern Africa, there is the Common Market for Eastern and Southern Africa (COMESA), with the Intergovernmental Authority on Development (IGAD) and the EAC as smaller inner groups. In Southern Africa, there are the Southern African Development Community (SADC) and the Southern African Customs Union (SACU). Northern Africa used to be the only subregion with a single scheme, the Arab Maghreb Union (AMU; UMA in French), but the later creation of the Community of Sahel-Saharan States (CEN-SAD) has brought it in line with the rest of Africa.

The AMU was established in 1989 by Algeria, Libya, Mauritania, Morocco and Tunisia by the Constitutive Treaty of the Union of the Arab Maghreb. It aim is to guarantee cooperation with similar regional institutions, participate in the 'enrichment of the international dialogue, reinforce the independence of its member states and safeguard their assets'. Within these wide terms, it aspired to become a CU before the end of 1995, a CM by 2000 and to achieve eventual political unity. Yet it is inactive, if not completely frozen, due to a deep rift between Algeria and Morocco over the Western Sahara.

The CEN-SAD was established in 1998, following a conference of political leaders in Tripoli, Libya, by Burkina Faso, Chad, Libya, Mali, Niger and Sudan. In 2000, it decided to emulate the EU, that is, to become an EconU. Since its establishment, the CEN-SAD has acquired 22 member nations. It now includes Benin (2002), the Central African Republic (1999), Comoros (2007), Ivory Coast (2004), Djibouti (2000), Egypt (2001), Eritrea (1999), Gambia (2000), Ghana (2005), Guinea (2007), Guinea Bissau (2004), Kenya (2008), Liberia (2004), Morocco (2001), Nigeria (2001), São Tomé and Príncipe (2008), Senegal (2000),

Sierra Leone (2005), Somalia (2001), Togo (2002) and Tunisia (2001). Mauritania was a member during 2008–12.

The ECOWAS was launched in 1975 by the signing of the Treaty of Lagos. It has 15 member states: Benin, Burkina Faso, Cape Verde, Ivory Coast, Gambia, Ghana, Guinea, Guinea Bissau, Liberia, Mali, Niger, Nigeria, Senegal, Sierra Leone and Togo. Mauritania was a member, but withdrew in 2000. Its aim is to create an economic and monetary union. Its revised treaty envisaged a mere CU by 2000, later delayed to 1 January 2003, and some member states have not even achieved an FTA.

The UEMOA was created by a treaty signed in Dakar, Senegal, in 1994 by the francophone member states of the ECOWAS: Benin, Burkina Faso, Ivory Coast, Mali, Niger, Senegal and Togo. They were joined by Guinea Bissau, a non-francophone country, in 1997. It is now a CU, introducing its CETs in January 2000, yet it also applies them to the rest of the ECOWAS.

The MRU was established in 1973 by Liberia and Sierra Leone in the Mano River Declaration. They were joined by Guinea in 1980, and in 2008 the Ivory Coast also agreed to join. Its aim is to foster economic cooperation, including a CU with certain cooperation in the industrial sector. Due to conflicts between the member nations (Sierra Leone Civil War, First Liberian Civil War, Second Liberian Civil War), MRU was dormant for a long time, but was reactivated on 20 May 2004.

The ECCAS was established in 1983 by the Brazzaville Treaty by Burundi, the Democratic Republic of the Congo, Rwanda and São Tomé & Príncipe. They were joined by Angola in 1999. After becoming operative in 1985, it was inactive for several years due to the non-payment of membership fees and the conflict in the Great Lakes region, but in 1998, the members decided to resurrect the organization.

The CEPGL was created in 1976 by the signing of the Agreement of Gisenyi by three countries: Burundi, the Democratic Republic of the Congo and Rwanda. Its purpose is to promote regional economic cooperation and integration, but it has been virtually inactive due to the conflicts within the bloc.

The CEMAC was founded in 1999 by six nations: Gabon, Cameroon, the Central African Republic, Chad, the Republic of the Congo and Equatorial Guinea. It has a common currency and has taken steps towards a CU.

The COMESA was established in 1994 by 19 countries that stretch from Libya in the north to Swaziland in the south. Of its member nations, Djibouti, Egypt, Kenya, Madagascar, Malawi, Mauritius, Sudan, Zambia and Zimbabwe formed an FTA in 2000. Burundi and Rwanda joined them in 2004, the Comoros and Libya in 2006 and the Seychelles in 2009. Note that of the member states of the EAC (first *truly* established in 1967), Kenya and Uganda are also members of the COMESA, while Tanzania also belongs to the SADC, having earlier withdrawn from the COMESA. The EAC and the COMESA, in the May 1997 Memorandum of Understanding, agreed to become a CU.

The SADC is the follower of the Southern African Development Cooperation Council (SADCC), created in 1980. Its membership comprises 15 nations: Angola, Botswana (since 1997), the Democratic Republic of the Congo, Lesotho, Madagascar (reinstated in 2014), Malawi, Mauritius (since 1995), Mozambique, Namibia (since independence in 1990), the Seychelles (was a member during 1997–2004 and rejoined in 2008), the Republic of South Africa (sine 1994), Swaziland, Tanzania, Zambia and Zimbabwe. In 1992, it became the SADC by the Windhoek Declaration and Treaty and initiated an FTA in 2000. In 2008, the SADC joined the COMESA to form the African Free Trade Zone.

Note that the IGAD (formed in 1996 to replace the equivalent Association on Drought and Development of 1986) and the Indian Ocean Commission (IOC, set up in 1982, with vague aims and ambitions, except for concentration on some functional cooperation areas such as fisheries and tourism) have agreed to adopt the COMESA's aims

Hence a unique characteristic of IEI in Africa is the multiplicity of overlapping schemes, made more complicated by the coexistence of intergovernmental cooperation organizations. For example, in West Africa alone, in 1984 there was a total of 33 schemes and intergovernmental cooperation organizations, and by the late 1980s, about 130 inter-governmental, multisectoral economic organizations existed simultaneously with all the above-mentioned IEI schemes.[11] That is why the United Nations Economic Commission for Africa (UNECA) recommended in 1984 that there should be some rationalization in the economic cooperation attempts in West Africa. Therefore, some would claim that the creation by all the African nations except Morocco of the African Economic Community (AEC) in 1991, and the African Union (AU) in 2001 by the Constitutive Act, are the appropriate response. The AU replaced the Organization for African Unity (OAU). However, that response would be incorrect, since the AEC not only officially endorses all the existing African IEI schemes but also encourages the creation of new ones while remaining silent on how they can all coexist.[12] When this uniqueness is combined with the proliferation of schemes, one cannot disagree with the declaration that '*Reculer pour mieux sauter* is not a dictum that seems to carry much weight…. On the contrary, if a certain level of [IEI] cannot be made to work, the reaction of policy makers has typically been to embark on something more elaborate, more advanced and more demanding in terms of administrative requirements and political commitment'.[13]

1.4.2 IEI in the Western Hemisphere

IEI in Latin America has been too volatile to describe in simple terms, since the post-1985 experience has been very different from that in the 1960s and 1970s. At the risk of oversimplifying, one can state that there are four IEI schemes in this region (see Map 1.1). Under the 1960 Treaty of Montevideo, the Latin American Free Trade Association (LAFTA) was formed between Mexico and all the countries of South America except for Guyana and Surinam. The LAFTA came to an end in the late 1970s, but was promptly succeeded by the Association for Latin American Integration (Associación Latinoamericana de Integración, ALADI or LAIA) in 1980. The Managua Treaty of 1960 established the Central American Common Market (CACM) between Costa Rica, El Salvador, Guatemala, Honduras and Nicaragua. In 1969, the Andean Pact (AP) was established under the Cartagena Agreement, forming a closer link between some of the least developed nations of the LAFTA, now LAIA.

Since the debt crisis in the 1980s, IEI in Latin America has taken a new turn. Mexico joined Canada and the United States in the North American Free Trade Agreement (NAFTA, see below) in 1993. Argentina, Brazil, Paraguay[14] and Uruguay, the more developed nations of LAIA, signed the Treaty of Asunción in 1991 to create MERCOSUR (Mercado Comùn del Sur or Southern Common Market). The MERCOSUR became a CU on 1 January 1995 and aimed to become a CM by 1995, but this has yet to happen. Bolivia and Chile became associate members in 1996, a move which Brazil saw as merely a first step towards the creation of a South American Free Trade Area (SAFTA), a counterweight to the efforts in the north (see below). Indeed, by 2004 the number of associates increased to six by including Colombia, Ecuador, Peru (2003) and Venezuela, and in 2006 Venezuela became an accessing member, with full membership in 2012. Guyana and Suriname became associate members in 2013. In 1999, The MERCOSUR reached agreement with the EU to start negotiations on an arrangement for free trade and investment between them, which is yet to be concluded. Also, on 29 April 2006, Cuba, Bolivia and Venezuela signed an agreement creating the Bolivarian Alternative for the Americas (ALBA) to thwart US plans for a Free Trade Area of the Americas (FTAA, see below).

There is one scheme of IEI in the Caribbean. In 1973, the Caribbean Community (CARICOM) was formed by practically all the nations in the area. The CARICOM replaced the Caribbean Free Trade Association (CARIFTA), which was established in 1968.

In 1988, Canada and the United States established the Canada–US Free Trade Agreement (CUSFTA or CUFTA), and, together with Mexico, they formed NAFTA in 1993, which started to operate from 1 January 1994. NAFTA is also the first scheme to include investment, and hence has started the present trend for the equal treatment of trade and investment in FTAs (see above). When George H. W. Bush was the US president, he suggested the enlargement of NAFTA to include the rest of the western hemisphere. He hoped to construct an FTAA, to be concluded by 1 January 2005, but due to a strong movement against increased poverty, led by Argentina, Bolivia, Brazil and Venezuela, this did not happen. Chile has been negotiating membership of NAFTA. It should be added that a Central American Free Trade Agreement (CAFTA), between the US, five Central American nations (Costa Rica, El Salvador, Guatemala, Honduras and Nicaragua) and the Dominican Republic was to take effect on 1 January 2006, but due to various inconsistencies in the process of legal reforms in these countries, bar the US, this did not happen.

1.4.3   IEI in the Asia-Pacific

Until recently, Asia did not figure prominently in the league of IEI schemes (see Map 1.1), but this was not surprising given the existence of such large (if only in terms of population) countries as China and India. Nevertheless, there was the Regional Cooperation for Development (RCD), a very limited arrangement for sectoral integration between Iran, Pakistan and Turkey. In addition, there was the Association of Southeast Asia (ASA), which was a collaborative effort between Malaysia, the Philippines and Thailand, and Maphilindo, which followed soon after, joining together Indonesia, the Philippines and Thailand. The Association for South-East Asian Nations (ASEAN), which is now comprised of ten member nations, was founded in 1967, but after almost a decade of inactivity, the ASEAN was galvanized into renewed vigour in 1976 by the security problems which the reunification of Vietnam seemed to present to its membership.[15]

The drive for the ASEAN's establishment and for its vigorous reactivation in 1976 was both political and strategic. However, right from the start, economic cooperation was one of the most important aims of the ASEAN; indeed, most of the vigorous activities of the group since 1976 have been predominantly in the economic field, and the admission of Vietnam in 1995 is a clear manifestation of this. Moreover, at the fourth ASEAN summit, held in Singapore in January 1992, the ASEAN initiated the ASEAN Free Trade Area (AFTA), which laid out a comprehensive programme for intramember nations' tariff reductions, to be implemented in phases by 2008. This was completed in 2002, six years ahead of schedule. In the meantime, the programme of tariff reductions has been broadened and accelerated, and a host of 'AFTA Plus' activities initiated, including efforts to eliminate NTBs and to harmonize customs nomenclatures, valuation and procedures, and develop common product certification standards. In addition, the ASEAN later signed framework agreements for intraregional liberalization of trade in services and for regional cooperation in intellectual property rights (IPRs), and on 23 August 2006 its trade ministers agreed on a EU-style association by 2015 instead of 2020. On 20 October 2007, the ASEAN Charter was adopted, which aims to 'strengthen democracy, enhance good governance and the rule of law, and to *promote and protect human rights and fundamental freedoms*, with due regard to the rights and responsibilities of the Member States of ASEAN' (italics added).[16] On 4 November 2002, the ASEAN and China signed a PTA, covering both trade and investment, to be completed by 2010 by the original six member nations, and by 2015 by the remaining four. Moreover, an ASEAN+3 PTA with an East Asian Community[17] in mind, was agreed with China, Japan and South Korea in 2003, but is yet to be finalized; likewise with an ASEAN+6 which includes Australia, India and New Zealand.

On 8 December 1985, the South Asian Association for Regional Cooperation (SAARC) was established by Bangladesh, Bhutan, India, Maldives, Nepal, Pakistan and Sri Lanka. Its aim is to accelerate the process of economic and social development of the members, but within the wider context of working together in a 'spirit of friendship, trust and understanding'. On 13 November 2005, at the thirteenth summit, held in Dhaka, Bangladesh, the SAARC agreed to admit Afghanistan as a member, to grant China and Japan observer status and to firmly commit to the realization of a South Asian Economic Union as well as an FTA (SAFTA).

In 1965, Australia and New Zealand entered into an FTA called the New Zealand Australia Free Trade Area. But, in 1983, it was replaced by a more important arrangement: the Australia New Zealand Closer Economic Relations and Trade Agreement (CER, for short). This has resulted in the complete elimination of all restrictions on goods and services between the two countries.

A scheme for the Pacific Basin integration-cum-cooperation was being hotly discussed during the 1980s. In the late 1980s, it was argued that given the diversity of countries within the Pacific region, it would seem highly unlikely that a very involved scheme of integration would evolve over the next decade or so. There did exist various fora involving governments, business and academics across the region,[18] but none could be deemed to be IEI schemes. However, in 1989 the Asia Pacific Economic Cooperation (APEC) forum was established by the ASEAN in addition to

Australia, Canada, Japan, New Zealand, South Korea and the US. These participants were joined by China, Hong Kong and Taiwan in 1991. In 1993, President Clinton galvanized it into its present form, and its membership increased to 18 nations with the addition of Chile, Mexico and Papua New Guinea. In Bogor, Indonesia, in 1994 the APEC declared its intention to create a free trade and investment area embracing its advanced member nations by 2010, with the rest to follow ten years later. The APEC tried to chart the route for realizing this vision in Osaka, Japan, in 1995, and came up with the interesting resolution that each member nation should unilaterally declare its own measures for freeing trade and investment; agriculture was completely left out of the reckoning. China immediately obliged by declaring that it would do this for a vast number of products, an act conditional on WTO membership, which China was negotiating at the time. In November 1998, Peru, Russia and Vietnam joined the APEC, increasing its total membership to 21 nations. In its 2004 meeting in Bangkok, Thailand, the APEC outlined its priorities as the promotion of trade and investment liberalization, the enhancement of human security and the use of the organization to help people and societies benefit from globalization. And at the 2010 summit, with the financial crisis in mind, its leaders declared their support for the goals of the Group of Twenty (G20) London 2009 Framework for Strong, Sustainable and Balanced Growth, by joining in their commitment to (a) work together to ensure that macroeconomic, regulatory and structural policies are collectively consistent with more sustainable and balanced trajectories of growth; (b) promote current account sustainability and open trade and investment to advance global prosperity and growth sustainability; (c) undertake macro prudential and regulatory policies to help prevent credit and asset price cycles from becoming forces of destabilization; and (d) promote development and poverty reduction as part of the rebalancing of global growth.

Officially speaking, the APEC aims to further enhance economic growth and prosperity, as well as strengthen the Asia-Pacific region. It claims to be the only intergovernmental grouping in the world that operates on the basis of non-binding commitments, open dialogue and equal respect for the views of all participants. It has no treaty obligations and reaches decisions by consensus and commitments entered into voluntarily.

One should add that since 2010, 12 of the 21 APEC nations (Australia, Brunei, Chile, Canada, Japan, Malaysia, Mexico, New Zealand, Peru, Singapore, the US and Vietnam) have been negotiating the creation of the Trans-Pacific Partnership (TPP). This would broaden the 2005

Trans-Pacific Strategic Economic Partnership Agreement (TPSEP or P4) between only Brunei, Chile, New Zealand and Singapore. The TPP aims to enhance trade and investment; promote innovation, economic growth and development; and support the creation and retention of jobs.

1.4.4 IEI in the Middle East

There are several schemes in the Middle East, but some of them extend beyond the geographical area traditionally designated as such. This is natural since there are nations with Middle Eastern characteristics in parts of Africa. The Arab League (AL) clearly demonstrates this reality since it comprises 22 nations, extending from the Persian Gulf in the east to Mauritania and Morocco in the west. Hence the geographical area covered by the scheme includes the whole of North Africa, a large part of the 'traditional' Middle East, as well as Djibouti and Somalia. The purpose of the AL is to strengthen the close ties linking Arab states, to coordinate their policies and activities, to direct them to their common benefit and to mediate in disputes between them. These are vague terms of reference, consistent with very limited achievements. For example, the Arab Economic Council, whose membership consists of all Arab Ministers of Economic Affairs, was entrusted with suggesting ways for economic development, cooperation, organization and coordination. The Council for Arab Economic Unity (CAEU), which was formed in 1957, had the aim of establishing an integrated economy of all AL states. Moreover, in 1964 the Arab Common Market was formed by Egypt, Iraq, Jordan and Syria, but in practice never got off the ground. The exception seems to be the Gulf Cooperation Council (GCC, officially referred to as the Cooperation Council of the Arab States of the Gulf), established on 25 May 1981, which is keen to stress that long-lasting and deep religious and cultural ties link its members and that strong kin relationships prevail amongst its citizens. The GCC claims to have concrete objectives as an economic and political policy-coordinating forum; has growing cooperation on, inter alia, customs duties, intellectual property protection, standard setting and intra-area investment; and has resolved most of the practical details for establishing a CU in 2003. In 2008, they launched a CM. The target date for introducing a single currency was 2010, but disputes regarding the location of the common central bank in Riyadh rather the United Arab Emirates (UAE) have put this on hold. Jordan applied for membership, Iraq did likewise in 2011, and Morocco has been invited to join. In short, the GCC wants to bring together the monarchical states of the Gulf and beyond to prepare the ground for them to join forces in the economic, political and military spheres.

With regard to economic integration in the Middle East, the UMA, which aims to create an organization similar to the EU, has already been mentioned in the context of Africa. But there is also the Arab Cooperation Council (ACC), founded on 16 February 1989 by Egypt, Iraq, Jordan and the Arab Yemen Republic with the aim of boosting Arab solidarity and acting as yet another link in the chain of Arab efforts towards integration.

1.4.5   IEI in Europe

The EU is the most noted of all IEI schemes (see Map 1.1). That is because the EU is almost a complete economic union (EconU, above): (a) it is practically a complete CM due to the 1987 Single European Market, SEM, which allows for the free movement of people, goods, services, capital and establishment; (b) it speaks with one voice in international trade matters; (c) 19 of its 28 Member States have the same currency (euro), with the European Central Bank (ECB) in charge of Eurozone monetary policy; (d) it has a system for monitoring and influencing fiscal policy, the Stability and Growth Pact (see Chapters 2 and 6); and (e) it has its own budget, financing a range of policies. Also, since the entry into force of the Treaty of Lisbon on 1 December 2009, it has (f) a single President of the European Council, and (g) a Foreign Policy Chief, called the High Representative (HR), who controls a vast diplomatic corps, now in the process of being established. And since the financial crisis of 2008, it has created (h) the European Financial Stability Facility (EFSF) and the European Stability Mechanism (ESM) to assist Eurozone nations in their troubles. Moreover, on 20 March 2014, it agreed to create a Single Resolution Mechanism for handling banking crises, having transferred in the previous year the powers to supervise the Eurozone's largest banks from the national regulators to the ECB, and thus it is close to having a Banking Union.

Also, of the six EU founding states, Germany (West), France and Italy were top ten world economies, the remaining three being Belgium, the Netherlands and Luxembourg. Since then, two such economies have joined, the UK and Spain, but recently Spain dropped one level. If one considers the top 25 world economies, the EU would account for ten of them in terms of both Gross National Income (GNI), using the World Bank's Atlas Method and GNI adjusted for Purchasing Power Parity (PPP; Table 1.3). Furthermore, the EU has proved a magnet for new members, so in addition to the founding member nations, known as the Original Six (hereafter, the Six), there are now an additional 22 member states. The EU of 28 continues to receive applications for membership; hence, it is set to include practically the whole of Europe and may go beyond the

Table 1.3 World's top 25 economies, 2013

	GNI (WB Atlas method) ($ billion)	GNI (PPP) ($ billion)
US	16,967.7	17,057.5
China	8,905.3	16,080.6
Japan	5,875.0	4,791.6
Germany	3,716.8	3,590.7
France	2,789.7	2,481.2
UK	2,506.9	2,292.2
Brazil	2,342.6	2,955.3
Italy	2,058.2	2,040.0
Russia	1,988.2	3,329.7
India	1,960.1	6,697.9
Canada	1,835.3	1,497.3
Australia	1,515.6	984.0
Spain	1,361.1	1,485.7
South Korea	1,301.6	1,679.1
Mexico	1,216.1	1,971.2
Indonesia	895.0	2,314.5
Turkey	820.6	1,405.7
Netherlands	797.2	726.0
Saudi Arabia	755.2	1,550.4
Switzerland	647.3	431.2
Sweden	567.3	428.4
Norway	521.7	338.2
Belgium	506.1	451.0
Poland	499.5	859.1
Iran	447.5	1,208.3

Source: Selected from the World Bank's World Development Indicators 2014.

geographical area if Turkey succeeds in joining in 2015 (see above and Chapter 2). None of the schemes just covered match this economic size and diversity.

Furthermore, the EU is the oldest IEI scheme in operation. Recall that 'involuntary' associations do not count (above). This longevity is part of the attraction of the EU.

Furthermore, the EU is prominent in terms of both world population and economy. Using 2008 and 2013, that is, pre-2008 global financial crisis and the latest available comparative data, calculated on a compilation from the World Bank (see Table 1.4), the population of EU27 in 2008 exceeded that of the US by about 193 million (63.5 per cent) and that of NAFTA (Canada, Mexico and US) by about 53 million (11.9 per cent), and was the third largest in the world, after China (1,357 million) and India (1,252 million). The equivalent figures for 2013 were 190.6 million (60.3

Table 1.4 A comparison of the EU, the US and NAFTA, 2008 and 2013

Scheme and US	Population (million)		GNI (WB Atlas method) ($ billion)		GNI (PPP) ($ billion)		GNI per capita ($)		GNI (PPP) per capita ($)	
	2008	2013	2008	2013	2008	2013	2008	2013	2008	2013
EU	496.7	506.7	17,455.10	16,444.20	16,015.40	17,332.10	35,142	32,454	32,244	34,206
US	304.1	316.1	15,006.70	16,967.70	14,794.20	17,057.50	49,348	53,678	48,649	53,962
NAFTA	443.8	473.6	17,566.60	20,019.10	17,720.50	20,526.00	39,582	42,271	39,929	43,524

Source: own calculations of data selected from the World Bank's World Development Indicators (2014).

per cent) and 33.1 million (7 per cent). The combined economic weight of the EU in 2008, in terms of GNI, converted using the World Bank's Atlas Method for exchange rates, exceeded that of the US by $2448.4 billion (16.3 per cent), but fell short of that of NAFTA by $111.5 billion (0.6 per cent) in 2013. Using the purchasing power parity (PPP) method, the EU did better than the US by 8.3 per cent, but performed worse than NAFTA by 10.7 per cent in 2008. In 2013, the equivalent figures were 1.6 and 18.4 respectively, that is, the EU performed better than the US, but worse than NAFTA. One should not read too much into the per capita differences since what is important is the number of EU nations that are in the top ten world economies, but the data is provided in the table. Needless to say, the overall picture indicates that the 2008 global financial crisis has impacted more severely on the EU relative to the US; hence, the 2013 data may not be 'normal', and thus the 2008 comparison may be more pertinent.

The EFTA is the other major scheme of IEI in Europe. To understand its membership, one has to know something about its history (detailed in chapter 2). In the mid-1950s, when the European Economic Community (EEC) of the Six plus the UK was being contemplated, the UK was unprepared to commit itself to some of the economic and political aims envisaged for that community. For example, the adoption of a common agricultural policy and the eventual political unity of Western Europe were seen as aims which were in direct conflict with the UK's powerful position in the world and its interests in the Commonwealth, particularly with regard to 'Commonwealth preference', which granted special access to the markets of the Commonwealth. Hence the UK favoured the idea of a Western Europe that adopted free trade in industrial products only, thus securing for itself the advantages offered by the Commonwealth as well as opening up Western Europe as a free market for its industrial goods. In short, the UK sought to achieve the best of both worlds, which is understandable, but such an arrangement was not acceptable to those countries seriously contemplating the formation of the EEC, especially France, which stood to lose in an arrangement excluding a common policy for agriculture (see Chapter 2). As a result the UK approached those Western European nations, which had similar interests with the purpose of forming an alternative scheme of IEI to counteract any possible damage due to the formation of the EEC. The outcome was the EFTA, which was established in 1960 by the Stockholm Convention, with the object of creating a free market for industrial products only. There were some agreements on non-manufacturers, but these were relatively unimportant.

The membership of the EFTA consisted of Austria, Denmark, Norway, Portugal, Sweden, Switzerland (and Liechtenstein) and the United

Kingdom. Finland became an associate member in 1961, and Iceland joined in 1970 as a full member. But Denmark, Ireland and the UK joined the European Community (EC; which is what the EEC became) in 1973; Portugal and Spain did so in 1986; and Austria, Finland and Sweden joined the EU in 1995. All the remaining EFTA countries, except Switzerland, that is, Iceland, Liechtenstein and Norway, now belong to the European Economic Area (EEA), a scheme introduced in 1992 which provides economic but not political membership in the EU, being part of the SEM without having a say in EU decisions.

Before the dramatic events of 1989–90, IEI schemes in Europe were not confined to the EU and the EFTA. The socialist planned economies of Eastern Europe had their own arrangement: the Council for Mutual Economic Assistance (CMEA), or COMECON as it was generally known in the West. The CMEA was formed in 1949 by Bulgaria, Czechoslovakia, the German Democratic Republic, Hungary, Poland, Romania and the Union of Soviet Socialist Republics (USSR), and they were later joined by three non-European countries: Mongolia (1962), Cuba (1972) and Vietnam (1978). In its early days, before the death of Joseph Stalin, CMEA activities were confined to the collation of the member nations' plans, the development of a uniform system of reporting statistical data and the recording of foreign trade statistics. However, during the 1970s the CMEA adopted a series of measures to implement a 'Comprehensive Programme of Socialist Integration', hence indicating that the organization was moving towards a form of integration based principally on plan coordination and joint planning activity, rather than on market levers.[19] The CMEA comprised a group of relatively small countries and one 'super-power', and the long-term aim of the association was to achieve a highly organized and integrated bloc, without any agreement ever having been made on how or when that was to be accomplished.

The dramatic changes that took place in the 1980s in Eastern Europe and the former USSR inevitably led to the CMEA's demise, this, together with the fact that the CMEA did not really achieve much in the nature of economic integration – indeed some analysts have argued that the entire organization was simply an instrument for the USSR to dictate its wishes to the rest.[20] However, soon after the USSR's breakup, 12 of the 15 former Soviet Republics created the Commonwealth of Independent States (CIS) to bring them closer together in a relationship originally intended to match the EU's, but to no avail because the relationship remains very limited. But since October 2011, Russia's president Vladimir Putin has been promoting the formation of a political and economic union, the Eurasian Union (EAU), between these nations. This is presently creating political turmoil in Ukraine, to which Putin has committed vast financial assistance and lower energy prices in return for tempting the country away from EU membership aspirations.

Before we turn from the topic of Europe, mention should be made of the Central European Free Trade Agreement (CEFTA), the Council of the Baltic Sea States (CBSS) and the Nordic Community. The CEFTA was originally formed by Czechoslovakia, Hungary and Poland in 1992, but with the EU enlargement, members have left when they joined the EU and new countries have joined, so it has moved southwards to include the republics of the former Yugoslavia,[21] Albania and Moldova. The CBSS involves 11 states, 9 EU states which border the Baltic, and Norway and Russia, and it focuses on cooperation but not economic integration. The Nordic Community involves five Nordic countries: Denmark, Finland, Iceland, Norway and Sweden.[22] The Nordic scheme is one of cooperation rather than IEI since its members belong to either the EU or the EEA through which economic integration is organized.

1.4.6 An intricate web of relationships

All these schemes are connected by an increasing number of PTAs between them and between individual members within them. This has resulted in an intricate web of interrelationships. Considering just the EU, since it is the main protagonist of PTAs, it has a special PTA, with cooperation and political dimensions, with the 79 African-Caribbean-Pacific (ACP) nations of the ACP-EU[23] arrangement (see Chapter 4). As already mentioned, the EU also has the EEA with three of the EFTA nations and more. Moreover, the EU has bilateral PTAs with countries all over the world, including Israel, Turkey and most African and Arab nations (see Map 1.2). If one thinks of the EU as being connected with wires to all these countries, one can understand why the term 'spaghetti bowl' has been used to describe this web of interrelationships. The bowl would be even more intricate if the Transatlantic Trade and Investment Partnership (TTIP), negotiations which started in 2013, becomes a reality. This is because it would allow for the free exchange of goods and investment between both NAFTA and the EU, with a total population of about one billion and GNI of just over \$36 trillion (see Table 1.4), although Canada and Mexico will have to negotiate separate deals.

1.5 The possible gains from IEI

Economists have identified several possible gains from IEI due to increased market size. At the FTA and CU levels, the gains can be attributed to (a) enhanced efficiency in production made possible by increased specialization in accordance with the law of comparative advantage; (b) higher production levels because of better exploitation of economies of scale; (c) an improved international bargaining position, leading to better terms of trade, that is, lower prices for imports and higher prices for exports; (d) enforced changes in economic efficiency brought about by enhanced competition; and (e) changes affecting both the amount and quality of the factors of production arising from technological advances, enhanced by the increased competition.

If the level of economic integration is to proceed beyond the FTA and CU levels, further sources of gain can be envisaged. (f) The increased factor mobility across the borders of member nations in a CM, on the understanding that factors move in search of better rewards, would increase GNI. (g) The coordination of monetary and fiscal policies in EcUs, which would enable their being carried out at lower cost, also would increase GNI. (h) The goals of near full employment, higher rates of economic growth and better income distribution becoming unified targets, would enable their achievement at lesser costs, hence also leading to higher GNI.

It should be stressed, that these are *possible*, not *guaranteed* gains. Indeed, one can even envisage scenarios in which IEI results in worse economic performance. For instance, in the case of gain (a) above, increased specialization in production may result in unemployment in the sector from which the extra resources are attracted, and the adjustment costs may prove prohibitive if the skills of those who lose their jobs are not suitable to those areas in which production is increased. Moreover, improved terms of trade would depend on what happens in the 'outside' world: the non-participants may decide to act together to undermine the power of the scheme of IEI. Furthermore, some companies may get 'fatter' through mergers and acquisitions in order to lessen the threat to their dominance by the increased number of firms due to IEI. Consequently, they may become both less efficient and exploit their position to the detriment of consumers, and hence reduce national incomes. Thus the gains or losses depend on the particular scheme of IEI.

These considerations are too technical to discuss in this book, so they will not be discussed further here except where appropriate. These topics are available elsewhere in detail.[24] However, it is instructive to briefly consider gain (a), because it highlights three basic considerations that lie at the very heart of the economic analysis of IEI.

Consider two identical commodities produced in three nations at constant costs per unit. In Table 1.5.1, the cost of beef per kg is given in cents (of either € or US $) for the UK, France and New Zealand (NZ). With a 50 per cent non-discriminatory tariff rate, the cheapest source of

Table 1.5.1 Beef: illustrating 'trade creation'

	UK	France	NZ
The cost per unit (cents)	90	80	70
UK domestic price with a 50% tariff rate	90	120	105
UK domestic price when the UK and France form a customs union	90	80	105

supply of beef for the UK consumer is the home producer. When the UK and France form a CU, the cheapest source of supply for the UK consumer becomes France. Given that French and UK beef is identical, the UK consumers would naturally stop buying UK beef, importing French beef instead. Assuming that the resources devoted to beef production in the UK are diverted to other economic activities, that is, no unemployment occurs in the UK, and there are no adjustment costs, the UK as a nation would save 10 cents per kg of beef. This is referred to as 'trade creation': the replacement of expensive domestic production by cheaper imports from the partner.

Next consider, under the same assumptions for beef, a different product, butter, on which the UK has a lower non-discriminatory tariff rate (25 per cent) relative to beef. As shown in Table 1.5.2, before the CU, NZ is the cheapest source of supply for both the UK consumer and government. This is because the UK government buys a kg of NZ beef at 70 cents, and although the UK consumer is charged 87.5, the difference of 17.5 cents is tariff revenue for the UK government, which can be returned to the UK consumer as a refund. Hence, in effect, both the UK consumer and government pay only 70 cents per kg. After the CU, France becomes the cheapest source for the UK consumer: 80 against 87.5 cents per kg. However, for the UK as a whole, there is a loss of 10 cents per kg: 80 against the 70 cents paid to NZ. This is called 'trade diversion': the replacement of cheaper initial imports from the outside world by expensive imports from the partner.[25]

Now consider a different situation for both beef (Table 1.5.3) and butter (Table 1.5.4). The cost of beef and butter per kg is the same as in

Table 1.5.2 Butter: illustrating 'trade diversion'

	UK	France	NZ
The cost per unit (cents)	90	80	70
UK domestic price with a 25% tariff rate	90	100	87.5
UK domestic price when the UK and France form a customs union	90	80	87.5

Table 1.5.3 Beef: illustrating 'unilateral tariff reduction'

	UK	France	NZ
The cost per unit (cents)	90	80	70
UK domestic price with a 50% tariff rate	90	100	105
UK domestic price with a non-discriminatory tariff reduction of 80% (i.e. tariff rate becomes 10%)	90	80	77

Table 1.5.4 Butter: illustrating 'unilateral tariff reduction'

	UK	France	NZ
The cost per unit (cents)	90	80	70
UK domestic price with a 25% tariff rate	90	100	87.5
UK domestic price with a non-discriminatory tariff reduction of 80% (i.e. tariff rate becomes 5%)	90	80	73.5

the previous examples and so are the initial UK tariff rates. But instead of the creation of a CU by France and the UK, the UK decides to simply unilaterally reduce its tariff rates without discrimination by 80 per cent: from 50 per cent to 10 per cent for beef and from 25 per cent to 5 per cent for butter. It can then be seen that the UK will achieve the same benefits of trade creation in the case of beef. As to butter, the UK continues to buy from NZ; hence, it avoids the losses from trade diversion that it would have incurred in the CU with France. This situation is referred to as a policy of 'unilateral tariff reduction' (UTR).[26]

This dangerously simple analysis[27] (since a number of simplistic assumptions have been made to prove the point, such as unit costs of production do not change after integration, the displacement of production does not create unemployment) has been the inspiration for a massive literature on CU theory. Yet the three concepts of trade creation, trade diversions and UTR lie at the very heart of the analysis of the economic effects of IEI and the discussion regarding whether or not IEI undermines multilateral free trade. Trade creation and trade diversion still form the basis for any empirical evaluation of the economic effects of IEI schemes.

1.6 Why IEI?

We shall see in Chapter 2 that the driving force behind the formation of the EU, the earliest and most influential of all existing IEI schemes, was the political unity of Europe with the aim of realizing eternal peace in the Continent. Some analysts would also argue that the recent EU attempts at more intensive economic integration can be cast in the same vein, especially since they are accompanied by one currency, the euro, a full-time president and a 'foreign policy supremo'. At the same time, during the late 1950s and early 1960s, IEI among developing nations was perceived as the only viable way for them to make some real economic progress; indeed, that was the rationale behind the UN's encouragement and support of such efforts. More recently, the drive for IEI has been the belief that the opening up of markets would enhance the economic performance of the countries involved. It is conceded that the gains would be even greater if pursued globally, but frustrations with the WTO's slowness in reaching agreement, due to the varied interests of its many participants, have led some to the conclusion that IEI would result in a quicker pace for negotiations since, by definition, it would reduce the number of parties involved. There are also practical considerations, such as countries may feel that IEI would provide security of markets among the participants.

1.7   Pertinent questions

Since the EU is the most significant and influential of all IEI schemes, several pertinent questions should be asked. What are the true reasons for the European nations' drive for IEI? How does the EU reach decisions? What institutions has the EU created to enable it to achieve its integration aims? What policies has the EU deemed desirable to meet its aspirations? How does the EU finance its policies? And what does the future hold for the EU? The answers to these questions will reveal the very nature of the EU and why it is important. Thus Chapter 2 is devoted to a short history of EU integration, narrating the journey taken by the Original Six in 1951 to become today's club of 28. Chapter 3 describes how the EU reaches its decisions and implements them. Chapter 4 provides a brief but comprehensive coverage of EU policies, but begins with a fuller coverage of the SEM since it impacts on all policies. Chapter 5 shows how the EU finances its policies and operations. Chapter 6 deals with the most vital aspect of the EU: the EMU and the single currency, the euro. Chapter 7 is devoted to the importance of the EU. And Chapter 8 examines what the leading EU politicians consider the future of the EU should be.

Recommended Reading

El-Agraa, Ali M. (1999) *Regional Integration: Experience, Theory and Measurement*, Macmillan, Basingstoke; Barnes and Noble, New York.
*Although this book was first published 16 years ago, most of the theoretical work remains intact and the schemes have been updated in this chapter.

2
The Passage to the EU

2.1 Introduction

It was established in Chapter 1 that the EU is the most significant and influential of all international economic integration (IEI) schemes. But why have the Europeans pursued IEI? That was one of the questions raised at the end of that chapter. The purpose of this chapter is to provide the answer.

A proper appreciation of why the EU has been created and how it has evolved would not be possible without an understanding of the history of European unity. This is because in a world presently dominated by immediate considerations, recently bordering on the purely economic, the driving force behind European integration is often forgotten, and attempts to reform existing policies and to steer the EU in new directions seem to be frustrated. Thus an overall perspective is warranted. This chapter provides this, and in two main sections. The first is devoted to a very brief history of European unity, brief since otherwise a whole book would be needed to cover just this topic. The second offers a bird's-eye view of the evolution of the EU.

2.2 A short history of European unity

Most, if not all, actual steps taken to achieve economic and political unity in Europe originated after the end of the Second World War in 1945. However, the idea of European unity is deeply rooted in European thinking. History shows that there have been a number of proposals put forward for creating it. In the fourteenth century, the idea of a united Christendom inspired Pierre Dubois to propose a European Confederation to be ruled by a European Council of wise, expert and faithful men.

In the seventeenth century, the Duke of Sully desired to keep peace in Europe by means of a European army. In 1693, William Penn, the English Quaker, then the eponymous governor of Pennsylvania, wanted the creation of 'an Imperial Dyet, Parliament or State of Europe', as he outlined in his *Essay towards the Present and Future Peace of Europe*. In the nineteenth century, Pierre-Joseph Proudhon was strongly in favour of the formation of a European Federation and predicted that the twentieth century would witness an era of federations, forecasting disaster in the absence of such a development.

Immediately after the First World War, politicians began to give serious consideration to the concept of European unity. For example, in 1923 Count Coudenhove Kalergi, the Austrian founder-leader of the Pan-European Movement, called for the formation of a United States of Europe,[1] his reason being the successful assertion of Swiss unity in 1848, the forging of the German Empire in 1871 and, most significantly, the independence of the United States in 1776.[2] And on 5 September 1929, in a renowned speech, delivered to the League of Nations Assembly in Geneva, French foreign minister Aristide Briand, with the backing of his German counterpart, Gustav Stresemann, proposed the creation of a European Union within the framework of the League of Nations, and reiterated this later, when he was prime minister, by declaring that part of his political manifesto was the building of a United States of Europe.

The main reason for the pursuit of European unity was to achieve lasting peace in Europe. It was realized that there was no other means of putting an end to the Continent's woeful history of conflict, bloodshed, suffering and destruction. However, economic reasons were also a contributing factor. These were influenced by the tradition of free trade and Adam Smith's argument, in his *An Inquiry into the Nature and Causes of the Wealth of Nations* (1776), that 'the division of labour is limited by the extent of the market', which the German philosopher Friedrich Naumann utilized to propose in 1915 that European nation states were no longer large enough to compete on their own in world markets; therefore, they had to unite in order to guarantee their survival.

Despite the fact that there was no shortage of plans for creating a united Europe, it was not until 1945 that a combination of new forces and an intensification of old ones prompted action. First, Europe had been at the centre of yet another devastating war, caused by the ambitions of nation states. Those individuals who sought and some of those who still seek a united Europe have always had at the forefront of their minds the desire to prevent any further outbreak of war in Europe. It was believed that if the nations of Europe could be brought closer together, such war would become unthinkable. Second, the Second World War left Europe economically exhausted, and this led to the view that if Europe were to recover, it would require a concerted effort on the part of the European states. Third, the Second World War also soon revealed that for a long time Western Europe would have to face not only a powerful and politically alien Union of Soviet Socialist Republics (USSR) but also a group of European nations firmly fixed within the Eastern European bloc. It was felt that an exhausted and divided Europe (since the war embraced co-belligerents) presented both a power vacuum and a temptation to the USSR to fill it. Fourth, the ending of the war soon revealed that the wartime allies were in fact divided, with the two major powers, the US and the USSR, confronting each other in a bid for world supremacy. Hence, it should come as no surprise to learn that members of the European Movement, who wanted to get away from intergovernmental cooperation by creating institutions leading to a Federal Europe, felt the need for a third world force: 'the voice of Europe'. This force would represent the Western European viewpoint and could also act as a bridge between the Eastern and Western extreme positions.

2.2.1   Concrete unity efforts

The first concrete move for regional integration in Europe was made in 1947 with the establishment of the Economic Commission for Europe (ECE), which was set up in Geneva as one of five regional organizations of the United Nations (UN). Its objective was to initiate and participate in concerted measures aimed at securing the economic restructuring of the *whole* of Europe. A year later in March, the UK, France, Belgium, the Netherlands and Luxembourg founded the Brussels Treaty Organization (BTO). In recognition of the newer USSR threat, the BTO was designed to create a system of mutual assistance in times of attack on Europe, but it simultaneously perpetuated the wartime alliance against Germany. The BTO took an Atlantic form in 1949 when the five nations, together with the US and Canada as well as Denmark, Iceland, Italy (significantly, since it had been an Axis power), Norway and Portugal, founded the North Atlantic Treaty Organization (NATO). The aim of NATO was, and continues to be, to provide military defence against attack on any of its members.[3]

Also, in 1948 the Organization for European Economic Cooperation (OEEC) was formed and was followed a year later by the Council of Europe. These initiatives marked the beginning of the division of Western Europe into two camps, with, on the one hand, the UK and some of the countries that later formed the European Free Trade Association (EFTA), and, on the other, Belgium, France, West Germany, Italy, Luxembourg and the Netherlands, usually referred to as the Original Six (hereafter, simply the Six), which subsequently established the European Economic Community (EEC). The main reason for this division was that the UK was less committed to Europe as a main policy area than the Six. This was because, until the second half of the 1950s, the UK was still a world power, which had been on the victorious side and a major participant in some of the fateful geopolitical decision-making at the time, and it still had the Empire to dispose of. Therefore, British policy was bound to incorporate this wider dimension: relations with Europe had to compete with Empire (later, Commonwealth) ties and with the *special relationship* with the US. In addition, the idea of a politically united Europe (as we have seen, in some quarters this meant a United States of Europe) was strongly held by the other countries, particularly by France and Benelux (Belgium, the Netherlands and Luxembourg agreed in 1944 to form a customs union – for a technical definition, see Chapter 1, Section 1.1 – which did not become effective until 1948). But, despite the encouraging noises made by Winston Churchill, British prime minister, both during the Second World War and after, this was not a concept that thrilled British hearts;[4] indeed, Churchill was advocating European unity for Continental Europe, not a Europe that included the UK.

The different thinking between the UK and the Six about the political nature of European institutions was revealed in the discussions leading up to the establishment of the OEEC and the Council of Europe. The Second World War had left Europe devastated. The year 1947 was particularly bleak: bad harvests in the previous summer led to rising food prices; the severe winter of 1946–7 led to a fuel crisis; the Continental countries were producing very little, and what was produced tended to be retained rather than exported, while imports were booming; hence, foreign exchange reserves were running out. It was at this juncture that the US entered the scene to present the Marshall Plan. General George Marshall proposed that the US make aid available to help the European economy find its feet and that the European governments 'should get together' to decide how much assistance was needed. In short, the US did not feel it appropriate that it should unilaterally decide on the programme necessary to achieve this result. Although it seemed possible that this aid programme could be elaborated within the ECE framework, the USSR felt otherwise. Soviet reluctance was no doubt due to the fear that if its satellites participated, this would open the door to Western influence. Therefore, a conference was convened without the USSR, and the Committee for European Economic Cooperation (CEEC) was established.

The US attitude was that CEEC should not just provide it with a list of needs. The US perceived that the aid it was to give should be linked with progress towards European unification. This is an extremely important point since it shows that right from the very beginning, the European Movement enjoyed the encouragement and support of the US. Of course, the driving force behind the US' insistence on European unity was its desire to establish a solid defence against any western advance by the USSR. In other words, the US did not insist on unity for unity's sake. Indeed, the US also asked that its multinational companies should have free access to European markets. The CEEC led in turn to the creation of an aid agency: the OEEC. Here, the conflict between the UK and the Six, especially France, came to a head over the issue of *supranationalism*. France in particular (and it was supported by the US) wanted to introduce a supranational element into the new organization. But what is supranationalism? It can mean a situation in which international administrative institutions exercise power over, for example, the economies of the member states, or in which ministerial bodies, when taking decisions (to be implemented by international organizations), work on a majority voting system rather than insisting on unanimity.

The French view was not shared by the British, who favoured a body that would be under the control of a ministerial council in which decisions should be taken on a unanimity basis. The French, on the other hand, preferred an arrangement in which an international secretariat would be presided over by a secretary-general who would be empowered to take policy initiatives on major issues. Significantly, the organization that emerged was substantially in line with the British wish for unanimity rule. This was undoubtedly a reflection of the UK's relatively powerful position in the world at the time and her close alliance with the US.

In the light of subsequent events, it is also interesting to note that the US encouraged the European nations to consider the creation of a customs union.[5] Although this was of considerable interest to some Continental countries, it did not appeal to the UK. In the end, the OEEC convention merely recorded the intention to continue the study of this proposal. For a variety of reasons, one of which was UK opposition, the matter was not pursued further.

The creation of the Council of Europe, with broad political and cultural objectives, including the notable contribution to protecting the individual through the *Convention for the Protection of Human Rights and Fundamental Freedoms* (its statute expresses a belief in a common political heritage based on accepted spiritual and moral values, political liberty, the rule of law and the maintenance of democratic forms of government), also highlighted the fundamental differences in approach between the countries which later founded the EEC, on the one hand, and the British and Scandinavians, on the other. The establishment of the Council of Europe was preceded by the Congress of Europe at The Hague in May 1948. This was a grand rally of 'Europeans', attended by leading European statesmen, including Winston Churchill. The Congress adopted a resolution calling for the giving up of some national sovereignty before the accomplishment of economic and political union in Europe. Subsequently, a proposal was put forward, with the support of the Belgian and French governments, calling for the creation of a European Parliamentary Assembly in which resolutions would be passed by majority vote. A Committee of Ministers was to prepare and implement these resolutions.

Needless to add, the UK was opposed to this form of supranationalism and in the end the British view largely prevailed. The Committee of Ministers, which was the executive organ of the Council of Europe, had sole power of decision and generally these were taken on the unanimity principle. The Consultative Assembly that came into existence was a forum (its critics called it a debating society), not a European legislative body. In short, the British and Scandinavian *functionalists* – those who believed that European unity, insofar as it was to be achieved, was to be attained by *intergovernmental cooperation* – triumphed over the *federalists* – those who sought unity by the radical method of creating European institutions to which national governments would surrender some of their sovereignty. The final disillusionment of the federalists was almost certainly marked by the resignation of Paul-Henri Spaak (below), a devoted European federalist, from the presidency of the Consultative Assembly in 1951.

The next step in the economic and political unification of Western Europe was taken without the British and Scandinavians. It was the creation in 1951 of the European Coal and Steel Community (ECSC) by the Six, and marked the parting of ways in post-war Western Europe. The immediate factor in these developments was the revival of the West German economy. The passage of time, the efforts of the German people and the aid made available by the US through the Marshall Plan all contributed to this recovery. Indeed, the West German economic miracle was about to unfold.

It was recognized that the German economy would have to be allowed to regain its position in the world, and that the Allied control of coal and steel under the International Ruhr Authority could not last indefinitely.

The fundamental question was how the German economy in the sectors of iron, coal and steel, which were the basic materials of any war effort, could be allowed to regain its former powerful position without endangering the future peace of Europe. The answer was a French plan, elaborated by Jean Monnet, a French businessman turned adviser (Box 2.1 provides a brief list of his contributions to European unity), but put forward by Robert Schuman, French minister of foreign affairs, in May 1950. The Schuman Plan was essentially political in character. It was brilliant since it sought to end the historic rivalry of France and Germany by making a war between the two nations not only unthinkable but also materially impossible. This was to be achieved in a manner that ultimately would have the result of bringing about that European federation which is indispensable to peace. The answer was not to nationalize or indeed to internationalize the ownership of the means of production in coal, iron and steel, but to create, by the removal of customs duties, import quota restrictions and similar impediments on trade and factors of production, a 'common market', the technical definition of which is in Chapter 1, in these products. Every participating nation in such a common market would have equal access to the products of these industries wherever they might be located, and, to reinforce this, discrimination on the grounds of nationality was to be forbidden.

Box 2.1   Jean Monnet

Jean Monnet was a pivotal architect of European unity and a founding father of the EU. A whole book would be needed to do justice to his career, but here is a brief highlighting of his vital contributions.

Monnet was born on 9 November 1888 in Cognac, France, into a family of brandy merchants. At the age of 16, he abandoned his university entrance examinations and moved to London to spend several years working with an agent of his father's firm, travelling on business trips to Scandinavia, Russia, Egypt, Canada and the US.

Monnet held the conviction that the Allies could not win the First World War unless Britain and France combined their war resources. After some setbacks in trying to achieve such an outcome, he proposed the Anglo-French Supply Commission to assist in coordinating the flow of these resources to the Allies and was chosen to run it from London. In recognition of his services, he was appointed in 1919 as Deputy Secretary General of the newly established League of Nations (LN), and the British government bestowed an honorary knighthood on him.

Disappointed with the LN for its laborious decision-making process and unanimity rule, he returned to business in 1923, managed to rescue the family business and in the process established himself as an international financier. He was credited with the economic recovery of several Central and Eastern European countries, helping stabilize the Polish zloty in 1927 and the Romanian leu in 1928. He was also instrumental in reorganizing the Swedish match industry as well as laying the foundations in 1929 of the Bancamerica-Blair in San Francisco. During 1934–6, he was invited to live in China by Chiang Kai-shek to help reorganize the railway network.

In December 1939, he was sent to London to oversee the collectivization of the British and French war industries and made chairman of the Franco-British Committee for Economic Coordination. In 1940, in the face of the German advance in June, he proposed to Winston Churchill to consider a 'proclamation of the indissoluble union of the French and British peoples' and, much to the surprise of Churchill, the proposal received 'great consent' by the War Cabinet, which approved a final draft of an Anglo-French Union and authorized its dispatch to Paul Reynaud's government by the hand of General de Gaulle, but Reynaud´ government resigned a few hours later without having the chance to debate the proposal.[6]

In August 1940, the British government sent him to the US as a member of the British Supply Council to negotiate the purchase of war supplies. Soon after his arrival in Washington, DC, he became an adviser to President Franklin D. Roosevelt. Convinced that the US could serve as 'the great arsenal of democracy', he persuaded the president to launch a massive arms production programme to stimulate the economy and supply the Allies with military resources. In 1941, Roosevelt, with the endorsement of British prime minster Winston Churchill, launched the Victory Programme, which marked the entry of the US into the war effort. After the war, John Maynard Keynes, the noted British economist, claimed that through his coordinating efforts, Monnet had probably shortened the Second World War by a year.

In 1943, he joined the National Liberation Committee (NLC), General Charles de Gaulle's French government in exile in Algiers. It is known that on 5 August of the same year, he declared to the NLC that there would be no peace in Europe, 'if the states are reconstituted on the basis of national sovereignty' because 'the countries of Europe are too small to guarantee their peoples the necessary prosperity and social development', hence the 'European states must constitute themselves into a federation' (.http://www.newworldencyclopedia.org/entry/Jean_Monnet)

The plan had a number of attractive features. First, it provided an excellent basis for solving the 'Saar problem': the handing back of the Saar region to West Germany was more likely to be acceptable to the French if Germany was firmly locked into such a coal and steel community. Second, the plan was extremely attractive to Germany since membership in the community was a passport to international respectability; it was the best way of speeding up the end of occupation and avoiding the imposition of dampers on the expansion of the German economy. Third, the plan was also attractive to the federalists, who had found the OEEC fell far short of their aspirations for the Council of Europe (its unanimity rule and that no powers could be delegated to an independent commission or commissariat were extremely frustrating for them), and, in any case, the prospects for the OEEC were not very good, since by 1952 the four-year Marshall Plan period would be over, and the UK attitude was that thereafter the OEEC budget should be cut and some of its functions passed over to NATO.

As it turned out, the ECSC was much more to the federalists' taste. This is because its executive body, the High Authority, was given substantial direct powers, which could be exercised without the prior approval of the Council of Ministers (the ECSC's second institution. It also had a Parliamentary Assembly, Court of Justice and Consultative Committee). Note that Monnet was made the first president of the High Authority and occupied his office during 1952–5.

The plan received favourable responses from the Six. The UK was invited to join but refused. Clement Attlee, British prime minister at the time, told the House of Commons, 'We on this side [of the House] are not prepared to accept that the most vital economic forces of this country should be handed over to an authority that is utterly undemocratic and is responsible to nobody'. However, the Six were not to be deterred, and in April 1951 the Treaty of Paris, valid for 50 years, was signed. The ECSC was born, and it embarked on an experiment in limited economic integration on 1 January 1952.

The next stage in the development of European unity was also concerned with Germany. When the Korean War broke out in 1950, the US, faced with the need to reduce its forces in Europe for deployment in Korea, put pressure on the Western European nations to do more to defend themselves against possible attack by the USSR. This raised the issue of a military contribution from West Germany, the implication being that Germany should be rearmed. However, France was opposed to this proposal, and was equally against Germany becoming a member of NATO. This was not a purely negative attitude. Indeed, René Pleven, French prime minister at the time, put forward a plan which envisaged that there would be no German army as such, but that there would be a European army to which each participating nation, including Germany, could contribute.

Britain was not against this idea, but did not wish to be involved. The Six were positively enthusiastic, and discussion began in 1951 with a view to creating a European Defence Community (EDC). It was envisaged that there would be a Joint Defence Commission, a Council of Ministers, a Parliamentary Assembly and a Court of Justice. In other words, the EDC institutions were to parallel those created for the ECSC.

The Six made rapid progress in the negotiations and the EDC Treaty was signed in May 1952.

Having gone so far, there were a number of reasons for further integrative efforts. First, the pooling of both defensive (NATO) and offensive capabilities (the EDC) inevitably reduced the possibility of independent foreign policies. It was logical to follow integration in defence with measures, which served to achieve political integration as well. Second, it was also desirable to establish a system whereby effective control could be exercised over the proposed European army. Third, there was also the Dutch desire that progress in the military field should be paralleled by more integration in the economic sphere as well. Therefore, the foreign ministers of the Six asked the ECSC Assembly, together with co-opted members from the Consultative Assembly of the Council of Europe, to study the possibilities of creating a European Political Authority.

A draft of a European Political Community (EPC) was produced in 1953 in which it was proposed that, after a period of transition, the ECSC political institutions and those proposed for the EDC be subsumed within a new framework. There would then be a European Executive responsible to a European Parliament (which would consist of a People's Chamber elected by direct universal suffrage, and a Senate elected by national parliaments), a Council of Ministers and a European Court to replace the parallel bodies created under the ECSC and EDC treaties.

This was a watershed in the history of the European movement. The Six had already successfully experimented in limited economic integration in the fields of iron, coal and steel; they had now signed a treaty to integrate defence; and they were about to proceed further by creating a community for the purposes of securing political unity. Moreover, the draft treaty proposed pushing economic integration still further by calling for the establishment of a general common market based on the free movement of commodities and factors of production.

However, on this occasion the success that had attended the Six in the case of iron, coal and steel was not to be repeated. Five national parliaments approved the EDC treaty, but successive French governments felt unable to guarantee success in asking the French Assembly to ratify. Finally, the Mendès-France government attempted to water down the treaty, but failed to persuade the other five nations. The treaty as it stood was therefore submitted to the French Assembly, which refused to consider it, and in so doing obviously killed the EPC too.

There were a number of reasons for the refusal of the French Assembly to consider the treaty. First, there was opposition to the supranational elements that it contained. Second, the French Left refused to consider the possibility of the rearmament of Germany. Third, the French Right refused to have the French army placed under foreign control. Fourth, British aloofness was also a contributing factor: one of the arguments employed by those who were opposed to the treaty was that France, fearing German domination, could not participate in the formation of a European army with Germany if the UK was not a member.

It is perhaps worth noting that the failure of the EDC was followed by a British initiative also aimed at dealing with the problem of rearming Germany in a way acceptable to the French. A series of agreements was reached in 1954 between the US, the UK, Canada and the Six under which the BTO was modified and extended: Germany and Italy were brought in and a new intergovernmental organization was formed – the Western European Union (WEU). These agreements also related to the termination of the occupation of Germany and its admission into NATO. As a counterbalance to the German army, the UK agreed to maintain specified forces on the Continent. In short, the gist of the agreements was to provide a European framework within which Germany could be rearmed and become a member of NATO, while also providing for British participation to relieve French fears that there would be no possible German predominance. It should be pointed out that the response of Eastern Europe to these agreements was a further hardening of the East/West division in the shape of the formation in 1955 of the Warsaw Pact (formally, the Treaty of Friendship, Co-operation and Mutual Assistance) by the USSR and its Eastern European satellites.

2.2.2 Unity via the back door

The year 1954 was a bad year for European unity since those advo-cating the creation of supranational bodies had suffered a reverse, and the establishment of the WEU, an organization cast more in the tradi-tional intergovernmental mould, had thereafter held the centre of the stage. However, such was the strength of the European Movement that by 1955 new ideas were being put forward. The relaunching initiative came from Benelux. Its members produced a memorandum calling for the establishment of a general common market and for specific action in the fields of energy and transport.

The basic idea behind the Benelux approach was that political unity in Europe was likely to prove difficult to achieve. It was the ultimate objective, but it was one that could be realized in the longer run. In the short and medium terms, the goal should be overall economic inte-gration. Experience gained in working together would then pave the way for the achievement of political unity, that is, political unity should be introduced through the 'back door'. The memorandum called for the creation of institutions that would enable the establishment of a European Economic Community (EEC).

These ideas were considered at the meeting of Foreign Ministers of the Six in Messina, Italy, in June 1955. They met with a favourable response. The governments of the Six resolved that work should begin with a view to establishing a general common market and an atomic energy pool. Moreover, a committee should be formed which would not merely study the problems involved but should also prepare the texts of the treaties necessary in order to carry out the agreed objectives. An intergovernmental committee was therefore created and, significantly enough, Paul-Henri Spaak (above), by then foreign minister of Belgium, was made its president: what a triumph for members of the European Movement.

The Messina resolution recorded that since the UK was a member of the WEU and had been linked with the ECSC, through an Agreement of Association in 1954, it should be invited to participate in the work of the committee. The position of the other OEEC countries was not so clear: the question regarding whether they should be invited to participate was left for a later decision by the Foreign Ministers of the Six.

The Spaak Committee held its first meeting in July 1955. British representatives were present, and then and subsequently played an active role in the committee's deliberations. However, as the discussions continued, differences between the Six and the UK became evident. The UK was in favour of a 'free trade area' (for a technical definition, see Chapter 1, Section 1.2) arrangement, while the Six were agreed upon the formation of a customs union: the Messina resolution had explicitly called for this type of arrangement. Moreover, the UK felt that only a little extra machinery was needed to put the new arrangement into effect: the OEEC, perhaps somewhat strengthened, would suffice. This view was bound to anger the federalists, who put emphasis on the creation of supranational institutions, which should help achieve more than just economic integration. These differences culminated in the withdrawal of the UK representatives from the discussions in November 1955.[7]

Meanwhile, the Spaak Committee forged ahead, although not without internal differences. For example, the French had apprehensions about the transition period allowed for the dismantling of the intramember tariffs, escape clauses, the harmonization of social charges and the level of the common external tariffs (CETs). They wanted high CETs, while the Benelux nations desired low ones.

The Spaak Committee reported in April 1956, and its conclusions were considered by the Foreign Ministers of the Six in Venice, Italy, in

May of the same year. However, the attitudes amongst the Six were not uniform. On the one hand, the French naturally liked the idea of an atomic energy community, given that France was the only country of the Six to have atomic energy then, but were not keen on the proposition for a general common market, while, on the other, the remaining five had reverse preferences. Nevertheless, in the end the Six agreed that the drafting of two treaties, one to create a general common market and another to establish an atomic energy community, should begin. Treaties were subsequently signed in Rome on 25 March 1957. These were duly ratified by the national parliaments of the Six. The EEC and Euratom came into being on 1 January 1958. Thus, in 1958 the Six belonged to three separate entities: the ECSC, the EEC and Euratom.

But what are the aims set out in these treaties? The overall guiding light is the achievement of 'an ever closer union' of Europe. The EEC's aims are stated in Article 3 of its Treaty and can be summarized as

a. The establishment of free trade between the Member States such that *all* impediments on intraunion trade are eliminated. The impediments included tariffs, import quota restrictions and export subsidies, as well as all measures that had an equivalent or similar effect (now generally referred to as non-tariff trade barriers – NTBs, see Chapter 1). Moreover, that Treaty called for the creation of genuine free trade and therefore specified rudiments of common competition and industrial policies.

b. The creation of an intra-EEC free market for all factors of production by providing the necessary prerequisites for ensuring factor mobility. These included taxes on, and subsidies to, capital, labour and enterprise.

c. The formation of common policies with regard to particular industries which the Member States deemed necessary to single out for special treatment: namely, agriculture (hence the Common Agricultural Policy – CAP) and transport (hence the Common Transport Policy – CTP).

d. The application of procedures by which the economic policies of the Member States could be coordinated and disequilibria in their balances of payments remedied.

e. The creation of a European Social Fund (ESF) to improve the possibilities of employment for workers and to contribute to the raising of their standard of living.

f. The establishment of a European Investment Bank (EIB) to facilitate the economic expansion of the EEC by opening up fresh resources.

g. The establishment of a common commercial policy vis-à-vis the outside world, that is, the creation and management of the CETs, the adoption of a common stance in multinational and multilateral trade negotiations, the granting of a Generalized System of Preferences (GSP[8]) treatment to imports of certain manufactured and semi-manufactured products coming from the least developed countries (LDCs) and the reaching of trade pacts with associated nations.

It should be noted that a period of transition of 12 years, divided into three four-year stages, was granted for the elimination of intra-EEC trade barriers and for the establishment of the CETs.

Euratom asked for (h) a common approach to atomic energy, but as already mentioned, at the time only France had such capabilities. We have already seen that the ECSC created (i) a common market for, and equitable access to, iron, coal and steel. Thus the totality of all these aims (a–i) depicted the bold integration aspirations of the Six at the time.

2.3 The journey to the EC

2.3.1 The EC

The ECSC, the EEC and Euratom each had its own institutions. These centred on a Council of Ministers (Council, hereafter) and a Commission (High Authority in the case of ECSC, see above), backed by a European Parliament (Assembly in the case of ECSC) and a Court of Justice. Although there were some differences of legal competences, it later became convenient to consider the three entities as branches of the same whole, with the EEC naturally becoming the dominant partner. When the Merger Treaty was passed in 1965, but entered into force in July 1957, it seemed more logical to refer to the whole structure as the European Communities (EC), or European Community, whose main constitutional base was the Treaty of Rome which created the EEC.

By the 1970s, however, it was clear that the EC needed institutional strengthening. The EC having completed the early tasks laid down in the treaties ahead of schedule,[9] further internal objectives had to be formulated and a way found to ensure that the EC could act more effectively on the international stage. The result was to bring national political leaders more closely into EC affairs by the introduction of summit meetings. These were formalized under the name of the European Council in 1974, but the first summit was held in 1969 (the end of the transition period), in The Hague, when the Member States agreed that they were then so interdependent that they had no choice but to continue with the EC. That decision provided the necessary political will to reach agreement on the development of the CAP, on budgetary changes, on embarking on an economic and monetary union (EMU, to be achieved in three stages, beginning in 1970 and completed in 1980 as per the Werner Report,[10] discussed in Chapter 6) and, most importantly, on the need to work on enlargement. At that time, this meant settling the teasing question of relations with the UK, which, as we have seen, had vexed the EC from the very beginning.

Moreover, it was recognized that the EC needed institutional development to match its growing international stature. Its existing international responsibilities neither matched its economic weight nor allowed effective consideration of the political dimensions of its external economic relations. Individual members still conducted most of their external affairs themselves and could easily cut across EC interests, and this was apart from the issue of whether the EC should begin to move into the field of wider foreign affairs. Since the Member States had very different interests, and often had conflicting views on relations with the US and the USSR, and on defence, it was clear that the EC was not ready to take over full competences. However, the foreign ministers of the Member States were asked to study the means of achieving further political integration, on the assumption of enlargement, and to present a report. Consequently, the EC began, gingerly, to move into political cooperation, with an emphasis on foreign affairs. This did not result in a common foreign policy, but it did mean that efforts were to be exerted to identify common aims, and it led to further institutional innovation alongside the EC institutions rather than as part of them, although the new and the old gradually came together.

A second landmark summit was held in 1972 (in Paris) and was attended by the three countries set to join in 1973: Denmark, Ireland and the UK. It devoted considerable attention to internal affairs and notably to the need to strengthen the EC's social and regional aims as part of an ambitious programme designed to lead to the EMU, thus to a full 'European Union'. It also saw a continuous need to act externally to maintain a constructive dialogue with the US, Canada and Japan, and for the Member States to make a concerted contribution to the Conference on Security and Cooperation in Europe (CSCE, which began in Helsinki, Finland, in July 1973 and issued its Final Act, or Helsinki Accord, in 1975, comprising the USSR and 35 European nations), which led to a 1990 Paris Charter on peaceful relations in Europe. The foreign ministers of the Member States were to meet more frequently to discuss this last issue. This meeting marked the realization that the heads of governments would have to meet more frequently than in the past. At first sight this seemed to strengthen the intergovernmental structure of the EC at the expense of the supranational element, but this was not really the case. Rather, it showed that the future was a joint one, that the international climate was changing and often bleak, and that if the Member States dealt with their internal economic difficulties alone, this could undermine the efforts of the EC to strengthen its economies. Informal discussion of general issues, whether economic or political, domestic or worldwide, was a necessary preliminary to action which often seemed stronger if it were to be EC-based. Through the summit meetings and the Political Cooperation Procedure (ECP) the subject matter coming to the EC steadily enlarged.

Indeed, 1969–72 can be described as a period of great activity. Apart from what has just been mentioned, in 1970 the Six reached a common position on the development of a Common Fisheries Policy (CFP), although total agreement was not to be achieved until 1982. Also, at another Paris summit in 1973, agreement was reached on the development of new policies in relation to industry and science and research. Moreover, the summit envisaged a more active role for the EC in the area of regional policy and decided that a European Regional Development Fund (ERDF) should be created to channel EC resources into the development of the EC backward regions. The UK demanded such a fund during the accession negotiations, expecting to get the most of it since it was the only country to have a 'regional policy' then, but events proved otherwise.[11] Furthermore, later in the 1970s, the relationship between the EC and its ex-colonies was significantly reshaped in the form of the Lomé Convention, which became the EU-ACP agreements when the Caribbean and Pacific ex-colonies were later added,[12] now managed as the EU Cotonou Agreement.

It was obvious from all these developments that the EC needed financial resources not only to pay for the EC day-to-day running but also to feed the various funds that were established: the ESF, ERDF and, most important of all, the European Guidance and Guarantee Fund (EAGGF) to finance the CAP. In 1970, the EC took the important step of agreeing to introduce a system that would provide the EC, and specifically the EC general budget, with its 'own resources', thus relieving it of the uncertainty of annual decisions on national contributions for its finances as well as endorsing its political autonomy in this respect. Another important step was the decision that the European Parliament (EP) should be elected directly by the people, not chosen by national parliaments. In addition, the EC decided to grant the EP certain powers over the

EC general budget, which proved to be a very significant development. Finally, but by no means least, was the development of the political cooperation mechanism. It is important not to forget that the dedicated members of the European movement had always hoped that the habit of cooperation in the economic field would spill over into the political arena, one aspect of which is foreign policy matters.

By the 1980s, it was clear that the political and economic environment in which the EC operated was changing fast. Tumultuous events in the former USSR and the countries of the Warsaw Pact threw the institutional arrangements of Western Europe into disarray and brought the need to reassess defence requirements, NATO's role and the continuance of the US presence in Europe. The unresolved issue of whether the EC needed a foreign policy, or at least some halfway house towards one, was sure to be raised once more. Meanwhile, the economic base upon which the EC had been able to develop became much more uncertain. Recession, industrial change, higher unemployment, slower growth and worries about European competitiveness undermined the previous confidence.

The twin issues of constitutional development and institutional reform continued to exercise EC circles, but little progress was possible and the EC seemed to be running out of steam. The deepening of the integrative process required action which governments found controversial, the new Member States – now including Greece (1981), Spain (1986) and Portugal (1986) – inevitably made for a less coherent group, while the recession hardened national attitudes towards the necessary compromise required for cooperative solutions. The EC finances were constrained (the EC budget amounted to less that 1 per cent of EC GDP; see Chapter 5) such that new policies could not be developed, and this in turn led to bitter arguments about the resources devoted to the CAP (which exhausted more than 75 per cent of the EC budget) and its inequitable impact, especially on the UK. Internal divisions were compounded by fears of a lack of dynamism in the EC economy, threatening a relative decline in world terms. Such worries suggested that a significant leap forward was required to ensure a real common market, to encourage new growth and at the same time to modernize the EC institutions.

2.3.2   The Single European Market

As the debate progressed, a major division emerged between those who were primarily interested in the ideal of political union and wished to develop the EC institutions accordingly, and those who were more pragmatic in approach and stressed the need for new policies. It was not until 1985 that the lines of agreement could be settled. These were brought together in the Single European Act (SEA), which became operative on 1 July 1987.

The SEA contained policy development which was based upon the intention of creating a true single market (usually referred to as the 'single European market' – SEM – and the 'internal market') by the end of 1992 (hence the popular term EC92), with free movement of goods, services, capital and labour (the so-called four freedoms) rather than the patchy arrangements of the past (above). The SEA also introduced, or strengthened, other policy fields. These included responsibilities towards the environment; the encouragement of further action to promote health and safety at work; the promotion of technological research and development (R&D); work to strengthen economic and social cohesion so that the weaker Member States could participate fully in the freer market; and cooperation in economic and monetary policy. In addition, the SEA brought foreign policy cooperation within its purview and provided it with a more effective support than it had in the past, including its own secretariat, housed in the Council building in Brussels. Institutionally, it was agreed that the Council would take decisions on a qualified majority vote (QMV) in relation to the SEM, research, cohesion and improved working conditions, and that in such cases the EP should share in decision-making. These developments were followed later by agreement regarding the control of expenditure on the CAP, which, as we have seen, had been a source of heated argument for a number of years and, most importantly, a fundamental change in the EC general budget.

The SEM provided a goal for the next few years, and the EC became preoccupied with the necessary preparations (300 directives had to be passed and then incorporated into national law for this purpose), giving evidence of its ability to work together as one unit. However, it also brought new complications. It raised the question of how much power should be held by the EC institutions, presented the Member States with heavy internal programmes to complete the changes necessary for the SEM, and exposed the very different economic conditions in the Member States, which were bound to affect their fortunes in SEM. Meanwhile, the unification of Germany in 1990 fundamentally changed its position within the EC by giving it more political and economic weight, but at the same time it was required to expend considerable effort eastwards.

A further challenge at the time came from new bids for membership (so far there has been one withdrawal: the position of Greenland was renegotiated in 1984, but it remains associated and has a special agreement to regulate mutual fishing interests). The SEM and the end of the Cold War finally convinced the doubters in Western Europe that they should try to join. This was both a triumph and an embarrassment for the EC in that it was preoccupied with its own internal changes and a belief that it had not yet fully come to terms with the southern enlargement, which had brought in Greece, Portugal and Spain. The reaction was mixed in that some Member States wished to press on with enlargement as a priority, while others wished to complete the SEM and tighten internal policies before opening the doors. A closer economic relationship was negotiated between the EC and the EFTA countries, except for Switzerland, to form the European Economic Area (EEA), on 2 May 1992, which was widely assumed to be a preliminary step towards membership, since it extended all EC privileges except in agriculture to these countries, but, understandably, without giving them voting rights. Austria, Finland, Sweden and Switzerland all formally applied between 1989 and 1992, and Norway followed them shortly afterwards. Switzerland's application remains on the table, which is odd, given its snub of the EEA.[13] Hungary, Poland and Czechoslovakia signed association agreements and hoped that they might join in a few years' time. Turkey and Morocco applied in 1987, although the former's application was laid aside and the latter's rejected. Cyprus and Malta applied in 1990. Later, most of the Central and Eastern European Countries (CEECs) expressed their desire to join, and formal negotiations were opened in 1998 with those most likely to succeed: Cyprus, the Czech Republic, Estonia, Hungary, Poland and Slovenia. However, the instability in the Balkans and the war in Kosovo showed the need to hasten the process and, at Helsinki in December 1999, it was agreed to open accession talks with Bulgaria, Latvia, Lithuania, Malta, Romania and Slovakia. Moreover, after 36 years of temporizing, it was also agreed at the same summit that Turkey should be a recognized candidate, but negotiations were then not expected to start for a very long time, since the EU wanted to see big improvements in Turkey's political and human rights behaviour, including the rights of Kurds and other minorities and the constitutional role of the army in political life, which might require changes in her constitution (these are known as the Copenhagen criteria, introduced in June 1993 at the Copenhagen summit; below). Therefore, there was then an active list of 13 candidates, which included Turkey, and a change in regime brought Croatia closer to joining this group.

It did not seem easy to generalize about the issues involved in admitting such a variety of countries for membership, but the brief history shows that integration was always meant to apply to all of Europe, although it would require a stretch of the imagination to claim that Turkey is in Europe. However, the EC already had a series of agreements with the applicants through which it provided aid and advice on development and reform; these are set out in Agenda 2000.[14] In particular, the EC was looking for economic reform, the development of democratic political institutions and the protection of minority and human rights as necessary preconditions for closer relationships before full membership (Copenhagen criteria). Partnership and cooperation agreements with Russia and the newly independent states were developed, but these did not include provisions for membership.

Clearly, an organization with such a large and varied membership would be very different from the original EEC of the Six, and challenged received wisdom as to its nature. This is one reason why pursuing the question of enlargement was made consequent upon the finalizing of the Maastricht Treaty (below) and agreement upon new financial and budgetary arrangements for existing Member States. Continuing issues about defence and the appropriate reaction to conditions in Central and Eastern Europe, the Gulf War and the collapse of Yugoslavia all suggested further considerations of foreign and defence capabilities were important.

2.3.3 The Treaty on European Union

It was therefore against a troubled background that the EC set up two Inter-governmental Conferences (IGCs) to prepare the way for a meeting of the European Council in Maastricht in December 1991, which produced a new blueprint for the future. It aimed to integrate the EC further through setting out a timetable for full EMU, introducing institutional changes and developing political competences, the whole being brought together in the Treaty on European Union (TEU, popularly known as the Maastricht Treaty), in which the EC should form a part of a wider European Union. Since this treaty was later added to and adapted as the 1997 Amsterdam Treaty, its details are discussed in the next section, but it should be stated here that it was signed on 7 February 1992 and came into force on 1 November 1993.

It is not surprising that the ratification process of the TEU, for which some have argued not a great deal of time was allowed, produced furious argument across Western Europe after Denmark, the first to begin the ratification process, rejected it by a mere 50.7 per cent in a referendum on 2 May 1992. Although each Member State had its own peculiar worries, a general characteristic, which the TEU made obvious, was the width of the gap between political elites and the voters in modern society. Even though political leaders rapidly expressed contrition that they had failed to provide adequate explanations for their moves, they seemed less able to accept that there were strong doubts about many of the proposed new arrangements as being the best way forward, and that a period of calm reflection, with less frenetic development, might in the end serve the EC and its people better.

2.3.4   The Amsterdam Treaty

The TEU left contentious problems for the Amsterdam conference to tackle. Although the hard core, comprising changes to the voting system in Council and the size of Commission, was not tackled (but the 2000 Nice Treaty and the 2009 Treaty of Lisbon did, below), the 1997 Amsterdam Treaty was useful in updating aims and policies, in clarifying the position regarding foreign and defence policies and justice and home affairs, and in strengthening the social side. The treaty itself modified the existing treaties, notably those on the EEC and the Union, and these, together with the *acquis communautaire* (legislation deriving from the treaties), can be considered as the EU constitution (see below). Supplementary treaties must be used when developments go beyond the existing ones. Past examples include changes in the budget procedures, agreements to admit new members and the SEM (above). In addition, a unique arrangement was attached to the Maastricht Treaty in 1991: an agreement and a protocol were annexed because the UK could not accept changes in the social field endorsed by the other Member States. The EC, that is, the EEC, the ECSC and Euratom, forms the most developed section (or, in current jargon, one of the EU three pillars, the other two being 'foreign and defence policies' and 'justice and home affairs') of the Union, and its legislation takes precedence over national decisions in the appropriate field. A moment's reflection will show that this is a necessary precondition for the EC to work at all. It would otherwise be impossible to create a single economic unit, to establish the confidence needed between the Member States or to handle external relations.

The Amsterdam Treaty gave the EU a more coherent structure and a modern statement of its aims and policies, and brought some necessary improvements in the working of the institutions. Naturally, it highlighted the new aspects, but these were not necessarily more important than more long-standing policies: for example, publicity was given to provisions on foreign and defence policy, yet they remained far less developed than arrangements in the economic sphere. Despite being thought of as a tidying up of the Maastricht loose ends, the treaty is a substantial document, but naturally greatly overlaps with Maastricht.

Thus it has three parts on substantive amendments to previous treaties, their simplification and modernization and their renumbering, ratification procedures and official language versions. In addition, there are an annex, 13 protocols, often dealing with very difficult issues, 51 declarations and 8 declarations by individual Member States.

The post-Amsterdam EU had broad objectives, but again these naturally overlapped with those in the Maastricht Treaty. The classic aim, set out long ago, is to lay the foundations of, and subsequently develop, the 'ever closer union'. It promoted economic and social progress, an aim which included the abolition of internal frontiers; better economic and social cohesion to assist the less-developed Member States to catch up with the EU average (facilitated by the creation in 1993 of a Cohesion Fund); and the EMU, complete with a single currency. It wished to assert an international identity through a common security and defence policy and new provisions designed to enhance this, and to draw closer to the WEU (above), which has been dormant since it was launched in 1954, by turning it into the equivalent of a EU defence force. Thus for the first time the EU was set to have a common defence policy with the implication that the WEU will eventually be responsible for implementing decisions of an inevitable political union. Appreciation for (or was it accommodation of?) NATO was reiterated by stating that the revival of the WEU is to be linked to NATO, thus ensuring a continued alliance with the US and Canada for the defence of Europe. It not only introduced a formal Union citizenship but also took steps to strengthen the commitment to democracy and individual rights, to promote equality and to combat discrimination. It had a procedure to be followed should a Member States appear to breach human rights. The treaty also established the EU as an area of free movement, security and justice, and attempted to establish clearer and more uniform rules in these fields. These goals were in addition to those in the EEC treaty. Internally, the EU had general economic objectives relating to the SEM; agriculture; transport; economic and social cohesion; a new emphasis on policy-making in employment; the social field; and environmental matters. The need for enhanced competitiveness for EU industry, the promotion of R&D, the construction of trans-European infrastructure, the attainment of a high level of health protection, better education, training and cultural development all found their place. Recognition is given to development policies, consumer protection and to measures in energy policy and tourism. There were, of course, a host of subsidiary and supporting objectives. All of these policies are tackled in Chapter 4.

After many arguments, the concept of flexible integration was brought out into the open. Articles 40, 43 and 44 (the TEU) allowed some Member States to establish closer cooperation amongst themselves with the aim of developing EU policies that not all the Member States wished to pursue, subject to veto by the dissenting Member States. This was fully endorsed in the 2000 Nice Treaty by stating that groups of eight (out of the then fifteen) or more Member States may pursue greater integration in certain areas. Such a move must be supported by a majority of the Member States, must not harm the interests of others and must allow the non-participating Member States to be involved in the discussion of developments, but without voting on them. There were some important examples of policies which were less than fully inclusive, amongst them membership of the single currency, the Danish opt-outs from the free movement provisions (although Denmark accepted the Schengen Principle dictating them) and from decisions with defence implications, and the British and Irish non-acceptance of the abolition of border controls.

The Maastricht conference touched fears of the creation of a super state. In an attempt to counter this, the subsidiarity principle was agreed during the Edinburgh summit in December 1992 and the Amsterdam Treaty tried to clarify it further. Article 5 (EC) explains that, where the EU does not have exclusive competence, it may proceed only if the Member States cannot pursue the action themselves or if it is an objective better achieved by EU action (later the proportionality principle was added to minimize the number of directives needed for action). A protocol attached to the treaty has tried to clarify how this concept should be applied and, in particular, insists that the reasons for action must be stated, EU action must be simple and limited and a report must be given to the EU institutions on what has been done. These provisions are meant as a check on an insidious growth of EU power, allowing it to slip in a direction that has never been agreed. Indeed, a Member State is given the right to bring a case to the Court of Justice when it believes that the EU is extending its powers unjustifiably.

One element in the debate about subsidiarity was doubt concerning the remoteness of decision-making in Brussels. There was a need to make the EU more responsive to the needs of the general public and more sensitive to the effects of the intrusiveness that EU legislation appeared to bring. The 'democratic deficit' is an issue that has long been discussed, and there are several ways of addressing it, of which greater powers to the EP is one (below and Chapter 3). Individuals have long had the right to petition the EP, and this has been supported by the appointment of an ombudsman, chosen by the EP, but independent of it.

One particular issue was the undermining of national parliaments, especially those that have an important legislative function and that have found it hard to devise ways for exercising control over the EU. In practice, they had been limited to scrutiny of proposals, which, once they are at an advanced stage, are very difficult to change. Some efforts have also been made, through scrutiny committees, to discuss general issues, thus helping to suggest policy positions for the future, while Denmark, in particular, has tried to define the parameters within which ministers may negotiate. A protocol of the Amsterdam Treaty tries to increase the influence of national parliaments. Associated with this was the general acceptance of the need to keep the public better informed and to provide access to EU documentation. A declaration attached to the Treaty stresses the importance of transparency, access to documents and the fight against fraud, with Article 255 (EC) giving citizens a right to access official documents. A further declaration accepts the importance of improving the quality of drafting in legislation. Over the years, efforts have been made, too, to help individuals question the EU. The right to petition the EP was buttressed by the establishment of an ombudsman (see above). A further change, directly affecting individuals, was to confer EU citizenship on the nationals of the Member States. Although such changes are intended to encourage a greater openness in decision-making, their implementation will take time. Actual decision-making in the Council remains private.

Flexible policies and subsidiarity have been tackled together, although they deal with very different circumstances, because they both suggest that the EU is still uneasily balanced between the two opposing views on how to organize Europe which have been so eloquently expressed since the end of the Second World War. To some observers the Amsterdam Treaty was one more step towards a federal Europe, but to others it was seen as a means of keeping a check upon this drive and retaining a degree of national governmental control. The final outcome remains uncertain.

2.3.5 The Nice Treaty

Hammered out over four bitter days and nights on the French Riviera, the Treaty of Nice of 11 December 2000 is both complex and insubstantial; one of its authors even called it 'lousy'. The treaty's main concern is with EU enlargement, especially with the institutional changes that would be needed to accommodate 12 to 15 new members (above). Since its provisions will not make sense until we have discussed the EU institutions, they will be dealt with in Chapter 3. Here it suffices to state that the treaty both amends QMV and extends it to new areas, including trade in services; asks the larger Member States to drop their second commissioner; limits the total number of commissioners to 20 after 2007; and proclaims the Charter of Rights, but without legal force.

One should add that the ratification of the treaty followed almost the same path as Maastricht's. The Irish, whose constitution demands a referendum on such issues, were the first to kick off the process and shocked everyone by rejecting it on 7 June 2001 by 54 per cent to 46 per cent. Although technically that meant the death of the treaty, the other Member States stubbornly went ahead with ratification, leading to a dramatic situation in 2002 when all but Ireland had ratified. However, in a second referendum on 20 October 2002, Ireland recorded an emphatic 'yes' (by 62.9 per cent against 37.1 per cent). This then set the tone for the Copenhagen summit of 12–13 December 2002 when it was agreed that (a united) Cyprus, the Czech Republic, Estonia, Hungary, Latvia, Lithuania, Malta, Poland, the Slovak Republic and Slovenia could join the EU on 1 May 2004; Bulgaria and Romania could join in 2007, provided they met the necessary criteria, which they have done; and Turkey could open accession negotiations immediately after the December 2004 summit pending a favourable report by Commission on its status on the Copenhagen criteria. Indeed, the ten countries signed accession treaties with the EU on 16 April 2003 at the Athens summit, ratified their accession treaties, nine of the countries through popular referendums, with Cyprus not needing one, and became members on 1 January 2004, but, alas, not a united Cyprus. And in the Brussels 16/17 December 2004 summit, in light of a positive report from the EU Commission, Turkey was given the go-ahead to start negotiations on 3 October 2005, which are expected to take ten years. It should be added, however, that the decision to grant Turkey the right to negotiate EU membership has since proved controversial: France has decided that it will hold a referendum on Turkey's membership, and many have attributed France's referendum rejection of the Constitutional treaty to this issue; the present German Chancellor Angela Merkel is not keen on full membership, preferring a 'privileged partnership'; and there are many who are not happy with Turkey's claims to being 'European' in terms of both geography and character. Also, in June 2005, the 'Thessaloniki agenda' was reaffirmed, allowing the assessment of progress towards EU membership of the western Balkan countries: Albania, Bosnia and Herzegovina, Croatia, the former Yugoslav Republic of Macedonia and Serbia and Montenegro, including Kosovo. Finally, on 26 September 2006 the Commission offered a positive report on the progress made by

Bulgaria and Romania, which led to endorsement by the Member States. They joined on 1 January 2007.

2.3.6 A Constitution for the EU?

At the Nice summit meetings it was decided to 'engage in a broader and more detailed analysis of the future of the EU, with a view to making it more democratic, more transparent and more efficient'. The ensuing debate culminated at the 2001 Laeken summit when, on 12 December, it was decided to create a convention for this purpose. On 28 February 2002, the Convention for the Future of Europe was set up under the chairmanship of ex-French president Valéry Giscard d'Estaing, with ex-Italian prime minister Giuliano Amato and ex-Belgian prime minister Jean-Luc Dehaene as vice chairpersons, to discuss the matter further and then report to an IGC in mid-2003. The convention had 105 delegates, representing the EU governments, parliaments and institutions, and was set two tasks: (a) to propose a set of arrangements to enable the EU to work when it has 25 to 30 Member States, and (b) to express the purpose of the EU, so that the citizens whom it is meant to serve will understand its relevance to their lives and, with luck, feel some enthusiasm for its activities.

Surprisingly, the Convention issued a draft constitution for the EU on 6 February 2003, with the contents being mainly about the consolidation of the various EU treaties, but they included proposals for the reform of existing EU institutions and on the future of the EU. A changed final draft was adopted on 20 June 2003 at the Thessaloniki summit, but although the December summit failed to endorse it, the Brussels June 2004 IGC did. Hence, it was set to become the EU Constitution when ratified by all the Member States. However, during the early months of 2005, both France (on 29 May) and the Netherlands (on 1 June) rejected it in national referendums (by, respectively, 55/45 per cent and 62/38 per cent); therefore, it was technically dead. However, as was the case with the Maastricht and the Nice Treaties, this was not a foregone conclusion. Indeed, 18 Member States, including Bulgaria and Romania, representing two-thirds of the then 27 Member States and 56.12 per cent of the EU population, went ahead and ratified the Constitution. Moreover, on 26 January 2007, the foreign ministers of 20[15] so-called friends of the Constitution declared in Madrid that, far from slashing the original treaty to make it more palatable to voters, it should be more ambitious, giving the EU a bigger role in social policy, fighting climate change and immigration, which attracted the new headline 'Use the Pen Not the Scissors'. Later, almost all of the other Member States went ahead with ratification. This in turn led to a new draft which removed some of the controversial terminology, that is, replacing 'constitution' with 'reform treaty', and accommodated certain demands by some Member States.

2.3.7 Treaty of Lisbon

The eventual outcome is the Treaty of Lisbon, signed on 13 December 2007 and scheduled for full ratification by the end of December 2008. Ireland was the first to put it to the test, and it rejected the treaty on 13 June 2008, by 53.4 per cent to 46.6 per cent, creating the by now familiar havoc. This led to 'a time for reflection' since the other Member States repeated the game of proceeding with ratification. To shorten the familiar game, certain accommodations were finally agreed on that led to a second and overwhelmingly successful Irish referendum on 3 October 2009, by 67.1 per cent to 32.9 per cent. But the final ratification did not happen until the 'eurosceptic', some would add eccentric, Czech president, Vaclav Klaus, had to be accommodated.[16] The treaty became final on 13 November 2009, operative from 1 December 2009, and it amends the two core treaties, the TEU and the Treaty establishing the European Community (see Teasdale and Bainbridge, 2012, for how the various treaties are amalgamated), with the latter renamed the Treaty of the Functioning of the European Union (TFEU).

Here, is a skeleton of the Lisbon Treaty – a skeleton since most of it simply incorporates what is in the previous treaties:

1. It sets out a single simplified EU treaty.
2. It creates a post of president of the European Council (see Treaty on the European Union, TEU, Article 9B.5), serving for 30 months, renewable once instead of six-monthly rotation.
3. It creates a post of EU foreign policy chief, officially called the High Representative (HR) of the Union for Foreign Affairs and Security Policy (TEU, Article 9E), popularly referred to as 'foreign policy supremo', who heads a to-be-created EU diplomatic service.
4. It gives greater scope for defence cooperation among the Member States, including procurement.
5. It gives new powers to the EP over legislation and the EU budget.
6. It enables national parliaments to ensure EU law does not encroach on the rights of the Member States.
7. It abolishes the national veto in some areas, including immigration and asylum policy.
8. It retains the national veto in tax, defence and foreign policy, and over financing the EU budget.

9. It introduces a new 'double majority' voting system for Council, requiring at least 15 Member States comprising 65 per cent of the EU population.

10. It introduces a mechanism for those Member States wishing to leave the EU.

11. It increases the power of the 'Eurozone' (the countries that have adopted the euro) to decide its own policies.

12. It incorporates an EU Charter of Fundamental Rights, including the right to strike, with legal provision limiting its application in national courts.

13. It reduces the size of the Commission starting in 2014, with commissioners sent from only two-thirds of the Member States on a rotation basis.

14. It raises the minimum number of seats in the EP for the small Member States from 4 to 6, and sets out a limit of 96 for the big Member States.

As mentioned, since a number of these points concern institutional changes, it makes more sense to discuss them in Chapter 3.

2.4 An unfinished passage?

The adherents to the original ideal of European unity would stress that, from what has been stated in this chapter, one cannot escape the conclusion that although the EU has not yet reached the finishing line, it has gone a long way towards achieving the dream of its founding fathers: the creation of a United States of Europe (Box 2.2 summarizes the time-pass of EU integration). They would add that the long march is easily explicable in terms of the difficulties inherent in securing the necessary compromises needed, while accommodating new members, and the tackling of unforeseen economic and political problems, from both within and without. They would concede that it would, of course, require a big leap from the present 'union' to a full European state, but that much has been achieved and that this vision has been and will continue to be the guiding light for European integration. They would also add that it behoves all those who would like to reduce the EU to a mere trading bloc to think twice. The EU has already gone far beyond this, and as the continuing problems of the Eurozone indicate, even to effectively maintain current economic integration may require further political developments. However, several member nations – most definitely the UK and, some would claim, many EU citizens (they have never been asked the question directly and straightforwardly) – do not share this view. They would insist that the EU has developed more than far enough, and would add that even though the creation of a powerful united European economy with most of its members using the same currency is a historic achievement, nothing further should ensue, certainly not political unity.

I shall leave it there since my own position, if it is not yet apparent, should not matter. It is what you believe in the light of the facts and your own deep reflection, as well as your personal vision that really matters. I shall, however, return to this issue in the final two chapters on the importance and future of European integration.

Box 2.2   A chronology of EU integration

1947

The Economic Commission for Europe was set up in Geneva as one of five regional organizations of the UN with the goal of initiating and participating in concerted measures aimed at securing the economic restructuring of the *whole* of Europe.

1948

* The Belgium, the Netherlands and Luxembourg (Benelux) customs union, agreed in 1944, became effective.
* In March, Benelux, France and the UK founded the Brussels Treaty Organization (BTO), designed to create a system of mutual assistance in times of attack on Europe.
* The Organization for European Economic Cooperation (OEEC) was founded to administer the Marshall Plan, aimed at making aid available to help the European economy find its feet, provided the European governments 'got together' to decide how much assistance was needed.

1949

The five BTO nations, together with the US and Canada as well as Denmark, Iceland, Italy (significantly, since it had been an Axis power), Norway and Portugal, founded the North Atlantic Treaty Organization (NATO), with the same BTO aims.

1950

In May, French foreign minister Robert Schuman, on the inspiration of Jean Monnet, offered the Schuman Declaration for cooperation in the production of coal, iron and steel, in order to make war between France and Germany 'not merely unthinkable but materially impossible'.

1951

The Treaty of Paris was signed by Benelux, France, West Germany and Italy (the Original Six) to create the European Coal and Steel Community, valid for 50 years, based on the Schuman Declaration, with a supranational High Authority (HA) to run it, a Council of Ministers to counterbalance the HA, a Parliamentary Assembly, a Consultative Committee and a Court of Justice. Monnet was appointed the first HA President.

1954

Germany and Italy were admitted into NATO, and the Western European Union was formed.

1957

On 25 March, two treaties were signed in Rome by the Original Six to establish, in a three-stage transition period of 12 years, a common market, the European Economic Community, and an atomic energy community, Euratom; both came into being on 1 January 1958 and each with five institutions: Commission, Council of Ministers, European Parliament, Court of Justice and Economic and Social Committee.

1960

In January, the European Free Trade Association (EFTA) for industrial products was established by the Stockholm Convention by Austria, Denmark, Norway, Portugal, Sweden, Switzerland and the UK.

1965

The Original Six signed the Merger Treaty, which entered into force on 1 July 1967, to combine the ECSC, EEC and Euratom, in order to become the European Community (EC) under a unified set of institutions: Commission, Council of Ministers, European Parliament, Court of Justice and Economic and Social Committee.

1969

The 12-year transition period successfully came to an end, and the Original Six decided to form a European Monetary Union (EMU, note that the abbreviation is the same as for economic and monetary union with the difference between the two explained in Chapter 6) in three stages, beginning in 1970 and completed in 1980, as well as to open the doors for new members. The EMU successfully completed the first stage and was progressing well towards the second when the Nixon Shock and the oil crisis led to its demise.

1973

Denmark, Ireland and the UK joined the EC after signing accession treaties in 1972 together with Norway, but a referendum in Norway rejected admission.

1979

The European Monetary System (EMS), a zone of monetary stability for narrow exchange rate variations of ±2.5 per cent, and a system of adjusting to keep within the agreed bands, the Exchange Rate Mechanism (ERM), was established.

1981

Greece became the tenth member of the EC.

1986

Portugal and Spain joined the EC to make it the club of 12.

1987

The EC adopted the Single European Act, which became operative on 1 July, to establish the legal requirements for the creation of the Single European Market (SEM) by 1992 with the four freedoms for the movement of goods, services, labour and capital.

1992

* The Treaty on the European Union (TEU), popularly known as the Maastricht Treaty, was signed on 7 February, with the aim of integrating the EC further through setting out a timetable for full EMU, introducing institutional changes and developing political competences. It had a rough ride due to the Danes rejecting it in a referendum in June, but was eventually ratified. The UK had an opt-out on the EMU.
* Austria, Finland and Sweden joined the EC to make it the club of 15.

1997

The Treaty of Amsterdam was signed, updating the EC aims and policies; clarifying the position regarding foreign policy (High Representative appointed), defence policy and justice and home affairs (JHA); and strengthening the social side, and it incorporated the Schengen agreement on frontier controls, but Ireland and the UK maintained op-outs. The UK ended its opt-out from the Social Charter.

1998

On 2 May, the Commission decided that 11 Member States qualified for the EMU.

1999

The EMU became a reality for 11 EC Member States, with the euro an official currency for the qualifiers.

2001

* Greece joined the Eurozone, extending its membership to 12.
* On 26 February, the Treaty of Nice was signed, amending the TEU, mainly on institutional matters.

2002

On 1 January, the national currencies of the Eurozone were replaced by the euro.

2004

Ten Central and Eastern European nations joined the EC to make the club of 25.

2007

* Bulgaria and Romania joined the EC, increasing its membership to 27.
* Slovenia joined the Eurozone, extending its membership to 13.
* On 13 December, the Treaty of Lisbon was signed, after problems with the constitutional treaty.

2008

Cyprus and Malta joined the Eurozone, extending its membership to 15.

2009

* Slovakia joined the Eurozone, extending its membership to 16.
* The Lisbon Treaty entered into force on 1 December, renaming the TEU as the Treaty on the Functioning of the European Union (TFEU), introducing many institutional changes, creating a permanent post of President of the European Council, enhancing the post of High Representative, introducing an exit clause and strengthening the national parliaments.

2010

* On 9 May, the European Financial Stability Facility (EFSF) was created to provide financial support to the Eurozone Member Nations in trouble after the 2008 financial crisis.
* In December, the European Stability Mechanism (ESM) was established as a permanent crisis resolution mechanism by issuing debt instruments to help finance loans to Eurozone countries in trouble.

2011

Estonia joined the Eurozone, extending its membership to 17.

2014

* Latvia joined the Eurozone, extending its membership to 18.
* Croatia joined the EU to elevate the club to its present 28 Member States.

On 20 March, the EU agreed to create a Single Resolution Mechanism for handling banking crises, having transferred in the previous year the powers to supervise the Eurozone's largest banks from the national regulators to the ECB, thus establishing a Banking Union.

Appendix

Table A2.1   EC intra-area tariff reduction (%)

Reduction date	Reduction based on the 1 January 1957 level	Cumulative reduction
1 January 59	10	10
1 July 60	10	20
1 January 61	10	30
1 January 62	10	40
1 July 62	10	50
1 July 63	10	60
1 January 65	10	70
1 January 66	10	80
1 July 67	5	85
1 July 68	15	100

Table A2.2   The establishment of the CETs (%)

Adjustment date	Industrial products		Agricultural products	
	Adjustment	Cumulative adjustment	Adjustment	Cumulative adjustment
1 January 61	30	30		
1 January 62			30	30
1 July 63	30	60		
1 January 66			30	60
1 July 68	40	100	40	100

Recommended Reading

Teasdale, Anthony and Bainbridge, Timothy (2012) *The Penguin Companion to the European Union*, Penguin Books, London.

Van Middelaar, Luuk (2013) *The Passage to Europe: How a Continent Became a Union*, Yale University Press, New Haven and London.

Young, H. (1998) *This Blessed Plot: Britain and Europe from Churchill to Blair*, Macmillan, Basingstoke.

3
Decision-making in the EU

3.1 Introduction

We now turn to the second and third questions raised at the end of Chapter 1. How does the EU reach decisions and what institutions has it created to enable it to achieve its integration aims? Obviously, the two questions have to be tackled together since decisions do not drop from the sky and decisions to promote EU integration have to be implemented through agreed channels.

The EU has a unique institutional structure, which is not surprising, given that it is neither a federal state nor a purely intergovernmental cooperative venture – vital facts often forgotten especially by the 'euroskeptics' who compare its institutions to their equivalents in single states. The EU Member States pool sovereignty in specific areas and delegate them to independent institutions, entrusting them with defending the interests of the EU as a whole as well as of both its Member States and citizens. The European Commission (Commission, hereafter) upholds the interests of the whole EU. The Council of the European Union (Council, hereafter) upholds those of the governments of the Member States through their ministerial representatives. The European Parliament (EP) upholds those of the EU citizens, who directly elect its members. And the Council of the European Union (European Council), made up of the Heads of State or the Governments of the Member States, offers general guidelines and decides on issues not dealt with elsewhere in the system.

The Commission, the Council and the EP, known as the 'institutional triangle', are flanked by the European Court of Justice (ECJ) and the Court of Auditors, as well as by three other bodies: the European Central Bank (ECB); the European Economic and Social Committee (EESC); and the Committee of the Regions (CoR). However, the EESC and CoR are purely advisory bodies. There is also the European Investment Bank (EIB), but it is a financial institution, not an institution in the sense of the EU treaties. Moreover, there are many agencies, created by specific legislation, to cater for specialized concerns, which are of a technical, scientific or managerial nature, such as the European Data Protection Supervisor (EDPS) and the European Ombudsman, although, strictly speaking, neither qualifies as a body.

This chapter provides basic coverage of the 'institutional triangle', because between them these three central institutions initiate and finalize most new EU legislation, and thus constitute the core of the EU legislative process. There is also briefer coverage of the EESC and the CoR because they have to be consulted, and hence are somewhat involved in the legislative process, although not in actual legislation. Moreover, there is a short description of the courts, especially the ECJ, because its rulings are in the nature of secondary legislation. Obviously, the Court of Auditors does not belong to this process, but an endnote is devoted to it for the interested reader.[1] The others are dealt with in some detail in the chapters in which they are most relevant. For example, the ECB is fully covered in Chapter 6. The EIB is dealt with in an endnote[2] and so is the Ombudsman[3] since they are obviously also not legislative actors. Moreover, due to the obvious nature of the EDPS, established in 2001, no further consideration is needed.[4]

3.2   Important actors

Before we explain these institutions, one should recall from Chapter 2 and above that the EU has the European Council which, since the adoption of the Treaty of Lisbon (Treaty on the Functioning of the European Union, TFEU) on 1 December 2009, has a full-time president[5] (see Treaty on the European Union, TEU, Article 9B.5) and a High Representative of the Union for Foreign Affairs and Security Policy[6] (HR), the so-called Foreign Policy Supremo (TEU, Article 9E). The European Council comprises the EU political leaders, the EU president and the Commission president, with the HR participating in its work when pertinent issues are under consideration. However, when necessary, the members may decide that each be accompanied by a minister, or a member of the Commission in the case of the Commission president. The European Council meets four time a year and is convened by its president, and he/she can call to order special meetings when required. The European Council is meant to provide the EU with the 'necessary impetus for its development' and to 'define the general political directions and priorities thereof', that is, it offers general guidelines and blueprints, but it has no legislative functions. However, it is the EU's highest decision-making body because it is only there that disputes between the Member States, over the common budget, expansion onto new policy areas, or the accession of new members can be settled.[7] The same applies in the case of disagreements in the Council (of Ministers). Also, it generally makes decisions by consensus unless otherwise required by the treaties, and elects its president by a 'qualified majority vote' (QMV, below).

The president of the European Council is expected to 'facilitate cohesion and consensus' within the European Council, present a report to the EP after each meeting and make sure that the EU is externally represented on common foreign and security policy (CFSP), naturally without prejudice to the powers of the HR. The appointment is full-time for 30 months and can be renewed once.

The HR assumes office for five years. The office holder also acts as a vice president of the Commission and controls a vast diplomatic corps, which is now in the process of being established. The HR is appointed by QMV in the European Council (and the president-elect of the Commission) and is later confirmed by the EP as a Commission vice president.

3.3 The Commission

The EU treaties assign the Commission a wide range of tasks, but these can be narrowed to four major roles. The Commission initiates EU legislation by proposing new legislation to the Council and the EP. It serves as the EU executive arm by administering and implementing EU policies. Jointly, with the ECJ, it acts as the guardian of EU treaties by enforcing EU law. And it acts as the EU spokesperson and negotiator of international agreements, especially in relation to trade and cooperation, such as the EU Cotonou Agreement, which links the EU with 79 African, Caribbean and Pacific nations (EU-ACP).

As the initiator of EU legislation, the Commission formulates proposals in several areas defined by the treaties. Due to the 'subsidiarity principle', such proposals should be confined to those in which action at the EU level would be more productive than at the national, regional or local level. However, once the Commission has lodged a proposal with the Council and the EP, these two bodies become the twin arms of the legislative authority, but the three institutions collaborate to try to achieve an agreement. Note that the Council generally reaches agreement by unanimity, only resorting to QMV for more controversial measures.

Also, the Commission carefully scrutinizes amendments by the EP before offering, where deemed appropriate, an amended proposal.

As the EU Executive, the Commission is involved in all the areas in which the EU is concerned. However, the role it plays assumes particular significance in certain fields. These include 'competition policy', in which it monitors cartels and mergers and disposes of or monitors discriminatory state aid; agriculture, in which it drafts regulations; and technical research and development (R&D), which it promotes and coordinates through the EU framework programmes. The Commission is also entrusted with the management of the EU general budget. The European Court of Auditors assesses the way in which the Commission discharges this responsibility (Chapter 5).

As the joint guardian of the EU treaties, the Commission has to see to it that EU legislation is properly implemented in the Member States. In doing so, it is hoped that it can maintain a climate of mutual, sincere cooperation so that all concerned, be they the Member States, economic operators or private citizens, can carry out their obligations to the full. If any Member State is in breach of EU legislation, say by failing to apply a EU directive, the Commission, as an impartial authority, should investigate, issue an objective ruling and notify the government concerned, subject to review by the ECJ, of the action needed to rectify the situation. If the matter cannot be dealt with through the infringement procedure, the Commission then has to refer it to the ECJ, whose decision is binding. Likewise, with the supervision of the ECJ, the Commission monitors companies for their respect for EU competition rules.

Until 2004, when the EU had 15 Member States, the Commission consisted of 20 members, one of whom was president and two were vice presidents. Two commissioners came from each of the then five large Member States and one from each of the remaining ten, that is, the number of commissioners was determined, roughly, by population size. However, the Nice Treaty required that the larger Member States should drop their second commissioner after 2005, so the number is now 28, including the president of the Commission and the HR since the entry into force of the Lisbon Treaty, which also dictates that, as of 1 November 2014, the number should be limited to two-thirds of the total, that is, 18 or 19 for the EU of 28, unless the European Council unanimously decides otherwise. But an intergovernmental agreement to maintain one commissioner per Member State (a compromise forced by the second Irish referendum) was later confirmed by a European Council decision.

All commissioners are appointed for five years (four until 1994) and have renewable terms of office. They are chosen for their *competence and capacity to act independently in the interest of the EU itself,* not of their own nations, but many scholars believe that in reality they favour their home country. They have been politicians in their own countries, often having held ministerial positions. The incumbent (since November 2014) Commission president, Jean-Claude Juncker, was prime minister of Luxembourg during 1995–2013. His immediate predecessor was José Manuel Barroso, who was not the first choice for his first term (2004–9), and was recruited while still prime minister of Portugal. Before them, Romano Prodi was prime minister of Italy (1996–8, and again during 2006–8). Before Prodi, Jacques Santer was prime minister of Luxembourg (1995–9). And the noted Jacques Delors was the French minister of economy and finance in 1981 (Table 3.1). After Delors, there was an informal 'gentlemen's agreement' between the Member States that the position of president of the Commission should go to 'one of them', but in 2014 the EP, citing the Lisbon Treaty, insisted that the leader of its largest party group, the European People's Party (EPP), Juncker, should be appointed (a process now called *spitzenkandidat*), and it succeeded despite strong opposition by the British prime minister, David Cameron (more on this below).

This political experience is necessary because the commissioners need to be familiar with the political scene and able to meet senior politicians on equal terms. Without this stature and ability to understand political pressures, they would lose the senses of touch and timing which are essential for effective Commission functioning. Indeed, two commissioners have been so assertive that they have been accused of exceeding their duties: Hallstein (1958–62 and 1962–7) for trying to give more powers to the Commission to build it into a government for Europe, and Delors (1985–9, 1989–93 and 1993–5) for attempting to impose his French socialist approach on the rest of the Member States. One has to recall, however, that Hallstein, the first-ever president of the Commission, was following in the footsteps of Monnet's and the Benelux countries' drive for the political unity of Europe, at a time when seeking the support of the European populace for a 'united states of Europe' was out of the question: who in his/her right mind would have attempted to seek the endorsement of the average person when the war devastation was so fresh in people's minds? As to Delors, his record speaks for itself, and many believe that his so-called misguided obsession with a 'socialist' Europe was shared by many EU organizations and citizens at the time. Of course, some would claim that all commissioners had become spent

Table 3.1   Presidents of the European Commission

Commission president	Term of office	National political position
Walter Hallstein (Germany)	1 January 1958 to 30 June 1967	Leading civil servant in the German Foreign Office in 1951 and de facto Foreign Minister thereafter
Jean Ray (Belgium)	30 June 1967 to 1 July 1970	Minister of Reconstruction 1949–50; Minister of Economy 1954–8
Franco Maria Malfatti (Italy)	1 July 1970 to 1 March 1972	Minister of Finance 1978–9; Minister of Foreign Affairs 1979–80; etc.
Sicco Mansholt (Netherlands)	1 March 1972 to 5 January 1973	Minister of Agriculture, Fishing and Food Supply 1945–58
François-Xavier Ortoli (France)	5 January 1953 to 5 January 1977	Finance Minister 1968–9
Roy Jenkins (United Kingdom)	5 January 1977 to 19 January 1981	Home Secretary 1965–7; Chancellor of the Exchequer 1967–70, etc.
Gaston Thorn (Luxembourg)	19 January 1981 to 6 January 1985	Prime Minister 1974–9; President of UN General Assembly 1975
Jacques Delors (France)	6 January 1985 to 24 January 1995	Economic and Finance Minister 1981–3; Economics, Finance and Budget Minister 1983–4, etc.
Jacques Santer (Luxembourg)	24 January 1995 to 15 March 1999	Finance Minister 1979–89; Prime Minister 1984–95
Manuel Marin (Spain; Interim)	15 March 1999 to 17 September 1999	President of the Spanish Parliament 2004–8
Romano Prodi (Italy)	17 September 1999 to 22 November 2004	Prime Minister 1996–8, 2006–8
José Manuel Barroso (Portugal)	22 November 2004 to 1 November 2014	Secretary of State for Foreign Affairs and Cooperation 1987–92; Prime Minister 2002–4
Jean-Claude Juncker (Luxembourg)	1 November 2014 to present	Minister of Finance 1989–2009; Prime Minister 1995–2013

forces in their own countries before joining the Commission, but against that others would counter by stressing that 'experience' does not vanish overnight and many politicians return to office in their home countries after serving on the Commission.[8]

The appointment process for the commissioners begins long before the EP elections. This is to allow time for the necessary EP procedure to approve the Commission. This procedure commences with the appointment of the Commission president, who is nominated by the Member States and has to be approved (elected) by the EP. For the 2014 Commission president, the EP insisted that the leader of its largest faction (Jean-Claude Juncker, below) should be appointed, but British prime minster Cameron objected strongly, on the grounds that Juncker is an 'old-fashioned' European federalist when Cameron wants the UK to opt out of the 'ever closer union'. Had Cameron succeeded, a stalemate would have arisen: since the EP has to approve the appointment, the EP would have refused to approve anyone else. The result is that it has now been firmly established that the EP will in future approve only its own candidate and has thus greatly enhance its institutional powers.

Once confirmed, the Commission president, following the nominations of the governments of the Member States, puts forward the remaining commissioners. The EP then gives its opinion on the entire college of 28 through an approval process. The new Commission assumes its official responsibilities soon after the EP has approved it, in the latest case, on 1 November 2014. Six of the commissioners were vice presidents on the Barroso Commission, but only the HR is mentioned in the Treaty, and the 2014 Commission has seven vice presidents, including the HR.

It is pertinent to add here that, following the exposure of ineptness and laxity of some parts of the Commission (Box 3.1), but more generally as a matter of rendering the 'executive' more accountable for its actions, the EP has taken the question of approval even more seriously. The EP has done so by subjecting nominees to detailed scrutiny, including their suitability for their intended posts (Box 3.2), the allocation of which is subject to discussions between the Commission president and the Heads of State and Government. Indeed, the EP succeeded in doing precisely that when Barroso, for his first term, proposed, on the nomination of Italy's Berlusconi government, Rocco Buttiglione for the justice and home affairs portfolio. By then, all the other positions had been agreed; hence, the ultimate solution was to withdraw Buttiglione altogether.

Box 3.1   The need to reform the Commission

Santer's Commission (1995–9) suffered the unique humiliation of having to resign nine months prematurely in March 1999. The resignation had been instigated by the EP following a report by a Committee of Independent Experts, which condemned the Commission and the Commission president for not assuming responsibility for financial irregularities and other acts of misconduct within their services. Serious allegations were also made against Commissioner Édith Cresson of France regarding the appointment of her former dentist to whom she was 'very close' for a research job within the Commission. Cresson's stubborn refusal to resign and the belief of several commissioners that resignation was necessary, if only to clear their names, left Santer with no alternative but to announce the resignation of the entire Commission, even though the EP had not censured it. Santer's Commission thereafter stayed on in a caretaker capacity.

Box 3.2   The EP forces a vital decision

After two days of arguing with the members of the EP (MEPs) over his proposing Rocco Buttiglione – a Catholic Italian conservative who was on the record as believing that homosexuality is a sin and that women should stay at home to raise children – as Justice Commissioner, a post which includes an anti-discrimination policy, Barroso had to back down. One hour before the EP was to vote, he told the MEPs that if the vote were to go ahead, on 27 October 2004, the outcome would 'not be positive'. Then, to loud cheers and clapping, he added that under 'these circumstances I have decided not to submit a new commission for your approval today'. He went on to say, 'I need more time to look at this issue and to consult with the [European] Council and consult further with you, so we can have strong support for the new Commission. It is better to have more time to get it right'. Then, displaying some of the diplomatic skills for which he was chosen to lead the new Commission, he uttered, 'Ladies and gentlemen, these last days have demonstrated that the European Union is an intensely political construction and that this Parliament, elected by popular vote across all of our member states, has indeed a vital role to play in the governance of Europe'. The crisis came to an end when the Italian prime minister, Silvio Berlusconi, urged by British prime minister Tony Blair, replaced Buttiglione with Franco Frattini.

It has also been made clear that the commissioners must work under the political guidance of the Commission president (Article 219 EC), while the commissioners have had to agree to resign if asked to do so by the Commission president. The procedures have enhanced the EP's powers considerably, since the EP can satisfy itself about Commission's programme and intended initiatives before giving its approval.

While these moves are intended to ensure a more efficient and accountable Commission, the episode has brought a latent contradiction to the surface. The Commission was designed as the powerhouse of EU political momentum. Although, as mentioned, this function is to some extent now shared with the European Council and the EP, it has been less effective in administrative and managerial functions in which its weaknesses have been exposed. This has led some critics to argue that reform should include a shift of responsibility away from policy and towards execution so that the Commission becomes more like a national civil service,[9] but the incumbent Commission president, Juncker, has categorically stated that he wants his Commission to be a 'political team'.[10]

Each commissioner is responsible for a portfolio, which in many cases is a mixture of policy areas and administrative responsibilities, called Directorates General (DGs). However, since there are 43 DGs and Services (Table 3.1), some commissioners have responsibilities for more than one portfolio. That does not mean that they are busier, since the workload for each department depends on its relative weight within the EU. Indeed, the less busy commissioners have been accused of increasing their workload by using their time to promote undesirable EU legislation and, in this respect, it should be noted that Juncker has appointed six Commission vice presidents (above) some of whom have assumed the responsibility of overseeing the work of such commissioners.[11] Also, Juncker and the six vice presidents will work together in a 'collegiate' fashion, and hence assume collective responsibility and eliminate the overenthusiasm of the previously less-worked commissioners. Table 3.2 gives the latest DG designations.

A director general is in charge of a DG, and under him/her are directors, followed by heads of unit. Each commissioner has a private office made up of his/her own chosen administrative staff and outside advisers, referred to as a cabinet, a word borrowed from the administrative practice of France. When the commissioner is away, the head of his/her private office, the *chef de cabinet*, will act on his/her behalf at the weekly meetings, held on Wednesdays in Brussels, but in Strasbourg during the EP plenary sessions.

Whereas in the UK, the principle of 'ministerial responsibility' indicates a close relationship between a minister and her/his official policy advisers, the EU cabinet system is one of a more detached association between them. To become part of a cabinet is highly desirable amongst the EU bureaucracy, due to the influence that its members can exercise on behalf of their bosses and access to the power at the senior

Table 3.2   EU DGs and services

Agriculture and rural development (AGRI)
Budget (BUDG)
Climate action (CLIMA)
Communication (COMM)
Communication networks, content and technology (CNECT)
Competition (COMP)
Economic and financial affairs (ECFIN)
Education and culture (EAC)
Employment, social affairs and inclusion (EMPl)
Energy (ENER)
Environment (ENV)
Eurostat (ESTAT)
Financial stability, financial services and capital markets union (FISMA)
Health and food safety (SANTE)
Humanitarian aid and civil protection (ECHO)
Human Resources and Security (HR)
Home Affairs (HOME)
Informatics (DIGIT)
Internal market, industry, entrepreneurship and SMEs (GROW)
International cooperation and development (DEVCO)
Interpretation (SCIC)
Joint Research Centre (JRC)
Justice and consumers (JUST)
Maritime affairs and fisheries (MARE)
Mobility and transport (MOVE)
Neighbourhood and enlargement negotiations (NEAR)
Regional policy (REGIO)
Research and innovation (RID)
Secretariat general (SG)
Services for foreign policy instruments (FPI)
Taxation and customs union (TAXUD)
Trade (TRADE)
Translation (DGT)

Services
Central library
European Anti-Fraud Office (OLAF)
European Commission Data Protection Officer
Historical archives
Infrastructures and Logistics – Brussels (OIB)
Infrastructures and Logistics – Luxembourg (OIL)
Internal Audit Service (IAS)
Legal Service (SJ)
Office for administration and payment of individual entitlements (PMO)
Publications Office (OP)

EU levels. Indeed, some key appointments became even more powerful than most other commissioners, such as *chef de cabinet* Pascal Lamy, who later became a very significant commissioner himself and is now head of the WTO.

The staff of the cabinet had traditionally come from the same Member Nation as the commissioner, for ease of communication, but this has changed. The personal cabinets of the commissioners have been opened to wider recruitment so that they are less obviously national enclaves attached to a particular commissioner. Reform of financial controls and stronger management systems have been put into place, and merit accounts for more, and nationality less, for promotion to senior posts. Personnel are to receive more training and be subject to tighter controls. The cabinet of Commission president José Manuel Barroso comprised 12 policy advisers coming from seven different Member States. His cabinet also included 23 assistants and 2 press spokesmen. It is generally understood that the appointees should not be confined to the same nationality as the commissioner and that a certain percentage should be women.

Over time, some DGs have acquired greater prestige than others. Not surprisingly, those who deal with core EU policies are most prominent, and as the EU has developed so has the possibility for conflict between the DGs over policy matters arisen. Agricultural, competition and regional and external trade policies, especially imports from the LDCs, are obvious examples. A new development brought in with the 1999 Commission was to have a senior commissioner responsible for the oversight of external affairs, whether of an economic or a political nature, but this is now the job of the HR (above). Once the Commission has reached a decision on a matter presented by the commissioner concerned, the decision becomes an integral part of its policy and will have the unconditional backing of the entire college, even if simple majority voting led to its adoption. In a sense, the Commission follows the British practice of 'collective responsibility', that is, it acts as a collegiate body, accepting responsibility as a group, but policy implementation rests mainly with the responsible commissioner, perhaps in association with two or more colleagues.

In carrying out its responsibilities, the Commission seeks the opinions of national parliaments, administrations, and professional and trade union organizations. For the technical details of its legislative provisions or proposals, it consults the experts who meet in the committees and working groups that it organizes. In carrying out the implementation of measures, the Commission is assisted by committees of representatives of the Member States. Also, it works closely with the EESC and CoR since it has to take into account their advice on many proposed legislative acts. The Commission also attends all the EP sessions, at which it must clarify and justify its policies, and regularly replies to both written and oral questions posed by the MEPs.

In some ways, both for interest groups and for the layperson wishing to make the effort, the Commission is more accessible than national administrations. This is in part because the consultation processes, although clumsy, do bring a wide range of people in touch with EU affairs. At the same time this puts a premium on the views of those who are effectively organized, like French farmers. Additionally, there is a well-established Commission policy of informing and educating the public in order to mobilize public opinion behind the integration process. This had not been very effective in the past, so that considerable unease remained and the Commission's success in establishing relations with bankers, industrialists and other interest groups had contributed to a widespread belief that the EU is an elitist institution far away from the ordinary citizen. However, the impression of remoteness has been greatly dented since the 2008 financial crisis and the Eurozone problems, and Commission initiatives are more or less daily news nowadays. But better information and public access to the Commission have been a priority since the Maastricht Treaty.

Finally, one should add that it is possible that the term 'Commission' may be confusing. This is because it is used to refer to both the college of 28 commissioners and to the entire institution with approximately 32,000 staff[12] (contrary to popular prejudice, this total is equivalent to that in a reasonable size ministry in any of the larger Member States). However, one should encounter no major difficulties identifying which commission is being referred to since it is easy to judge from the context.

3.4   The Council of the European Union

As mentioned in Chapter 2, the three Councils of Ministers, one each for the ECSC, EEC and Euratom, were merged in 1965. With the adoption of the Treaty on European Union (TEU; the Maastricht Treaty), the name was changed in 1993 to the Council of the European Union (hereafter simply Council; see above) to reflect the three EU pillars.

The Council consists of representatives of the governments of the Member States at the ministerial level (not officials, see TEU, Article 16[2]), who are accountable to their national parliaments and citizens;

hence, it is the embodiment of national interests. Representatives of the Commission always attend its meetings. Note that, although the Commission has no voting rights, it plays an active role in helping to reach decisions, and that it is here that it can perform an important mediating function between national viewpoints and its own, which, as we have seen, is intended to represent the general EU interest.

The Council meets in different 'configurations', the list of which is decided by the European Council. Presently, the Council has ten (there was no limit to the number before 1999, then capped at sixteen until June 2002) distinct subject-based such configurations that work in parallel. These are the General Affairs Council (GAC); Foreign Affairs Council (FAC); Economic and Financial Affairs Council (ECOFIN), including budget; Justice and Home Affairs (JHA), including the Civil Protection Council; Employment, Social Policy, Health and Consumer Affairs (ESPCO) Council; Competitiveness (internal market, industry, research and space) Council; Transport, Telecommunications and Energy Council; Agriculture and Fisheries Council; Environment Council; and Education, Youth, Culture and Sport Council (including audio-visual matters). The FAC and the GAC, consisting respectively of foreign ministers and a mixture of foreign and European affairs ministers, are enshrined in the TEU (Article 16[6]) and each meets once a month, usually back to back. Also, the ECOFIN and the Agriculture and Fisheries Council meet once a month. There are regular but less frequent meetings of the remaining six Councils, the frequency depending on the number and urgency of the issues under consideration. Occasionally, joint, so-called jumbo, meetings of all ten Councils are held when issues cross the responsibility boundaries of any one Council. The FAC used to be referred to as the Senior Council, but the Lisbon Treaty of 2009 has bestowed this on the GAC, now explicitly entrusted with a general coordinating role within the system 'to ensure consistency in the work of the different Council configurations' (TEU, Article 16[6]).

Note that the FAC discusses issues emanating from the Common Foreign and Security Policy (CFSP) and other external policy domains, such as external trade (the Common Commercial Policy) and development policy. Article 16.6 of the Lisbon Treaty dictates that the FAC should 'elaborate the [EU]'s external action on the basis of the strategic guidelines laid down by the European Council and ensure that the [EU]'s action is consistent' (Article 16.6 TEU). The FAC meets periodically in the form of defence or development ministers.

Thus, unlike the Commission, the Council is not made up of a fixed body of people. The Council is located in Brussels, and most of its meetings are held there, except during April, June and October when they take place in Luxembourg.

Since membership of the Council varies according to the subject matter under review, this has led to problems for the Member States. These arise because EU issues are handled by different, various, ministers, each minister briefed by her/his own civil servants, so it becomes hard for any government to see its EU policy as a coherent whole. In turn, coordination within the government machine becomes problematic. For the EU, too, the greater specialization of business creates difficulties, for it has become far more difficult to negotiate a package deal whereby a set of decisions can be agreed, and each Member State has gains to set off against its losses, although in the long run governments need to show the benefits they have won.

The presidency of the Council rotates, with each Member State holding it in turn for a period of six months, and the chairmanship of the many committees alters correspondingly. The presidency plays an active role as the organizer of the Council's work and as the chairperson of its meetings; as the promoter of legislative and political decisions; and as an arbiter between the Member States in brokering compromises between them. It has become the practice for each Member State to try to establish a particular style of working and to single out certain matters to which it wishes to give priority. Since any chairperson can influence business significantly, the president may occupy an important, albeit temporary, role. The president also fulfils some representational functions towards other EC institutions, notably the EP.

The Council has six major responsibilities. It is a twin arm of the legislature, together with the EP, through the 'co-decision procedure', now called the 'ordinary legislative procedure' (Section 3.5). The Council coordinates the broad economic policies of the Member States. It also concludes EU international agreements. Together with the EP, it has authority on the EU general budget. On the basis of general guidelines from the European Council, it used to take the necessary decisions for framing and implementing the CFSP, but this task has now gone to the HR. And it coordinates the activities of the Member States as well as adopts measures in the area of 'judicial and home affairs' (JHA).

It may prove helpful to elaborate on three of these roles. With regard to its decision-making powers, the Council generally speaking only acts on a proposal from the Commission (see above), and in most cases acts jointly with the EP in the context of ordinary legislative procedure, consultation or assent procedure (Section 3.5). Under the ordinary legislative procedure, the Council and the EP share legislative authority in general areas, which include the completion of the internal market (SEM), environment and consumer protection, non-discrimination, free movement and residence and the combating of social exclusion. However, the Council plays a dominant role when it comes to JHA when it relates to essential components of national policy, since both the EP and the Commission have a more limited role in this area. Also, although the Commission is entrusted with the enforcement of EU legislation, the Council may reserve the right for it to perform executive functions.

The Maastricht Treaty introduced economic policy coordination, to achieve this task. Each year, the Council adopts draft guidelines for the economic policies of the Member States, which are then incorporated into the conclusions of the European Council. They are then converted into a Council recommendation and accompanied by a multilateral surveillance mechanism. This coordination is performed in the context of the EMU, in which the Economic and Financial Affairs Council (ECOFIN) plays a leading role.

Finally, with regard to the joint responsibility of the Council and the EP for the EU general budget (Chapter 5), each year the Commission submits a preliminary draft budget to the Council for approval. Then a reading, followed by conciliation, allows the EP to negotiate with the Council the modification of certain items of expenditure and to ensure that budgetary revenues are allocated appropriately. In the case of disagreement with the EP, the Council is entrusted with making the final decision on the so-called 'compulsory expenditures', relating mainly to agriculture and financial commitments emanating from the EU agreements with non-Member States. However, with regard to 'non-compulsory expenditures' and the final adoption of the whole budget, the EP has the final say.

The decisions of the Council are taken by unanimous vote or by simple or QM vote (above), with QMV being the most common. When QMV is used, each Member State is endowed with a number of votes. The votes are weighted so that at least some of the smaller Member States must assent. For the EU of 28, the distribution of the votes is 29 each for France, Germany, Italy and the UK; 27 for Poland and Spain; 14 for Romania; 13 for the Netherlands; 12 each for Belgium, the Czech Republic, Greece, Hungary and Portugal; 10 each for Austria, Bulgaria and Sweden; 7 each for Croatia, Denmark, Finland, Ireland, Lithuania and Slovakia; 4 each for Cyprus, Estonia, Latvia, Luxembourg and Slovenia; and 3 for Malta. A decision requires a majority of the Member States and a minimum of 260 votes (73.9 per cent of the total of 352), and the blocking minority is 91 votes. The proviso is added that a Council member can request verification on whether the Member States constituting the 260 votes represented at least 62 per cent of the total EU population. If not, the decision cannot be adopted. Thus a decision requires a triple majority. This general picture is reinforced in the Lisbon Treaty, which defines QMV from 1 November 2014 to be at least 55 per cent of the Council members, comprising at least 15 of them and representing Member States comprising at least 65 per cent of the EU population. That being the case, one is left wondering why the complicated arithmetical formula is needed, unless one is interested in the trivial pursuit of playing exercises with them.

As a final word on QMV, one should add that its proponents often claim that it is a device meant to ensure that the large Member States cannot impose their wishes on the smaller Member States. However, it can equally be claimed that it is a system which prevents majority opinion from being stymied by a few smaller nations, which is what could happen in the case of a decision requiring a simple majority of the EU nations, that is, needing 15 out of the 28, or of course unanimity.

The Council is served by its own secretariat and is supported by an important body called the Committee of Permanent Representatives (COREPER). Originally, the membership of COREPER comprised senior representatives from the Member States holding ambassadorial rank.[13] But today, there are two such committees: COREPER I, consisting of deputy heads of mission and dealing largely with social and economic issues, and COREPER II, comprising heads of mission (Ambassador Extraordinary and Plenipotentiary) and dealing largely with political, financial and foreign policy issues. These bodies prepare the work of the Council, except for agricultural matters, since these are entrusted to the Special Committee on Agriculture. The Council is also assisted by working groups, which consist of officials from the national administrations of the Member States.

In 1966, it was agreed that it would be desirable for the Commission to contact the governments of the Member States via COREPER before deciding on the form of an intended proposal. As a result of its links with both the Council and Commission, COREPER is involved in all major stages of EU policy-making. Many matters of policy are in fact agreed by COREPER and reach the Council only in a formal sense. While this is one way of keeping business down to manageable proportions, it has meant that the Council itself has become concerned only with the most important matters or those which may not be of great substance, but which are nevertheless politically sensitive. In the past, this encouraged domestic media to present the Council meetings as national battles in which there had to be victory or defeat, and politicians too became extremely adept at using publicity to rally support for their point of view. As a result, the effect became the opposite of that originally intended when it had been thought that the experience of working together would make it progressively easier to find an answer expressive of the general good, and for which majority voting would be a suitable tool. Instead, conflict of national interests was often a better description. The Council also encountered practical problems. The great press of business, the fact that ministers can only attend to Council business part-time, the highly sensitive nature of their activities and the larger number of members all contributed to a grave time lag in reaching policy decisions, and the move towards QMV was one measure designed to overcome this difficulty. Fortunately, today the media does not report on most Council meetings, so this problem does not arise; indeed, the media has taken its attention away to the European Council meetings, due to the above-mentioned attributes.

3.5 The European Parliament

Originally, the EP was a consultative rather than a legislative body, since the Council had to seek its opinion, but without obligation, before deciding on a Commission proposal. It did have the power to dismiss the entire Commission, but because it did not possess the right to appoint commissioners, many analysts did not attach much significance to this. However, as mentioned in Chapter 2 and above, the EP acquired budgetary powers in 1970, financial provisions powers in 1975 and the right to elect the president of the Commission in 1992. Also, the SEA gave it more powers in 1986 and the Maastricht (1992), Amsterdam (1997) and Lisbon (2009) treaties have turned the EP into a true legislative body as well as strengthened its role as the democratic overseer of the EU.

The EP acts together with the Council in formulating and adopting certain legislation emanating from the Commission. Here, the most common path is through the ordinary legislative procedure (above) in the Lisbon treaty (Article 294 TFEU), which gives equal weight to both bodies and results in the adoption of joint acts (Figure 3.1). In the case of disagreements between the two, conciliation committees are convened to find common ground. The equal legislative procedure applies particularly in the case of the Single European Market (SEM) (the four freedoms, especially the free movement of workers); technological research and development; the environment; consumer protection; education; culture; and public health.

Also, the approval of the EP is needed in certain areas. These include accession by new member nations; association agreements with non-member countries; decisions affecting the right of residence for EU citizens; its own electoral procedures; and the task and powers of the ECB.

Moreover, although the Commission remains the main instigator of new legislation, the EP also provides significant political momentum, especially through its examination of the annual programme for the Commission and asking it to submit appropriate proposals.

With regard to the EU general budget, the EP and Council are the key players. Each year, the Commission has to prepare a preliminary draft budget, which has to be approved by the Council. Then two readings ensue, providing the EP with the occasion to negotiate with the Council the amendment of certain items of expenditure, although such amendments are generally subject to the financial constraints of the budget, and to ensure that the budgetary resources are appropriately allocated. Finally, it is the EP that has the right to adopt the final budget, which needs the signature of the president of the EP before it can come into force. Also, the EP's committee on budgetary control is entrusted with monitoring the implementation of the budget, and each year the EP grants a discharge to the Commission for the implementation of the budget for the previous year.

Thus the EP of today performs three important functions *together* with the Council: it legislates; shares authority on the EU general budget; and elects the president of the Commission, and approves the nominations of the president of the EU and commissioners. Independently, it has the right to censure the Commission, forcing its resignation, and exercises political supervision over all the institutions. Moreover, as we have seen, it holds the executive accountable.

The EP operates in three different places. It meets in Strasbourg, where it is officially seated, for its plenary sessions, which all members (MEPs) must attend. Its 21 parliamentary committees (covering everything from women's rights to health and consumer protection), which prepare work for the plenary sessions, hold their meetings in Brussels, and additional plenary sessions are held there too. Its secretariat is located in Luxembourg. This set-up has attracted harsh criticism not only for its inconvenience and money and time wasting, due to the travel and accommodation expenses involved, but more importantly for making it difficult for the EP to become a more coherent and effective organization. It is often claimed that the reasons for these locations are mainly historical, going back to the creation of the ECSC, EEC and Euratom, but the history was no accident, given the prestige the EP extends to the

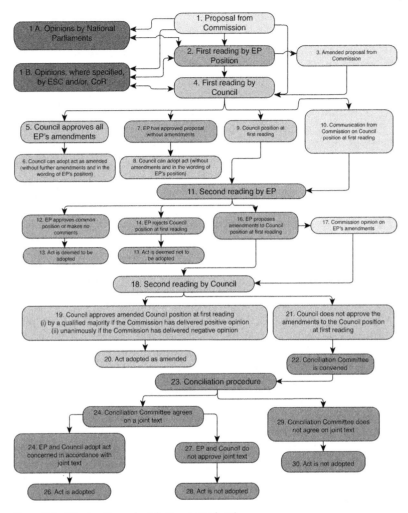

Figure 3.1   The 'ordinary legislative procedure'

countries in which it is located and the economic value of having EU institutions operate in one's country.

The EP is still in an evolutionary stage and cannot be expected to follow the path of national parliaments, which, in any case, differ among themselves. Some[14] have suggested that it should become a merely advisory body, just falling short of the powers of the British House of Lords, on the assumption that the EU is not a single state. Others[15] argue for the creation of a second chamber consisting of representatives of national parliaments, determined by lot and with its only power to be the blocking of centralizing legislation. But such propositions would not be consistent with the very nature of the EU as a dynamic association still in the making (Chapter 2). The EP operates in a different environment, and its power struggles, so far, have been with the Council and Commission rather than with national parliaments.

The EP had its first elections by direct universal suffrage in 1979. Elections are based on a system of proportional representation and are held either on a regional basis (as in, for example, Belgium, Italy and the UK) or nationally. The EP elected in May 2014 has 751 members (MEPs; Table 3.3). Ninety-six MEPs come from Germany (population of 82 million); 74 from France (66 million); 73 each from Italy (61 million) and the UK (63 million); 54 from Spain (46 million); 51 from Poland (39 million); 32 from Romania (21 million); 26 from the Netherlands (17 million); 22 each from Belgium (11 million), the Czech Republic (11 million), Greece (11 million), Hungary (10 million) and Portugal (11 million); 20 from Sweden (10 million); 18 from Austria (8 million); 17 from Bulgaria (7 million); 13 each from Denmark (6 million), Finland (5 million) and Slovakia (5 million); 11 each from Croatia (4 million), Ireland (5 million) and Lithuania (3 million); 8 each from Latvia (2 million) and Slovenia (2 million); and 6 each from Cyprus (1 million), Estonia (1 million), Luxembourg (1 million) and Malta (0.3 million). The total number of MEPs in the previous EP was 765, but the Lisbon Treaty dictates that in future the number of MEPs should not exceed 750 plus the EP's president (elected for 30 months), hence the 751 of today, and that no country should have fewer than 6 MEPs or more than 96 (Germany had 99 before 2014). As the figures indicate, the national distribution of the MEPs is roughly proportional to the populations of the Member States.

The MEPs are elected for a term of five years, and each has several parliamentary assistants. Once elected, they are organized in EU-wide political, rather than national groups, although in some cases national identity remains very strong. This has created serious problems because the MEPs are elected on a national basis according to their national party affiliations. Thus voters choose them not on an EU agenda, but rather on the basis of their disaffection with their own domestic parties. This became very clear in the 2014 EP elections when national concerns over immigration led to the success of fringe and anti-EU parties far beyond expectations (see the Introduction).

There are seven groups (Table 2.2): the European People's Party (Christian Democrats), with 220 MEPs; the Progressive Alliance of

Table 3.3 Members of the European Parliament elected in June 2014

	EPP	S&D	ALDE	G/EFA	ECR	GUE/ NGL	EFD	NA	Total
Austria	5	5	1	3				4	**18**
Belgium	4	4	6	2	4			1	**21**
Bulgaria	7	4	4		2				**17**
Croatia	5	2	2		1				**11**
Cyprus	2	2				2			**6**
Czech Republic	7	4	4		2	3	1		**21**
Denmark	1	3	3	1	4	1			**13**
Estonia	1	1	3	1					**6**
Finland	3	2	4	1	2	1	1		**13**
France	20	13	7	6		4	1	23	**74**
Germany	34	27	4	13	8	8		2	**96**
Greece	5	4			1	6	2	5	**21**
Hungary	12	4				2		3	**21**
Ireland	4	1	1		1	4			**11**
Italy	17	31				3	17	5	**73**
Latvia	4	1		1	1		1		**8**
Lithuania	2	2	3		1	1	2		**11**
Luxembourg	3	1	1	1					**6**
Malta	3	3							**6**
Netherlands	5	3	7	2	2	3		5	**26**
Poland	23	5			19			4	**51**
Portugal	7	8	2			4			**21**
Romania	14	16	2						**32**
Slovakia	6	4	1		2				**13**
Slovenia	5	1	1						**8**
Spain	17	14	8	4		11			**54**
Sweden	4	6	3	4		1	2		**20**
United Kingdom		20	1	6	20	1	24	1	**73**
Total	**220**	**191**	**68**	**50**	**70**	**52**	**48**	**52**	**751**

Note: EPP is a group of the European People's Party (Christian Democrats); S&D is a group of the Progressive Alliance of Socialists and Democrats; ALDE is a group of the Alliance of Liberals and Democrats for Europe; Greens/EFA is a group of the Greens and European Free Alliance; ECR is a group of the European Conservatives and Reformists; GUE/NGL is a group of the European United Left and Nordic Green Left; EFD is the group of the Europe of Freedom and Democracy; and NA is the Non-attached.

Socialists and Democrats, with 191; the Alliance of Liberals and Democrats for Europe, with 68; the Greens and European Free Alliance, with 50; the European Conservatives and Reformists, with 70; the European United Left and Nordic Green Left, with 52; the Europe of Freedom and Democracy, with 48; and the Non-attached, with 52. Twenty-five MEPs from at least one quarter of the EU member nations are needed for a group, and no member can belong to more than one group. Each group appoints its own chairperson, bureau and secretariat. Belonging to a group is important because the groups attract funding and receive guaranteed seats on committees.

Since the ideologies of the different factions in a group are not identical, one may wonder how such motley collections ever get anything useful done. The response would be that in reality they do agree on many issues, but of course the pace at which they do so is dictated by the time needed to reach consensus. Moreover, for the EP to be effective, it has proved necessary to have such large coalitions.

3.6   The courts

3.6.1   The European Court of Justice

There are three reasons why the ECJ is needed. First, a body of legal experts is indispensable for ensuring that the EU institutions act in a constitutional manner, fulfilling the obligations laid out for them by the treaties. Second, a court is essential for seeing that the Member States, firms and individual citizens observe the (increasing number of) EU rules. And a court at the EU level is vital for guiding national courts in their interpretation of EU law, hence for ensuring that EU legislation is uniformly applied.

The court system consists of three courts, the ECJ, the General Court and the Civil Service Tribunal, all seated in Luxembourg.[16] The ECJ has twenty-eight judges, one from each Member State. The Judges are appointed upon agreement by the governments of the Member States, following the consultation of a panel responsible for providing an opinion on the suitability of each candidate. The judges are appointed for a six-year term of office, which is renewable. The judges choose one of themselves as their president, who is appointed for three years. The judges also appoint a registrar for a six-year term of office.

There are nine advocates general, who are responsible for (a) preliminarily investigating a matter and (b) presenting publicly and impartially reasoned opinions on the cases brought before the ECJ to help the judges in reaching their decisions. Each judge has a cabinet to take care of administrative responsibilities, and its members are recruited directly by the judge. A cabinet comprises three law clerks to the ECJ and two to the General Court (see below). Clerks help the judges draw up their reports and draft their rulings. The registrar heads the ECJ administrative service and is also responsible for the procedural following of cases (see below).

In carrying out its responsibilities, the ECJ has a wide jurisdiction that it exercises in the context of various categories, the most common of which are

a. request for preliminary rulings when national courts ask the EJC to interpret a point of EU law;
b. actions for failure to fulfil obligations brought against governments of the Member States for failing to apply EU law;
c. actions for annulment against EU laws deemed to violate EU treaties of fundamental rights;
d. actions for failure to act brought against EU institutions for failing to make decisions required of them; and
e. direct actions brought by individuals, companies or organizations against EU decisions or actions.

A few words on how business is handled by the ECJ may be in order. After cases are lodged with the registry, they are distributed among the judges. A specific judge and advocate general assume responsibility for each case. A judge, appointed as *juge rapporteur*, has to write a report for the hearing, providing a summary of the legal background to the case and the observations of the parties to the case submitted in the first written phase of the procedure. In light of the reasoned opinion of the responsible advocate general, the *juge rapporteur* writes a draft ruling, which is then submitted to the other EJC members for examination. Thus the procedure has both a written and an oral phase. The advocate general then submits his/her conclusion, that is, reasoned opinion, before the judges deliberate and deliver their judgment on the case.

The ECJ sits as a full court, a Grand Chamber of thirteen judges, or a Chamber of three or five judges, depending on the nature, complexity or importance of the case. Chambers of five have three-year presidents; those of three have one-year presidents. The full court considers cases prescribed by its statutes, such as the dismissal of a member of the Commission; a Grand Chamber deals with a request by a member state or an institution and exceptionally important cases; and the other chambers deal with the rest. An ECJ judgment is reached by majority decisions and is pronounced at public hearings. There is no expression of 'dissenting opinions', and all the judges partaking in the deliberations must sign the judgment.

3.6.2 The General Court

Because the ECJ had been too busy to reach quick decisions, essential for a smooth operation of the integration process, the SEA introduced a Court of First Instance in 1989, renamed the General Court in 2009. The court deals with

a. cases brought by ordinary or legal persons against acts of the EU institutions, bodies, offices or agencies (which are addressed to them or are of direct and individual concern to them) and against regulatory acts (which concern them directly and which do not entail implementing measures) or against a failure to act on the part of those institutions, bodies, offices or agencies; for example, a case brought by a company against a Commission decision imposing a fine on that company;
b. cases brought by the Member States against the Commission;
c. cases brought by the Member States against the Council relating to acts adopted in regard to State aid, 'dumping' and acts by which it exercises implementing powers (see Chapter 5);
d. cases seeking compensation for damage caused by the EU institutions or their staff;
e. cases based on contracts made by the EU which expressly give jurisdiction to the General Court;
f. cases relating to EU trademarks;
g. appeals, limited to points of law, against the decisions of the European Union Civil Service Tribunal (below); and
h. actions brought against decisions of the Community Plant Variety Office or of the European Chemicals Agency.

The court's rulings are subject to appeal, within two months, to the ECJ on points of law only.

The General Court has the same number of judges as the ECJ, that is, 28, and they are subject to precisely the same conditions. The judges choose one of themselves as their president for a three-year term. They also appoint a registrar for a six-year term of office, but the registry relies on the services of the ECJ for its administrative and linguistic tasks. Although it has no advocates general, in exceptional circumstances, a judge may be appointed for the task. The General Court sits in Chambers made up of five or three judges, but in some cases, of a single judge. It may also sit as a Grand Chamber of 13 judges or as a full court of 28 judges when the legal complexity or importance of the case so dictates. In reality, over 80 per cent of the cases brought before the Court are dealt with by Chambers comprising three judges. The presidents of the five-judge Chambers are elected from amongst the judges concerned for a three-year period.

3.6.3 The European Civil Service Tribunal

In 2004, the Council decided to establish the European Union Civil Service Tribunal (Tribunal, hereafter), comprising seven judges, appointed by the Council for six-year terms of office, which are renewable. Their appointment follows a call for applications and the consultation of a panel of seven persons selected from former members of the ECJ and the General Court together with lawyers of repute. In making the appointments, the Council must ensure a balanced composition based on broad geographical representation of the Member States and the national legal systems represented.

The election of the president and the registrar and their terms of office match those of the General Court. Likewise for the registry, that is, it makes use of the services of the ECJ for its other administrative and linguistic needs. But it sits in Chambers of three judges; however, when the complexity or importance of the questions of law which are raised, justifies it, a case may be referred to the full court. Also, in cases determined by its Rules of Procedure, the Tribunal may sit in a Chamber of five Judges or as a single Judge.

Since 2012, the Tribunal has been able to secure the assistance of a temporary judge in order to cover the absence of one who is prevented, on medical grounds, from participating in the disposal of cases for a period of at least three months. In other words, the judge in question is not suffering from total disablement.

The Council makes a list of three temporary judges on a proposal from the president of the ECJ. The three judges are chosen from among former Members of the ECJ, the General Court or the Tribunal.

The Tribunal deals with disputes involving the EU civil service. This jurisdiction used to belong to the EJC, but was transferred to the Court of First Instance upon its establishment in 1989. It has jurisdiction to

a. hear and determine at first instance disputes between the EU and its staff concerning not only questions relating to working relations in the strict sense (pay, career progress, recruitment, disciplinary measures and the like) but also the social security system (sickness, old age, invalidity, accidents at work, family allowances, etc.); and
b. deal with disputes between all EU bodies or agencies and their staff, such as between Europol, the Office for Harmonisation in the Internal Market (OHIM) or the EIB and their staff.

In other words, the Tribunal may not hear and determine cases between national administrations and their employees.

The decisions of the Tribunal may, within two months, be subject to an appeal, confined to questions of law, to the General Court.

3.7   The European Economic and Social Committee (EESC)

The Economic and Social Committee (ESC), frequently referred to as the European ESC (EESC), was first established in 1957 at the time of the signing of the two treaties of Rome, creating the EEC and Euratom. The EESC is a forum for organized EU civil society. It comprises the various categories of economic and social activity such as employers, unions and the self-employed, together with representatives from community and social organizations (in particular, producers, farmers, carriers, workers, dealers, craftsmen, professional occupations, consumers and the general interest). These have organized themselves into three groups: group I, which consists of employers' representatives from both the private and public sectors; group II, the workers group, the vast majority of whom come from national trade union organizations; and Group III, the various interest group, which is a miscellaneous group, including members from farmers' organizations, small and medium-sized enterprises (SMEs), various NGOs, etc.

The EESC plays an important role of a general consultative and informative nature. The Commission, Council and EP (since the Amsterdam Treaty) seek the opinions of the EESC on a broad range of legislative proposals. Since 1972, the EESC itself also has been able to formulate its own opinions on issues it deems important. It also offers 'exploratory opinions' when approached by the Commission or the rotating presidency of the Council or the EP to discuss and make suggestions on an issue which could lead to a Commission proposal. Most recently, the EESC was asked to draft an opinion on the social aspects of the EMU by the president of the European Council.

The TEU endowed the EESC with a status akin to that of the other EU institutions, especially in terms of its procedural rules, budget, the reinforcement of its right of initiative and the management of its staff with the secretariat general. But it is not an EU institution as such. The EESC saw a broadening in its field of action, notably in social matters, in 1997 as per the Amsterdam Treaty.

The EESC has 353 members, appointed by the Council through lists forwarded by the governments of the Member States. But the Lisbon Treaty has set an upper limit of 350 in 2015. Each member is appointed (can be reappointed) for four years and acts independently in a personal capacity in the interests of the whole EU. The national distribution of the 353 members is such that France, Germany, Italy and the UK have 24 members each; Poland and Spain have 21 each; Romania has 15; Austria, Belgium, Bulgaria, the Czech Republic, Greece, Hungary, the Netherlands, Portugal and Sweden have 12 each; Croatia, Denmark, Finland, Ireland, Lithuania and Slovakia have 9 each; Estonia, Latvia and Slovenia have 7 each; Cyprus and Luxembourg have 6 each; and Malta has 5.

The EESC is housed in Brussels, but although most of its meetings and plenary sessions are held there, meetings are also scheduled in other locations. It has a plenary assembly, a bureau, the three groups just mentioned, six sections (dealing with the main EU activities), a consultative commission on industrial change and a secretariat general, with a staff of about 700 officials, including translators. It elects its own 40-member bureau, president and two vice presidents from the three groups in rotation, who hold office for two-year terms. The president acts as its external representative.

In reaching a decision, the EESC follows a certain procedure. When the president receives a request for an opinion from the Council, the Commission or the EP, the bureau lodges it with the appropriate section. The section then sets up a study group, consisting of about 12 persons, and appoints a 'rapporteur', who is assisted by up to four experts in the field. Based on the group's recommendations, the section adopts its opinion on a simple majority basis, and this is then considered in the plenary session, which decides likewise before addressing it to the requesting institution. Usually about ten plenary sessions are held every year.

3.8 The Committee of the Regions

The Committee of the Regions (CoR) was set up in 1994, following the TEU, in response to demands by several Member States that regional and local authorities should be directly involved in deliberations at the EU level. In many countries these authorities enjoy wide-ranging powers, either because of the federal structure of the country concerned or by virtue of legislative or constitutional measures adopted over the past few decades; hence, they are in direct touch with the average EU citizen, whose involvement in EU affairs, as we have seen in Chapter 2, has been a major issue. The TEU specifies that members of the CoR must hold a regional or local authority electoral mandate or be politically account-able to an elected assembly, but must act independently.

The CoR is an advisory body to the Council, the Commission and the EP, and its main work entails advancing its own opinions on Commission proposals. Also, as is expected, it ensures that the subsidiarity and proportionality principles are safeguarded. Moreover, the Council and Commission must consult it on any issue of direct relevance to local and regional authorities, and it can initiate its own opinions on matters of particular concern to itself and lodge them with either, or with the EP. Hence, the committee's work is guided by three principles: subsidiarity, proximity to citizens and partnership between those involved at all levels.

The structure and procedures of the committee resemble those of the EESC in most respects. The exceptions are fourfold. First, for every one of the 353 (350 from 2015) members, there is an alternate. Second, as just mentioned, the members are mainly politicians, either elected or exerting influence on local or regional authorities. Third, the members are assigned to six specialist commissions (set up by each Plenary Assembly; hence, their designation varies with each term) whose job is to prepare for the six annual plenary sessions (it also holds two extraordinary meetings, each in the member nation acting as president at the time), which decide its 'opinion'. Fourth, its bureau consists of its president; the first vice president; twenty-eight other vice presidents, one from each Member State; twenty-eight other members; and the leaders of its political groups. The bureau has three seats each for France, Germany, Italy, Poland, Spain and the UK; one for each of the remaining 22.

3.9   Types of EU decisions

It should be clear from all of the above that all the major EU institutions have a part to play in the decision-making process, depending on a modus vivendi existing between them to allow the process to operate. The proposals deemed adopted are jointly signed by the president of the EU and the presidents of both the Council and the EP. The latter signs the budget into being. It is, however, at the Council that outcomes are declared. Formally, an EU 'action' results in a regulation, a directive, a decision, a common action/position, a recommendation or an opinion (Article 288 TFEU; see Chapter 2). Other measures, such as 'conclusions', 'declarations' and 'resolutions', can be adopted. A regulation is directly applicable and binding in its entirety in all the Member States without the need for any national implementing legislation; hence, it is automatic EU law. A directive binds the Member States to the objectives to be achieved within a certain period of time, while leaving the national authorities the choice of form and means to be used. Thus directives have to be implemented by national legislation in accordance with the procedures of the individual Member States. The Commission deems it vital that the Member States should speed up transposition and proposes fines under the special penalty regime established by Article 260(3) of the TFEU. There were 56 directives to transpose in 2012, 131 in 2011 and 111 in 2010, with the late transposition infringements being 447, 1,185 and 855 for the respective years. In 2012 (data for later years is not available), Belgium and Poland were at the top of the offenders' list, with 34 each, followed by the Cyprus and the UK (25 each), Austria and Portugal (23 each) and Finland (21). The least offender was the Netherlands (6), followed by Sweden (7). The remaining Member States had between 8 and 19 offences.

A decision, which is a more specific act and often administrative in nature, is binding in all its facets only for the party to which it is addressed, whether it be all the Member States, an individual Member State, an enterprise, an individual or individuals. Recommendations and opinions have no binding force, but they express detailed EU preferences on an issue. Formal acts, notably regulations and directives, are constantly adding to EU law. The majority of legislation is now directives: in 2012, there were 1,769 regulations and 1,420 directives relating to only the SEM.[17]

Note that the Council and the EP may empower the Commission to adopt specific decisions to implement the detailed provisions of a regulation or directive, in accordance with what is in effect administrative law, known as the comitology process. Also, Article 106.3 of the TFEU permits the Commission to adopt a limited number of decisions in its own right with regard to competition policy. And, concerning the CFSP, decisions may be proposed by the High Representative or by the Member States to be adopted by the Council.

3.10   Does Brussels dictate?

The moral of the story is that, with regard to the actual legislative process, the initiatives come from the Commission, based on its annual work plan and its five-year programme. And, in the cases in which the European Council of the Heads of State or Government of the Member States has offered blueprints or general guidelines, these will be included, after a careful examination by the Commission has turned them into appropriate 'proposals'. Once a draft of a proposal is made, the Commission has to consult the Member States, through COREPER, as well as the EESC and the CoR, which represent respectively the EU citizens and local government associations. When the draft is finalized, it goes to both the Council of Ministers and the EP, and the two, through the ordinary legislative procedure, have to seek agreement. The agreed proposal is final and is announced at the Council. Thus it would be inaccurate to argue that Brussels rules the waves since the EU governments, citizens and local associations are all involved in the decision-making process. The accusation that the parliaments of the Member States are not afforded much time to debate a proposal is unwarranted and for three reasons. The first is already mentioned: the governments of the Member States are involved in the EU decision-making process and so are aware of the nature of the proposal. It is therefore their responsibility to inform and consult their parliaments. The second is that the national parliaments are themselves not so availed in all legislation emanating from their own governments, so why should EU legislation be treated differently? Of course, this does not mean that debate is not desirable; rather, only that there is no special reason why EU legislation should be debated longer, especially when the life of a parliament is limited.

The third is of the essence and so needs to be stated fully. In response to demands by the national parliaments for more EU democratic legitimacy, the 2009 Lisbon Treaty has conferred a number of new rights and powers on them. These rights can be classified into three categories. The first is 'information rights', meaning that the national parliaments have the right to receive information directly from the EU institutions concerning not only EU legislative acts (Article 12.a of the TEU) but also EU legislative programmes, Commission consultative documents on legislative matters, Council minutes of its deliberations on legislative acts and the annual report of the Court of Auditors (Protocol 1, on the role of National Parliaments in the European Union).

The second is the right to object to EU acts on subsidiarity grounds (Article 5.3 and Protocol 2 on enhanced subsidiarity and proportionality). The Protocol charts a subsidiarity early warning mechanism that affords the national parliaments the opportunity to object to EU legislative proposals with a view to having them amended or withdrawn. National parliaments may submit a 'reasoned opinion' within eight weeks to the institution proposing the draft legislative act, usually the Commission, outlining why the proposal does not comply with the principle of subsidiarity. If a third or more of the EU national parliaments submit reasoned opinions (the threshold drops to a quarter for legislation in the field of cooperation in criminal matters), the originating institution is usually bound to review its proposal with a view to maintaining, amending or withdrawing it. This is called the 'yellow card' mechanism (Article 7.2 of the Protocol). If more than half the Member States submit reasoned opinions and the institution decides to maintain the proposal, it must submit a reasoned opinion in support of this decision to the Council and the EP, each of which can strike down the proposal. Under this Protocol, national parliaments can apply to the ECJ, via their Member State governments, for judicial review of EU legislation on the grounds of infringement of the subsidiarity principle. The Protocol also has a 'red card' mechanism, which applies to only the ordinary legislative procedure. This is activated when a simple majority of the national parliaments complain (27 votes out of 54). That matches that for the yellow card, but adds that if the Commission insists on maintaining the proposal, it should send a justified opinion to the EP and the Council to carry out a final subsidiarity review. The proposal is not given further consideration if either the Council (by a majority of 55 per cent of the members) or a majority in the EP deem that the proposal is incompatible with the subsidiarity principle (Article 7.3).

Recommended Reading

Rose, Richard (2013) *Representing Europeans: a Pragmatic Approach*, Oxford, Oxford University Press.

Teasdale, Anthony and Bainbridge, Timothy (2012) *The Penguin Companion to the European Union*, 4th edition, Penguin Books, London.

Vaubel, Roland (2009) *The European Institutions as an Interest Group*, Institute of International Affairs, London.

4
EU Policies

4.1 Introduction

As can be seen from the number of the EU Commission's Directorates General (DGs; Table 3.1), the EU has a wide range of policies. These policies can be classified into three main groups. The first covers areas that constitute the very foundations needed to facilitate a properly operating Single European Market (SEM). There are six such areas: (a) competition rules; (b) industrial and competitiveness policy; (c) tax harmonization; (d) transport policy; (e) energy policy; and (f) environmental policy. Industrial policy is included because variations in it would be tantamount to affording differing protection to national domestic industry. The absence of tax harmonization would have consequences equivalent to those of disparate industrial policies. Similar considerations apply to transport, energy and the environment. Of course, transport and energy are also dealt with as industries in their own right, as well as providers of social services, and the environment is treated in terms of tackling pollution and the consequent health benefits.

The second group comprises all the EU policies that address certain structural aspects of the EU economy and society. The EU affords special treatment to those in the (g) agricultural sector, hence the Common Agricultural Policy (CAP); the (h) fishing industry, thus the Common Fisheries Policy (CFP); and the (i) depressed regions, hence the Common Regional Policy (RP), as well as deals with EU-wide social problems, especially (j) unemployment, hence the Social Policy. These areas are not only financed by the EU but also claim the bulk of its general budgetary resources (see Chapter 5).

The final group covers the external relations of the EU. One of these caters for the (k) EU trading relations with its major partners within the context of the Common Commercial Policy (CCP), run by the European Commission on behalf of all the EU Member States. Another covers the (l) EU relations with the developing world in terms of trade, aid and preferential trading arrangements.

Obviously, a whole book would be needed to tackle these policies in some detail and depth. But here the intention is to provide merely a general description of them. Those readers interested in a full coverage and discussion of these policies can find it in my EU text.[1] The chapter deals with the policies in the order given above, but does not devote equal space to each of them simply because some need more explanation than others and some have wider implications and effects than others. However, since the SEM is the reason for the majority of the policies, a fuller discussion of the SEM is of the essence; hence, the next section is devoted to it.

4.2   The SEM

Unlike many areas of EU policy-making, the SEM has been seen in a positive light, perhaps because it has been central to EU development. However today, amid widespread disillusion with the EU, even the SEM is seen as 'less popular than ever, more needed than ever'.[2] The SEM is an important stepping stone on the route from the customs union to a fully fledged economic union, and many regard the European Monetary Union (EMU, see Chapter 6) as the last stage and thus the final piece in the jigsaw of 'negative' integration. The SEM is defined as 'an area without internal frontiers in which the free movement of goods persons, services and capital is ensured' (Single European Act, SEA, 1987; Article 12). This means that borders should disappear within the EU: goods, services, capital and people should be able to move between the Member States as they move between regions within a country. This requires the removal of customs and passport controls at borders; the elimination of any national barriers to the sale of other EU countries' goods and services; and the ending of any national controls on the movement of capital. This is a very extensive agenda that has such wide implications that, as we shall see in the rest of this chapter, the subject of virtually every EU policy area has been affected by its developments.

4.2.1   Why the SEM?

There were provisions for a single market in the 1957 EEC Treaty: Article 3 required the removal of not only all internal tariffs and quotas but also 'of all other measures having equivalent effect', and 'obstacles to freedom of movement of persons, services and capital'. The procedure to eliminate these non-tariff barriers (NTBs) was harmonization or the approximation of laws (EEC Treaty, Article 100). After the successful early completion of the customs union, internal factors and external events conspired against the completion of the single market. The EEC economy was under strain in the 1970s because of the world recession associated with the oil price shocks of 1973 and 1979; rapid changes in technology; the changing structure of the world economy; and the emergence of significant new competitors, first Japan and then the newly industrializing countries of South East Asia. With growth slow or negative and unemployment rising rapidly, national governments tried to protect their economies, but with tariffs fixed by the General Agreement on Tariffs and Trade (GATT) and the EEC Treaty commitments, only NTBs could be used; this was the 'New Protectionism'. Barriers went up within as well as outside of the EEC, and these economic strains made countries much less willing to agree to integration initiatives in general and harmonization in particular.

The progress of harmonization was extremely slow for other reasons. It proved difficult to reach agreement on what were often complex technical issues, which were politically sensitive and the subject often of long-standing national legislation. For example, it was difficult to agree on a definition for chocolate because in the UK significant amounts of non-cocoa fat could be added, but in the rest of Europe this was not the case. So an agreed definition was seen as either undermining Continental European standards or requiring UK manufacturers to change their products. The UK was able to hold up the process in this instance because harmonization required unanimous agreement in the Council. Harmonization was also seen in some countries as over-regulation. The Treaty also allowed national measures 'on grounds of public morality, public policy or public security; the protection of health and life of humans, animals or plants; the protection of national treasures possessing artistic, historic or archaeological value; or the protection of industrial and commercial property' (Article 36). This was exploited by some Member States to restrict trade. As a result, between 1969 and 1985, the EC managed to adopt only 270 directives. This was too slow to bring about any reduction in technical barriers because new regulations were being introduced at a faster pace by the governments of the Member States.

Gradually attitudes towards the single market began to change. There was concern over the performance of the EC economies, slow growth and the falling share of world exports of hi-tech goods. Big business began to see the segmentation of the EC market into national markets as hampering their international competitiveness. They were unable to get long production runs to keep costs down and to spread the costs of research and development (R&D). The Round Table of European Industrialists was particularly influential in lobbying national governments and the Commission. The limitations of nationalistic economic policies were being revealed by generally poor performance and failures, such as President François Mitterrand's abortive attempt to expand the French economy from 1981 to 1983. The European Monetary System (EMS) was seen as a successful example of what could be achieved by European cooperation. There was also support for further integration demonstrated by the European Parliament (EP) majority in favour of the Draft Treaty of European Union in 1984. The awkward partner in the EC, the UK, was also prepared to cooperate on further integration for three reasons. First, in 1984 a more permanent solution to the UK's budgetary problems was agreed. Second, the SEM was in tune with the free market orthodoxy of the time, particularly with the Thatcher government's philosophy. Third, the UK prime minister, Margaret Thatcher, believed that there were large potential gains for the UK from freer trade in services, especially for financial services in the City of London.

The new Commission in 1984, presided over by Jacques Delors, was pushing at an open door when it chose the SEM as the priority for its period in office. Lord Cockfield (from the UK), the vice president of the Delors Commission who was responsible for the SEM, drew up the *Internal Market White Paper*[3] (at the time a novel approach for the EC), setting out an ambitious, but feasible strategy including a legislative programme designed to sweep away cross-border restrictions and to restore the momentum of economic integration. The Commission stressed three main features that would characterize the SEM programme:

a. Minimum harmonization – New Approach Directives restrict harmonization to essential requirements (health, safety, environmental and consumer protection). The general harmonization method, originating in too rigid an interpretation of the Treaty was to be abandoned; in most cases, an 'approximation' of the parameters was sufficient to reduce differences in rates or technical specifications to an acceptable level.
b. The deadline of 31 December 1992, combined with regular monitoring, was designed to speed progress.

   c. Qualified Majority Voting (QMV) was to apply to most SEM measures, but not to fiscal (tax) provisions, the free movement of persons or the rights of employed persons.

   d. Control of the emergence of new NTBs.

   e. Mutual recognition, facilitated by the landmark judgement by the European Court of Justice (ECJ) in the Cassis de Dijon case: goods which are 'lawfully' made and sold in one EU [Member State] should in principle be able to move freely and go on sale *anywhere* within the EU, and the same was true of tradable services such as banking or insurance.

   f. European standards are to be developed, but (except where they coincide with legal requirements) their absence should not be allowed to restrict trade. The detailed technical definition of these requirements should, where possible, be entrusted to European standards' institutions.

To make the SEM for the EU like a national market required the removal of three types of barriers: physical, fiscal and technical. Physical barriers were checks at borders for the control of the movement of persons for immigration purposes; customs borders were required due to differences in indirect taxes; animal and plant health was protected by inspections at borders; and checks on lorries and drivers were ostensibly for safety reasons and to enforce national restrictions on foreign hauliers. Considerable expense was incurred in preparing the documentation needed, and there were delays at borders, further increasing the cost of inter-EU transport. Fiscal barriers were needed to check the goods crossing borders because differences in indirect taxes, value added tax (VAT) and excise duties on alcohol, tobacco and so forth, were dealt with by remitting these taxes on exports and imposing them on imports.

   Technical barriers cover an enormous range of measures that affect trade. The most pervasive of these are technical regulations and standards. *Regulations* are legal requirements which products must satisfy before they can be sold in a particular country; these cover health, safety and environmental requirements. Regulations are also important in relation to services (see below). *Standards* are not legally binding in themselves; they are technical requirements set by private standardization bodies like DIN in Germany, BSI in the UK and AFNOR in France. Although they are only voluntary, they often assume a quasi-legal status because they are used in technical regulations and in calls for tender in contracts. They are also important in marketing a product. The existence of different regulations and standards imposed additional costs on the EU producers, who had to make alterations to their products before they could sell them in other Member States.

Another technical barrier related to *public procurement*: private sector purchases by governments. Governments frequently discriminated against bids from firms in other Member States for a variety of reasons: strategic (e.g. weapons); support of employment; encouragement of emerging high-tech industries, to maintain employment; and so on. However, such policies imposed costs on both the public authorities (who ended up paying more than they need to) and on firms (because the market available for selling their goods was too limited). One consequence was too many producers, making it difficult to achieve an optimum scale in industries such as defence, electricity generating and telecommunications equipment.

Technical barriers were the main impediment to trade in *services*. For a range of services from plumbing to legal services the problems related to the recognition of qualifications and the rights to establish businesses. For *financial services*, trade was limited by government regulatory measures. In banking, there were particular problems with establishing capital adequacy. Insurance could not be sold in most Member States unless the insurer had a local permanent establishment. Capital movements were controlled by several Member States, which interfered with free trade in financial services.

What made the SEM programme remarkable was its broad aims and ambitions, and the development of a clear approach to achieving them. It embraced measures as diverse as animal health controls and the licensing of banks; public procurement and standards for catalytic converters for car exhausts. It covered not just traditionally tradable services such as banking, insurance and transport but also the new areas of information, marketing and audio-visual services. With regard to transport, the agenda included the 'phasing out of all quantitative restrictions (quotas) on road haulage', and further liberalization of road, sea and air passenger services through the fostering of increased competition. The aim for audio-visual services was to create a single EC-wide broadcasting area.

4.2.2 An evolving programme

The White Paper contained 300 proposals for legislation. By the 1992 deadline, 95 per cent of the measures were in place. However, this was not the end of the process since additional legislation was needed: to close the remaining gaps in the SEM, for example, finance, energy and services; to update and improve the existing legislative framework, in order to ensure it achieves its objectives; and to minimize the administrative burdens on business. Existing legislation needs to be transposed, *directives* need to be incorporated into national legislation, and this can take a considerable time.[4] Continuing vigilance is needed to ensure the implementation of existing legislation; enforcement is the responsibility of national governments and sometimes this is problematic. In addition to legislation, there is the enormous task of developing European standards, which is still far from complete.

By the end of 2012 there were 1,420 directives and 1,769 regulations related to the SEM,[5] which gives some idea of the increased coverage of the programme. Despite this, the Commission continues to identify areas in which further progress is needed. These can broadly be divided into three categories: the traditional SEM; extension beyond its traditional boundaries or into new areas; improvement of the context within which the SEM operates. The free movement services, standards, consumer rights, network industries; reduction of tax obstacles; public procurement; improvement in conditions for small and medium-sized enterprises (SMEs), including simplifying the regulatory environment; cross-border debt recovery, a Statute for a European Private Company, and EU patents are all traditional SEM issues. Extensions include the digital single market and the green industry. The context is both economic and political. The 1985 White Paper recognized that the measures to reduce barriers should be accompanied by an expanding market and a flexible market. So the SEM can be seen as both complementary to and dependent upon the Lisbon process. Politically, if the SEM is to operate effectively, there should be a consensus on its importance and its continued development.

Another important issue, which relates to political support, is SEM integrity, the extent to which the existing measures apply and are enforced. Most SEM legislation takes the form of directives, which means that national legislation is necessary to introduce the measure. As a result, two problems occur: first, failure of transposition by national governments to pass the necessary legislation by the deadline contained in the directive; and, second, incorrect transposition, that is, national legislation does not comply with directives. These two problems mean that 1.5 per cent of directives do not apply correctly across the whole EU. This percentage is improving, but it still remains an issue for the operation of the SEM. The effectiveness of the SEM is also compromised by the problem of enforcement. Measured by infringement proceedings, in cases in which the Member States are brought before the ECJ for failing to correctly apply the legislation, only limited progress is being made. So the SEM rules for the most part apply and are enforced, but further improvements can and should be made.

4.2.3 The services market

A major SEM disappointment has been the limited extent to which the services markets have been integrated. In 2012 services accounted for just over 74 per cent of output and 70 per cent of employment in EU27. The limited impact of the SEM in this area is illustrated by the low proportion of Gross Value Added (GVA, roughly equal to GDP less taxes on production plus subsidies to products) that is traded and the low level of foreign direct investment (FDI) in services industries, which seem to be related to regulatory problems.

The EU has sought to open up the services market with two particular measures: a general services directive and the Financial Services Action Plan (FSAP). The barriers to cross-border trade in non-financial services remain high. National regulatory regimes are very different and complex, with a high level of discretion by the Member States, and there is little confidence that they would not be used to protect domestic companies. In sectors such as accountancy, retailing, wholesale trade and information technology (IT) services, barriers remain high and the gains from their elimination significant.

The original proposal for a services market directive[6] sought to extend the principle of mutual recognition to services: a company able to operate a service in one Member State should in principle be able to operate that service in any other Member State. The directive proposed various measures to achieve these ends: freedom of establishment (easing of administrative requirements); freedom of movement (country of origin principle and rights of recipients to use services in other Member States); and measures to establish consumer confidence in services provision. Coming as they did at a time of growing economic nationalism, these proposals proved so controversial as to be labelled the 'Frankenstein directive', in a pun on the name of Frits Bolkstein, the Internal Market Commissioner at the time. There were concerns over social dumping: social standards (minimum wages and health and safety) would be undermined because foreign services companies could use cheap foreign workers employed on lower standards. Particular concerns were raised over the regulation of private security and social care in which the vetting of workers' suitability, for example, for criminal convictions, could be undermined.

Although there were some problems with the directive, these criticisms were exaggerated. The Posted Workers Directive[7] requires employers to pay the minimum wages and satisfy employment conditions, including health and safety, of the host country, although it would have still been possible to employ foreign workers at below-normal wages for the service. Are standards that much lower in other countries? Wages are lower, but whether standards are lower is questionable. A lot of the criticisms are special pleading by interest groups.

These objections have resulted in a significantly modified services directive.[8] The modification includes a considerable number of exemptions from the directive: in addition to the original exemptions on financial, electronic communication networks and transport services, are added health care and pharmaceutical services, audio-visual services whatever their means of transmission, gambling services, social services in the area of housing, childcare and support to families and persons in need. The other significant modification is that the principle of regulation by country of origin has gone to be replaced by the freedom to provide services. The original proposal for mutual recognition was important since it would potentially have made the cross-border services provision much more straightforward, because it meant that cross-border services providers would only have to satisfy one set of regulations. But under the agreed directive, two sets of regulations are going to have to be satisfied. Provided requirements of non-discrimination, necessity and proportionality are met, national authorities may regulate foreign services' providers. There are some useful requirements on the authorization regime, such as a single point of contact, charges and processing time. The impact of the directive will only become apparent later, but these modifications are likely to significantly reduce its impact by increasing the difficulty of establishing new services provision in another Member State. These difficulties are such that some suggest that from a legal view little has changed, which implies that the benefits of the measure will be limited.

4.2.4   Financial services

The integration of financial markets is an essential SEM component: it not only yields direct benefits but it is also essential for the SEM as a whole. The Cecchini Report (1988)[9] attributed as much as a quarter of the potential gains for the EC GDP from the SEM to the liberalization of financial services. The SEM review in the mid-1990s[10] was markedly less optimistic, largely because remaining regulatory and other barriers had inhibited the emergence of genuine pan-EU provision of services. This was especially the case for retail financial services, but some barriers also remained in other areas and there was limited cross-border consolidation of the financial services industry. This led in 1999 to the FSAP to restore the impetus towards financial integration, because the potential gains from greater capital market efficiency were being lost. There is still plenty of potential for further integration of financial markets, and this will substantially enhance economic growth.

The first legislative phase of the FSAP is now complete: all the original measures have been adopted and transposed. The Lamfalussy Directives on securities markets are all adopted, but a few Member States still need to complete transposition of a few directives. But the process continues, with a further 13 directives adopted, only 2 of which have been transposed in all the Member States.

With the legislative programme still recent, it is early to judge the impact of FSAP. The one study that has been published[11] found evidence that FSAP was having an impact in the three areas examined (banking, securities and insurance), but it was difficult to evaluate because of the financial crisis and the short time the measures had been in operation.

The financial crisis has fundamentally changed the environment within which financial market integration is occurring. The EU has responded by changing financial legislation in the areas of deposit guarantees, capital requirements and credit rating agencies, and further measures are in the pipeline. One fundamental change has been the development of a new EU supervisory financial framework consisting of a European Systemic Risk Assessment Board, and three new supervisory authorities dealing with banks, insurance/pensions and securities markets. Regulation will still be by national authorities, but more closely monitored at the EU level. How effective this framework will prove is questionable, but it does mark a significant step towards EU regulation of financial markets.

4.2.5 Assessment of the SEM

The assessment of the SEM has two aspects: (a) the evaluation of the extent to which it has been achieved and (b) the measurement of its effects on economic performance.

4.2.5.1 *The extent of integration in the single market*

There is a very wide range of potential measures of the extent of integration in the SEM, but two stand out for their generality: price convergence and the extent of trade. A further indicator that needs examination is FDI because, particularly in services, FDI could be a substitute for trade.[12]

The SEM makes trade easier between the Member States, which should make it harder to maintain price differences between national markets. Arbitrage and consumer cross-border trade should be much easier in the SEM. There was price convergence in EU15 associated with the SEM from 1989 to 2000, but since 2000 there has been some divergence. The new Member States show signs of price convergence both within their group and with EU15.

The SEM should cause price convergence by increasing the proportion of output that is traded. Intra-EU15 exports increased their share of GVA (above) rapidly after the introduction of SEM measures, and this growth has continued. Extra-EU15 exports increased their share of GVA from 1992, but at a slower rate than for intra-EU15 trade. The greater rate of increase of intra-EU share of GVA is a clear indication of the effect of the SEM, because extra-EU15 exports should have been boosted by the faster growth of non-EU GDP. Both intra- and extra-EU15 imports fell in 2009 as a result of the crisis, but the fall in extra-EU15 exports is less as EU15 GDP fell more than world GDP. The high level of intra-EU15 merchandise trade is a strong indication of the success of the SEM in integrating EU's economy.

The situation with trade in services is very different: both intra- and extra-EU imports have low shares of GVA in services, and while there is some growth, trade remains at a very low level. Given that a significant proportion of services is non-tradable, a lower share of GVA traded is to be expected. But the low overall growth and the fact that intra-EU15 trade in services is growing no faster than extra-EU15 trade is an indication that the integration of services markets has not been achieved. Trade is of course not the only indicator. The effects of integration could occur in the absence of trade if foreign services providers set up in other economies, but this does not seem to be happening (see Section 7.3.1). This is also indicated by the significant difference in services trade between countries.

These conclusions relate to EU15. The new Member States have higher overall levels of trade and growth of trade for both goods and services. Here, it is difficult to disentangle the impact of the SEM from the impact of enlargement, but they do seem to be more willing and able to exploit the potential of the SEM.

The SEM should increase the amount of FDI as companies locate and concentrate production at least cost locations in the EU; invest in new local production for markets which have to be served locally (e.g. retailing); and as market competition is reconfigured by mergers that were previously off limits. An acceleration of intra- and extra-EU15 FDI can be noted in 1998. This was a time of booming FDI across the world, but from 1999 on intra-EU15 FDI began to significantly exceed outward FDI, and a clear gap between the two has been maintained. The timing of this development indicates that the single currency has had a significant role in encouraging intra-EU FDI. While there is some tendency for FDI to decline with distance, other factors affecting FDI would tend to encourage extra- rather than intra-EU FDI, for example, differences in labour costs and market access. Extra-EU15 FDI has risen continuously, indicating that the SEM is attractive to non-EU multinational companies.

4.2.5.2   *The SEM and economic performance*

The rationale for the SEM is that it reinforces the market opening principle of the Common Market by focusing not just on existing trade flows but also on subjecting hitherto protected sectors to greater cross-border competition. In so doing, it establishes a number of channels for improved resource allocation and efficiency gains that, in turn, offer the promise of improved economic performance. The economic gains are both micro- and macro-economic. Achieving these benefits will require some dislocations: unemployment can result from the changes needed to achieve overall benefits. The benefits and costs of SEM are analogous to the benefits of the formation of customs unions sketched in Chapter 1.

4.2.5.3   *Empirical research on the SEM: Commission studies*

There are three major problems in estimating the effects of the SEM. First, the very wide nature of the programme means that its effects are spread across the whole EU economy. Second, both the implementation of the SEM and businesses' response take considerable periods of time. One estimate suggests that by 2007 less than half the long-term income gains had been achieved.[13] For example, the elimination of barriers will encourage the relocation of production to least-cost sites within the EU, but this is a slow process. Third, these two problems compound the general difficulty of identifying the counterfactual: what would have happened in the absence of the SEM. The SEM is not exogenous since some economic integration would have occurred in its absence, but how much? These general benefits of the SEM are calculated as part of the measurement of the effects of EU integration, but these are too complicated, so only a short summary of the potential size of the effects is included here. Those interested in the full picture are advised to turn to the mentioned EU book.

The Cecchini Report is based on economic research carried out on behalf of the Commission,[14] highlighting the benefits of the SEM in the run-up to the 1992 deadline. The study predicted the total potential gain for the EC12 to be 4 per cent to 7 per cent of EC GDP and 2 to 5 million jobs. It is important to emphasize the speculative nature of this exercise and the fact that it was undertaken by a Commission keen to underscore the benefits of the flagship policy. Compared with this very optimistic picture, the findings of the second major exercise conducted by Commission in the mid-1990s have to be regarded as a disappointment. Enormous effort was put into this research, which comprised some 38 studies, in addition to a business survey.[15] The headline figure this time was that the SEM had raised EU GDP by just over 1 per cent by 1994 and had increased employment by about half a million.

Why was there such a difference in the assessed impact? The Commission identified three main problems. First, it was too soon to observe the medium-term effects of the SEM (above). Some SEM measures were not implemented until 1994–5, but also economic agents had not yet had time to adjust. Second, the data that could be used were, at best, only up to 1994 and thus only allowed a very short assessment period. Third, separating out the relatively small and incremental of market integration is difficult. While the impact of the SEM on economic performance was disappointing, surveys of the opinions of company representatives reported a strong and significant impact of the SEM on output and employment. In particular, the protection the SEM programme provides against the introduction of new barriers and the re-fragmentation of the market were seen as important, thus, indicating the role of the SEM in protecting existing gains rather than providing new ones.

On the tenth anniversary of 1992, the Commission was keen to celebrate the achievements of the SEM. It produced new estimates indicating that the SEM had raised EU GDP in 2002 by 1.8 per cent, and increased employment by 1.46 per cent, which means that around 2.5 million extra jobs had been created.[16] A 2002 independent academic estimate more or less confirms these (Table 4.1), but also provides average, lower and upper limits, as well as projections to 2022. And a 2007 another such estimate finds the gains during 1992–2006[17] to have been an increase of 2.2 per cent in GDP and 1.4 per cent in employment (about 2.75 million jobs). The latest estimates by the Commission (2013b) indicate an increase in EU GDP of 2.13 per cent (about €233 billion) and a 1.3 per cent extra boost to EU employment (2.77 new jobs). These indicate a significant but far from earth-shattering impact of the SEM, undermining the Commission's explanations for the low estimates in 1996. The idea that the SEM would transform EU economic performance has proved to be wide of the mark: there is no indication in the

Table 4.1 Simulation results of the total SEM effects

Scenario	Additional employment (1,000 of persons) in			Additional GDP (€billion) in		
Year	2002	2012	2022	2002	2012	2022
Average	164.5	203.1	214.0	2,450.6	2,463.8	2,463.8
Lower Bound	105.6	127.5	158.4	1,733.9	1,741.5	1,741.5
Upper Bound	223.2	264.2	273.3	3,189.2	3,202.3	3,202.3

Source: Selected from Selgado (2002) and Nataro (2002).

growth of output or productivity over this period that would support this contention.

It is only with the availability of a longer run of post-1992 data and the gradual refining of techniques that more reliable estimation of the overall effects of the SEM has become possible. A good recent example[18] suggests that internal market integration including the customs union has raised EU GDP by 2 per cent to 3 per cent but that the effect differed significantly between countries, amounting for example to 4 per cent to 6 per cent for the Netherlands.

4.2.6 SEM success and problems

In political terms, the SEM must be regarded as a success. Despite some foot-dragging in the implementation of key measures, the strategic aim of opening up goods markets has been consistently advanced and has retained wide political support. Although, in a sense, the SEM will never be fully completed, because there will always be barriers that give some advantage to indigenous producers, there can be little doubt that the EU has moved a long way. The scope of the SEM has also expanded significantly to encompass most production. Economic nationalism and protection remain potent forces and the development of the SEM continues to be a battle with these forces. The pace of regulation has slowed, and the emphasis has gradually shifted to quality of regulation, implementation and enforcement.

Although much of the rhetoric surrounding the SEM has been about liberalization and deregulation, with the implication that it is principally concerned with *negative* integration, the reality is more complex. In a number of areas, the outcome has been more a recasting of the regulatory framework than dismantling it, and the resulting regulatory style is one that reflects European values.

In economic terms, the outcome of the SEM is much less clear-cut: ultimately its objective was to raise the performance of the EU economy, by raising productivity growth. To paraphrase Robert Solow, you can see the SEM programme everywhere but in the productivity statistics.[19] The interesting issue is, why? Various responses are possible: the limited progress in services, the long-term nature of the project and the difficulties of implementation. An alternative view is that the SEM's impact may have been a transitory shock with little long-term impact on productivity growth. A balanced view might be that expectations were overblown and limited, but worthwhile benefits have been achieved. It is also important to note that the SEM is merely part of an increasingly globalized world market, generally subject to liberalization and deregulation. Ultimately these developments may have more profound impacts on economic performance. Indeed, European companies' search for competitiveness in this market was at the heart of the SEM, and in this sense it has been successful, enabling large companies to emerge and be competitive in the globalized economy. The SEM remains central to the EU, and despite its apparently limited economic impact, it is a powerful attraction for potential members and a model for its many imitators.

4.3 Policies facilitating the SEM

As mentioned, we begin by considering the six policies that lay the foundations for a properly functioning SEM.

4.3.1 Competition rules

Competition policy is mainly concerned with protecting the market mechanism from breaking down. It does so by promoting competitive market structures and policing anticompetitive behaviour, thereby enhancing both the efficiency of the economy as a whole and consumer welfare in particular. In the EU, this objective is pursued by means of enforcing prohibitions against (a) anticompetitive agreements between different companies and (b) anticompetitive behaviour by companies that are large enough, either individually or jointly, to harm competition by means of independent behaviour. The objective is also pursued by means of (c) vetting mergers between previously independent companies to verify whether they are likely to result in non-competitive market structures.

The EU competition policy has three important characteristics that are not commonly found elsewhere. First, it aims not only to protect the competitive process as such but also to promote and protect market integration between the EU Member States. Second, apart from addressing private distortions of competition, it also curbs distortions of the market process by its Member States, notably as a result of state aid. Both result from the third distinguishing feature of EU competition policy: it is implemented in a multilevel political system, that of the EU and its Member States. In this context, it is worth noting that, although until recently the application of EU competition rules was highly centralized in the hands of the Commission, due to its exemption monopoly for agreements infringing the cartel prohibition, this changed fundamentally in May 2004. A decentralized system based on enforcement by, and coordination between, the 28 national competition authorities was established.

But why does the EU need a competition policy? The reasons for introducing competition rules have varied, both between different jurisdictions and over time. The first set of modern competition rules is contained in the US Sherman Act (1890). These rules were adopted as the result of political concern over the railroad, oil and financial 'trusts' emerging in the US at the end of the nineteenth century, generating an economic concentration of power that threatened to upset the popular consensus underpinning the economic as well as the political system of that country. In various European states from the early twentieth century onwards, national competition rules typically sought to provide protection against the socially and therefore politically undesirable results of 'unfair' competition. In some cases, the legislation concerned even enabled public authorities to impose the terms of existing private cartel agreements on entire economic sectors, as an alternative to state-designed market regulation, for example, in order to control prices.

American ideas about competition policy that were more critical of restraints were exported to both Germany and Japan after the Second World War, when the Allied occupation forces imposed new anti-monopoly legislation to curb the influence of the financial-industrial combines that were widely seen as having powered the war effort of these two countries. For similar reasons, coal and steel being the essential components of the war industry of the time, anti-trust provisions were introduced into the 1951 Treaty of Paris that created the European Coal and Steel Community (ECSC), which, unlike the EEC Treaty, included the control of concentrations from the outset. This check on concentrations of economic power was therefore in line with the objective of the ECSC of eliminating the threat of future wars between the participating Member States.

Competition rules were likewise introduced in the 1957 EEC Treaty, albeit for a different reason. In this case, the competition rules served primarily to ensure that the removal of restrictions on trade between the Member States (tariffs and NTBs) would not be replaced by cartels between undertakings following national lines. This is why competition rules addressed to undertakings were introduced into what at the outset was still regarded as an international treaty between independent states.

Initially, therefore, EU competition rules essentially served to complement an interstate trade policy of reducing trade barriers and promoting market integration. From this starting point, promoting market integration has developed into an overriding rationale of EU competition policy, alongside that of maintaining 'effective competition' and, more recently, promoting the consumer interest. The integration rationale has had a profound impact on the orientation of EU competition policy that has at times led it into conflict with the emerging economic consensus favouring efficiency considerations.

However, although EU competition policy is increasingly driven by economic considerations, its origins are found in European law, and it must evidently operate within the constraints of its legal framework. This framework consists of the substantive, procedural and institutional rules that govern EU competition policy. It is important to understand that the framework only applies to 'undertakings'.

The legal basis of EU competition policy is found, first of all, in the TFEU itself (101–6 and 107–9). Second, it is found in implementing legislation adopted by the Council and the Commission in the form of regulations and directives, which develop in particular the wide-ranging powers of the Commission in this field, notably Council Regulation 1 of 2003. Council Regulation 139 of 2004 provides the framework for merger control by the Commission. In addition, an increasing number of notices and guidelines that are not formally binding provide essential information on the manner in which the Commission intends to apply EU competition policy. By issuing such guidance, the Commission increases the predictability of its policy – allowing undertakings and their legal advisers to take EU competition law constraints into account, while at the same time facilitating the enforcement of EU competition law between private parties and at a national level.

The ultimate arbiter of the various rules, and on whether the Commission policy remains within the bounds of its powers, is the ECJ. It decides only on points of law. The ECJ becomes involved either directly on a 'pre-judicial' reference by a national court, or in judicial review proceedings following a first appeal against the Commission decisions to the EU's General Court, which establishes the facts. In principle, the standards applied are those of administrative review of policy: that is, they focus on formal competence to act, on respect for the rights of the defence and enforcing minimum standards of reasoned rationality. The ECJ and General Court have nevertheless on a number of occasions led the way in demanding higher standards of economic argument, rather than more formal reasoning, from the Commission.

Finally, as a result of the 'modernization' exercise from 1 May 2004 onwards all national competition authorities (NCAs) and national judges in the Member States (i.e. the national courts) now have explicit powers (and the obligation) to apply the legal exception clause of Article 101.3 TFEU (formerly the exemption provision), which is 'efficiency based', concerning 'antitrust (cartels and dominance abuse)'. Under the old Regulation 17 of 1962, parties could obtain such an individual exemption exclusively from the Commission. Article 9.1 of Regulation 17 conferred 'sole power' on the Commission 'to declare Article [101.1] inapplicable pursuant to Article [101.3] of the Treaty'. Following modernization, Article 101.3 is now directly applicable. This may give rise to increased requests by national courts for the pre-judicial rulings on points of law by the ECJ that are an important mechanism to ensure the coherent application of EU competition law and policy. It is expected that competition rules will be enforced much more effectively. The exemption has actually become a legal exception, so it is, largely, self-enforcing. The NCAs and national courts are now also competent to apply anti-trust rules to behaviour within their jurisdictions that has a EU dimension. Needless to add, this model of decentralization could not apply equally to state aid (see next subsection), in which the Commission retains monopoly on exemption, because this would ask national public authorities to police themselves.

4.3.2   Industrial and competitiveness policy

Industrial and competitiveness policy (ICP) can be defined as government policy designed to improve a country's economic performance. This includes a very broad range of government policies both 'horizontal', to provide a supportive environment for business (fiscal, competition, regional, social, labour and environmental policies, etc.), and vertical, designed to favour particular sectors of the economy.

ICP has fluctuated over time. From 1950 to1979, the prevailing orthodoxy was that government could and should correct market failures, and so microeconomic intervention in specific industrial sectors was normal. Thus in the 1970s, the response to structural change in the world economy was protection of companies and industries in difficulty, and European industrial policies aimed to create European super-firms to compete with the US giants. The failure of these policies to raise EU industrial performance, as well as the failure of individual companies, meant that by the 1980s, the effectiveness of government action was increasingly questioned. By the early 1990s, in the Commission's view, ICP should promote adaptation to industrial change in an open and competitive market. So company- and sector-specific policies were viewed with suspicion, and ICP supported competitive markets in general. Today, the consensus is between these extremes of extensive intervention and reliance on market forces: ICP can be a helpful tool to improve economic performance, provided it is used sparingly and carefully.

Competition rules (above) are really part of ICP because decisions affect the structure of industries by controlling mergers and joint ventures and preventing cartels. And as mentioned above, CP includes the control of state aid to industry, which is an important part of ICP.

Traditional industrial policy uses subsidies/tax breaks, protection, regulation and public procurement. ICP includes also deregulation, education reform, subsidization of infrastructure and research. Over time, with the tightening of trade rules in the GATT/WTO and within the EU, ICP instruments have shifted from tariffs to NTBs. ICP measures either permit the local firms to raise their prices to enjoy a hidden subsidy or offer them subsidies that directly reduce the cost or raise the quality of their inputs, such as labour and research. Regulations can be implicit or explicit instruments of ICP. For example, the adoption of the GSM (Global System for Mobile Communication) standard for mobile phones helped EU firms to an early dominance of this industry.

The EU has a role in all these areas of industrial policy. It is the major actor in external trade policy, and it has a shared but growing competence over regulatory policy, supervision of state aid and limited but increasing subsidies in such areas as research as well as competition policy. A discussion of these is beyond the scope of this chapter, but is readily available in Chapter 14 of my EU text.[20] What is needed, however, is a brief summary of what is described as an important EU initiative in ICP: the Lisbon Strategy.

The development of the ICP could be characterized as moving from support of specific initiatives to a general improvement of EU competences. This switch reflects changing views on the way to improve economic performance. The conventional wisdom is that the improvement of individual aspects of economic policy is not enough and interaction between policies is crucial; therefore, for example, reform of labour policies works more effectively when product markets are reformed. This leads to the idea that the competitiveness of the economy requires a very broad range of policies. Since the late 1990s, internal and external factors have led to economic reform in this general sense, becoming one of the key items on the EU's policy agenda. Economic reform is seen to be urgently required if the EU is going to be able to meet the social and economic aspirations of its citizens and fulfil its global obligations.

The EU was seen as being 'confronted with a quantum shift from globalization and the challenges of a new knowledge-driven economy'.[21] The EU needed to ensure that its economy and society are able to meet new challenges and to maintain/improve their global competitiveness. Strong pressure was exerted by some Member States (e.g. Spain and the UK) to move forward on the liberalization agenda. The introduction of the euro in 1999 strengthened the argument for more flexibility in the labour, product and capital markets, and introduced a new sense of urgency to reform.

The LS was the culmination of a number of EU developments. The introduction of an 'Industry' title in TEU (1992; Article 173) gave the EU a broad mandate to promote the competitiveness of European industry by improving its ability to adjust to structural change, encouraging the SMEs, favouring cooperation between enterprises and increasing the effectiveness of the EU's R&D. The Treaty of Amsterdam (1997) provided the legal basis for 'developing a coordinated strategy for employment and particularly for promoting a skilled, trained and adaptable workforce and labour markets responsive to economic change' (Article 145). These objectives are to be achieved by the 'open method of coordination'. Under the UK's presidency, the Cardiff European Council agreed that the *Broad Economic Guidelines* introduced under the EMU process should be developed as a key tool for economic recovery and self-sustaining, non-inflationary growth.[22] This Council also highlighted the need for fresh initiatives to promote entrepreneurship and competitiveness, especially encouraging small businesses and innovation, improving the skills and flexibility of the labour market and making the capital market more efficient. The 1999 Cologne European Council shaped the agenda for the planned Lisbon Council by arguing that 'the jobs of the future will be created by innovation and the information society'.[23]

The Lisbon European Council brought together these initiatives in a comprehensive policy strategy. There was a new strategic goal for the next decade: 'to become the most competitive and dynamic knowledge-based economy in the world, capable of sustainable economic growth with more and better jobs and greater social cohesion'.[24] Achieving this goal requires an overall strategy aimed at (a) preparing the transition to a knowledge-based economy and society by better policies for the information society and R&D, as well as by stepping up the process of structural reform for competitiveness and innovation and by completing the SEM; (b) modernizing the European social model, investing in people and combating social exclusion; and (c) sustaining a healthy economic outlook and favourable growth prospects by applying an appropriate macro-economic policy mix.[25]

The LS operated during 2000–10 and a midpoint evaluation was very critical: 'Lisbon is about everything and thus nothing'.[26] The midterm review of the policy[27] recognized these problems and sought to make the policy more focused and to raise its status. Lisbon 2 had three priorities concentrating on growth and jobs: making Europe a more attractive place to invest and work, completing the SEM and business-friendly regulation; knowledge and innovation for growth (Figure 4.1 provides the rates of growth of GDP for the EU Member States and comparator countries for several years; note how the 2008 financial crisis has dented EU growth) and raising expenditure on R&D; creating more and better jobs, by raising the labour force's adaptability, education and skills. Even this slimmed agenda involved a multiplicity of objectives, which widened further when concerns over the downgrading of environmental and social aspects led to their being reemphasized in the agreement on the revised agenda.[28] The Commission also tried to achieve more by 'bending' other policies such as competition and structural policy to achieve the LS' objectives.

The Commission has proposed a new strategy, 'Europe 2020: A strategy for smart, sustainable and inclusive growth',[29] which has been adopted

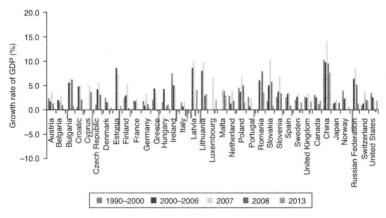

Figure 4.1 Average percentage growth of GDP for the EU and comparator countries (various years)

by the 2010 European Council. This looks awfully like Lisbon 3, with targets for the employment rate of 75 per cent,[30] R&D 3 per cent of GDP, the environment, education and reductions in poverty. To overcome some of the LS' problems, national targets will vary according to starting points, and there will be closer monitoring. But doubts remain that this will be sufficient to overcome the weaknesses of the LS.

From this brief discussion of the ICP, it can be concluded that it has always suffered from the ability of interest groups to exploit policy so that their interests rather than the public good are served, and this problem remains. The developing ICP also suffers from two other major problems. The first is the difficulty of achieving a coherent policy when so many conflicting views have to be reconciled. The second is the difficulty of ensuring that policy is implemented when major elements remain national responsibilities. The first problem led to the rather ramshackle edifice of the LS, which tried to be all things to all people. Furthermore, it is difficult to achieve the consistency required of a policy which seeks to change long-term economic performance. The second problem is one of delivery: the implementation of the LS policy is largely in the hands of the Member States whose policies do not seem to have been significantly changed by the LS. One cannot be optimistic that the Europe 2020 initiative will be any more successful.

4.3.3 Tax harmonization

EU tax harmonization is the agreement and application of common rules for taxation across the EU. This involves three separate aspects: first, the object of taxation – what is to be taxed; second, the tax base – agreement on the calculation of what is to be taxed; and third, harmonization of rates. Tax harmonization in the EU has so far been very limited, with an agreed base for the VAT, and minimum rates for VAT, alcohol, cigarette and energy taxation, in addition to some agreements to limit unfavourable interaction between national tax systems (Table 4.2 shows the basic tax rates).

The government plays a very important role in modern economies: in 2011/12 (the latest year for comparable data), tax revenue accounted for 35.7 per cent of EU28 GDP, but the percentage varies between 26 per cent in Lithuania to close to 48 in Denmark (Table 4.2). Normally tax and government expenditure is primarily the responsibility of the highest tier of government, the federal or central government. This is not the case in the EU, since the Member States control most tax revenue and are responsible for most government expenditure. This makes the EU unusual because there is a large variation of taxes and government expenditures in a single market.

Table 4.2   EU tax rates (2014) and total tax revenue (2011–12)

EU Member State	Maximum income tax rate (%)	Standard VAT rate (%)	Corporation tax rate (%)	Total tax revenue % GDP
Austria	50.00	20.00	25.00	42.0
Belgium	50.00	21.00	33.99	44.1
Bulgaria	10.00	20.00	10.00	27.2
Croatia	40.00	25.00	20.00	26.6
Cyprus	35.00	18.00	12.50	35.2
Czech Republic	22.00	21.00	19.00	34.4
Denmark	55.56	25.00	24.50	47.7
Estonia	21.00	20.00	0.00	32.2
Finland	53.00	24.00	20.00	43.4
France	45.00	20.00	33.30	43.9
Germany	45.00	19.00	30.18	38.7
Greece	42.00	23.00	26.00	32.4
Hungary	16.00	27.00	10.00	37.0
Ireland	41.00	23.00	12.50	38.9
Italy	45.00	22.00	27.50	42.5
Latvia	23.00	21.00	15.00	27.6
Lithuania	42.00	21.00	15.00	26.0
Luxembourg	40.00	15.00	28.59	37.2
Malta	35.00	18.00	35.00	34.5
Netherlands	52.00	21.00	20.00	38.4
Poland	32.00	23.00	19.00	32.4
Portugal	46.50	23.00	15.00	33.2
Romania	45.00	24.00	16.00	28.2
Slovakia	19.00	20.00	22.00	28.5
Slovenia	50.00	22.00	17.00	37.2
Spain	42.00	21.00	30.00	33.4
Sweden	56.60	25.00	22.00	44.3
UK	45.00	20.00	23.00	36.1

Notes: The rates are general guides since there are higher income tax rates on incomes above a certain level, reduced VAT rates and also some qualifications regarding the corporation tax rates concerning distributed/undistributed profits as well as changes in the rates in the future in some Member States.

There are two basic types of taxation: direct and indirect. Direct taxes, such as income and corporation taxes, are levied on wages and salaries (income taxes), or on the profits of business (corporation tax, CT). Direct taxes are not intended to affect the prices of commodities or professional services. Indirect taxes are levied specifically on consumption and are, therefore, in a simplistic model, significant in determining the pricing of commodities.

Taxes can act as NTBs on international trade as well as affect the international movement of factors of production. Therefore, to complete the

SEM and to realize the four freedoms for the movement of goods, services, persons and capital, some degree of tax harmonization is required in the EU.

The other reason for tax harmonization is that the ability of national tax systems to raise revenues, and the efficiency effects which they have, are affected by the tax regimes in the other Member States. For example, the revenue from tobacco taxation will depend upon the rates of taxation in neighbouring Member States; thus, there can be positive or negative spillovers/externalities between the tax systems of the Member States. The movement of factors of production can be influenced by government tax and expenditure policies. The administrative and compliance costs for the government and taxpayers may be affected, and the ability of national governments to pursue redistributive policies is constrained. Tax harmonization in the EU is the alignment of tax bases, rules and rates to reduce the harmful interactions between the different tax systems.

The EU adopted the VAT as its turnover tax and a common base was agreed. Having chosen the tax and the tax base, the EU had to decide on the tax jurisdiction using either the 'destination' or the 'origin' principle.[31] The EU decided to use the destination principle, which is consistent with undistorted intra-EU trade, provided that customs controls remain. This decision ensured that the EU continued to have separate national markets divided by physical borders. Changes were needed once these physical borders were eliminated in the SEM.

The EU is still a long way from achieving the approximation of VAT rates envisaged in the SEM White Paper.[32] All countries respect the minimum standard rate of 15 per cent, with a range from 15 per cent in Luxembourg and Cyprus to 25 per cent in Denmark and Sweden. Lower rates vary between 0 and 10 per cent, with the majority of countries operating multiple-rate VAT. A long list of exceptions considerably complicates the system.

As to excise duties, there are large differences in rates between the Member States, and excise duties are important for their governments, being the fifth most important source of revenue. The importance of excises varies substantially between the Member States, ranging between about 5 per cent and 18.3 per cent of tax revenue.

Energy taxes vary significantly between forms of energy, where the energy is used and among the EU countries. The most heavily taxed is fuel for transport. Although the tax on unleaded gasoline varies between €0.35 in Romania to €0.713 in the Netherlands, there is little possibility of cross-border shopping or smuggling, so this does not raise issues related to tax harmonization. Differences in the excise duties on commercial diesel fuel can affect competition in road transport, in which goods in one country can be transported by lorries buying their fuel in another. The extent of such problems has been limited by a reasonable degree of similarity of rates; 23 Member States have rates between €3 and €4.55 per litre of normal diesel fuel. Belgium, Germany and the UK are out of line, with rates of €5.80, €6.55 and €6.28 per litre respectively. Since these countries are exceptions, the solution seems to lie in their own hands.[33]

While the heavier taxation of road transport can be justified as a means of paying for roads, concentrating tax on one energy use makes little sense in a wider environmental context. To reduce distortions caused by the haphazard taxation of energy, a directive applying minimum tax rates to all energy products was agreed in 2003.[34] This applies to fuel used for transport or heating, not when used as raw materials, and it allows differential taxation between private and commercial use. While it irons out some distortions and encourages energy efficiency, this is very far from a comprehensive carbon tax.

This indicates that further reform of indirect taxes in the EU is desirable. The operation of VAT is complicated by multiple rates, which seem to have little merit. The transitional regime for the collection of VAT worked reasonably well, but is now under pressure from growing fraud, and tackling this will either complicate the existing system or require a more fundamental change to the origin system. Differences in excise rates are a cause of substantial smuggling from both within and outside the EU. Further harmonization, with reductions, particularly in the highest rates, seems the only answer here.

The CT is imposed on company profits and thus on capital. Since capital is potentially mobile, there are concerns that the movement of capital will undermine national CT, hence governments' revenue.[35] The received wisdom that tax competition would inevitably lead to a race to the bottom has, however, been questioned on both theoretical and empirical grounds. Not all capital is mobile, and governments have consequently sought to tax immobile corporations while reducing burdens on mobile capital. The widening of the CT base and the lowering of rates can be seen as a move in this direction. In addition, the CT is only one of the factors affecting choice of location, and if there are offsetting benefits, then the CT can still be collected. These benefits could be agglomeration economies leading to a differential return on capital. Alternatively, the benefits could derive directly from the effects of government expenditure on productivity. If this view is taken, then tax competition has the benefit of encouraging government expenditure, which benefits the economy while constraining wasteful expenditure.[36]

CT rates have been reduced in the EU, but this is not necessarily the result of tax competition. The rates vary between 10 per cent in Bulgaria and Cyprus to 35 per cent in Malta in 2012. Microeconomic evidence does seem to suggest that the CT is a factor affecting location decisions for the Member States: head offices and foreign subsidiaries are attracted to low tax jurisdictions. There is in addition evidence of a significant shift of profit from high- to low-tax jurisdictions, and that it occurs within the EU.

The CT has other economic effects: the higher rate on dividends favours profit retention. Since interest can be allowed as a cost before the calculation of profit, the CT encourages the use of debt rather than equity for finance. This is reinforced by financial innovation blurring the distinction between equity and debt. This will tend to make it more difficult for new firms to raise capital, because profit will be retained by existing firms rather than recycled via dividends. Also, the limited credit history and asset bases for the collateral of new firms make it difficult for them to borrow.

4.3.4 Transport policy

Transport is an integral part of any economic or social structure. It is also a major industry in its own right. It employs about 10 million people, accounting for about 4.5 per cent of the EU workforce. It constitutes about 4.6 per cent of EU GDP. The manufacture of transport equipment adds another 1.5 per cent to EU employment and 1.7 per cent to EU GDP. And it accounts for about 30 per cent of EU energy consumption. From an economic perspective, however, the crucial point about transport is its role in facilitating trade and in allowing individuals, companies, regions and nation states to exploit their various comparative advantages. The contemporary upsurge of interest in supply chain management, just-in-time production and the like has led to a wider appreciation of the general need to enhance the efficiency of EU transport if the EU is to compete successfully in the globalized economy.

The importance of having some form of a CTP as an integral part of EU economic and political integration goes back to the 1951 ECSC Treaty. The development of such a policy has been slow, sporadic and incomplete. National interests, geography, already-established institutions, new technologies, available infrastructure and changing demand patterns have hindered progress. While a CTP was one of the major common policies in the 1957 EEC Treaty, little of substance happened for three decades.

The EU's focus on transport policy has shifted with time. The ECSC was concerned with the efficiency of freight railways because of its importance in the carriage of bulk commodities. But after the EEC Treaty, trucking became the main concern because of its role as a mover of manufactures. Air transport grew in relevance as globalization increased from the 1990s. And more recently, attention has turned to less environmentally intrusive transport and to fuel efficiency. With these shifts in modal priorities have come accompanying changes in the types of policy areas given special attention, with, in broad terms, concerns about subsidies and economic pricing of operations shifting to matters of market access and economic regulation, and then to challenges in the provision and pricing of infrastructure, and recently to more socially oriented subjects.

The major forward movement in the CTP came with the creation of the SEM in the 1990s that allowed free supply of transport services across the borders of the Member States, and the subsequent support of the development of Trans-European Networks (TENs) that have begun to provide the infrastructure to physically allow more intra-EU transport. The more recent trends in the CTP have included (a) taking more account of the social and environmental implications of transport in such things as pricing, regulation and investments, and (b) beginning to develop policies to improve the efficiency of extra-EU transport by giving the Commission powers to negotiate with non-Member States.

4.3.5   Energy policy

Energy has been central to the EU ever since its inception: witness the creation of the ECSC in 1951 by the Treaty of Paris, and Euratom in 1957 by one of the treaties of Rome. The details of these treaties (and their rationales) are covered in Chapter 2, but their significance for energy policy is clear enough. The ECSC reflected the dominance of coal in the energy balance of the Member States (as well as its role in the steel industry): by tackling coal, most European Community (EC) energy supply and demand issues were addressed. Euratom sought to foster cooperation in the development of civil nuclear power, then perceived as the main source of future energy requirements. Moreover, both were in principle geared towards the creation of free and integrated markets in these sectors: the ECSC, being a 'common market' (CM, see Chapter 1), sought to abolish all barriers to trade between the Member States while controlling subsidies and cartel-like behaviour amongst producers, and Euratom aspired to do likewise for nuclear products.

A CM for other energy sectors was addressed in the 1957 EEC Treaty. While the EEC was oriented towards more or less competitively structured sectors, it also applied to the more oligopolistic (competition among few dominant sellers) or monopsonistic (competition among few dominant buyers) sectors such as oil, gas and electricity. Accordingly, in addition to being subject to the EEC Treaty's general provisions on opening up markets, these energy industries' special characteristics were covered by the Treaty's provisions on state enterprises and their conduct. Presently, there is the DG Comp investigation of Gazprom for abuse of a dominant position, which, if set aside (as seems likely) for political reasons, would be bad for competition policy. It would also leave the EU exposed to the possibility of energy blackmail by Russia.

The question of the EU's dependence on Russia for energy[37] is tied up with the question of fracking. Fracking has the potential to make the world oil and natural gas markets sufficiently competitive that both Russia and the Organization of Petroleum Exporting Countries (OPEC) member states will lose any ability to leverage market power in energy for economic or political advantage. It is then inevitable that fracking will be used in the EU, regardless of its environmental impact.

The UK is enthusiastic about this, while France has formally banned fracking and Germany has informally done so. However, the Member States that are holding back will certainly reverse their positions. The challenge for the EU is to reconcile imperatives for energy independence with environmental concerns.

There is greater consensus, leaving aside France and the UK, about shrinking the role of nuclear power. Fracking may make this feasible. If the Continental countries hold fast to a no-fracking policy, then without nuclear power, either the real price of energy will be allowed to rise, which will shackle growth, or the price of energy will be held below market-clearing levels for political reasons, and there will be brownouts and energy shortages.

The gap between the intentions expressed in the treaties and the outcomes, however, has been a large one for energy, more so than for most other parts of the economy. The attempts by the Commission to develop a 'common energy policy' (CEP) of any sort, let alone one reflecting the ideals of the treaties, have proved to be of only limited success. The governments of the Member States have grudgingly left energy sectors to the marketplace when energy markets seemed to be working well. When they suffered disorienting shocks (all too often) they intervened directly, or tried to do so. Throughout, the Commission has been true to its vocation, seeking to lay the foundations for a single EU energy market. The results have been mixed in terms of coping with periodic crises, and have impeded the development of an effective CEP.

4.3.6   Environmental policy

There was no specific reference to environmental protection in the 1957 EEC Treaty. It was not until the inclusion of the environmental chapter in the Single European Act (SEA) in 1987 that the legal basis for a EU environmental policy was fully established. The subsequent development of environmental policy was substantial, spurred by the accession of Austria, Finland, and Sweden in 1995, which saw the EU embrace three Member States with a high level of commitment to environmental protection. However, the enlargements of 2004 and 2007 included ten Central and Eastern European countries (CEECs) with significant environmental problems. The scope and influence of the EU has grown at the same time as recognition that more needs to be done to protect the environment. The policy has developed through a series of Environment Action Programmes.

Environmental protection is only one aspect of the EU's actions to move towards a broader and more wide-ranging strategy to achieve the goals of sustainable development. The 1999 Treaty of Amsterdam provided an explicit reference to sustainable development for the first time,[38] and the 2001 European Council adopted the EU's first Sustainable Development Strategy (SDS). The SDS commits the EU and its Member States to actions that will safeguard the earth's capacity to support life, offering a high level of environmental protection and respecting the limits of the planet's natural resources. Other objectives included social inclusivity, with a healthy and just society running a competitive eco-efficient economy and meeting international commitments. The guiding policy principles thus place human beings at the centre of policy through promoting public awareness and the involvement of business and social partners in making sustainable choices.

In an area as complex and diffuse as the environment, the promotion of policy coherence at the different levels of governance was seen as important, as was the policy integration. The core economic principles upon which the EU's environmental policy is founded are (a) using the best available knowledge;[39] (b) applying the precautionary principle, which suggests that it is best to take action to deal with potential environmental problems on the best available information since it might well be too late if problems such as extreme climate change are left until the actual disaster arrives; (c) decoupling resource use from economic growth; and (d) making the polluters pay for the damage they cause (the Polluter Pay Principle, PPP). Environmental policy should therefore be seen in the context of a greater integration of EU policies within a wide spectrum of policy and mission.

The EU has increasingly favoured the use of market-based instruments (MBI) to enhance environmental performance. Such economic instruments include (a) *pollution charging*, which can be used as an instrument in areas such as water pollution either for cleaning up the related pollution or, as in more recent times, as a way of encouraging an improved environmental performance; (b) *indirect taxation*, to be applied depending upon whether the production or use of a good is environmentally friendly or not; (c) *subsidies*, to be used as incentives to improve environmental performance and which can take the form of direct payment, tax allowances or the provision of low-cost services (their use tends to be limited because subsidies run counter to PPP); (d) *financial penalties*, which are related to the enforcement of environmental laws whereby a failure to comply can lead to a fine, ideally at least as high as the benefits gained from damaging the environment; (e) *creating artificial markets*, by using tradable permits which include the use of emission trading schemes; and (f) *deposit schemes*, which involve charging customers for items such as packaging, but then giving a refund on their return in order to encourage recycling.

Many businesses and legislators prefer regulation because it offers a more consistent approach to environmental standards, and unlike most MBIs, firms do not pay for remaining pollution emissions once they meet the required standard. But MBIs are believed to be more flexible and effective because they offer an incentive to achieve improved environmental outcomes. MBIs can (a) take account of the fact that where different polluters have different marginal costs of abatement, they can minimize the total cost of achieving the desired reduction in abatement; (b) offer an incentive to innovate such that both the production process and the environmental standards are improved; (c) allow choices to be made about the cost of intervention and the environmental benefits that can be gained; (d) avoid excessive government interference into the business of private companies; (e) avoid many of the burdens of environmental protection falling upon the public purse; and (f) present governments with a way of raising money.

A few words on the EU Emissions Trading System (ETS) are in order. The release of greenhouse gases[40] is a classic example of market failure associated with a public good, in which the atmosphere exhibits both non-rival and non-excludable features. That is, additional users of the atmosphere do not impact upon fellow polluters, and it is difficult to exclude polluters unless specific action is taken against them. The EU has attempted to control emissions by allowing polluters that own permits to 'use' the environment, but at a price. If they do not have sufficient permits to meet their needs, they must purchase them from other producers who have a surplus. Over time, the number of permits will be reduced, forcing up their price, encouraging businesses to reduce their level of emissions. This so-called cap-and-trade system accepts that there will be pollution, but the extent of the damage must be reduced by charging a price for the environment so that firms internalize a social cost within their pricing system, something which was regarded as free in the past. The advantage of the ETS is that there is a market for permits that allows those businesses that can reduce their emissions cheaply to trade surplus permits to those that cannot. So heavy polluters must pay if they are less efficient or have less scope to reduce emissions. The idea behind the scheme is to create a scarcity of permits, so that those companies that reduce their emissions can sell them to others that find it not cost effective to reduce their pollution. In the longer term, even those that find it expensive to reduce emissions may choose to invest in improved technology.

Since the launch of the ETS there have been doubts about its effectiveness. The ETS is complex and difficult to understand in an operational context, leading to a degree of inefficiency. As the ETS has operated over time, there have been a number of cases of fraud, involving as much as €5 billion. This fraud undermines the ETS' integrity and suggests that more needs to be done to make the operation of the ETS transparent.

4.4   Policies for structural aspects of the economy and society

This section is devoted to the four policies dealing with certain aspects of the EU economy and society.

4.4.1   Common agricultural policy (CAP)

Although most economists praise the advantages of free markets, the agricultural sector in most countries has been more or less regulated by specific policies for centuries. Four reasons have for a long time been advanced for this special treatment: concern with food security; the low level of agricultural incomes; agricultural inefficiency; and instability of agricultural markets. Lately, two more reasons have been added: food safety and environmental concerns. Different European countries had devised different policies to cater for these.

Unlike the other schemes of international economic integration, the EU has extended free trade between its Member States to agriculture and agricultural products ever since the 1957 EEC Treaty. Agricultural products are defined as those of the soil, stock farming and fisheries, as well as those of first-stage processing directly related to them, although fisheries has developed into a policy of its own. Moreover, the EU treaties ask for the establishment of a 'common agricultural policy' (CAP) among the Member States. This is because different policies would act as NTBs on the sector.

The CAP is based on two basic principles. The first is the principle of financial solidarity, which means that CAP activities are financed out of a common budget. The second is the principle of preference for agricultural products, which means that EU consumers should exhaust domestically produced foods before turning to imports.

There are three constraints on CAP policymakers. The first is the international trade agreements, earlier under the GATT and recently the World Trade Organization (WTO). Indeed, the EU had to change its policies for most agricultural products as a result, policies which had led to the infamous butter mountains and wine lakes. The second is the budget constraint since the finances devoted to the CAP are not unlimited. The third is the influence of non-agricultural groups.

The CAP has an extremely complex set of instruments and regulations, which have changed greatly since the days of its inception. Here, mention is made of only the present system. Those readers interested in how it developed over the years are advised to turn to earlier editions of the previously mentioned EU book. The instruments are (a) import regulations, comprising variable and specific import tariffs, ad valorem tariffs, tariff rate quotas and preferential access; (b) export regulations; and (c) domestic market regulations, which include intervention purchases, direct payments production quotas and consumption subsidies. These measures are still in place, but have become less effective over time. To these must be added those for rural development (below). The quota systems for milk and sugar will be abolished in 2015 and 2017.

Some information on direct payments is in order. Direct payments, introduced to compensate farmers for significant price cuts starting in 1993, are still in place, although domestic prices are higher in recent years than before the drop in institutional prices due to increased world market prices. Payments were tied to either land or number of animals.

In 2003, the Council decided to introduce a major change in direct payments called the single farm payment scheme. The Commission had proposed simplifying the market and price policy by summing up all the different entitlements of individual farmers by direct payments and introducing one single payment, based on past payments, and completely decoupled from production. Moreover, the proposal foresaw making the entitlement for payments tradable. The Council was not able to reach such a wide-ranging agreement. However, the principle was accepted, but the Member States were allowed to introduce some coupled payments for some periods or to introduce coupled payments when there is a serious drop in regional production. Moreover, countries can link payment to area and pay a flat rate at the national level, possibly differentiated with respect to arable or grassland. Furthermore, the Member States were allowed to introduce limitations on the tradability of the payment entitlements.

In 2003, it was also decided to introduce 'compliance measures'. Farmers have to meet various conditions (environmental, animal welfare and others) in order to receive payments. It is claimed that the direct payments have become greener. Starting in 2014, 30 per cent of payments are made for using 5 per cent of agricultural land of individual farms for environmental purposes. In addition, payments have been modified to protect farmers of small farms more than those of large farms.

Finally, it should be added that a rural development policy was formally created under *Agenda* 2000.[41] This introduced what is called the 'second pillar of the CAP'. Some of the policy instruments have been in place as part of EU structural policy since the 1970s, but most of them were introduced in the 1990s. The rural development policy has three objectives: (a) to improve the competitiveness of the agricultural sector; (b) to protect the environment and landscape; and (c) to improve the living standards in rural areas and support diversification. There is a menu of more than 40 measures from which the countries may select as many as they want. However, they have to keep total payments within the national envelope (the budget allocated to them from the Commission), and the total expenditure for the individual measures has to be co-financed by individual Member States. Moreover, the projects have to be approved by the EU. The basis for approval is the submitted National Rural Development Plans and the specifics of the project.

The list of instruments (Figure 4.2) shows that agriculture is considered the main sector that should be supported when aiming at rural development. Indeed, the preamble of the regulation makes it clear that the focus should be on agriculture or activities closely related to agriculture. Moreover, it is clearly stated that payments to farmers in cases of environmental measures should be calculated on the basis of income forgone, and could surpass income forgone by as much as 20 per cent.

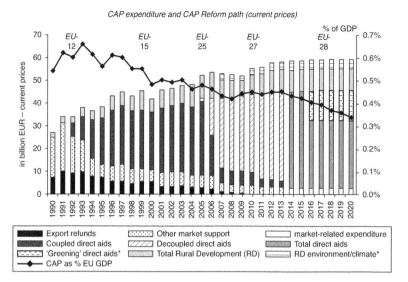

Figure 4.2 Breakdown of EU expenditure on agriculture, to be found at http://
ec.europa.eu/agriculture/cap-post-2013/graphs/graph1_en.pdf

Note: Precise amounts for 2014–2020 may vary according to Member State implemantation
plans.

4.4.2 Common fisheries policy (CFP)

It is logical for the EU to have a 'common fisheries policy' (CFP) since
much fishing activity is conducted across and beyond national territorial
waters, and fish take no notice of national boundaries. And, although
the EU's fisheries sector, comprising fishing, fish processing and aquaculture, is small in terms of both production (less than 1 per cent of EU
GDP) and employment (about 0.4 per cent of total EU employment),
the EU fishing industry is the world's fourth largest, and, vitally, fishing
activity tends to be concentrated in peripheral regions in which there is
often little alternative employment and the industry and its representatives tend to be highly fragmented.

The CFP has evolved since 1970, but was not formalized until 1982
and has been operative from 1983. It has four aspects: (a) *marketing*,
which includes common marketing standards, the institution of a
price support system and the establishment of producers' organizations
(POs); (b) *structural assistance*, with the aim of promoting 'harmonious
and balanced development' of the industry, the 'rational use of marine
resources' and multi-annual guidance programmes; (c) *conservation*, which

is the responsible exploitation of living marine resources on a sustainable basis, taking into account its implications for the marine ecosystem and socio-economic implications for producers and consumers, the two main conservation policies being quotas/total allowable catches (TACs) and technical instruments; and (d) *external relations*, based on fisheries partnership agreements (FPAs) with non-member states, which include reciprocal arrangements over fishing rights, access to surplus stock, access to stock in return for financial compensation, and more recently the development of joint enterprises.

The EU's financial assistance for communities dependent on fisheries is provided by the European Fisheries Fund (EFF), which forms part of the EU structural funds. The EU's aid for fishing now systematically requires some form of co-funding from the Member States and is conditional on meeting fleet decommissioning targets.

Fisheries policymaking is characterized by a multilevel system of governance, ranging from the international arena, in which a legal framework is set by the international fisheries regime, to the European, national, regional and local levels, which are responsible for the implementation and much of the monitoring of policy.

The CFP has been in a process of reform since 1983 with the EU's Mediterranean enlargement, when a commitment was given to review the CFP and in particular the principle of relative stability in 2002. The 2002 reforms, which apply until 2013, include (a) the adoption of a longer-term perspective to fisheries management by setting multi-annual targets instead of the annual exercises of the past; (b) renewed and stricter commitment to capacity reduction and control to bring fleets in line with available resources; (c) the importance of ecosystem management and the precautionary principle to 'ensure exploitation of living aquatic resources and of aquaculture that provides sustainable economic, environmental and social conditions'; (d) an increasing role for industry and stakeholders through the setting up of regional advisory councils (RACs); (e) simplified and streamlined regulations for easier and fairer application; and (f) EU aid, which should support coastal communities as the industry restructures while fleet overcapacity is reduced. The reform process for 2013 is still underway, but is not expected to result in any radical changes.

4.4.3 Regional policy

EU regional policy (RP) traces its origins to the decision in 1975 to create the European Regional Development Fund (ERDF) on the behest of the UK during its accession negotiations. The policy subsequently underwent minor reform in 1979 and 1984,[42] followed by a major reform in

1989.[43] The 1989 reform was specifically designed to accompany the introduction of the SEM and integrated a number of previously separate EU funding mechanisms, renaming them the 'structural funds': the ERDF, together with the European Social Fund (ESF), the Guidance Section of the European Agricultural Guidance and Guarantee Fund (EAGGF) and, from 1994, a Financial Instrument for Fisheries Guidance (FIFG), renamed the European Fisheries Fund (EFF) in 2007. The Cohesion Fund, also created in 1994, acts in many ways like one of the structural funds, although it is not in fact strictly one of them.

The RP continues to this day to be operated in its essential characteristics on the basis of the reform to the structural funds introduced in 1989. The reformed policy provided the basis for further reforms in 1994 (designed to accompany steps towards the EMU;[44] and 1999, designed to prepare the way for enlargement to include the Central and Eastern European Countries, CEEC[45]). The 1994 and 1999 reforms both incorporated massive increases in funding for the RP, resulting in its status being the second-largest EU policy. The 1999 reforms were for the programming period 2000–6. Further reforms accompanied the two multi-annual financial frameworks (see Chapter 5), covering the 2007–13 and 2013–20 periods.

The 2007–13 RP, renamed the 'cohesion policy', has operated in all of its essential characteristics on the basis of the major reform to the structural funds of 1989. In order to ensure that funding is as precisely targeted as possible (the principle of *concentration*), since 1989 the structural funds have been given the task of attaining specific *priority objectives*. At one time there were no fewer than seven priority objectives. During 2007–13, these were cut back to just three.

Objective 1 (called the 'lagging regions' objective between 1989 and 2006, and the 'convergence' objective in 2007–13) was focused on the most disadvantaged EU regions (i.e. those whose GDP per capita – at purchasing power parities – is under 75 per cent of the EU average) and was designed to help them to catch up (i.e. 'converge') with the rest of the EU. This objective was by far the most generously funded of the three, commanding some 81.4 per cent of total funding in 2007–13 (€282.9 billion at current prices) and with less stringent requirements than for the other objectives in terms of percentages of investment costs met and national matching funding targets.

Since the EU sets the criterion for eligibility for Objective 1 regions, the EU, not the Member States, effectively determined such regions. Within EU15, the Objective 1 regions were concentrated in the southern Mediterranean and in parts of Ireland and the UK. The accession of the new Member States (NMS12) in 2004/7 brought in a huge swathe of regions that were automatically eligible. Indeed, apart from Malta and Cyprus only small enclaves within NMS12 (e.g. Prague) were *not* automatically eligible for assistance.

Although the RP budget was increased for the 2007–13 programming period, the sheer scale of regional problems in the NMS12 meant that a major shift eastwards had to be incorporated in funding arrangements for 2007–13. Many regions in Western Europe, particularly in Finland, Greece, Ireland, Italy, the UK and Sweden, which had formerly enjoyed Objective 1 funding, found that they lost this in 2007. These are referred to as 'phasing in' and 'phasing out' regions. Phasing in regions are those whose growth rates prior to 2007 had been sufficient to lift their GDP per capita values above the Objective 1 threshold and hence would in any event have lost Objective 1 status after 2007. Phasing out regions, sometimes called 'statistical effect' regions, in 2007–13 were those unfortunate to have fallen foul of the fact that the accession of the 12 much poorer NMS in 2004/7 led to a significant fall in overall average GDP per capita in the EU. These are therefore regions which would have retained their status in 2007–13 had the EU remained at EU15, but which found themselves exceeding the 75 per cent GDP per capita criterion for Objective 1, which had by 2007 become based on the lower EU27 average. Some transitional assistance continued in 2007–13 for the phasing in and phasing out regions in EU15, but this is quite small (only €11.4 billion and €14.0 billion respectively).

Objective 2 in 2007–13 was called the 'regional competitiveness and employment' objective. The name reflected the desire to use the RP not only as a means of providing relief for very poor regions but also of helping the EU as a whole to maintain its competitiveness in an increasingly competitive global trading environment. During the 2007–13 period, the RP was expected to throw its weight behind the so-called EU 'Lisbon Agenda' objectives – growth, competitiveness and environmental sustainability. The name of Objective 2 closely reflected the Lisbon Agenda ideals, and the Commission's detailed guidelines for the RP in 2007–13 were based very firmly on growth and competitiveness aims.[46] The types of policies favoured by Objective 2 were also very much focused on competitiveness – policies to stimulate innovation, the knowledge society, entrepreneurship, the protection of the environment and the enhancement of workers' skills.

The areas eligible for Objective 2 in 2007–13 comprised all regions other than Objective 1 (i.e. effectively a 'non-regional' objective). This was, however, misleading because the Member States were allowed to establish their own priorities and eligible areas (within the budget limits set by the Commission). In practice a diverse range of regions got support, including regions suffering from industrial (i.e. manufacturing) decline, certain disadvantaged rural areas, certain urban areas suffering severe economic, social and environmental problems, fishing communities in decline, and a series of regions suffering 'geographical handicaps', such as islands, mountainous regions and the very remote outermost EU regions (Azores, Canary Islands, Madeira, Guadeloupe, Réunion, Martinique and French Guyana). Objective 2 was much less generously funded than Objective 1, being allocated only €55 billion for the 2007–13 period, which was only 15.8 per cent of the RP budget (see Chapter 5).

Finally, there was Objective 3: 'European territorial cohesion'. This has been allocated only a small pot of money (€8.7 billion or 2.5 per cent of the 2007–13 RP budget) to stimulate cross-border and transnational economic development initiatives. It was built on previous small, yet successful cross-border schemes funded under a programme called 'Interreg', but was in fact rather more significant than either its name or small budget suggests. As mentioned, the EU has long been concerned with reducing economic and social disparities. However, in the 2007–13 period, a commitment to 'territorial cohesion' was added to economic and social cohesion.

As well as the commitment to concentration of assistance and much closer coordination of the activities of the EU's financial instruments, the RP which has emerged in the aftermath of the 1989 reforms places great emphasis on four further principles. They are the use of a system of multi-annual programmes of assistance, the need for a close partnership between all of those involved in the RP, a commitment to subsidiarity (the retention at the EU level of the minimum necessary powers), and a desire that EU money should be a genuine supplement to RP spending by the Member States (additionality). None of these principles was entirely new to the 1989 reform package, but the 1989 reforms represented the first comprehensive attempt to create an RP 'delivery system' that would allow the principles to be achieved. These four great principles continue to underpin the RP.

The current programming period is for 2014–20 (Map 4.1 shows the cohesion policy eligible areas, which are identical to those for 2007–13). Despite real threats around 2011, the RP remains substantial, with a reformed cohesion policy funded by €351.8 billion. This is being aimed at 'creating growth and jobs, tackling climate change and energy dependence, and reducing poverty and social exclusion'. It is to be assisted

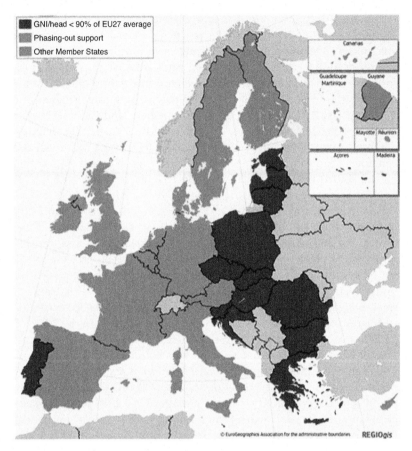

Map 4.1 Cohesion policy eligible areas, 2014–20 to be found at http://ec.europa.
eu/regional_policy/what/future/eligibility/index_en.cfm

through targeting the ERDF at such key priority areas as lending support
to SMEs, doubling the financing for this from €70 billion to €140 billion
over the seven years. There will also be more emphasis on the delivery of
results, with a larger 'performance reserve' in all the EU's structural and
investment funds that provide incentives for good projects, together
with efficiency in cohesion policy, rural development and that the fisheries fund will be linked to economic governance in order to encourage
compliance by the Member States with the EU's recommendations. Thus
the focus on the economic goals of the Lisbon Agenda is continued and
reinforced.

It should be added that the 2014–20 programme has three regional types: (a) less developed regions (again under 75 per cent of GDP per capita); (b) transition regions (75 per cent to 90 per cent); and (c) more developed regions (over 90 per cent). It contains a bigger 'performance reserve' to encourage better practice (and less corruption!). The direct focus of RP on Europe 2020 is through four key growth priorities (innovation/research; digital agenda; SMEs; and low carbon economy) and eleven thematic ones.

4.4.4   Social policy

Social policy is a broad term, which can encompass government policies on education, health, employment, social security, social exclusion and the like.[47] There are very wide divergences in these policies in the Member States, and because they are related to the nature of society and considered sensitive, they are issues of high political salience. This meant that a uniform policy was not possible and that decision-making powers had to remain with the Member States.

In the 1957 EEC Treaty, social policy was restricted to the free movement of labour[48] and to gender equality in payment terms. And, because of the political sensitivities in these areas, the Member States insisted on unanimous decision-making. These two policies were established in the 1960s, but further initiatives were limited until the SEM in the 1980s. The SEM encouraged further social policy development for two reasons. First, there were fears that the SEM competition would encourage a race to the bottom in social policy areas affecting companies' costs, such as working conditions. Second, there was a desire to show that the SEM was not just about big business, but that it benefited working people too. Thus the 1987 SEA included working conditions as part of the EC policy and began to extend QMV to these 'traditional' areas of social policy.

This process was further developed by the 1989 Social Charter, which led to an extension of the EU social policy in the Maastricht Treaty, a process carried through in the subsequent Amsterdam, Nice and Lisbon Treaties. This means that today the free movement of labour, gender equality, working conditions, worker information/consultation, modernization of social protection, public health and coordination of social security are all areas of EU social policy, and hence are decided by QMV, with the ECJ ruling on the application of legislation.[49] Other areas are potentially within the EU remit but require unanimous agreement by the Member States; they include anti-discrimination, social security, protecting workers' rights and the employment of third country nationals. Some of these areas as well as others are subject to a separate mode of policy development: the Open Method of Coordination (OMC). So although it is still true that welfare considerations remain national, with the EU not responsible for individual entitlements, the sovereignty of the Member States in social policy is increasingly constrained within a Europeanized multi-tiered policy process.

Although social and employment policies remain very differentiated across the EU, there is a view that there is a distinctive 'European social model' (ESM), which is differentiated from the US market-driven model. The ESM involves generous benefits and a high level of rights for workers, with the US model being very limited in both respects. The ESM is justified not only on social grounds but also in efficiency terms: it is argued that workers' greater attachment to the companies for which they work results in higher productivity and a better trained workforce. The US model is supposed to protect workers by encouraging high levels of job creation as a result of the flexibility of the workforce and a more entrepreneurial culture. The challenge to the ESM is in maintaining the benefits in the face of a recession with rising unemployment and an ageing population. The challenge for the EU is in generating jobs to replace those that have been lost in the recession. The ESM has influenced EU employment policy, which has to try to balance high benefits and workers' rights with sufficient flexibility to try to improve employment performance, but whether this has been successful is arguable.

Today, EU social policy is largely concerned with employment policy and for four reasons. First, unemployment is very high in the Member States, especially in those hard hit by the 2008 financial crisis (Figure 4.3 also provides information for comparator countries). Second,

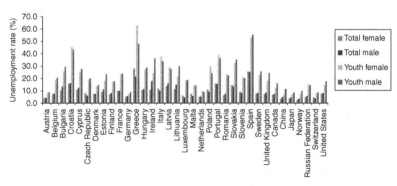

Figure 4.3 Total and youth female and male unemployment in the EU and comparator countries, 2012

employment encompasses many of these areas of social policy. Third, the complex nature of EU decision-making is well illustrated in the employment arena. Fourth, employment policy is the most important aspect of social policy, not only for economists but also for specialists in other social disciplines. Employment policy has also become increasingly important in the EU as the result of a generally deteriorating employment performance and the consequent EU desire to be seen as taking action on this important issue. The SEM has limited the room for manoeuvre in employment policy by the Member States and increased the importance of ensuring that competition is fair. The EMU has meant that the Eurozone countries can no longer rely on changes in exchange rates to remain price competitive, so the ability to adjust depends upon wage rates being flexible.

4.5   Policies for external relations

Finally, this section considers two policies. The first concerns EU trade relations with its major partners within the context of the CCP run by the Commission on behalf of all the EU Member States. The second is about the EU relations with the developing world in terms of trade, aid and preferential trading arrangements.

4.5.1   External trade policy

The EU's external trade policy involves nearly one-fifth of world trade. Hence an understanding of the principles and practice of the EU's trade policy, the CCP, is of vital importance for understanding the EU's role and impact on the global economy.

The CCP is shaped by the EU's obligations (and reciprocal rights) under the WTO, which has been administering the GATT since 1995. As mentioned in Chapter 1, the purpose of the WTO is to establish and monitor the rules for trade policymaking in its member countries and to encourage the liberalization of trade through successive rounds of trade negotiations to reduce tariffs and other barriers (NTBs) to trade in goods and services. One of its core principles is that of most-favoured nation (MFN) treatment, which means that member countries undertake not to discriminate in their handling of imports originating in different members. The EU played a major role in the Uruguay Round Agreement conducted under the auspices of the GATT. It was among the strongest proponents of the further comprehensive round of trade negotiations that was initiated in Doha, Qatar, in November 2001, which is yet to be concluded. The difficulties in reaching an agreement in the Doha Round have, however, revived the tension between the EU's commitment to multilateral trade liberalization through the WTO and its ongoing concern with regional and bilateral agreements outside that organization.

While initially the EU trade policy mainly consisted of tariffs and import quota restrictions on goods, the importance of the former has gradually diminished and today is marginal with the exception of tariffs on agricultural products. Hence, agriculture still remains a sensitive area both in multilateral liberalization negotiations and bilateral agreements in which the coverage in agricultural goods is often not the same as in manufacturing goods. While tariff protection has waned, NTBs have assumed increased importance; hence, the SEM. But the SEM is a family affair, so there is still scope for realizing further global integration through the removal of NTBs between the EU and its trading partners.

The CCP has also developed a highly complex set of trade relations with third countries, reflecting in part the way in which the granting of trade preferences (the Generalised System of Preferences, GSP) was virtually the sole instrument of the EU foreign policy in the past. This resulted in a hierarchy of preferential trading schemes, determined by a mixture of trade, strategic and foreign policy concerns, in which the conflicting interests of the Member States, as well as hard bargaining between the EU institutions and the Member States, have played an important role. Apart from tariff reductions, the EU has also facilitated access to its own markets to numerous countries by establishing a complex system of preferential trade agreements (the spaghetti bowl phenomenon). This complexity reflected in part the way in which the granting of trade preferences was virtually the sole instrument of EU foreign policy in the past. This led to a hierarchy of preferential trading schemes, determined by a mixture of trade, strategic and foreign policy concerns in which the conflicting interests of the Member States, as well as hard bargaining between the EU institutions and the Member States, have played an important role.

Because NTBs have become so disruptive to trade, policy areas relating to regulatory issues have become increasingly relevant to international trade. Thus the Commission's 'Global Europe: Competing in the World' (CEU, 2006f) set out some main policy objectives for the CCP that address the challenges of globalization. The main objective is to define a trade policy that will both stimulate growth and create jobs in Europe. It also defines some of the links between the EU's external and internal policies and emphasizes the importance of the multilateral and bilateral liberalization processes as well as the CCP's role in achieving competitiveness. It calls for the CCP to address, among other issues, NTBs, liberalization of trade in services and the securing/protecting intellectual property rights (IPR). Throughout, the importance of external liberalization is emphasized, which is well illustrated by the statement 'openness to others, and their openness to us, are critical and mutually reinforcing factors in European competitiveness'.

The Commission has the sole responsibility for the EU's external trade relations and is in charge of the negotiations with the outside world in consultation with a special committee appointed by the Council. All trade agreements are subject to Council approval but increasingly so jointly with the European Parliament, especially after the changes introduced by the Lisbon Treaty in December 2009 (the 'ordinary legislative procedure').

There are important challenges ahead for EU trade policy. The EU needs a secure system of rules for international trade given that the EU relies heavily on trading with other nations. This implies the need for an efficiently functioning dispute settlement system at a multilateral level. Due to the increasing relative importance of NTBs, there is an increasing need to address the problem arising from divergence in regulatory systems between countries; indeed, these lie at the very heart of the ongoing negotiations between the EU and the US for an Atlantic Trade and Investment Partnership (TTIP). The economic downturn coupled with concerns about food and energy security makes these issues even more challenging to tackle.

Some recent changes introduced in the Lisbon treaty, such as the reinforcement of the EU's external actions by the new High Representative and the extension of the scope of the CCP to include FDI, might facilitate future negotiations in the area of trade. However, the precise form of the EU's future external policy will depend on several factors. Among these are that the increasing heterogeneity among the Member States is likely to make it more difficult to reach consensus by them and that the current economic crisis might lessen the enthusiasm for further integration.

4.5.2 The EU and the developing world

The EU's economic size and its role in world trade mean that it is a key player in structuring the global economic environment for developing countries (DCs) through its aid and trade policies. The EU Member States are the largest trading partner of the DCs, absorbing about one-fifth of their exports and accounting for a similar portion of their imports. Also, they provide about 56 per cent (as against 19.1 per cent and 6.7 per cent for the US and Japan respectively) of total official development assistance (ODA) worldwide. Moreover, the EU has a significant indirect influence through its active participation in international organizations that manage the world economic system, for example, the World Bank, the WTO and, before it, the GATT. Furthermore, the EU development cooperation policy is comprehensive in its approach, including free trade agreements (FTAs), ODA and political dialogue,[50] with important and even radical changes having been adopted by the EU in its development policy: the TFEU dictates that the relationship should be firmly based on the principle of poverty eradication, and calls for all the EU policies that impinge on the DCs to do likewise. But more significant than all these considerations is that the EU's relationship with the DCs goes back to the time of the creation of the EEC, when the ex-colonies of especially the French had to be accommodated before the 1957 Rome Treaties could become a reality, with the admission of the UK and the Iberian nations extending and enhancing it to encompass African, Caribbean, Latin American and Asian nations, leading to the 2003 ACP-EU Cotonou Agreement which comprises the EU and 79 nations (see Chapter 1).

The major thrust of the EU's trade policy towards the DCs is a move away from the autonomous preference-based and regionally discriminatory trade arrangements of the past to a more horizontal but differentiated policy emphasizing reciprocal FTAs with low- and middle-income DCs and duty- and quota-free access now offered to all the least developed countries (LDCs) under the 'everything but arms' (EBA) policy (presently for bananas, rice and sugar). The EU argues that FTAs will have positive outcomes for the partner countries, through encouraging a more efficient allocation of resources and greater competition, and by creating a more attractive location for FDI. However, some potential drawbacks should be noted.

For the ACP and the Mediterranean partners, entering into an FTA is an asymmetric liberalization process. For manufacturing products, these countries already enjoyed duty-free access to the EU markets (although in the case of the Mediterranean countries ceilings operated for sensitive products such as textiles and clothing), so the main impact is the unilateral removal of trade barriers on EU exports entering partner country markets. While consumers and producers who will now have the possibility of importing cheaper intermediate products will benefit, many firms, particularly SMEs, may be forced to close, with a consequent rise in unemployment. Also, the continued barriers to agricultural trade in the agreements, which is the sector in which many of the partner countries have their comparative advantage, make adaptation to the required structural changes more difficult. Some fear that a consequence of this asymmetric liberalization may be trade diversion in favour of EU exports, which would add to the economic costs of these agreements for the EU partners.

Proponents of these agreements therefore emphasize the likelihood of dynamic gains, particularly that the contractual nature of these agreements will lower uncertainty by locking in trade liberalization policies in the partner countries, thus helping to attract greater FDI flows. Also potentially important are the provisions to tackle NTBs, thus lowering the transactions cost of trade and reducing the impact of regulatory trade barriers. For the ACP countries, a further issue that has to be addressed is the reduction in tariff revenues as duties on EU imports are eliminated. This could curtail government spending when increased support for industrial restructuring and assistance to cushion the costs of transitional unemployment is required, unless other means to broaden the tax base are found.

The EU announced a self-imposed moratorium on new FTA initiatives prior to the 1999 Seattle WTO Ministerial Council in order to focus EU efforts on promoting the new WTO multilateral trade round. Following the suspension of the Doha Round negotiations in July 2005, the EU indicated a revision of this position in its 'Global Europe' document the next year (CEU, 2006f). This document noted that the EU's existing FTAs serve its neighbourhood and development interests well, but its trade interests less so. The content of existing agreements is too limited, in that they fail to address regulatory and 'behind the border' trade barriers. The EU does not have agreements with the world's most dynamic markets, particularly in Asia, while many of these priority markets are negotiating FTAs with its competitors (such as the ASEAN members with China, Japan and Korea and each other, or Korea with the US, concluded in June 2007), threatening the EU with a loss of market share. The document therefore announced the EU's interest in concluding a range of further FTAs, particularly with countries with significant market potential and in which existing barriers to EU exports were high. Based on these criteria, the document highlights agreements with ASEAN, the Gulf Cooperation Council, India, Korea, Mercosur and Russia as of direct EU interest. While the document at the same time restates its commitment to a successful conclusion of the Doha Round, it clearly signals that the EU is 'open for business' when it comes to concluding a range of FTAs with the DCs in the future.

Three further points need mentioning. First, the proliferation of the EU's special trade relationships with the DCs and groups thereof has devalued the preferential trade cooperation schemes, and the WTO has criticized these as discriminatory. There is therefore a need for a new approach which strengthens regional trade cooperation; avoids discrimination; and promotes the overarching objective of poverty eradication.

Second, the EU is carefully watching how China is expanding its cooperation with the DCs, and China's role in this regard will have a major impact on the future of the EU's relationships with the DCs. The EU is aiming to make human rights a stronger factor in its preferential trade agreements with the DCs.

Third, it should be noted that the EU's ODA is provided by both the Commission and the Member States, which combine to provide the about 56 per cent of total global ODA. In 2013, despite continued budgetary constraints due to the 2008 crisis and its aftermath, the collective EU ODA increased to €56.5 billion from €55.3 billion in 2012, accounting for 0.02 per cent of EU GNI. The total for the Member States increased from €50.7 billion in 2012 to €53.6 billion in 2013, that is, from 0.39 per cent to 0.41 per cent of EU GNI. This means that the Commission manages 10 per cent of all ODA. The Member States implement their own bilateral and multilateral programmes in addition to the EU's, which are managed by the Commission. The Commission is a strong protagonist of government-to-government aid, providing general budgetary support to further good governance. It allocates only a very small proportion of its programme to basic health and education. Because the EU's ODA is so significant, the chapter ends with more on it: Box 4.1 explains the EU's combined efforts to the financing of EU ODA and political accountability; and Figure 4.4 reveals how the EU compares with the other member nations of the Group of Eight (G8); and Table 4.3 shows its evolution over 2012–15.

Recommended Reading

Ali M. El-Agra (2011) *The European Union: Economics and Policies*, Cambridge University Press, Cambridge.

Box 4.1   EU ODA: financing sources and political responsibility

Sources of financing

The EU's external assistance programme has two distinct sources of funding: funds allocated through the EU budget and contributions by the Member States outside the EU budget to the European Development Fund (EDF).

Decisions on budget funds are made with the involvement of the Council of the EU, the European Parliament (EP) through the 'ordinary legislative procedure (see Chapter 3) and the Commission. The final decision is made by the EP, but within the limits/ceilings agreed in the financial perspective. The EDF funds are contributed by the Member States on a voluntary basis according to a specific distribution key, and decision-making power rests with the Council without any legal basis for involvement of the EP and the Commission. The funds are, however, managed by the Commission on behalf of the Member States. The EDF funds are allocated solely to the ACP nations and overseas countries and territories (OCTs), while aid via the EU budget is provided mainly to non-ACP countries. Budgetary assistance is allocated according to either a geographical or a thematic approach under specific budget headings.

Political responsibility

Responsibility for the EU external assistance used to be divided among five Directorates General ([DGs], see Chapter 3): Development, which provided policy guidance on development policy and was responsible for aid to the ACP states; EuroAid-Cooperation Office; Humanitarian Aid; Enlargement, which provided pre-accession assistance for potential future members in the western Balkans; and External Relations, which was responsible for the remaining external assistance mainly to Asian, Latin American and Mediterranean countries. However, in the 2014 Commission, EU development aid is implemented by the DG responsible for EuropeAid Development and Cooperation (DEVCO).

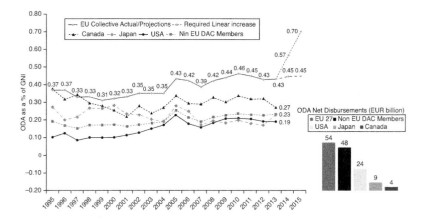

Figure 4.4 A comparison of EU and non-EU G8 ODA contributions to be found at http://www.consilium.europa.eu/uedocs/cms_data/docs/pressdata/EN/foraff/137320.pdf

Source: OECD/DAC data for 1995–2013 when available; Commission simulation based on information provided by EU Member States or based on agreed EU commitments 2015.

Table 4.3 The EU's ODA for 2012–15 by Member State and in totals to be found at http://www.consilium.europa.eu/uedocs/cms_data/docs/pressdata/EN/foraff/137320.pdf

Member State	2012		2013		2014		2015		2015 commitment		2015 financial gap	
	EUR million	% of GNI	EUR million	% of GNI	EUR million	% of GNI	EUR million	% of GNI	EUR million	% of GNI	EUR million	% of GNI
Austria	860	0.28	882	0.28	1393	0.43	1386	0.42	2,328	0.70	942	0.28
Belgium	1,801	0.47	1,718	0.45	1,731	0.44	1,745	0.43	2,843	0.70	1,099	0.27
Bulgaria	31	0.08	37	0.10	46	0.11	56	0.13	140	0.33	83	0.20
Croatia	15	0.03	32	0.07	26	0.06	27	0.06	217	0.33	190	0.27
Cyprus	20	0.12	19	0.11	19,5	0.13	19.5	0.13	51	0.33	32	0.20
Czech Republic	171	0.12	160	0.11	156	0.12	156	0.11	458	0.33	302	0.22
Denmark	2,095	0.83	2,206	0.85	2,181	0.82	2,181	0.79	2,748	1.00	567	0.21
Estonia	18	0.11	23	0.13	28	0.15	30	0.15	66	0.33	36	0.18
Finland	1,027	0.53	1,081	0.55	1103	0.55	1069	0.52	1,448	0.70	379	0.18
France	9,358	0.45	8,568	0.41	10327	0.48	10,588	0.48	15,428	0.70	4,840	0.22
Germany	10,067	0.37	10,590	0.38	10,779	0.37	10,971	0.37	20,996	0.70	10,025	0.33
Greece	255	0.13	230	0.13	198	0.11	170	0.09	1,293	0.70	1,123	0.61
Hungary	92	0.10	91	0.10	90	0.10	94	0.10	322	0.33	228	0.23
Ireland	629	0.47	619	0.45	600	0.43	554	0.38	1,015	0.70	461	0.32
Italy	2,129	0.14	2,450	0.16	2,618	0.17	3,152	0.20	11,306	0.70	8,154	0.50
Latvia	16	0.08	18	0.08	18	0.07	19	0.07	87	0.33	68	0.26
Lithuania	40	0.13	39	0.12	40	0.11	41	0.11	125	0.33	84	0.22
Luxembourg	310	1.00	324	1.00	316.37	0.96	324	0.93	348	1.00	24	0.07

Malta	14	0.23	14	0.20	13	0.19	**14**	**0.19**	24	0.33	10	0.14
The Netherlands	4,297	0.71	4,094	0.67	3,816	0.61	**3,990**	**0.62**	4,499	0.70	509	0.08
Poland	328	0.09	357	0.10	224	0.06	**232**	**0.06**	1,346	0.33	1,114	0.27
Portugal	452	0.28	365	0.23	**353**	**0.22**	**341**	**0.21**	1,163	0.70	822	0.49
Romania	111	0.08	101	0.07	134	0.09	**139**	**0.09**	500	0.33	362	0.24
Slovak Republic	62	0.09	64	0.09	71	0.10	**77**	**0.10**	249	0.33	172	0.23
Slovenia	45	0.13	45	0.13	43	0.12	**44**	**0.12**	118	0.33	74	0.21
Spain	1,585	0.16	1,656	0.16	1,341	0.13	**1,085**	**0.10**	7,306	0.70	6,220	0.60
Sweden	4,077	0.97	4,392	1.02	4,348	1.00	**4,557**	**1.00**	4,557	1.00	–	–
UK	10,808	0.56	13,468	0.72	14,304	0.70	**14,961**	**0.70**	14,961	0.70	–	–
EU15 Total	**49,749**	**0.42**	**52,643**	**0.44**	**55,408**	**0.44**	**57,074**	**0.44**	**92,238**	**0.72**	**35,164**	**0.27**
EU13 Total	**964**	**0.10**	**1,000**	**0.09**	**908**	**0.09**	**948**	**0.09**	**3,704**	**0.33**	**2,756**	**0.25**
EU28 Total	**50,713**	**0.39**	**53,643**	**0.41**	**56,316**	**0.42**	**58,022**	**0.42**	**95,942**	**0.69**	**37,920**	**0.27**
EU Institutions ODA	13,669		11,995									
Of which:												
Imputed to Member States	9,125		9,122									
Not Imputed to Member States	4,544	0.04	2,873	0.02	3,249	0.02	3,675	0.03				
Collective EU ODA(1)	**55,257**	**0.43**	**56,517**	**0.43**	**59,599**	**0.44**	**61,697**	**0.44**				

> Gap between 2013 collective EU ODA and collective 2015 target 0.7%
> Target in EUR Million 97,830
> Gap in EUR Million 41,314

5
The EU General Budget

5.1 Introduction

We now turn to one of the final questions raised at the end of Chapter 1: how does the EU finance its policies? The answer to the question requires an examination of the EU's general budget, but recall from Chapter 3 that EU institutions, such as the European Investment Bank (EIB), carry out specific EU policies which are financed by their own loans, hence they do not fall under the EU's general budget; the interested reader is therefore advised to turn to that chapter (endnote number 2).

The EU general budget (hereafter budget)[1] has always been an issue of high political salience. The Member States are naturally concerned with their contributions to and receipts from it. Until 1988, the political significance of the budget was also heightened by inter-institutional rivalry within the European Community (EC). The right to approve the budget, one of the more significant powers of the European Parliament (EP), was used as a lever to force concessions from the Council. This problem has been resolved through gradually increasing the EP powers by making it more directly involved in the budgetary planning.

The budget is also a window on the EU as a political and economic institution. In the early years, it was very small and financed from national contributions. With the development of EU policies, in particular the 'common agricultural policy' (CAP), expenditure rose and 'own resources' were introduced in 1970. There followed a period of expenditure growth, principally on agriculture. The late 1970s and the early 1980s were plagued by disagreements over the budget between the institutions and in relation to the UK's contribution. The resolution of this British problem was accompanied by measures to control agricultural expenditure, and was one of the factors that facilitated the development of the 'single European market' (SEM). The SEM and the EU's Mediterranean enlargement led in 1988 to the Delors I budgetary package. This was a comprehensive revision of the budget that increased expenditure. Following agreement on the Treaty on European Union (TEU), the budget was further modified by the Edinburgh Agreement, which was the Delors II package. This was accompanied by a radical CAP reform and further expanded the budgetary resources in order to accommodate more expenditure on structural policies, internal policies (particularly research) and on external action, recognizing the impact of the changes in Central and Eastern Europe. The reduced dynamism in the EU in the second half of the 1990s is reflected in budgetary developments. It took eight years to agree on relatively modest resources to finance EU enlargement in 2004 and 2007.

This chapter commences with a non-technical survey of the economic theory of the state since it is fundamental for a proper appreciation of the budget and the role it plays. Equally important is an understanding of fiscal federalism and its application to the EU, so this comes next. A consideration of the EU budgetary system follows. Then the budget revenues and expenditures are explained and the problems facing the budget are examined. The chapter finishes by considering budgetary limitations.

5.2 The economic theory of the state

Traditionally, the role of the state is delineated in three branches: allocation, distribution and stabilization. These days the regulatory role of the government is also stressed.

The government's role in allocation is the result of externalities, which are costs and benefits that arise in production but which do not directly affect either the producer or the consumer, that is, they are suffered without compensation or are enjoyed free of charge by third parties. Air pollution is an externality: when coal was the major source of energy, households and firms burnt coal without thinking of its effects on the atmosphere. It took government intervention in the UK, in the form of Clean Air Acts, to encourage the burning of smokeless fuel to solve this problem of urban air pollution. What is crucial about externalities is that in the absence of government intervention, their costs/benefits are non-rival and non-excludable. Non-rivalry occurs when one person's benefit/cost from a service does not limit other peoples' enjoyment/suffering. Such non-rivalry implies that access to benefits should not be limited by price or other means. If it is not possible to prevent access to a service to individuals who have not paid, then the service is non-excludable: it is generally not possible to finance the service privately because it cannot be charged for – the so-called free-rider problem. With public goods such as defence, all the benefits are non-rival and non-excludable, so governments finance them from general taxation. The allocative role of government involves the provision or subsidization of services where externalities are significant.

The regulatory role of the state overlaps with that of allocation, by setting rules in markets to make them work in the interests of society. So regulation encompasses competition policy, the rules for natural monopolies, the safety of products, financial services, etc. The reason for government regulation is either that there are problems with the operation of markets, with competition, or that there are informational problems. For example, with financial services, there is a case for regulation because of systemic risk: the government has to ensure the viability of key financial institutions in a crisis, while avoiding moral hazard[2] in its underwriting of banks in difficulties. Financial services also need to be regulated because of information problems related to the complexity of the product, so consumers need to be protected from fraud and misrepresentation.

The distributive role of government recognizes the fact that markets are compatible with very unequal distributions of individual income levels, which are unacceptable to modern societies. Redistribution occurs as a result of equity, insurance and special interest. Equity justifies the redistribution of income from rich to poor in accordance with society's views on fairness. Insurance is a payment to people with particular adverse circumstances: unemployment, sickness and retirement. The political power of special groups may also enable them to obtain redistribution in their favour, which is the case with farmers in the EU. Redistribution takes place via a progressive tax system,[3] a progressive benefit system and the provision of public services that are subsidized or free of charge. Central governments also redistribute income among regions. Part of this is explicit through grants and transfer mechanisms, but most occurs via the operation of national taxation, social security systems and the provision of government services. Governments provide insurance against unemployment and sickness and pensions for the elderly, even though this can be purchased privately. However, market provision is unlikely to cover all eventualities (e.g. long-term unemployment) and many individuals, particularly those at greatest risk, would be unable to pay the necessary premiums. Thus the government provides social insurance partly as an allocative measure because of gaps in the market, but largely for redistributive reasons.[4]

The government's stabilization role is the use of monetary and fiscal policy to try to achieve the objectives of full employment, price stability, economic growth and balance of payments equilibrium. Today there is much less confidence in government's ability to stabilize the economy. Many governments have delegated authority over monetary policy to independent central banks, because it is believed that better decisions will result from technocrats, freed from short-term political considerations. Similarly, difficulties with the accurate timing and magnitude of discretionary fiscal policy have led governments to rely on automatic stabilization.

Although these arguments provide a clear justification for state intervention in the economy, its extent is subject to discretion, with the size of the public expenditure and the extent of public services varying widely among nation states. While part of this variation is due to differences in the level of development, much is the result of history, national values and institutions.

5.3   Fiscal federalism

Choices have to be made not only about the extent of the public sector but also the level of government at which the activity takes place. The traditional theory of fiscal federalism examines the factors that will determine the choice of the level of government that will undertake the various economic tasks of the state.[5] The theory assumes that each level of government cares exclusively about the welfare of its constituents. An efficient system of fiscal federalism would then balance the advantages and disadvantages of provision at various levels of government, and allocate competences accordingly.

The principal advantage of decentralization is that the lower the level of government, the easier it is to assess the preferences of local residents, so the provision of services can be better tailored to their requirements. The existence of different subnational units of government (regions) means levels of taxation and public services can be varied. The central government not only has informational problems but it also has a limited ability to differentiate policies across jurisdictions.[6] Democratic accountability is also best achieved with decentralized government, in which the correspondence between those who benefit from public expenditure and the taxpayers who fund it is most apparent.[7]

Centralized public services may offer benefits provided the preferences of citizens in different jurisdictions are similar. The policies of one region may have effects on other regions (spillovers), and the central government can take account of these interactions. When there are economies of scale, that is, when the cost per unit diminishes with the volume of the service produced, central government provision may be more efficient.[8] Centralization can be used to achieve uniformity in public provision, which may be regarded as important for equity and efficiency, for example, in health and education. There are also centralization advantages in relation to taxation. Generally, immobile tax bases should finance state/local government. Since mobility is potentially a problem with the major sources of taxation – personal income, corporate profits, social security and to an extent the taxation of consumption – state/local government financial autonomy is limited. Local variation in taxation is, however, possible provided differences in rates are not too great and where subnational jurisdictions are large. The ability to finance public services will, therefore, vary across jurisdictions. The national government can reduce these inequalities to acceptable levels. Redistribution is difficult to achieve at the local level because the rich would tend to migrate to low-tax jurisdictions (the poor might migrate to high-benefit-level localities).

If the assumption of a benevolent government is relaxed, then a government may also pursue its own ends, which will not always coincide with those of the society. Governments have considerable discretion because parliamentary oversight is imperfect and elections infrequent. If this is the case, decentralization may be advantageous because it increases the options available to citizens (moving to a different jurisdiction), promoting competition between jurisdictions and providing an additional mechanism for achieving efficiency in the provision of public services. This argument is particularly strong in relation to the EU because of the strength of national democracy and concerns over the EU democratic deficit.

The Commission has examined the implications of fiscal federalism for the EU on three occasions, all related to the Economic and Monetary Union (EMU).[9] These reports mark a gradual retreat from a significant public finance role for the EU. In a later assessment, the Commission[10] downgraded the importance of redistribution, emphasized decentralization and subsidiarity and suggested that a budget of 2 per cent of EU GDP was sufficient for the EMU.

The large gap between public finances in the EU and existing federations is indicated by a comparison between the EU and federal expenditure. Even in the leanest federation, Switzerland, federal government expenditure amounts to about 17 per cent of GDP compared with just 1 per cent in the EU. In Germany, the percentage is about 29 per cent, in Australia about 23 per cent and in the US about 20 per cent. The EU has significant responsibility in relation to only one area that is important to federal government expenditure: economic affairs (agricultural, industrial and regional policy, research and development [R&D]). In the other important areas of defence, education, health and social security, it has virtually no role. Interest payments do not arise for the EU. Since the EU cannot run deficits (see Section 5.5), it does not have debt to service.

These comparisons indicate that the EU is currently very far from even a decentralized federation like Switzerland. Given the crucial differences between the EU and other federations, the latter are unlikely to provide an appropriate template. The next section considers the characteristics of the EU that will affect its economic role and what that role should be.

5.4   The EU and fiscal federalism

The EU is not a nation state. It is made up of individual Member States, each with its own institutions, history, culture and languages. Thus the evolving EU constitution is very different from that of national federal states, and it is probable that the economic role and budget of the EU will remain distinct. One aspect of the EU distinctness is the difference in income levels between the Member States, which are important for the provision of public services, especially social security. The non-economic differences between the Member States present problems for common policies in other areas such as defence/security and education.

The dispersion of income levels is much wider in the EU than in the US, which makes it unlikely and undesirable that the EU could have a significant distributional role. It is unlikely because redistribution would involve taxpayers in one Member State supplementing the income of citizens of another Member State. Besides the questionable political acceptability, the practical difficulties are immense, for example, how much should differences in income be reduced?

Where does this leave the EU's current re-distributional role in the structural policies? The political stability of the EU in general and of the EMU in particular, is dependent upon a reasonable degree of cohesion in the EU. While this probably does not require equality of income levels,[11] what is needed is that the poorer countries are at least converging on the rich. Convergence in income levels is not automatic, and so some effective aid policy can be justified.[12]

There is no compelling externality or economies-of-scale argument for a significant EU involvement in health and education. With regard to defence, a more compelling case can be made for a larger EU role. Defence is the classic public good, and with war between the EU Member States increasingly unlikely, defence is against external threats to the EU as a whole, or is related to peace-keeping/making beyond the EU. There is public support for the development of an EU defence policy.[13] There are a number of obvious difficulties, such as the reluctance of governments to cede sovereignty over such a sensitive area, whether the public would be supportive of European armed forces, and the role of the EU neutral countries. Similarly, there are strong reasons for an important EU role in fighting organized crime and terrorism, for which there is again public support.

Beyond these areas,[14] the EU's economic role would seem to be confined to competences that are already part of its responsibilities, such as overseeing the SEM, operating competition policy and regulation more generally, and also R&D policy in which EU programmes are justified because there are potentially important economies of scale.[15] External action is really part of foreign policy and related increasingly to defence. The current EU role in agricultural policy is more questionable. There seems little reason for the EU to be paying direct agricultural subsidies, so agricultural expenditure could shrink, with the EU's role confined largely to regulation and trade policy. These arguments tend to suggest that there is a case for some limited expansion of the budget, if the EU were to acquire a significant defence role. It would, however, remain small – much smaller than that of existing federations. The conclusion must be that, at the present stage of development, a limited budget seems well suited to the EU requirements. The EU has still to ensure that the operation of this limited budget is fair and efficient. These are the issues to which this chapter now turns.

5.5   Budget rules and procedure

There are five basic principles derived from the treaties under which the EU budget operates:

1. *Annuality* – The budget is only for the one year, so expenditure has to be made in that year. This prevents the build-up of long-term commitments, but has caused some problems because much EU expenditure is now on multi-annual programmes. The practical resolution of this problem has been the use of commitments for future years, which strictly do not have to be honoured, but which in practice usually are.

2. *Balance* – Revenues must cover expenditure, and deficit financing is not possible. If expenditure is going to exceed revenue, additional resources have to be raised by supplementary or by amending budgets in the current year. Surpluses at the end of the year are carried over to the next year as revenue.[16] The EU is not allowed to borrow to finance its own expenditure, but can use its triple-A credit rating to borrow for loans.[17] Most of these loans take place via the European Investment Bank (EIB). These capital transactions are financially self-supporting and do not breach the principle of EU budgetary balance.
3. *Unity* – All expenditure is brought together in a single budget document.
4. *Universality* – All EU revenue and expenditure are to be included in the budget, and there are to be no self-cancelling items.
5. *Specification* – Expenditure is allocated to particular objectives to ensure that it is used for the purposes the budgetary authority intended. There is some possibility for transfers between categories for the effective execution of the budget.

These rules indicate the extent to which the Member States wanted to limit the EU competence in this sensitive area of government activity. So they ensure maximum control by the Member States and minimum discretion for the EU.

The budgetary procedure laid out in the 1971 Budget Treaty[18] contained the seeds of discord in decision-making. This treaty granted the EP the responsibility for the final approval of the budget,[19] a power the EP was determined to use. So in the early 1980s, the annual budgetary cycle was one of frequent disputes between the institutions. Two developments resolved this situation: first, the increased EP powers which commenced with the Single European Act (SEA, see Chapter 2) in 1987; second, new budgetary procedures introduced with the 1988 Delors I package. This contained two innovations that continue to this day: a multi-annual financial perspective (now, framework) and an inter-institutional agreement on budgetary procedure. The Treaty of Lisbon (TFEU) shifted these procedures from soft to hard law, so that the Council and the EP agree the budget in a co-decision-type procedure (the 'equal legislative procedure' described in Chapter 3) and the budget perspective has legal force.

The current financial framework 2014–20,[20] approved after two years of bitter negotiations, contains agreed ceilings on broad categories of expenditure (below) and for the budget overall. Actual levels of expenditure are set by the annual budget, which must be within the financial framework limits. This budget has to be accepted through the procedure laid down in the treaties: preliminary draft budget from the Commission, and co-decision, and if necessary conciliation, between the Council and the EP (Figure 5.1). With the broad parameters of the financial framework, the agreement of the annual budgets since 1998 has been straightforward. The decisions on the financial framework are, however, far more hard fought.

5.6   EU budget revenue

Tax systems should be fair, efficient and transparent. Fairness can only be evaluated on the basis of consistent principles to decide tax liability.[21] There are two dimensions of fairness or equity – horizontal equity and vertical equity. Horizontal equity – the identical treatment of people in equivalent positions – implies that those with the same level of income and similar circumstances should pay the same amount of tax. Vertical equity requires the consistent treatment of people in different circumstances. In general, equity is taken to imply a progressive tax system. Depending upon how the EU raises its revenues, this could apply to taxes on individuals, or it could apply to the Member States.

Efficiency requires that the tax system should minimize harmful market distortions. Low collection and compliance costs are important additional aspects of tax efficiency. Transparency requires that the tax system should be simple to understand, so that taxpayers are aware of their tax liability and how this is determined. This requirement of transparency is essential for democratic accountability. This section will consider the development of the EU revenue system and how it matches up to these requirements, but first a brief comparison will be made between the EU revenue system and those of federal governments.

The EU does not have a financing system like that of federal states. The amount of truly independent tax revenue is extremely low, and taxation remains predominantly under the control of the Member States. Federal governments typically raise a large part of their revenue from taxation of income directly through the personal income tax system (about 10 per cent of GDP in the US and Australia, and 5 per cent in Germany) or indirectly through the social security system (about 10 per cent in the US and 15 per cent in Germany). The corporation tax, VAT/general sales taxes and excises are other important sources of tax revenue for federal governments. None of these revenue sources are available to the EU.

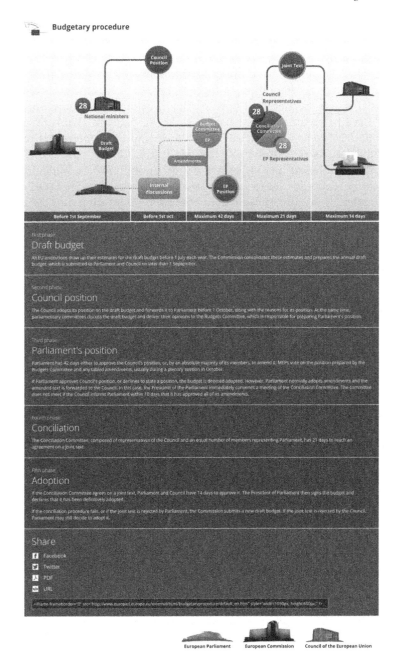

Figure 5.1 EU budgetary procedure, provided courtesy of the offices of the European Parliament in London

The EEC was initially financed like other international organizations by fixed national contributions, but the EEC Treaty provided for the development of a system of 'own resources'. The significance of this was that the EEC would have financial autonomy, by acquiring financial resources distinct from those of the Member States. This proved controversial, and it was not until April 1970, just before negotiations opened for the first enlargement, that agreement was reached. This provided for the EEC to be financed by duties on agricultural imports and sugar production, revenue from the Common Customs Tariff (CCT, the CETs of Chapter 1) and VAT up to 1 per cent of the harmonized base. Agricultural levies and customs duties, called traditional own resources (TOR) are naturally EU revenue because they arise from EU policies: the CAP and the Common Commercial Policy (CCP). In a common market, it is difficult to assign these revenues to individual Member States because goods imported through a Member State in which the duties are paid may then be sold in another in which the actual burden or incidence of the tax occurs. This is referred to as the 'Rotterdam problem', so called because Rotterdam is the port of entry for many goods that are then sold in other Member States, notably Germany. As the Member States have not used the harmonized base, the VAT contribution has always rested on 'artificial' calculation, so it amounts to being just a particular way of calculating a national contribution.

The original own resources system had a number of problems as a system of finance for the EEC. At first, revenue expanded as the call-up rate of VAT increased, but once the 1 per cent limit was reached, revenue grew comparatively slowly. The TOR revenue was constrained by falling agricultural imports as the EEC food self-sufficiency levels increased, decreasing tariff rates, expanding EEC membership to the EC and the extension of preferential trade agreements with third countries. The VAT base also grew slowly because it excluded government expenditure and savings, which tend to expand over time. It was regressive because these elements tend to increase with income. So the system was not equitable; contributions to the budget were not related to income per capita. The UK in particular seemed to be contributing more than its fair share, because of its high level of imports from outside the EU, and a relatively low level of government expenditure and savings.[22] Raising the VAT limit to 1.4 per cent in 1984[23] increased revenue, but this was only a temporary solution that did not address the problems of lack of buoyancy or of equity in contributions.

The own resources system was made more equitable and more buoyant by the introduction in 1988 of the fourth resource. The base for own resources is now expressed as a percentage of EU GNI, currently 1.24

per cent. The EU revenue now comes from the four own resources and miscellaneous revenue:

a. *Duties on agricultural imports and sugar production.* Agricultural duties are tariff revenue on imports of agricultural goods. Sugar levies are a tax on the production of sugar beyond quota limits.
b. *Common Customs Tariff* (CCT). The revenue from the EU taxes on non-agricultural imports, the importance of which has diminished due to the general lowering of tariffs and since 1999, when the share retained by national governments to cover the cost of collection rose from 10 to 25 per cent.[24]
c. *VAT* revenue of 0.3 per cent of VAT on the harmonized base. To make VAT fairer, the VAT base has since 1992 been capped at 50 per cent of GNI for member states whose per capita GDP is less than 90 per cent of the EU average.
d. *The GNI resource.* The revenue raised from TOR and VAT is subtracted from total EU expenditure and the difference is expressed as a percentage of EU15 GNI, with each Member State contributing an amount equal to this percentage of its GNI.[25] With the revenue from other sources diminishing as a percentage of GNI, this resource is becoming the dominant source of EU revenues, accounting for 73.4 per cent in 2013.

Table 5.1 provides the figures and percentages for EU revenues in 2013 (the data for 2014 will not be available until late in 2015), and Figure 5.2 shows the development of the revenues for 1958–2013.

This system of finance ensures that the EU revenue grows in line with GNI and is reasonably fair, because contributions are roughly proportional to GNI.[26] The exceptions are Belgium and the Netherlands (the Rotterdam problem) and the UK (due to its correction mechanism explained in full below). The increasing dependence on GNI-based contributions means that the EU has largely gone back to a system of national contributions.

Table 5.1   Sources of EU revenue, 2013

	€ million	%
Net Customs duties and agricultural levies	18,755	14.1
VAT resources	15,030	11.3
GNI resources	97,503	73.4
Miscellaneous revenues	1,549	1.2
Total	**132,837**	**100**

Source: Adapted from CEU (2013).

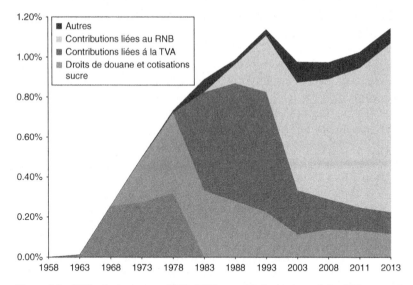

Figure 5.2   EU budget revenue 1958–2013, provided courtesy of the EU's general budget Directorate via offices of the EU in London

5.7   EU budget expenditure

The development of budgetary expenditure follows the development of the EU policies. For a long time the budget was dominated by agricultural expenditure (about three-quarters; Figure 5.3), partly because other policies were underdeveloped, but also because the CAP became expensive to operate. Until the late 1980s, agricultural expenditure grew rapidly, but it has since been stabilized because of CAP reform and limits being placed on agricultural expenditure. As enlargement increased the EU heterogeneity, it was felt necessary to introduce a greater redistributive element into the budget by expanding and concentrating expenditure on structural operations (cohesion). Part of this additional expenditure was financed by increased revenue, but the stabilization of agricultural expenditure freed resources for structural policies. Expenditure on research has increased as a result of concerns over EC competitiveness. The ending of the Cold War led to increased expenditure as the EU sought to bring stability to Central and Eastern Europe, initially with pre-accession expenditure and subsequently with expenditure on internal policies, as they became new member states.

The annual budget expenditure in 2014 amounted to €142.6 billion and comes under four main headings (see Figure 5.4). The first is 'smart

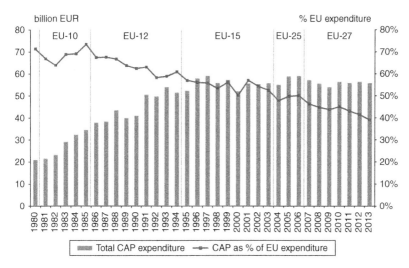

Figure 5.3 CAP expenditure in total EU expenditure, to be found at http://ec.europa.eu/agriculture/cap-post-2013/graphs/graph1_en.pdf

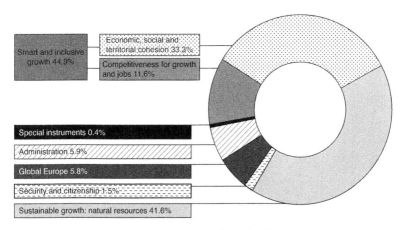

Figure 5.4 EU expenditure in 2014, to be found at http://europa.eu/about-eu/basic-information/money/expenditure/index_en.htm

and inclusive growth', claiming 44.9 per cent of total EU expenditure. This combines two elements: 'economic, social and territorial cohesion' (33.3 per cent) and 'competitiveness for growth and jobs' (11.6 per cent). The second is 'sustainable growth: natural resources', which claimed 41.6 per cent of total expenditure, the bulk of which supports

Table 5.2 Multiannual financial framework for the EU28, 2014–20

COMMITMENT APPROPRIATIONS	2014	2015	2016	2017	2018	2019	2020	Total
(1) Smart and inclusive growth	**60,283**	**61,725**	**62,771**	**64,238**	**65,528**	**67,214**	**69,004**	**450,763**
(1a) Competiveness for growth and jobs	15,605	16,321	16,726	17,693	18,490	19,700	21,079	125,614
(1b) Economic, social and territorial cohesion	44,678	45,404	46,045	46,545	47,038	47,514	47,925	325,149
(2) Sustainable growth: natural resources	**55,883**	**55,060**	**54,261**	**53,448**	**52,466**	**51,503**	**50,558**	**373,179**
of which: market related expenditure and direct payments	41,585	40,989	40,421	39,837	39,079	38,335	37,605	277,851
(3) Security and citizenship	**2,053**	**2,075**	**2,154**	**2,232**	**2,312**	**2,391**	**2,469**	**15,686**
(4) Global Europe	**7,854**	**8,083**	**8,281**	**8,375**	**8,553**	**8,764**	**8,794**	**58,704**
(5) Administration	**8,218**	**8,385**	**8,589**	**8,807**	**9,007**	**9,206**	**9,417**	**61,629**
of which: administrative expenditure of the institutions	6,649	6,791	6,955	7,110	7,278	7,425	7,590	49,798
(6) Compensations	27	0	0	0	0	0	0	27
TOTAL COMMITMENT APPROPRIATIONS	**134,318**	**135,328**	**136,056**	**137,100**	**137,866**	**139,078**	**140,242**	**959,988**
as percentage of GNI	1.03	1.02	1.00	1.00	0.99	0.98	0.98	1.00
TOTAL PAYMENT APPROPRIATIONS	**128,030**	**131,095**	**131,046**	**126,777**	**129,778**	**130,893**	**130,781**	**908,400**
as percentage of GNI	0.98	0.98	0.97	0.92	0.93	0.93	0.91	0.95
Margin available	0.25	0.25	0.26	0.31	0.30	0.30	0.32	0.28
Own resources ceiling as a percentage of GNI	1.23	1.23	1.23	1.23	1.23	1.23	1.23	1.23

Source: Figures obtained from the EU website.

the CAP and related areas. The third is 'global Europe', which covers such areas as enlargement and humanitarian aid, claiming 5.8 per cent. The fourth is 'administration', amounting to 5.9 per cent. Given that total expenditure is equal to 1.08 per cent of EU GNI and administration is only 5.9 per cent of total expenditure, one wonders about the basis for the accusations over a 'bloated' Brussels bureaucracy (see Chapter 3). Note that because these headings have changed over the years, it is not possible to have a figure for total EU budgetary expenditure equivalent to that for total revenue (Figure 5.1).

It should be added that the 2014–20 Multiannual Financial Framework sets similar annual amounts to those for 2013, with the total for the seven-year period amounting to €959,988 million, just short of the 'dreaded' €1 billion (see Table 5.2). However, the budget for 2014 represents a reduction of about 6 per cent relative to that of 2013, a true departure from ever-increasing budgets. The percentages for the five expenditure items are respectively: 39, 47, 2, 6 and 6. The 'commitments' ceiling amounts to 1 per cent of EU GNI compared to 1.12 per cent for the 2007–13 framework. The ceiling for 'payments' is to be 0.9 per cent of EU GNI compared to 1.06 per cent for 2007–13.

5.8   Operating budgetary balances

A Member State's operating budgetary balance (OBB) is the difference between the amount it contributes to the EU's own resource revenue and what it receives from allocated expenditure.[27] The Commission's position on OBBs has changed: it used to argue that national concerns with OBBs are mistaken, and that the budgetary costs and benefits are an inaccurate measure of the costs and benefits of EU membership.[28] While this is true, it is irrelevant. Whatever the overall costs and benefits of membership, the EU should be equitably financed. Another frequent observation is that the budget is too small to matter. However, the absolute amounts involved are very large: EU expenditure is greater than the GNI of the ten new Member States. Unlike national budgets, which are largely transfers from one group within the national economy to another, payments to the EU represent imports and reductions in GNI, and receipts from the EU represent exports and additions to GNI. The Commission now accepts that OBBs can be unfair and that there needs to be a correction mechanism.[29]

Although the percentages change every year, the 12 richest Member States, with GNI per head between 103 and 244 per cent of the EU average, have OBBs between 0.33 and −0.32 per cent of GNI. The budget thus has a rather haphazard impact: overall it is redistributive, but the relationship between OBBs and GNI is weak as is the budget's redistributive effect.

National governments are very well aware of their OBBs, and if they think they are being treated unfairly, it is understandable that they will demand that the situation be resolved. The most noted example of this is the British problem, a recurrent issue from 1973 when the UK joined the EEC until its resolution on the persistence of then-British prime minister Margaret Thatcher in 1984, unfortunately with a rebate (correction) specific to the UK. The rationale for the rebate was due to two main points. The first was that because a high percentage of the EU budget then was spent on support of the CAP (80 per cent, now about 41 per cent), when the UK had, and continues to have, a relatively small agricultural sector and imported much from outside the EEC, hence contributed much to the EU budgetary revenues through agricultural levies, thus it received very little EEC financial support. The second, and more vital, was that then the UK was the second poorest out of the then ten Member States.

The UK's correction for budgetary imbalances is calculated in a complicated way. In a current year, the correction is arrived at on the basis of the imbalance in the previous year. The imbalance is equal to the percentage share of the UK in VAT and GNI payments minus its share in total allocated expenditure. This is then multiplied first by total allocated expenditure and again by 0.66.[30] The correction is then financed by an increase in the own resource contributions by the other Member States, and not surprisingly they strongly resent this. Austria, Germany, the Netherlands and Sweden all have their contributions to make up for the rebate capped at 25 per cent of the amount that would otherwise apply.

Since 1984, the UK's position within the EU has changed substantially. Today, it is the eleventh-richest of twenty-eight, a point emphasized by the fact that the ten new Member States with very low levels of GNI per capita are contributing to the UK rebate. This development has led to increasing pressure from France and the poorer newer Member States for scrapping the rebate. Consequently, British prime minister Tony Blair in December 2005, agreed to concede 20 per cent of the rebate for the 2007–13 period provided three conditions regarding the funds involved are met: (a) they did not contribute to agricultural payments; (b) they were matched by contributions by the other Member States; and (c) they were only for the new Member States. Nevertheless, without the rebate, the UK would be the second-largest proportional net contributor to the EU budget.[31]

5.9   The EU budget and enlargement

When countries join the EU, they will make contributions to the budget and be recipients of EU expenditure. So enlargement involves negotiations among the existing Member States over the budgetary arrangements that will prevail after enlargement. These will have to take some account of the new Member States because after membership they will be involved in further budgetary negotiations.[32] The Original Six had relatively similar income levels, but enlargement has substantially increased the number and importance of relatively poor Member States. This was particularly the case in the 2004 and 2007 enlargements, which placed large potential demands upon the budget because of three characteristics of the countries involved: low income levels, the large total size of their populations and the importance of agriculture. Since contributions to the budget are roughly related to GNI, only a small amount would be added to EU revenues from own resources, but EU expenditure, with unchanged policies, would have risen significantly because of the demands on the structural and agricultural budgets. The EU15 Member States were unwilling to finance this by increasing contributions and against large reductions in their receipts from EU expenditures. So additional expenditure in the new Member States was limited and expenditure in other areas was to be tightly controlled.

The Brussels Agreement[33] finalized the financial arrangements for enlargement. It contained four principal elements. First, there was to be no extra expenditure for enlargement. Second, direct agricultural payments were to be extended to the new Member States. Third, the CAP guarantee expenditure from 2007 to 2013 was to be kept below that for 2006 plus 1 per cent per annum. Fourth, if forecast cash flow under the budget is less than in 2003 for any new Member State, compensation will be offered.

This was the starting point for the negotiations on the 2007–13 financial framework, which required unanimous agreement among the EU25 Member State. These negotiations needed to reconcile four contradictory demands: (a) additional 'enlargement expenditure'; (b) extra expenditure in new priority areas; (c), large net contributions to be reduced; and (d) unwillingness among the EU15 Member States to increase their net contributions or to reduce their net benefits. The only area of near unanimity was that the UK rebate should be reduced, a concession the UK was only prepared to make in conjunction with CAP reform. The Commission's initial proposals were for a modest expansion of expenditure:[34] 15 per cent in real terms over 2007–13 compared to

2006. Under the new categorization of expenditure by objective rather than by policy (above), the greatest absolute expenditure increase was in the sustainable growth, competitiveness (mainly R&D) and cohesion. Also expenditure on external action was to increase substantially. On the revenue side a generalized correction mechanism was proposed.[35]

The deal which was reached[36] followed the familiar pattern of expenditure restriction, limited reform, side payments, the postponement of difficult issues and the adjustment of the UK rebate. The overall growth of the budget was reduced substantially so that instead of the proposed 15.6 per cent increase, real expenditure on average for 2007–13 was to be only 2.7 per cent higher than in 2006. All categories of expenditure were to be reduced, with the largest cuts in competitiveness, citizenship, and the EU as a global partner. The two largest items of expenditure – agricultural market and cohesion expenditure – fare better, with only marginal cuts in agriculture. The cohesion budget was to grow significantly. There was a further marginal modification when agreement was reached on a limited budgetary response to the economic crisis with the European Economic Recovery Plan, which provided accelerated payments of €5 billion of expenditure on energy interconnections and rural broadband.[37]

The demands from Austria, Germany, the Netherlands and Sweden for reductions in their net contributions were partially met by the constraint in overall budgetary expenditure. They also benefited from reductions in the VAT contributions, and in the case of the Netherlands and Sweden, from reductions in their GNI contributions. The positions of the new Member States were enhanced by the concentration of structural funds on the poorer Member States and poorer regions. These provisions were partially financed by reductions in the UK rebate, which remained in full on all expenditure except that relating to the new Member States, where the UK's maximum extra contribution was to be €10.5 billion and from 2009 the UK would contribute fully to the non-CAP market expenditure, that is there would be no budgetary rebate on this category of expenditure.

5.10   Budgetary limitations

The multi-annual financial frameworks seem to have established a pattern of a low overall growth of expenditure based on the expansion of GNI. Indeed, the 2014–20 framework has reduced expenditure by 4 per cent, the first-ever reduction. This, together with gradual decline of spending on the CAP, permits the growth of expenditure on structural and other priority areas, within tight expenditure constraints, but funda-mental budgetary reform eludes the budget.

The budget faces the challenges of equity and the future development of the EU. The problem of equity is vital because Member States will block future developments with budgetary implications unless the EU financing and expenditure system is fair. Further CAP reform would help make the EU budget fairer and would release funds for the expansion of other policies. Structural operations can be justified as facilitating convergence and providing a visible EU response in problem regions. Generally, the concentration of funds should be enhanced, but all the Member States should continue to receive some structural funding; it would be undesirable to create subgroups of client and donor Member States within the EU. These changes would make the EU budget fairer, but with the EU likely to continue with a narrow range of financial resources and expenditure policies, equity in the EU budget can only be achieved by a generalized redistribution mechanism. This would ensure that net contributions were related to GNI per head in a consistent and equitable manner. Failure to resolve these issues means that the EU budget is still concentrating on dealing with past CAP and regional problems rather than developing the EU of the future, for example, laying more emphasis on R&D and environmental expenditure.

The role of federal budgets in a monetary union is considered in Chapter 6. The EU budget cannot have a significant role in fiscal policy because it is too small and it has to be balanced. The way in which the budget operates also makes it unsuitable for providing aid for regions badly affected by recessions; regional and cohesion expenditure only adjusts slowly to changing economic circumstances and is targeted on the poorest regions. So the budget does not currently fulfil the functions normally undertaken by federal budgets in monetary unions.

That the EU does not have a budget comparable to existing federations is both unarguable and unsurprising. It is unarguable because of the requirement of balance, its small size, the composition of expenditure and the fact that it is financed largely by national contributions, not its own taxes. It is unsurprising because the EU is very far from a political federation, made up as it is of nation states determined to preserve a significant degree of national sovereignty. Thus the expenditure and revenues of the EU tier of government will continue to develop slowly. The most important areas of federal government activity will remain national because there are few clear advantages and many problems in moving provision to the EU. This is not to suggest that there should be no further EU-level development of policies. The strongest arguments here relate to internal security and the CFSP. The likelihood is, therefore, that EU budgetary responsibilities will remain limited.

Recommended Reading

Oates, W. E. (ed.) (1977) *The Political Economy of Fiscal Federalism,* Lexington Books, Toronto.
—— (1999) 'An Essay in Fiscal Federalism', *Journal of Economic Literature*, 37 (3).
Commission of the European Union (annual), *EU Budget Financial Report.*

6

Economic and Monetary Union

6.1 Introduction

I now tackle the final question raised at the end of Chapter 1: what does the future hold for the EU's 'economic and monetary union' (EMU). The answer requires an understanding of what the EMU means, what problems it has been facing and the prospects for its future survival.

As mentioned in Chapter 1, and highlighted by the Eurozone ('euro area' in the EU jargon, but given that this book is addressed to the educated average person, I shall follow the popular usage) crisis, the EMU is by far the most challenging commitment for any scheme of economic integration. This chapter deals with it comprehensively in three steps. Section A provides a conceptual analysis of EMUs; Section B deals with the current and planned development of the EMU; and Section C appraises its operation. The chapter begins by explaining the differences between the 'monetary' and 'economic' facets of EMU.

6.2 Disentangling the concepts

The acronym EMU is often misinterpreted as *European* Monetary Union. This is understandable because the largest element of EMU (economic and monetary union) has been the setting up of the EU's monetary union, with the establishment of a single currency, the euro, and the European Central Bank (ECB). Indeed, the provisions of the treaty setting this up are heavily dominated by the monetary element of EMU.

However, in a unitary country or even a fairly federally weak one, economic *and* monetary integration involves having a countrywide fiscal policy as well as a single monetary policy. Arrangements vary as to how much of fiscal policy is handled at the country/federal level and how much at lower 'regional' levels. But the norm is for government expenditure and revenue at the federal level to dominate and for some limitations on what the 'regions' can do, even in very loose federations. The EU, however, has not attempted this level of integration. The centralized budget amounts to only around 1 per cent of EU GNI, which does not constitute a real macroeconomic policy instrument. It is a structural budget whose form is largely set for periods of seven years. It is thus both too small and too inflexible to be used in any sense to manage the path of the EU economy in either real or nominal terms.

The EU adopts a different approach, in constraining the ability of the members of its EMU (hereafter, 'Eurozone') to run independent fiscal policies. There are three types of constraints. The first is laid down in the Treaty on the European Union (TEU or Maastricht Treaty), as part of the conditions for Eurozone membership – the so-called 'Maastricht criteria'. These constraints, considered in detail in Section B, were designed to impose prudence on fiscal policy so that no one country's debt could start to raise the interest rates or lower the credit ratings of the other member countries. They relate to the ratio of debt to GDP to ensure long-run sustainability and to the ratio of the government deficit to GDP to exclude short-term pressures.

The second set of constraints operationalizing the membership requirements for the continuing behaviour of the Eurozone countries is the Stability and Growth Pact (SGP). To this, three innovations have been added since the 2008 financial crisis: the 6-pack, 2-pack and Stability, Coordination and Governance (TSCG). The coordination among the members takes place through the framework of ECOFIN (Council of the EU ministers of financial affairs), assisted by the Commission, and includes the ability to impose financial penalties on members that do not adhere to the prudent limits.

While the SGP coordinates fiscal policy to some extent through its constraints, the third aspect of policy among the Eurozone members is a more positive form of cooperation. This occurs through the annual setting of the Broad Economic Policy Guidelines (BEPGs). Here, there is not only discussion among the members to try to set a framework for policy consistent with the EU's longer-term objectives but also an informal dialogue between the fiscal and monetary authorities. Since 2012 this has been augmented by a much tighter set of constraints under the label of the 'European Semester' (section C).

The ability to levy taxation is one of the key elements of economic independence, and the EU Member States have only agreed fairly limited constraints on their individual behaviour. These relate to the nature of indirect taxation (VAT and specific duties), largely a facet of the treatment of trade and the Single European Market (SEM). It has been very difficult to get agreements on the nature of the taxation of income from capital and of company profits. Agreement on levels of taxation of personal incomes is even further from realization, as they range widely across the countries. It has, however, been possible to agree that reductions in the level of non-wage taxes on labour would assist the overall EU economic strategy.

Taken together, these measures represent limited coordination, which affects the nature of the conceptual discussion on monetary integration. Fiscal policy in the EU is neither a single coordinated policy nor a set of uncoordinated national policies run for the individual benefit of each Member State. Indeed the degree of automatic or discretionary coordination is difficult to estimate before the event. This makes the assessment of the impact of monetary integration somewhat uncertain.

6.3A   The conceptual analysis of monetary integration

6.3A.1   What is monetary integration?

Monetary integration has two essential components: an exchange rate union and capital market integration. An exchange rate union is established when members have what is in effect one currency. The actual existence of one currency is not necessary, however, because, if members have *permanently* and *irrevocably* fixed exchange rates among themselves with currencies exchangeable at par and at no cost, the result is effectively the same. But having a single currency makes the permanence and irrevocability more plausible as there would be severe repercussions from exit, not just the need to produce new coins and notes. Giving the impression of permanence is a crucial ingredient for a monetary union. Quasi-monetary unions, such as 'currency boards', which permit the continuation of the domestic currency but backed by another currency, tend to be less stable. This is because a currency board offers the abandoning of the backing currency as a way out of a crisis. In the same way, exchange-rate unions between more equal partners have tended to back the two currencies by a common medium, such as silver or gold, a link which can also be broken.

Exchange rate integration requires convertibility: the *permanent* absence of all exchange controls for both current and capital transactions, including interest and dividend payments (and the harmonization of relevant taxes and measures affecting the capital market) within the EMU. Complete convertibility for trade transactions is essential for free trade amongst the members, which is an integral part of economic union. Convertibility for capital transactions is related to free factor mobility, and is therefore an important aspect of capital market integration, which is necessary in 'common markets' (CMs; like the SEM), but not for CUs or free trade areas (FTAs). Nevertheless the patterns of both trade and production are affected by controls on capital transactions.

Monetary integration includes three elements: (a) a common monetary policy; (b) a common pool of foreign exchange reserves and a common exchange rate policy; and (c) a single central bank or monetary authority (MA) to operate these policies. If these elements are not included, monetary integration would be deemed a *pseudo* exchange rate union.[1]

There are important reasons for these elements. A country entering a fixed exchange rate system gives up monetary policy autonomy because such policy must be used to maintain the exchange rate. In a fixed peg system, the country to which the others peg has monetary autonomy, but the other countries have to adjust their monetary policy to maintain the fixed exchange rate. This monetary policy may not suit the economic circumstances of the other countries in the system.

One of the reasons for supporting the EMU was that a *common* monetary policy aimed at the average of the Eurozone as a whole might be more suitable for the other economies rather than the German monetary policy that had dominated the European Monetary System (EMS, Section B). Monetary policy conventionally targets inflation and controls interest rate to adjust economic activity to achieve the inflation target. To control interest rates, the MA must also control the money supply, which also implies control of foreign exchange reserves because of the interaction between foreign exchange operations and the money supply. The exchange rate hence becomes the MA's responsibility. So in a monetary union the single MA must take responsibility for four elements of monetary policy: interest rates, money supply, foreign exchange reserves and exchange rate. This has two further consequences. First, the rate of increase of the money supply must be decided jointly. Beyond an agreed amount of credit expansion, allocated to the central bank of each member nation, a member has to finance any budget deficit in the union's capital market at the ruling interest rate. This eliminates inflationary monetary financing. Second, the balance of payments of the entire union and hence the exchange rate with the outside world must be regulated at the union level, entailing a common pool of exchange reserves.

With a single currency the members can all have a say in the setting of policy. With a reference currency, the tendency will always be for the country whose currency it is to dominate the decision-making, as the others will have to follow or leave the arrangement. A tighter arrangement is likely to give them explicit rights in decision-making, perhaps even including a veto.

6.3A.2 The gains and losses from monetary integration

6.3A2.1 Gains from monetary integration

The gains from monetary integration could be purely economic, non-economic (e.g. political) or both. Some of the non-economic benefits are obvious. For example, it is difficult to imagine that a complete political union could become a reality without the establishment of a monetary union. However, because political, security and other issues are obvious, the discussion will be confined to the economic benefits, which can be briefly summarized as follows:

1. A common pool of foreign exchange reserves economizes their use, since it is unlikely that members will go into deficit *simultaneously*, so one country's surplus can offset another's deficit. Intra-union trade transactions will no longer be financed by foreign exchange, so the need for foreign exchange is reduced for any given trade pattern. Monetary integration may in itself lead to an increase in intra-trade at the expense of trade with non-members.[2]
2. The adoption of the euro has transformed that currency into a major world medium that competes with the US dollar and Japanese yen. The advantages of such a currency from seignorage[3] are well established, but not huge. Whether the euro will supplant much of the role that the US dollar has been as an international vehicle currency is a moot question.
3. Transactions costs incurred when one currency is exchanged for another are avoided within a monetary union, leading to a saving in the use of resources. The high costs individuals incur when making foreign exchange transactions would seem to suggest these costs are large. These gains are, however, thought to be small (the Commission estimated them in 1990 at 0.2–0.5 per cent of EU GDP).
4. Competition in the SEM is enhanced by the single currency because of the greater transparency and certainty it provides. Prices can be more easily compared across national borders, so competition is intensified. Differences in prices and costs between locations become more apparent, so production can shift to where costs are lowest.
5. There is normally a clear interest rate gain for the smaller and previously high-inflation countries, if the area as a whole has credible

institutions and policies. These countries will be able to borrow at lower interest rates because inflation expectations are reduced and because of the greater efficiency of deeper capital markets in monetary unions.

6. There are also advantages for free trade and factor movements. Stability of exchange rates enhances trade, through reduced price uncertainty, encourages capital to move to where it is most productively rewarded, and encourages labour to move to where the highest rewards prevail. While hedging can tackle the problem of exchange-rate fluctuations, it has a cost, but the evidence suggests that hedging costs and penalties from uncertainty are relatively minor, except for smaller companies that tend not to hedge. The much greater advantage is that it seems to cement integration, encouraging greater trade and foreign direct investment (FDI).

7. The integration of the capital market has a further advantage. If a member of a monetary union is in deficit, it can borrow directly on the union market using the capital inflow to finance the deficit, while adjustment takes place. Indeed, this help may occur automatically under the auspices of the common central bank

8. When a monetary union establishes a central fiscal authority with its own budget, then the larger the size of this budget, the higher would be the scope for fiscal equalization. Regional deviations from internal balance (the desired level of income and employment) can be financed from the centre. Centralized social security payments, financed by contributions or taxes on a progressive basis, would have stabilizing and compensating effects, modifying any harmful effects of monetary integration.

These benefits of monetary integration are unquestioned, but there is disagreement about their extent. Some give little weight to the psychological benefits of dealing with a single currency. However, there is no consensus with regard to the costs.

6.3A2.2   *Losses from monetary integration*

The losses from monetary integration have been elaborated in terms of the theory of optimum currency areas (OCAs).[4] The OCA message is simple:[5] two countries gain from having a single currency when the benefits of the elimination of exchange rate risks and enhanced price transparency outweigh the costs of adjusting to country-specific (asymmetric) shocks due to loss of control over their own interest and exchange rates. *OCA is not about the overall costs and benefits of monetary*

integration; it is a cost-benefit analysis of the impact of monetary integration.
The theory sets out the conditions that would limit the costs:

1. price/wage flexibility, which would enable markets to clear fully, thus offsetting the need for the lost policy instruments;
2. labour/capital mobility, which would compensate for the adjustments that the lost policy instruments would achieve;
3. financial market integration, which would cater for inter-area payments imbalances and enhance long-term adjustment through wealth effects;
4. open economies, meaning members have high export/income ratios and trade mainly with each other, thus benefitting from fixed exchange rates between them;
5. production spread across a variety of goods and services, which would insulate against fluctuations in the demand for individual commodities, dispensing with the necessity for frequent changes in the terms of trade (prices of exports over prices of imports) by way of exchange rate changes;
6. similarity of production structures, which ensures similar shocks, eliminating the need for individually tailored policies;
7. similarity of inflation rates, which would minimize payment imbalances; and
8. a considerable degree of fiscal integration, which would make it easier to eliminate divergent shocks through fiscal transfers.

It is not necessary to have all eight criteria for an area to be a net benefit, because an acceptable performance in one criterion may compensate for a poorer performance on another. For example, a high degree of labour mobility would reduce the need for a high degree of wage flexibility.

The extent of the loss caused by membership of a monetary union is determined by combined criteria,[6] which render price adjustments through exchange rate changes less effective or less compelling: (a) openness to mutual trade; (b) diverse economies; and (c) mobility of factors of production, especially of labour.

Greater openness to mutual trade implies that most prices would be determined at the union level, which means that relative prices would be less susceptible to being influenced by changes in the exchange rate. An economy more diverse in terms of production would be less likely to suffer from country-specific shocks, reducing the need for the exchange rate as a policy tool. Greater factor mobility enables the economy to tackle *asymmetric shocks* via migration, hence reducing the need for adjustment through the exchange rate.

The EU nations score well on the first criterion (a) since the ratio of their exports to their GDP is 20 per cent to 70 per cent. They also score well in terms of the second criterion (b), even though they are not all as well endowed with oil or gas resources as the Netherlands and the UK. As to the third criterion (c), they score badly. Labour mobility in the EU is low due to, inter alia, the Europeans' tendency to stick to their place of birth, not only nationally but also regionally. There is also a tendency for migration to be temporary and only involve part of a larger family. It is only in the last decade that there have been noticeable movements from the new Member States to some of the older Member States.

Although there is no definitive estimate of the costs due to the relative lack of labour mobility, it is generally thought to be considerable. However, it would have to be very large to offset the gains from monetary integration. In any case, much of the problem from lack of mobility is as relevant among the members as between them. It therefore requires addressing through structural policy in each member regardless of monetary integration, or regardless of membership of the EU itself for that matter. Tackling the problem has become more important since the late 1960s and will remain so in the face of faster rates of technical change in products and production methods. In part, it is a consequence of globalization, so it is a change that will have to be made in any case.

The benefits from a single currency tend to rise with integration, since, for example, intra-EU trade, which has been rising with integration over time (as Figure 6.1 shows, the percentage share of total exports for the Original Six going to each other rose from 46.1, 25.1, 29.2, 24.9, 41.6 in 1957 for respectively Belgium [Luxembourg's data was originally included in Belgium's], France, Germany, Italy and the Netherlands to 75.9, 61.8, 62.8, 57.1 and 77.1 in 2009, just before the 2008 global financial crisis started to impact on the data. Figure 6.2 provides the shares of imports, which reveal a similar trend[7]) will be conducted at lesser cost, while the losses from ceding the exchange rate as a policy variable decline with time. Changes in the exchange rate are needed to absorb asymmetric shocks, but these shocks will become less asymmetric as integration deepens. Thus, for countries seriously and permanently involved in monetary integration, sooner or later a time should arrive when the benefits will exceed the costs. The OCA ideas are really about 'feasibility', rather than 'optimality'.[8] And although methods were developed for identifying the suitability of various EU nations for monetary integration,[9] such methods only succeed in ranking suitability rather

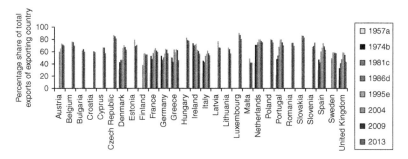

Figure 6.1   Share of trade with EU countries: exports

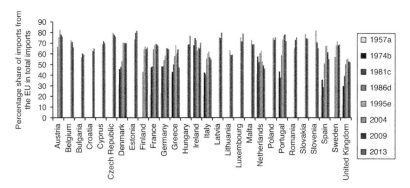

Figure 6.2   Share of trade with EU countries: imports

than calculating actual costs/benefits, which would indicate where the line separating included from excluded countries should be.[10] In any case, the conditions, such as the necessary market flexibility, can also be created *after* the event; hence, they are *endogenous*, that is, dependent on the process itself.[11]

In many respects, the key policy choice issue relates to uncertainty about the future. If a prospective member of a monetary union could be certain that the economies would grow more closely together, in the sense of becoming more economically similar (symmetrical in the economics jargon), and that there was the chance of having a serious external shock that affected only one of them or both in opposite directions, worries about a single monetary policy being inappropriate would be reduced. However, a priori, such developments can only be assessed; they cannot be known. Take the case of Finland, for example. One of the factors swaying the authorities in favour of membership in the EU's EMU was that it would force generally favourable changes in labour market behaviour.[12] In other words, knowing that the exchange rate mechanism is not available to accommodate asymmetric shocks may actually cause people to change their behaviour so that the impact of the shocks is reduced to acceptable levels.

Furthermore, there is a tendency to ignore positive asymmetric shocks. In such cases the impact of the favourable shock will be magnified by membership of a monetary union. Out of the union, such a shock would increase the demand for the currency as investors from other countries sought to join in the benefits. The surge in demand would probably push the domestic central bank into raising interest rates to head off any inflationary pressure, thereby also raising the exchange rate and reducing the expected rate of growth. Inside the EMU, the capital inflow will have a much more limited impact on the exchange rate as it relates only to a part of the union. Similarly the response of monetary policy will be negligible. Knowing that there will be no offsetting policy changes will in turn help keep down inflationary pressures. Such an experience seems to have occurred with the favourable technology shock or 'Nokia phenomenon' in Finland. The growth/inflation combination that occurred in the early EMU years was considerably more favourable than that which prevailed in earlier decades. Other factors, such as the continuing impact of the collapse of the former Soviet Union and the banking crisis in the early 1990s, may also have been influential but the evidence is at the very least suggestive. Nevertheless the higher inflation in the more rapidly growing Member States in the period since the Eurozone was formed resulted in serious competitiveness problems by the time of the GFC.

However, what has been clearly illustrated by the Eurozone in recent years is the consequence of not moving towards labour and product market flexibility as rapidly as had been hoped. Under these circumstances, countries can move to greater imbalances with respect to each other because the exchange rate and monetary policy correction mechanisms are no longer available.

6.3A.3   Fiscal policy in monetary unions

OCA theory deals purely with structure, but the role of fiscal policy in monetary unions is an essential component of their relative success. Durable EMUs are characterized by large central budgets that facilitate fiscal policy and transfers between regions. Fiscal policy is not just the manipulation of the balance between government expenditure and revenue so as to influence the aggregate demand in the economy, but it can also target aspects of the economic system that are not functioning efficiently. This has three elements in the EMU: the overall fiscal situation, interactions and transfers between members. Macroeconomic policy is more effective if monetary and fiscal policies are coordinated. This was apparent in the recent recession, starting in 2007, in which a loose monetary policy needed to be augmented by a fiscal stimulus. However, without coordination there is no guarantee that the fiscal policies of individual members responding to their individual macroeconomic situation will provide the suitable overall fiscal stance, particularly if some countries do not have the resources to cope with their own problems adequately.

Interactions between members can occur in two ways, first the potential effect of national fiscal policy on the EMU's monetary policy and second absorption. If national fiscal policy of some EMU members is too loose, then this could lead the MA to raise interest rates at the expense of the more prudent members.

The issue of absorption is more complex. A country's current account balance (CA) is equal to national income (output) minus absorption: the national use of goods and services in consumption, government expenditure and investment. Thus the CA is equal to net private saving plus the government fiscal balance (government revenue minus government expenditure).[13] So the national fiscal stance affects other countries in the EMU via their balance of payments. For example, Germany's high level of private saving more than offsets the modest fiscal deficits, and the country has a large surplus on CA. With most EMU trade being internal, the counterpart of this large surplus is deficits in other Eurozone members. So there is an important interaction between national fiscal positions, CA and national macroeconomic situations. In an EMU with a large central budget, the effects of these regional imbalances would be at least partially offset by fiscal transfers between regions.

With automatic transfers from the central or federal budget, fiscal policy acts as a means of interregional risk sharing by transferring resources between regions. On the whole, these transfers do not take the form of equalization payments; rather, they are simply the consequence of having fiscal systems that redistribute from the advantaged to the disadvantaged, often without regard to location. Such transfers perform three types of function: intertemporal stabilization, interregional insurance and interregional redistribution. The first two stabilize regional incomes, and the third reduces inequalities in income levels between regions. Intertemporal stabilization makes smoother the fluctuations in regional income levels due to the stabilization of the national economy by movements in the national public sector deficits: increasing the deficit when the economy turns down and moving towards surplus when it picks up. Interregional insurance transfers tax revenue from fast-growing regions to slow-growing ones when economic cycles are imperfectly correlated between regions. Interregional redistribution involves the transfer of resources from more to less prosperous regions, so it is related to levels of rather than changes in income.

These three functions relate to three problems regions face in the EMU: asymmetric shocks, competitiveness and differences in regional income. Differences in regional income levels relate to long-term economic growth, not stabilization. They have turned out to be very important in the Eurozone as rapid increases in income by the lower income countries as they converge has led to higher inflation there and to increasing CA imbalance. Asymmetric shocks and competitiveness relate to stabilization, so are an EMU issue. Regions within the EMU that face an adverse asymmetric shock have this partially offset by higher receipts from and lower payments to the federal budget, but how important is this stabilization? Initial research[14] indicated that interregional flows of public finance were important in reducing fluctuations in regional income, but more recent research suggests that federal taxes and transfers only reduce regional income fluctuations by 10 per cent in the US.[15] The national economies[16] of the Eurozone remain diversified so their vulnerability to asymmetric shocks and, consequently, the need for interregional stabilization is less than in the US. The greater separation of the EU Member States may also enhance the potential for differences in rates of wage and price inflation: an effective alternative adjustment mechanism (above). By comparison with the US, European national economies lack adjustment mechanisms such as labour mobility and cross-border capital holdings and flows. Moreover, the recent 2007 recession indicates that the vulnerability of national economies, to even symmetric shock, can vary substantially.

By contrast, competitiveness issues loom much larger for a monetary union since the separation of national economies makes wider divergences in wage/price inflation possible. The ability to reduce these divergences may also be more difficult if they are related to structural features of the economy. In the absence of changes in the exchange rate, the adjustment of competitiveness is a long and painful process, with lower growth and higher unemployment being needed to bear down on inflation. If these are insufficient to adjust competitiveness, then the EMU could find itself with nations having persistently high unemployment and lower income levels, in the same way that nation states have such regions, for example the Mezzogiorno in Italy. This indicates that the EMU may require fiscal transfers from prosperous to problem nations.

Government deficits lead to government debt, which is an issue for EMUs. National governments can adopt a relatively relaxed attitude to their debt, because the debt in developed countries is predominantly held by national citizens and institutions, and in the worst case, the debt could be repaid by expanding the domestic money supply.[17] Membership of the EMU changes the nature of government debt: foreign financing of debt within the EMU may increase because it is denominated in the same currency. With the money supply controlled by the ECB, national governments can no longer service their debts by creating money. Therefore, the EMU encourages looser fiscal policy, but makes its debt consequences more serious. A nation with high government debt in the EMU would have to increase taxes and reduce government expenditure. This would reduce national income, making servicing the debt more difficult. The hope would be that this deflation would restore price competitiveness and expand demand in the private sector, but this is a slow and uncertain process. This is of course a description of the current dilemma of Greece. It follows that it is important that countries enter EMUs with manageable government debt and that there are mechanisms to prevent the excessive accumulation of debt.[18]

A successful EMU either requires a significant central budget or very tight controls on national governments budget and limits on debt, facets the Eurozone has not had in the past.

6.3A.4   Important aspects of EMU

This section emphasizes three facets of the EMU. The first is that the development of the EMU has to be seen in the light of both the longer term and the wider political context. Narrow short-run economic assessments can make the decisions that have been taken look illogical. The second is that the EMU is expected to change the behaviour and structure of the European economy. Assessment of the likely impact therefore has to include these structural changes. Many traditional models that have been used to assess the impact of integration either do not take this into account adequately or have sometimes been used in ways that ignore these essential structural components of the process of change. And the third is that, while the focus on the monetary aspect of the EMU is understandable, it is the 'economic' 'E' in EMU that is both the more complex issue and the key to the ultimate success of the enterprise.

Hence Sections B and C appraise both the development of the EU's EMU over the last 40 years, and the way in which it is currently operating and will, in light of these three observations.

6.3B   The development of the EU's EMU

The aim of achieving EMU, although enshrined in the TEU, hence in the Treaty of Lisbon, is not a new phenomenon for the EU. This section provides a historical review of the route the EU has taken. The route followed has been a combination of seeking the economic benefits from increasing integration, paving the way for what some hoped to be the political unity of Europe, and the more immediate economic needs and shocks along that path. Nevertheless, the initial ideas, sketched out as early as 1970, bear striking similarities to what has eventually been accomplished.

The section begins by considering the first attempt at the EMU, based on the 1971 Werner Report, which committed the then-EC Member States to achieving it in three stages, beginning in 1971 and finishing in 1980. After examining the reasons for its failure, the section goes on to tackle the 1979 EMS, a limited arrangement aimed at dealing with the monetary upheavals of the time by creating a zone of monetary stability. It then turns to the revival of the EMU in the two Delors reports, which culminated in its formal adoption in the 1992 TEU, again to be achieved in three stages beginning in 1990 and finishing in 1997 or 1999 at the very latest. It then looks into how it has progressed and why some Member States remain outside the Eurozone.

6.3B.1   The Werner Report

From 1967, the prevailing world order for exchange rates, established as part of the Bretton Woods agreement in 1944, began to fall apart. Until that point the system of having exchange rates that were 'fixed' but adjustable occasionally, when the existing rate was shown to be unsustainable, had worked rather well. Fixity permitted fluctuations within 1 per cent of a peg with the US dollar, which in turn was convertible for gold at $35 per ounce. Despite some initial repositioning after the war, the number of occasions on which the pegs had been changed meant that the system had seemed credible. The contrast with problems after the First World War, with hyperinflation in Germany and then the deflationary impact of trying to return to the gold standard, was striking. However, while the early problems lay with other countries' trying to stabilize themselves with respect to the US, the problem in the 1960s was that the US, hindered by the cost of the Vietnam war, was no longer able to act as the anchor for the international system.

Other countries therefore had to look elsewhere for stability. While the main initial thrust was towards a reform of the Bretton Woods system, the EC looked at the possibility of trying to create a locally stable system with the same sort of architecture for itself. In 1969, during The Hague summit, the original six Member States (the Six) decided that the EC should progressively transform itself into an EMU, and set up a committee, led by Pierre Werner, then prime minister of Luxembourg, to consider the issues involved. The Werner Committee presented an interim report in June 1970 and a final report in October of the same year. The latter became generally known as the 'Werner Report', and was endorsed by the Council in February 1971.

According to the Council resolution,[19] the EC would

1. constitute a zone in which persons, goods, services and capital would move freely, but without distorting competition, or creating structural and regional imbalances.[20]
2. form a single monetary entity within the international monetary system, characterized by the total and irreversible convertibility of currencies; the elimination of fluctuation margins of exchange rates between members; the irrevocable fixing of their parity relationships. These steps would be essential for the creation of a single currency, and would involve a Community-level organization of central banks.
3. hold the powers and responsibilities in the economic and monetary field that would enable its institutions to ensure the administration of the economic union. To this end, the necessary economic policy decisions would be taken at the EC level and the necessary powers would be attributed to community institutions.

The EC organization of central banks would assist, in the framework of its own responsibilities, in achieving the objectives of stability and growth in the EC.

As progress was made in moving closer to the final objectives, EC instruments would be created whenever they seemed necessary to replace or complement the action of national instruments. All actions would be interdependent. In particular, the development of monetary unification would be backed by parallel progress in the convergence, and then the unification of economic policies.

The Council decided that the EMU could be attained during that decade, if the plan had the permanent political support of the governments of the Member States. Implementation was envisaged in three stages, with the first beginning in 1971 and the third completed by 1980. The Council made quite clear how it envisaged the process leading to full EMU (emphasis added):

a. The first phase should begin on January 1, 1971, and could technically be completed within three years. This phase would be used to make [the EC] instruments more operational and to mark the beginnings of [the EC's] individuality within the international monetary system;
b. The first phase should not be considered as an objective in itself; it should be associated with the complete process of economic and monetary integration. *It should therefore be launched with the determination to arrive at the final goal;*
c. In the first phase, consultation procedures should be strengthened; the budgetary policies of [the Member States] should accord with [the EC] objectives; some taxes should be harmonized; monetary and credit policies should be coordinated; and integration of financial markets should be intensified.

The EMU launched by the EC in 1971 was thus consistent with the requirements for a full EMU discussed in the Section A. While the problems of integrating product markets may not have been clear then, the intention to have the free flow of capital and labour rather than just free trade and ordered payments is set out, foreshadowing later developments.

Although the 1971 venture failed, after an earlier than expected successful negotiation of the first phase and making some progress during the second, the failure was not due to lack of commitment, determination or both. The Nixon Shock, the first oil shock and the enlargement shock (the admission of three new members, Denmark, Ireland and the UK, each bringing with it its own unique problems) were the real culprits. The first step in coordinated monetary management had been that the EC Member States would keep all their bilateral exchange rates within 2.25 per cent of each other. Their joint rates would therefore move quite closely together in a 'snake' around the US dollar, which was still treated as the numeraire of the system, and since the rate itself fluctuated, this led to the term 'snake in the tunnel'. (The Smithsonian Agreement that was in force at the time limited each currency's fluctuation with respect to the US dollar to 2.25 per cent. Thus without the 'snake', the EC currencies could have moved up to 4.5 per cent from each other. Price changes of that magnitude would be difficult to absorb and hence would have violated the degree of stability required within the EC.) Not only were the lira, sterling and the French franc unable to hold their parity within the first year or so but the Smithsonian Agreement itself had collapsed into generalized floating by 1973.

6.3B.2   The EMS

The EMS was the next step towards the EMU, but it was devised to counter the monetary upheavals of the 1970s by creating a 'zone of monetary stability'. The route to the EMS was a fairly short one. The idea was floated not by the Commission, but by the German chancellor, Helmut Schmidt, and the French president, Valéry Giscard d'Estaing, and was discussed in the Council in Copenhagen in April 1978. Roy Jenkins, Commission president, had called for such a corrective initiative in a speech in Florence the previous October. By 5 December the Council had adopted the idea, in the form of a resolution 'on the establishment of [EMS] and related matters', after a period of intensive discussion.

The EMS, which started operating in March 1979, was introduced with the immediate support of six of the EC Member States at the time. Ireland, Italy and the UK adopted a wait-and-see attitude. Ireland and Italy needed 'time for reflection', which required a broader band of permitted fluctuation of ±6 per cent when they did enter, and the UK expressed a definite reservation. Later, Ireland and Italy joined the system, while the UK expressed a 'spirit of sympathetic cooperation'.

The main features of the EMS, given in the annex to the conclusions of the EC presidency;[21] are set out in Box 6.1.

In essence, the EMS is concerned with the creation of an EC currency zone within which there is discipline for managing exchange rates. This discipline is known as the 'exchange rate mechanism' (ERM), which asks a member nation to intervene to reverse a trend when 75 per cent of the allowed exchange rate variation of ±2.25 per cent is reached. This is similar to what happened within the preceding 'snake' arrangements. The crucial differences were, however, twofold. First was the creation of the ECU as the centre of the system against which divergence of the exchange rate was to be measured. The ECU followed on directly from the European Unit of Account as a basket of *all* EC currencies, not just those participating in the ERM (1ECU = 1EUA). Weights in the basket, based on economic importance in the system, were revised every five years.[22] The ECU was the means of settlement between the EC central banks. Second, the EMS was to be supported by a European Monetary Fund (EMF), which, within two years, was to absorb the short-term

---

Box 6.1   Provisions of the EMS (OJC, 1971)

(1) the EMS ... will be at least as strict as the 'snake'. In the initial stages ... member countries currently not participating in the 'snake' may opt for somewhat wider margins around central rates. In principle, intervention will be in the currencies of participating countries. Changes in central rates will be subject to mutual consent. Non-member countries ... may become associate members of the system. The European Currency Unit (ECU) will be at the centre of the system; ... it will be used as a means of settlement between EEC monetary authorities.

(2) An initial supply of ECUs (for use among [the EC] central banks) will be created against deposit of US dollars and gold on the one hand ... and member currencies on the other hand in an amount of a comparable order of magnitude.

(3) Participating countries will coordinate their exchange rates policies *vis-à-vis* third countries. To this end, they will intensify the consultations in the appropriate bodies and between central banks participating in the scheme. Ways to coordinate dollar interventions should be sought which avoid simultaneous reserve interventions. Central banks buying dollars will deposit a fraction (say 20 per cent) and receive ECUs in return; likewise, central banks selling dollars will receive a fraction (say 20 per cent) against ECUs.

(4) Not later than two years after the start of the scheme, the existing arrangements and institutions will be consolidated in a European Monetary Fund.

(5) A system of closer monetary cooperation will only be successful if participating countries pursue policies conducive to greater stability at home and abroad; this applies to deficit and surplus countries alike.

---

financing arrangements operating within the snake, the short-term monetary support agreement that was managed by the European Monetary Cooperation Fund (EMCF), and the medium-term loan facilities for balance-of-payments assistance. The EMF was to be backed by approximately 20 per cent of national gold and US$ reserves and by a similar percentage in national currencies. The EMF was to issue ECUs to be used as new reserve assets, and an exchange-stabilization fund able to issue about US$50 billion was to be created.

It is clear from the above that the EMS asks neither for permanently and irrevocably fixed exchange rates between the member nations, nor for complete capital convertibility. Moreover, it does not mention the creation of a common central bank to be put in charge of the member nations' foreign exchange reserves and to be vested with the appropriate powers. Hence the EMS is not an EMU, although it could be seen as paving the way for one.

6.3B.3   The success of the EMS

The survival of the EMS belied the early scepticism, and there is little dispute that the EMS was something of a success. There was, however, a period from 1992 onwards when it looked as if the EMS might collapse altogether, just at the time that the final push to EMU was being agreed upon (see below). This success can be seen as embodied in three principal achievements.

First, despite occasional realignments and fluctuations of currencies within their pre-set bands, it seems that the EMS succeeded in its proximate objective of stabilizing exchange rates, not in the absolute sense, but in bringing about more stability than would have been enjoyed without it. Moreover, up to 1992, this was done without provoking periodic speculative crises of the Bretton Woods system. This stability had two elements. Not only did the number of realignments in the central rates fall (with one minor exception there were none in the five years following 1987) but also the variation of exchange rates between the ERM countries fell much faster than that of those outside, even in the early period up to 1985.[23] Just having scope for realignments meant that, unlike the 'snake', a parity change did not entail a confidence-shaking exit from the system.

Second, the claim is made for the EMS that it provided a framework within which member countries were able to pursue counter-inflationary policies at a lesser cost in terms of unemployment and lost output than would have been possible otherwise. The basis of the claim is that the structure of the EMS began to attach a measure of 'reputation' to countries that managed to avoid inflation and hence the depreciation of their exchange rates. This element of loss of reputation through 'failure' may have reduced the expectation of inflation and hence made counter-inflationary policy less 'costly'. However, estimates of the change in the 'sacrifice ratio' (ratio of the rise in unemployment to the fall in inflation in a period) do not indicate any improvements compared to countries outside the ERM (which were also successful in lowering inflation), although, as generally expected, the sacrifice ratios did rise as inflation fell.

Third, while it is claimed that nominal exchange rate stability was secured, it is also argued that the operation of the EMS prevented drastic changes in *real* exchange rates (or 'competitiveness'). This is contrasted with the damaging experience in this respect of both the UK and US over the same period. However, in one sense, it may merely have encouraged countries to put off necessary realignments, leading ultimately to the drastic changes and crisis in 1992/3.

Finally, while it was not an immediate objective of the EMS as such, the ECU became established as a significant currency of denomination for bond issues, which is testimony to the credibility of the EMS and the successful projection of its identity. In part, the use of the ECU in international bond issues may have reflected its role as a hedge by being a currency 'cocktail'. It also provided a means of getting around some of the currency restrictions in force, particularly in France and Italy. The high point for new ECU issues was 1991, and external issues never recovered after the 1992/3 crisis.

However, these achievements were not unqualified. For example, the 'divergence indicator' mechanism for triggering intervention before the limits of the band was reached did not withstand the test of time.

The enforced changes to parities in and after September 1992 considerably reduced the EMS' credibility and called into question the validity of the idea of approaching monetary union through increasingly fixed exchange rates while having no controls over capital flows. Although the widening of the bands to ±15 per cent in August 1993 appeared to remove much of the effective distinction between the ERM and freely floating exchange rates, the practice was a very considerable convergence and a system which took only limited advantage of the flexibility available.

6.3B.4　The Delors Report and the Maastricht Treaty

By 1987 the EMS, and the ERM within it, appeared to have achieved considerable success in stabilizing exchange rates. This coincided with legislative progress towards the EMU on other fronts. The EC summit held in Hanover on 27 and 28 June 1988 decided that, in adopting the Single European Act (SEA), the EC Member States had confirmed the objective of 'progressive realisation of economic and monetary union'. The heads of state agreed to discuss the means of achieving this in their meeting in Madrid in June of the following year, and to help them in their deliberations, they entrusted to a committee chaired by Jacques Delors, then Commission president, and composed of the central bank governors and two other experts, the 'task of studying and proposing concrete stages leading towards this union'. The committee reported just before the Madrid summit and its report is referred to as the Delors Report on EMU.

The committee concluded that the creation of the EMU must be seen as a single process, but that this process should be in stages, which progressively led to the ultimate goal. Thus the decision to enter upon the first stage should commit a Member State to the entire process. Emphasizing that the creation of EMU would necessitate a common monetary policy and require a high degree of compatibility of economic policies and consistency in a number of other policy areas, particularly in the fiscal field, the report pointed out that their implementation would require changes in the Treaty of Rome and consequent changes in national legislation.

According to the report, the first stage should be concerned with initiating the process of creating the EMU. During this stage there would be a greater convergence of economic performance through the strengthening of economic and monetary policy coordination within the existing institutional framework. The economic measures would be concerned with the completion of the SEM and the reduction of existing disparities through programmes of budgetary consolidation in the Member States involved and more effective structural and regional policies. In the monetary field, the emphasis would be on the removal of all obstacles to financial integration and on the intensification of cooperation and coordination of monetary policies. Realignment of exchange rates was seen to be possible, but efforts would be made by every Member State to ensure the functioning of other adjustment mechanisms was more effective. The committee was of the opinion that it would be important to include all the EC currencies in the EMS' ERM during this stage. The 1974 Council decision defining the mandate of central bank governors would be replaced by a new decision indicating that the Committee of Central Bank Governors itself should formulate opinions on the overall orientation of monetary and exchange rate policy.

In the second stage, which would commence only when the Treaty had been amended, the basic EMU organs and structure would be set up. The committee stressed that this stage should be seen as a transition period leading to the final stage; thus, it should constitute a 'training process leading to collective decision-making', but the ultimate responsibility for policy decisions would remain with national authorities during this stage. The procedure established during the first stage would be further strengthened and extended on the basis of the amended Treaty, and policy guidelines would be adopted on a majority basis. Given this understanding, the EC would

a. establish a medium-term framework for key economic objectives aimed at achieving stable growth, with a follow-up procedure for monitoring performances and intervening when significant deviations occurred;

b. set precise, although not yet binding, rules relating to the size of annual budget deficits and their financing; and

c. assume a more active role as a single entity in the discussions of questions arising in the economic and exchange rate field.

In the monetary field, the most significant feature of this stage would be the establishment of the European System of Central Banks (ESCB) to absorb the previous institutional monetary arrangements. It was envisaged that the formulation and implementation of a common monetary policy would take place in the final stage, during which exchange rate realignments would not be allowed, barring exceptional circumstances.

The second stage would require inter alia (a) national monetary policy being executed in accordance with the general monetary orientations set up for the EC as a whole; (b) a certain amount of foreign exchange reserves being pooled and used to conduct interventions in accordance with the guidelines established by the ESCB; and (c) the ESCB having to regulate the monetary and banking system to achieve a minimum harmonization of the provisions necessary for the future conduct of a common monetary policy.

The final stage would begin with the irrevocable fixing of exchange rates of the Member States and the attribution to the EC institutions of the full monetary and economic consequences. It is envisaged that during this stage the national currencies will eventually be replaced by a single EC currency. In the economic field, the transition to this stage would be marked by three developments: (a) the EC structural and regional policies may have to be further strengthened; (b) the EC macroeconomic and budgetary rules and procedures would have to become binding; and (c) the EC role in the process of international policy cooperation would have to become fuller and more positive. In the monetary field, the ESCB would assume full responsibilities, especially for (a) the formulation and implementation of monetary policy; (b) exchange-market intervention in third currencies; (c) the pooling and management of all foreign exchange reserves; and (d) technical and regulatory preparations necessary for the transition to a single EC currency.

The EC summit that opened in Madrid on 24 June 1989 decided to call a conference that would determine the route to be taken to the EMU. On the opening day of the summit, Margaret Thatcher, British prime minister, was surprisingly conciliatory. Instead of insisting that the UK would join the ERM 'when the time is ripe', she set out five conditions for joining: (a) a lower UK inflation rate and in the EC as a whole; (b) abolition of all exchange controls (at the time and for two years after, Italy, France and Spain had them); (c) progress towards the SEM; (d) liberalization of financial services; and (e) agreement on competition policy.

Since these were minor conditions relative to the demands for creating EMU, all the Member States endorsed the report and agreed on 1 July 1990 as the deadline for the commencement of the first stage.

The three-stage timetable for the EMU did start on 1 July 1990 with the launching of the first phase of intensified economic cooperation during which all the Member States were to submit their currencies to the ERM. The main target of this activity was the UK, whose currency was not subject to the ERM discipline. The UK joined in 1991 but withdrew from it in 1992, as did Italy.

The second stage is clarified in the TEU. It was to start in 1994. During this stage the EU was to create the European Monetary Institute (EMI) to prepare the way for an ECB, which would start operating on 1 January 1997. Although this was upset by the 1992 turmoil in the EMS, the compromises reached at the Edinburgh summit of December 1992 (deemed necessary for creating the conditions which resulted in a successful second referendum on the TEU in Denmark and hence in the UK ratification) did not alter the TEU much.[24] The TEU already allowed Denmark and the UK to opt out of the final stage. However, in a separate protocol, all the then-12 EC Member States declared that the drive to a single currency in the 1990s was 'irreversible'.

A single currency (the euro), to be managed by an independent ECB, was to be introduced as early as 1997 if 7 of the then-12 EC Member States passed the strict economic criteria required for its successful operation, and in 1999 at the very latest. These conditions were as follows:

1. *Price stability*. Membership required 'a price performance that is sustainable and an average rate of inflation, observed over a period of one year before the examination, that does not exceed by more than [1.5] percentage points that of, at most, the three best performing' EC [Member States]. Inflation 'shall be measured by means of the consumer price index on a comparable basis, taking into account differences in national definitions'.
2. *Interest rates*. Membership required that, observed over a period of one year before the examination, a [Member State] has had an average nominal long-term interest rate that does not exceed by more than two percentage points that of, at most, the three best performing

[Member States] in terms of price stability. Interest rates shall be measured on the basis of long-term government bonds or comparable securities, taking into account differences in national definitions.

3. *Budget deficits.* Membership required that a Member State 'has achieved a government budgetary position without a deficit that is excessive' (Article 109j). However, what is to be considered excessive is determined in Article 104c.6, which states that the Council shall decide after an overall assessment 'whether an excessive deficit exists'. The protocol sets the criterion for an excessive deficit as being 3 per cent of GDP. However, there are provisos if 'either the ratio has declined substantially and continuously and reached a level that comes close to the reference value; or ... the excess over the reference value is only exceptional and temporary and the ratio remained close to the reference value'.

4. *Public debt.* The requirement is that the ratio of government debt should not exceed 60 per cent of GDP, with the following proviso: 'unless the ratio is sufficiently diminishing and approaching the reference value at a satisfactory pace'. Whether such an excessive deficit exists is open to interpretation and is decided by the Council under qualified majority voting (QMV). In helping the Council decide, the Commission is to look at the medium term and quite explicitly can have the opinion that there is an excessive deficit if there is risk, 'notwithstanding the fulfilment of the requirements under the criteria'.

5. *Currency stability.* Membership required that a Member State has respected the normal fluctuation margin provided for by the exchange-rate mechanism [ERM] ... without severe tensions for at least two years before the examination. In particular, [it] shall not have devalued its currency's bilateral central rate against any other [Member States'] currency on its own initiative for the same period.

There is little rationale for these convergence criteria. The inflation criterion is not based on achieving some sustainable position such as the 'non-accelerating inflation rate of unemployment (NAIRU), so inflation could be convergent simply because the economy is out of internal balance over the examination period. There is no way to evaluate whether a 60 per cent of GDP public debt is better or worse than some other percentage. Normally the criterion used for assessing the debt level of a country is its 'sustainability', which is subject to a wide range of considerations. One easy rationalization is that 3 per cent of GDP happened to be the average level of public investment at that time, and the Member States deemed this percentage acceptable. It is often also accepted that investment, which has an equivalent financial rate of return, can be sustainably financed by a budget deficit. Assuming that this is a long-term situation, a compound rate of interest of 5 per cent per annum results in a public borrowing of 60 per cent of GDP,[25] which was also the average at the time.

The important requirements for a stable system are that no Member State should be able to run its economy in a way that increases the cost for the others. Provided that the minimum standard set is high enough, then the Eurozone as a whole will get the finest credit ratings/lowest interest costs. Unless there is some means of differentiation, then the single exchange and interest rate for the EMU will reflect the aggregate behaviour. In a more developed federal system, it becomes possible to have two sorts of public debt. Then states have the ability to raise their own debt, but subject to limits and very explicitly without a guarantee from the federal authorities. The US shows noticeable spreads for local and state debt and some states have indeed got into difficulty.

The timing of these convergence tests has been crucial. If they had occurred in 1992, only France and Luxembourg would have scored full marks (five points). The others would have scored the following: Denmark and UK four points each; Belgium, Germany and Ireland three points each; the Netherlands two points; Italy and Spain one point; Greece and Portugal no points. The position at the end of 1996 was even worse since only Luxembourg qualified. Thus the third stage of EMU did not begin by the earlier date of 1997. What is extraordinary is the turnaround by the final qualifying date of 1998. Then only one country, Greece, was deemed not to qualify, and even Greece was able to qualify at the first reassessment in 2000 (although it has been subsequently revealed that some of the statistics involved were knowingly inaccurate, see endnote 3, p. 267).

The data on which the decision on 2 May 1998 was based (Table 6.3) was deemed, in the opinion of the Commission, to indicate that 11 nations had passed the test. Of the remaining four, three (Denmark, Sweden and the UK) had already decided not to join in the first wave, and Greece was not in the running. The Commission's interpretation of the performance of the Member States was clearly 'flexible' (the EMI, which was also charged with issuing a convergence report, was of exactly the same opinion).[26]

Fourteen Member States had government deficits of 3 per cent of GDP or less in 1997: Austria, Belgium, Denmark, Finland, France, Germany, Ireland, Italy, Luxembourg, Netherlands, Portugal, Spain, Sweden and

Table 6.1 EU member states' performance with regard to the convergence criteria

	Inflation	Government budgetary position						Exchange rates	Long-term interest rates[d]
	HICP[a]	Existence of an excessive deficit[b]	Deficit (per cent of GDP)[c]	Debt (per cent of GDP)				ERM participation	
					Change from previous year				
		1998	1997	1997	1997	1996	1995	March 1998	January 1998
Reference Value	2.7[e]		3	60					7.8[f]
Austria	1.1	yes[g]	2.5	66.1	-3.4	0.3	3.8	yes	5.6
Belgium	1.4	yes[g]	2.1	122.2	-4.7	-4.3	-2.2	yes	5.7
Denmark	1.9	No	-0.7	65.1	-5.5	-2.7	-4.9	yes	6.2
Finland	1.3	No	0.9	55.8	-1.8	-0.4	-1.5	yes[h]	5.9
France	1.2	yes[g]	3	58	2.4	2.9	4.2	yes	5.5
Germany	1.4	yes[g]	2.7	61.3	0.8	2.4	7.8	yes	5.6
Greece	5.2	Yes	4	108.7	-2.9	1.5	0.7	yes[i]	9.8[l]
Ireland	1.2	No	-0.9	66.3	-6.4	-9.6	-6.8	yes	6.2
Italy	1.8	yes[g]	2.7	121.6	-2.4	-0.2	-0.7	yes	6.7
Luxembourg	1.4	No	-1.7	6.7	0.1	0.7	0.2	yes[k]	5.6
Netherlands	1.8	No	1.4	72.1	-5.0	-1.9	1.2	yes[g]	5.5
Portugal	1.8	yes[g]	2.5	62	-3.0	-0.9	2.1	yes[g]	6.2
Spain	1.8	yes[g]	2.6	68.8	-1.3	4.6	2.9	yes[g]	6.3
Sweden	1.9	yes[g]	0.8	76.6	-0.1	-0.9	-1.4	no	6.5
UK	1.8	yes[g]	1.9	53.4	-1.3	0.8	-1.3	no	7
EU (15)	1.6	yes[g]	2.4	72.1	-0.9	2	3		6.1

Notes: [a] Percentage change in arithmetic average of the latest 12-monthly harmonized indices of consumer prices (HICP) relative to the arithmetic average of the 12 HICP of the previous period; [b] Council decisions of 26.09.94, 10.07.95, 27.06.96 and 30.06.97; [c] A negative sign for the government deficit indicates a surplus; [d] Average maturity ten years; average of the last 12 months; [e] Definition adopted in this report: simple arithmetic average of the inflation rates of the three best-performing member states in terms of price stability plus 1.5 percentage points; [f] Definition adopted in this report: simple arithmetic average of the 12-month average of interest rates of the three best-performing member states in terms of price stability plus two percentage points; [g] Commission-recommended abrogation; [h] Since March 1998; [i] Average of the available data during the past twelve months; [j] Since November 1996; [k] Since October 1996.

Source: CEU (1998e, table 1.1, p. 34).

the UK. The Member States had achieved significant reductions in the level of government borrowing, in particular in 1997, aided by the favourable phase of the economic cycle.

In 1997, government debt was below the TEU reference value of 60 per cent of GDP in four Member States: Finland, France, Luxembourg and the UK. According to the TEU, countries may exceed this value as long as the debt ratio is 'sufficiently diminishing and approaching the reference value at a satisfactory pace' (above). This was deemed to be the case in almost all the Member States with debt ratios above 60 per cent in 1997. Only in Germany, in which the ratio was just above 60 per cent of GDP and the exceptional costs of unification continued to bear heavily, was there a small rise in 1997. All countries above the 60 per cent ratio were expected to see reductions in their debt levels. The Commission concluded that *the conditions were in place for the continuation of a sustained decline in debt ratio in future* years.[27]

6.3B.5   The transition to the EMU

When exchange controls were removed as part of stage 1 of the progress to the EMU, the EU experienced severe potential strains from two directions. First, a protection against speculation was lost. Second, because interest parity was no longer prevented, interest rates everywhere were tightly linked as the amount of expected depreciation was confined by the bands of permissible fluctuations of the currencies against one another. Because Germany was by far the largest EMS economy, this meant that interest rates, and hence monetary policy, everywhere in the system were dominated by Germany. Unless Germany in turn tempered its monetary policy by concern for the economic situation in other countries, this could turn out to be unacceptable, as indeed it proved in 1992–3.

These problems were addressed. With regard to the problem of speculation, it was agreed to ease the situation by requiring that, in the event of need, a strong currency country should extend automatic lending to a weak currency country. While initially this applied only when intervention took place at the edge of the band, after the agreement at Nyborg in September 1987, it also applied inside the margin before a currency reached its limit. These new provisions were successfully tested by a speculative run on the French franc in the autumn of 1987. The Bundesbank lent heavily to the Banque de France, but the lending was rapidly repaid once the speculation subsided and confidence returned. The problem of excessive German dominance was only resolved by moving on to full EMU. The Nyborg provisions called for much closer monetary cooperation, involving more continuous exchange of information, and interest rate movements within the EMS after that time displayed a high degree of synchronization. Progress towards a degree of common decision-making was less evident. The anxiety of France on this score, however, led to important initiatives. First, France called upon Germany to discuss economic policy on a regular basis, and an economic council was set up for this purpose. Second, it was a French initiative that led to the setting up of the Delors Committee on the requirements for full EMU, whose recommendations were endorsed by all 12 EC Member States in June 1989, leading to the TEU.

The path that the EMS participants agreed to follow thus called for increasing intervention resources and other devices to combat the threat of speculation and for increased economic and monetary cooperation between the Member States, eventually leading to the creation of the ECB.

A second means of attaining a greater measure of independence from the dominant power by enlarging the bands of exchange rate fluctuation was used in 1993. Other steps, such as retaining a measure of exchange control, would have been possible, given the increasing popularity in the late 1990s of the idea of putting 'sand in the wheels' of international financial transactions in order to limit their volatility. But these would have been a step away from the final goal.

The forecast threat to the system duly occurred in September 1992. Uncertainty about the outcome of the French referendum on the TEU contributed to speculation against the weakest currencies in the ERM: the pound sterling and the lira. Neither was able to resist the pressure despite substantial increases in interest rates. By the summer of 1993, not even the French franc could survive the pressure, and the bands had to be widened to ±15 per cent to allow it to devalue without realigning within the system.

Other currencies also came under pressure and were forced to devalue. There was considerable pressure on the French franc in September 1992, but it survived, aided by substantial intervention by the Bundesbank on its behalf. It is arguable that all the currencies that were devalued were in some sense overvalued in terms of their long-term sustainable values. However, the problem was not merely one of domestic inflation by the devaluing countries, but of the special problems of the dominant German economy leading to a divergence from the domestic objectives of the other Member States.[28] German interest rates were driven up by the need to finance German unification over and above the willingness to raise taxes. With the tight linkage of the EMS interest rates, other Member States also had to have rates that were high in real terms.

In the UK case, it was clearly a relief that the ERM constraints could be broken. Interest rates had already been progressively cut to the point that sterling was close to its lower bound. A domestic recession was being exacerbated by the inability to use monetary policy to alleviate it. On exiting, the UK interest rates were lowered by four percentage points in virtually as many months.

The EMS suffered considerably through being unable to organize an orderly realignment of exchange rates. The mechanisms existed, but political pressures meant that the Member States could not agree among themselves. Blame has been placed in a number of quarters: on the Bundesbank for not taking greater account of the impact of its policy on other Member States and on the UK for not being sincere in trying to maintain parity within the bounds. But the basic weakness of the system remained: that trying to have narrow bands without exchange controls is really not sustainable when there are substantial shocks to the system. This was admitted in practice by widening the bands.

The EMS remained intact after the devaluations of September 1992 and the widening of the band to ±15 per cent in August 1993, and slowly regained credibility. Despite three devaluations of the peseta and the escudo between November 1992 and March 1995, the participating currencies moved back into closer alignment. At the end of 1996, all bar the Irish punt were within the ±2.25 per cent band. Although sterling and the drachma remained outside the ERM and the Swedish krone did not join, Italy rejoined in November 1996, and Finland (in October 1996) and Austria (in January 1995) also became participants.[29]

As has been noted, the EMS survived through to its replacement by the Eurosystem at the start of 1999 primarily because of the determination of the EU governments to qualify for the EMU under the TEU criteria. The restraints on fiscal policy from needing to keep deficits below 3 per cent of GDP and debt below 60 per cent of GDP (or make credible progress towards 60 per cent) simultaneously helped inflation converge and the Member States get their business cycles in line, while the steady development of the SEM integrated them further.

In part, the reason why stage 3 of the EMU did not begin in 1997 was simply that the convergence period after the shocks of 1992–3 was just too short, particularly for countries like Sweden and especially Finland, for which the shocks were greatest, but the evolution of the general economic cycle was not favourable. From then onwards, however, convergence was easier. Just as the adverse circumstances in the mid-1990s were bad luck, so the EU was extremely lucky that 1996–8 was a period of very considerable stability. Even the Asian crisis did not have a marked effect, and decreased the chance of importing inflation from the rest of the world.

Once financial markets felt that fiscal convergence and the EMU were likely, this expectation brought the required convergence in real interest rates. Had the Member States that experienced the greatest difficulty in converging not joined then, it is likely that they would have experienced considerable pressures in the period immediately after the decision. The loss of credibility involved would have made joining at a subsequent date much more expensive than it was for those who were successful earlier on.

The establishment of the Eurozone also created three groups of countries within the EU: those that are in the area, those that are outside but expect to join at some date in the future and those that are outside but have no plans to join. In one sense, all the Member States that are outside the area, except Denmark and the UK, fall into this second group, as they are supposed to join as soon as they have met the convergence criteria, which are still the same as those applied originally under the TEU. Thus, rather than the more logical idea of converging to the performance of the existing Eurozone Member States, inflation convergence is still required to that of the three best-performing members of the EU as a whole, which on some occasions have all been non-area Member States. While Denmark and the UK have a derogation from this requirement to join, it appears that Sweden is at present a de facto member of the third group as well, since membership was decisively rejected (by 14 percentage points) in a referendum on 14 September 2003. The ten new Member States that joined the EU in May 2004 and the two that joined in 2007 varied in their enthusiasm for how fast they wished to join the Eurozone, with Estonia, Lithuania and Slovenia indicating that they wished to join at the first opportunity. Latvia and then Cyprus and Malta also opted for rapid entry, but others set more cautious timetables. Slovenia entered in 2007, Cyprus and Malta in 2008, Slovakia in 2009, Estonia in 2011 and Latvia in 2014. Lithuania narrowly failed in its bid to join in 2007, but was successful on 1 January 2015.[30]

The Eurosystem has created an extension of the ERM labelled ERM II, which the Member States that wish to adopt the euro should join during the convergence period. Thus the six countries mentioned above (Cyprus, Estonia, Latvia, Lithuania, Malta and Slovenia) joined, along with Slovakia, which entered in November 2005. Denmark is also participating in ERM II voluntarily, but operating in a tighter band. The rules are similar to those that faced the 1995 new members (Austria, Finland and Sweden) under the original ERM. Their currencies did not form part of the ECU basket, and hence if their exchange rate moved with respect to the other members, it did not affect the value of the ECU itself. Membership was notional for Estonia and Lithuania as they had currency boards based on the euro, and their exchange rates with it were completely fixed. Latvia also had a fixed peg to the euro from 2005.

A central value is agreed between the ECB and a Member State for the exchange rate with the euro, and the actual rate should then remain within the same 2.25 per cent range that prevailed within the ERM. Realignments are possible and indeed have already happened for Greece (upwards). However, the convergence requirement is not precise. In its 2006 Convergence Report, the ECB explains its application of the TEU provisions as 'whether the country has participated in ERM II for a period of at least two years prior to the convergence examination without severe tensions, in particular without devaluing against…the euro'. However, actual membership is not compelled for the full period: 'absence of "severe tensions" is generally assessed by (a) examining the degree of deviation of exchange rates from the ERM II central rates against the euro; (b) using indicators such as exchange rate volatility vis-à-vis the Eurozone and their development; and (c) considering the role played by foreign exchange interventions' (p. 17).

ERM II is thus a rather one-sided affair, very much reminiscent of the early days of the original ERM. It is for the applicants to adjust to the behaviour of the Eurozone. The euro monetary policy is run without regard to their problems. It is the ECB that determines the parities (Section C). The ECB (and the Commission) will offer an opinion on whether convergence has occurred. In the case of Greece, the government was keen to go ahead with euro membership as soon as possible. It was accepted for membership in June 2000 and joined at the beginning of 2001 (above). Even if all of the 12 new Member States were to join ERM II, the system would still be highly skewed in favour of the original 11 members in terms of relative economic size. In some ways, dependency actually strengthens the system, as it makes stable alternatives substantially more costly for the applicants. Thus not only will they have a strong incentive to try to remain in the system and not follow policies that are likely to lead to downward realignments, but the existence of these incentives will be obvious to everybody else as well, thereby increasing the credibility of the commitment. However, experience since 2009 has shown that there is a reciprocal pressure from credibility on the other Member States to make sure that no one is forced out; otherwise, the membership of the weaker Member States may start to look tenuous as well.

Some new Member States found ERM II difficult, as they were still undergoing a major process of structural change and have not in some cases achieved sustainably low inflation. As with the original ERM, the weaker new Member States will experience real exchange rate increases that will ultimately force them into realignments. Adopting a currency board based on the euro may offer greater credibility. Convergence will be easier the more heavily integrated they are with the Eurozone. Particularly in the case of the former Soviet bloc countries, the economic ties further east were thoroughly broken and hence they were more integrated with the Eurozone than sheer geography might dictate. This reduces worries about asymmetric shocks compared with countries like the UK with substantial economic linkages outside the Eurozone or Poland in which the domestic economy is relatively large.

Transition is likely to be slow in some cases, particularly for those countries that have not yet been accepted for EU membership, so ERM II is also likely to be a relatively long-lived arrangement. However, in many cases, new Member States have felt they would rather complete the process of adjustment within the EMU than outside. The credibility and hence much lower real interest rates offered by membership may very well be thought to outweigh the gains from exchange rate flexibility. Massive changes in their labour markets are known to be inevitable; therefore, there is a willingness to accept the pressures on non-monetary and non-fiscal routes to adjustment that have presented considerable difficulties for many of the current EU Member States.

6.3B.6   The decision over EMU membership

This subsection addresses two questions: a sensible strategy for the new Member States in the face of the EMU membership criteria, and the decision of Denmark, Sweden and the UK to stay out of the Eurozone. Both questions reflect clearly on the economic logic of membership of the EMU for potential and existing members.

It might appear odd, prima facie, in purely economic terms that the UK, Sweden and Denmark have chosen to stay out of stage 3 of the EMU, while other countries that seem less convergent on standard OCA criteria (Section A), such as Finland, Greece and the Irish Republic have chosen to join. Setting aside the political issues, there are three simple economic reasons that help explain the decisions, but the case of the UK stands out for a further reason. The UK is larger in economic terms than the other five countries mentioned above taken together. It is the only EU Member State with a world-scale financial market.

The simple economic reasons are the following:

1. Life on the outside has been successful. It is very difficult in the case of Denmark, for example, to point to the extra costs from staying outside but shadowing the euro very closely, except in terms of forgoing a seat at the table (both in the ECB and the Euro Group). With little right of veto, the impact of a single small country is rarely going to be decisive.

2. Some of the joining countries, particularly Finland, have put a much higher weight on the expectation that euro membership would change behaviour for the better. Furthermore, in the case of both Finland and the Irish Republic the expectation has been that membership would support their propensity for faster-than-average growth by offering lower real interest rates and dampening inflationary pressures through the threat of competition.

3. It is better to adjust first, making use of the extra flexibility available, and join second.

One might wish to add two further reasons. The first is a much more pessimistic view of the secondary benefits that could accrue under a more complete EMU than in the partial or 'pseudo' union. This would be particularly true for countries that expect to be net payers rather than net recipients. The second is that, if a country feels that it is already more flexible than its potential partners, membership and a tendency towards common behaviour might actually be retrogressive and result in a structure that generates slower growth. Some of this flavour emerges from the UK discussion.

The new Member States that are still outside face a rather different balance of interests. In general, their economic position and policies are less credible than those of the Eurozone; hence, they will get clear benefits from lower interest rates. Similarly the constraints that qualifying imposes on fiscal policy will provide helpful external pressures that domestic political conditions might otherwise find difficult. Most of the countries, Poland excepted, are also small, which limits their ability to build up an effective anchor for inflation on their own. They tend to meet many OCA criteria, with the exception of real convergence, and their trade pattern is strongly integrated with the EU. It is really only one main factor that inhibits their rushing to join stage 3 of the EMU before something goes wrong. They have low price levels, wages and output per head, and expect to grow faster than the existing Eurozone Member States over at least the next 20–30 years (i.e. real convergence will take some time). This in turn will therefore mean that their rate of inflation is likely to exceed that of current members. While this gives them a straightforward problem of meeting the convergence criteria – they would have to go through a period of unusually low inflation that looks sustainable – it also poses problems of whether it is better to adjust partly through the nominal exchange rate. The Czech Republic in particular regards it as beneficial to keep domestic inflation low by inflation targeting, which means that it will have comparable inflation to the Eurozone, but some exchange rate appreciation. Countries that join early can only make such adjustments through the real exchange rate, or the 'true value' of the rate.[31] If the process were smooth, this might not matter, but if it overshoots, then adjustment through an independent exchange rate may well prove easier than having to rely entirely on fiscal policy to disinflate, as Greece, Ireland, Cyprus, Spain and Portugal have been experiencing in recent years.

As noted earlier, it is largely an empirical question as to whether a country can achieve structural change rapidly without inflating. The Baltic States already know how easy/difficult it is to adjust when they get asymmetric shocks that do not affect their partners,[32] as they have faced both the Russian crisis of 1998 and the global financial crisis without the system collapsing. Other countries, including Poland and particularly Hungary, have experienced more difficulty, both in fiscal restraint and, in Hungary's case, in maintaining a smooth exchange rate regime. The Czech Republic also encountered difficulties in the aftermath of the Asian crises, as there was a general move of investors away from higher-risk countries.

The most common exposition of the problem is to refer to what is called the Balassa-Samuelson effect, which points out that prices of highly traded goods will tend to be at international levels round the world. Typically they will also show productivity growth relative to domestic services. Hence achieving balanced growth across the industrial spectrum will tend to involve non-traded goods and services rising in relative price. It may prove difficult for market forces to manage this without excess inflation in the price level as a whole. There have been a variety of estimates of the size of this effect, but something of the order of 1 per cent a year or a little more seems to be widely accepted.

Taken together, this means that the Member States that are pegging to the euro will want to join early and will hope that at some stage they will meet the convergence criteria, as they have nothing to gain from being outside except leaving the peg, which would be a serious blow to credibility and have a cost for several years to come. Inflation-targeting countries on the other hand, along with countries that are managing the real exchange rate, are likely to want to wait longer until they are closer to real convergence. At that point, nominal exchange rate movements are likely to be compatible with the convergence criteria.

6.3B.7 The UK

The UK declined to participate in the operation of the EMS to begin with, out of a belief that the EMS would be operated in a rigid way that would threaten the UK, with its high 'propensity to inflate', with a decline in its competitiveness, especially vis-à-vis Germany.

Opposition on different grounds was propounded by the incoming Conservative government headed by Thatcher, which wished to bring inflation down and reasoned that if the instruments of monetary policy (principally interest rates) were to be directed at reducing the rate of growth of the money supply, they could not simultaneously be used to target the exchange rate in the absence of exchange controls.

Events were to turn out somewhat paradoxically. The first phase of the Thatcher government's monetary experiment was associated with a very marked *appreciation* of the exchange rate, so competitiveness would have been *better* preserved inside the EMS; indeed, the deep recession that soon set in, was attributed by many observers to be this cause. In particular, the exchange rate would be steadier and competitiveness more assured, while inflation would be dragged towards the modest German level. This view gained momentum as official British policy towards the exchange rate as a target changed and as it became clear that monetary policy was no longer aimed in single-minded fashion solely at controlling the supply of money.

In late 1986, the UK started 'shadowing the EMS', keeping the sterling exchange rate closely in line with the Deutschmark. This policy initiative lasted for just over a year. By the end of February 1988, following a well-publicized exchange of views between the Chancellor of the Exchequer and the prime minister, sterling was uncapped. Higher interest rates, invoked as a means of dampening monetary growth and in response to forecasts of inflation, caused the exchange rate to appreciate through its previous working ceiling. The incident underlined the inconsistency between an independent monetary policy and an exchange rate policy. Even when sterling ultimately went into the ERM in October 1990, it appeared to be with considerable reluctance.

The ERM membership only lasted until September 1992, when markets pushed sterling out of the system (above). It did not rejoin, even when a government with a more favourable attitude was elected in May 1997.[33] The issue had been overtaken by whether the UK should join the EMU. While a close shadowing of the euro, as has been followed by Denmark, could make sense in its own right to help acquire greater stability, the main reason for such a policy would be as part of the preconditions for Eurozone membership. The UK monetary policy was focused on an explicit inflation target of 2.5 per cent a year in May 1997. Pursuit of this target with only narrow bands of 1 per cent either side almost inevitably meant that the UK monetary policy would vary from the ECB's, with its medium-term target of inflation 'less than but close to' 2 per cent (Section C).

The UK government decided that it would recommend euro adoption in a referendum to the British people provided five tests, set in 1997, were met. Performance against these tests was first evaluated in October of the same year by the UK Treasury, and the results showed that the UK economy had neither sufficiently converged with the rest of the EU economies nor was flexible enough. The tests were repeated in June 2003 with a negative result, but the government said it would try again. However, since the Labour Party lost in the general election in 2010, the tests are no longer UK government policy.

The tests were straightforward. The first was about business cycles and economic structures being compatible 'so that we and others could live comfortably with euro interest rates on a permanent basis'. The second related to whether there would be 'sufficient flexibility to deal with' any problems if they emerged. The third concerned whether euro adoption would 'create better conditions for firms making long-term decisions to invest in Britain'. The fourth was about what the impact of euro adoption would be 'on the competitive position of...the UK's financial services industry, particularly the City's wholesale markets'. The last summed up the other four since it was about whether euro adoption would 'promote higher growth, stability and a lasting increase in jobs'.

However, when announcing these tests in October 1997, the Chancellor, Gordon Brown, added that the Treasury must decide that there is a 'clear and unambiguous' economic case for recommending British euro adoption. Since that would be unlikely in any circumstances, it would seem that this addition has been made to ensure that any decision on the matter would be based on purely political grounds.

Clearly another factor that would determine the UK's economic performance for years to come needed to be added: namely, the value at which sterling would enter the euro. Contrary to popular perception, this did not need to be the prevailing market exchange rate.

Several other assessments of the UK's readiness to join were also made.[34] While all agreed that the British economy had been converging with the Eurozone, the overall assessment was firmly negative, although leaving open the opportunity for reassessment. The problem was straightforward. There was (is) no general public support for euro membership, so it would be pointless to incur the embarrassment of a defeat, or follow Sweden into an extended period of non-membership following a referendum. The relative success of the UK economy would inevitably influence the economic judgment over the appropriate timing of entry. A clear and unambiguous case can never be made, as the result depends on a comparison of two hypothetical futures that are unknowable by definition and cannot even be validated after the event. Moreover, even if the economic case can be established, it will ebb and flow as the performances of the EU and the UK economies move relative to each other. The final decision is, therefore, bound to be a political rather than an economic one and will continue to be so since the Conservative-Liberal Democratic coalition government that came into power in 2010 does not see eye to eye on this issue or on even membership of the EU itself. Indeed, British prime minister David Cameron has promised a referendum on EU membership in 2017 (see Chapter 8).

6.3B.8   The future of the EMU

Only a few years before it occurred, conclusions on the prospects for the EMU in the EU were cautious. In 1996, when the time for assessing whether stage 3 could start at the beginning of 1997, it was not even worth looking, as only one country, the smallest, qualified under the Maastricht criteria. Just two years later, the ECB was up and running, and 11 Member States had both qualified and decided upon membership. By 2002, the notes and coins of the euro currency were in circulation, and the national currencies of the Member States, by then increased to 12, had been withdrawn. There was a large element of luck in the specific timing, but nevertheless one must conclude that the process to the EMU has been a remarkable success. It is difficult to tell whether those framing the Maastricht Treaty a decade earlier really believed their efforts would turn out so well, especially since previous attempts had run into difficulty.

It will be some time before it is possible to estimate the EMU's degree of success in economic terms. However, any such assessment will always be highly contested, as it rests on comparison with a hypothetical alternative that did not occur. The years 1999 and 2000 were good years, not just in the Eurozone, but also more generally. The years 2001 and 2002 saw a serious setback, which continued in many parts of the Eurozone, with the overall economy only turning up clearly in 2006, not long before the disaster of the 2008 global financial crisis, which put about as harsh a pressure on the system as one could devise. Public support for the EMU has risen and fallen with the general economic climate, regardless of whether the EMU was actually causal. It is difficult to gainsay the beneficial impact on those countries that previously faced problems of credibility in their macroeconomic policy. In the same way, those that did not change that behaviour or their structural flexibility sufficiently have reaped the consequences and put pressure on all the other countries as well. The enthusiasm of some of the new Member States for moving on to membership of stage 3 as soon as possible after joining the EU, and the caution of some of the others, continue to illustrate the debate.

The debate on the impact of the global financial crisis is left to the next section, as it deals with the 'E' in the EMU while this section has concentrated on the 'M'.

6.3C   The operation of the EMU

The EU's EMU has four broad ingredients: the euro and the European single monetary policy (SMP); the coordination of the European macroeconomic policies through the SGP, the European Semester, Fiscal Compact and related processes; the completion of the SEM; and the operation of the structural funds and other cohesion measures. Since the last two have already been discussed in, respectively, Chapters 4 and 5, the first two are considered here.

Although the euro did not come into existence until 1 January 1999 and then only in financial markets, most of the characteristics of stage 3 of the EMU were operating once the ECB opened in June 1998. The ECB, in the form of the EMI, had been preparing for the day with all the EU national central banks (NCBs) since 1994. The form of the coming SMP was already known by 1998, both in framework and instruments. In the same way, much of the framework for the operation of the economic coordination among the Member States had been developed with the SGP of July 1997 and the commencement of the Broad Economic Policy Guidelines (BEPG) in 1998. The generalized framework was incorporated into the Treaty of Amsterdam (October 1997). There was thus no great break in behaviour at the beginning of 1999, especially since the main qualification period under the TEU convergence criteria had related to 1997. However, the SGP effectively broke down in 2003 and had to be revised in 2005 after a period of debate (above). The sovereign debt crisis that was precipitated by the global financial crisis in 2009 has resulted in a major strengthening of both the mechanisms for fiscal prudence and the requirements for structural balance.

This section begins by looking at the provisions for the SMP, then considers those for policy coordination, before exploring how they have worked. The EMU weathered the global financial crisis quite well until 2010, when problems for the most exposed Member States, particularly Greece, imposed strains on the whole system and prompted extraordinary measures and a rapid step forward in the closer integration of macroeconomic policies.

6.3C.1   The Eurosystem and the euro

The institutional system behind the SMP is quite complex because it has to deal with the fact that some EU Member States are not (yet) participants in stage 3 of the EMU. The TEU sets up the ESCB, which is composed of all the national central banks (NCBs) in the EU and the ECB, sited in Frankfurt. The ECB and the NCBs of the Eurozone form the Eurosystem, which is what is running the monetary side of the Eurozone. The term 'Eurosystem' has been coined by the constituent central banks so as to make the set-up clearer. It is not in the TEU. The body responsible for the ECB and its decisions, including monetary policy, is the Governing Council, which is composed of the governors of the participating NCBs and the six members of the Executive Board, who provide the executive management of the ECB. The Executive Board is composed of the president and vice president and four other members, responsible for the various parts of the ECB, which are labelled Directorates General in the same manner as the Commission. The ECB also has a General Council, which is composed of the president, vice president and the governors of *all* the EU NCBs, whether participating in the Eurozone or not. Thus the General Council has 30 members (28 governors + 2), but the Governing Council has 24 members (18 governors + 6) and it will increase in size as more Member States join the Eurozone.[35] A representative from the Commission and from the EU presidency may also attend, but not vote. Figure 6.3 summarizes the structure.

The Eurosystem is relatively decentralized compared to the US Federal Reserve System, although the names for the various institutions imply the opposite relative structures. The central institution in the US, the Board of Governors of the Federal Reserve System, which is the controlling body, having powers over the budgets of the 12 Federal Reserve Banks, does not have another label for its staff and administrative operations. The seven governors of the Federal Reserve Board hold a voting majority on the monetary policy-making body, the Federal Open Market Committee (FOMC), in which only the president of the New York Fed

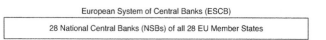

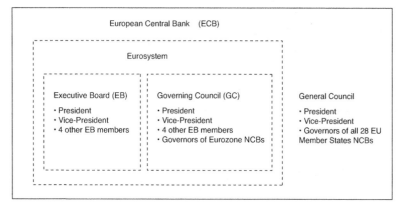

Figure 6.3   European System of Central Banks (ESCB)

and five of the presidents of the other Fed Banks, by rotation, can vote (although all are present at each meeting and may speak).[36]

The Eurosystem, on the other hand, operates through a network of committees, in which each NCB and the ECB has a member.[37] The ECB normally provides the chairman and the secretariat. It is the Governing Council that takes the decisions, but the Executive Board coordinates the work of the committees and prepares the agenda for the Governing Council. Many of these committees meet in two compositions, one for the Eurosystem and one for the whole ESCB, depending on the subject.

To complete the confusion over labels, the Eurosystem has a Monetary Policy Committee, but unlike the UK and many other central banks around the world, this is not the decision-making body on monetary policy. It organizes and discusses the main evidence and discussion papers to be put before the Governing Council on monetary matters.

There are, however, some key characteristics of this structure and other elements of the institutional set-up of the Eurosystem, which have important implications for policy. As the Delors Committee (above), which designed the set-up for the Eurosystem, was composed almost entirely of central bank governors, it is not surprising that it is very well adjusted to the current views about the needs of monetary policy. First of all, although the TEU sets down the objective of monetary policy (maintaining price stability) – in general terms – the Eurosystem has a high degree of independence from political influence in exercising responsibility. Not only is the taking or seeking of advice explicitly prohibited but the Governing Council members are protected in a number of ways in order to shield them from interest group pressures. First of all, they have long terms of office – eight years in the case of the Executive Board, and not renewable – so that they are less likely to have any regard for their prospects for their next job while setting monetary policy. Secondly, the proceedings are secret so that people cannot find out how they voted.[38] Each member is supposed to act purely in a personal capacity and solely with the aim of price stability at the Eurozone level in mind, without regard to national interests. No system can ensure this, but a well-designed one substantially increases the chance of this happening. Thirdly, the Eurosystem is explicitly prohibited from 'monetizing' government deficits.

The point of trying to achieve this independence is simply 'credibility' – to try to maximize the belief that the Eurosystem will actually do just what it has been asked to do – namely maintain price stability. The stronger that belief can be, the less 'costly' monetary policy will be. If people do not believe that the ECB will be successful, they will base their behaviour on that belief. Hence price and wage setters who believe that there will be increases in inflation substantially beyond what the ECB says it will deliver, will set their prices with that higher outcome in mind. That means that the ECB then has to struggle against that belief, thereby entailing high interest rates. Hence, even though the ECB may intend exactly the same outcomes in both cases, it does not have to run such high interest rates to achieve them if it is 'credible'.

This credibility comes from other sources as well as independence. The structure of the Governing Council is strongly reminiscent of that of the Bundesbank. The Bundesbank was highly successful in maintaining low inflation. By having a similar structure, the Eurosystem has been able to 'borrow' much of the Bundesbank's credibility.

6.3C.1.1 *The monetary policy of the Eurosystem*

The Eurosystem is further assisted in the inherent credibility of its policy by having a single simple objective of price stability laid down by the TEU. If a central bank has multiple objectives, it will have difficulty explaining the balance between them, especially when they conflict. There was a short period of confusion at the outset over exchange-rate policy, as the Eurosystem is not responsible for the regime, only the execution. However, it rapidly became clear that since exchange-rate policy and the objective of monetary policy are inextricably linked, one of the two must have primacy, and ministers made it clear that it was price stability that was the driving force. The other common objectives for a central bank of maximizing employment and the rate of economic growth – in this case expressed as 'without prejudice to the objective of price stability, ... the ESCB shall support the general economic [EU] policies' – are clearly subservient.

However, for monetary policy to be credible, it is necessary that the objective should be clear enough for people to act on, and that the central bank's behaviour in trying to achieve that objective, should be both observable and understandable as a feasible approach to success. Here, the ECB had to define the objective since the TEU's concept of price stability is far too vague to be workable. They opted for inflation over the medium term of less than 2 per cent. They also defined the inflation they were talking about as that in the harmonized index of consumer prices (HICP). After a swift clarification that this meant that zero inflation was the lower bound, the specification was widely criticized for being too inexact (compared with other central banks). Not only is the length of the medium term not spelt out, it is also not clear how much and for how long prices can deviate from the target. Nor is there any indication of how fast inflation should be brought back to the target after a shock hits. In 2003, the target was reappraised and 'clarified' as being 'less than but close to 2 per cent'.

This means that a range of policy settings would be consistent with such a target. Policy is thus inherently not very predictable – something the Governing Council has sought to offset by trying to give clear signals about interest rate changes. Despite the inevitably diffused structure of decision-making with 24 independent decision-makers, the Eurosystem has come to offer a single explanation of how it regards the working of the economy and the appropriate response to it. One facet of the Eurosystem strategy that came in for criticism was what is known as the 'two-pillars' approach. Rather than adhering to any specific model or suite of models, the Eurosystem announced that it would base its decisions on a wide range of indicators under two pillars. The first of these assigned a prominent role to money and has included a 'reference value' for the growth of broad money (M3). The second was a broadly based assessment of the outlook for price developments. In the 2003 reappraisal, it was made clear that the monetary pillar was assigned a medium-term role and acted as a cross-check on the broad-based assessment that underpins policy decisions. While some controversy remains, this brings the Eurosystem policy more into line with thinking in other central banks. If anything, the problems of the 2008 global financial crisis have stimulated new interest in the monetary pillar.

Assigning money such an important role by at least some of the members of the Governing Council was inevitable, given that this was the Bundesbank's policy as well as that of some other successful predecessor NCBs. The particular reference value of 4.5 per cent growth (based on the sum of the expected medium-term inflation of around 1.5 per cent, the expected rate of growth of around 2 per cent and the drift in the velocity of circulation of money[39] of around 1 per cent) proved a problem, as it has been exceeded almost all of the time and a lot of effort has had to be spent explaining the discrepancies. Similarly, the price assessment began as a narrative rather than a firmly based discussion of options and their possible outcomes. However, the process has developed steadily. The Eurosystem publishes its forecasts (broad macroeconomic projections) twice a year, with updating by the ECB staff in the intervening quarters. Although these are 'staff' forecasts and do not necessarily represent the views of the Governing Council, they are increasingly being used as a basis for explaining policy. The decentralized structure of the Eurosystem would make any closer 'ownership' of the forecasts by decision-makers impossible.

The Eurosystem is, of course, in good company. The US Federal Reserve has multiple objectives and has only recently quantified its target for the price level/inflation. It only publishes the staff forecasts by the Board of Governors with a lag.

Thus far, policy has been generally successful, but between mid-2000 and 2011 inflation was stubbornly above 2 per cent. It is possible to blame the rapid rise in oil prices and some other shocks, but the deviation reached the stage at which it had an effect on expectations (as calculated from French index-linked bonds). At that point, the Governing Council reacted by raising interest rates ahead of a clearly revealed recovery in the economy. This helped enhance the Eurosystem's reputation as an inflation fighter, but has been controversial in some political circles.

It is difficult to tell whether the Governing Council members have, either explicitly or unconsciously, as a result of their backgrounds, tended to promote monetary policy decisions that supported the particular economic conditions in their country of origin rather than in the Eurozone as a whole. Complex models of coalitions have been developed in the literature, raising worries about whether those voting in favour are sufficiently representative of the Eurozone as a whole. The first reason why this is not relevant is that the Governing Council has not been voting on these issues. It has operated by consensus, in the sense that decisions are taken when the majority in favour is such that the minority withdraws its objection and does not feel the need to register dissent in some public manner.

The possible objection to that form of behaviour is not some form of country bias, but rather that it might engender conservatism in policymaking. Since the records of the debates are not published, there is no way of finding out whether the particular structure has inhibited or delayed action. The simplest way of judging the issue is to look at the voting records in the FOMC, where the results are published with a lag. Here, it is immediately clear that deep divisions over what to do are relatively unusual. Most of the time there is not only no division at all, but also no proposal to change policy. When there are divisions, the number of dissenters, even before the vote in the debate, tends to be quite small. The problem is thus predicated on a much more random and indeed contentious approach to policymaking than is actually the case.

There has been strong pressure on the Governing Council to be more open and publish the minutes of its discussions, as this would inhibit the members from following obviously national interests. However, it is not at all clear what the impact would be. Publishing minutes or resolutions leads to more formal proceedings or taking positions for the sake of having them recorded, if the US and Japanese experiences are anything to go by. If the real discussion is pushed outside the meeting into informal subgroups and consultations, the result can be counterproductive and it will be even more difficult to sort out which opinions were responsible for which decisions.

6.3C.2   The coordination of fiscal and other macroeconomic policies

Operating a single monetary policy for a diverse area has proved quite tricky. Policy that is well suited to some economies has been ill suited to others. It is important to be clear about the extent of the differences. It has been shown[40] that in some Member States the exchange rate is at least twice as important as a determinant of inflation (as compared with interest rates). Similarly, the length of time it takes for the impact of policy on inflation to exert its full effect also varies by a factor of two. Thus, if the main problem lies in a region in which policy has both a relatively small and a relatively slow effect, a policy based on the average experience of the Eurozone would not be very efficient.

The problem is further complicated because the main economic relationships involved are non-linear and asymmetric. To spell this out a little: whereas a low unemployment or positive output gap has quite a strong upward pressure on inflation, high unemployment and a negative output gap has a considerably smaller downward impact for the same-size difference. This means that simply adding up inflation rates and growth across the Eurozone and exploring aggregate relationships will be misleading. The analysis needs to be at the disaggregated level and then summed using the appropriate estimates of the effect in each region or Member State.

However, once one looks at fiscal and structural policy, these differences become even more important because they have to offset the differential impact of monetary policy. The coordination of fiscal and other policies therefore needs not merely to permit different policy setting by each Member State, subject to the constraints of prudence, but to expect them.

6.3C.2.1   *The coordination processes for macroeconomic policies*

The structure of the 'economic' side of macroeconomic policymaking thus involves constraints from following policies that could harm the system as a whole. Until the rapid development of macroeconomic policy coordination in 2011–13, following the problems of the sovereign debt crisis, the system consisted of the Excessive Deficit Procedure (EDP) with the SGP and the system of enhanced policy learning or soft coordination under the BEPG. The annual BEPG formed the framework for bringing together three main elements: (a) the orientation of general fiscal policy (the EDP, the SGP and multilateral surveillance); (b) the European Employment Strategy (the Luxembourg process); and (c) the actions on structural reforms (the Cardiff process[41]).

There was actually a fourth process, the Cologne process, which involved an informal exchange of views twice a year between, inter alia, the current, past and future presidents of ECOFIN, the Employment and Social Affairs Councils, the ECB, the Commission and the social partners. These processes were named after the location of the meeting places at which they were agreed.[42] The coordination was somewhat broader than this, because the annual SEM reviews were also taken into account by the Economic Policy Committee (EPC); the committee of officials responsible for overseeing the Cardiff process. This is not to be confused with the Economic and Financial Committee (EFC), also composed of officials, which undertakes the preparation and offers advice for the decision-making of ECOFIN.

The whole annual process has now been deepened and expanded under the title of the European Semester, so called because it largely takes place in the first part of the year. This has involved developing the SGP by setting out a clearer longer-term basis for bringing each Member

State's debt under control, a much closer appraisal of their annual budgets by the Commission and an Excessive Imbalance Procedure (EIP) if too many of a range of indicators suggest that their economy is developing in an unsustainable manner that will potentially destabilize the Eurozone as a whole.

The general longer-term approach, spelt out in some detail in the Conclusions of the Lisbon Council in 2000, was to set '*a new strategic goal for the next decade: to become the most competitive and dynamic knowledge-based economy in the world, capable of sustainable economic growth with more and better jobs and greater social cohesion*' (p. 1, italics in the original). This involved aiming to change the structure of the development of the EU so that it could achieve a rate of growth of 3 per cent a year (without inflationary pressure), which should have been enough to bring down unemployment or increase employment to acceptable levels over the course of a decade. The key ingredients in this were continuing structural reform (overseen by the Cardiff process), a labour market strategy (Luxembourg) and the development of the appropriate fiscal incentives through a sound budgetary system within the Member States.[43] Despite a thorough appraisal and rethink at the halfway stage, the strategy showed only limited success and was finally swept aside by the 2008 global financial crisis that rendered its targets irrelevant. However, it has been replaced by the Europe 2020 programme, which adopts a similar, but somewhat more focused aspirational approach to the next decade.

Outside the EDP and the EIP, these processes do not compel, but by agreeing objectives, setting out how each Member State intends to achieve the objectives, and evaluating progress, particularly through annual reports by the Commission, they act as considerable moral suasion. The meetings and the annual round of plans and evaluations enable the Member States to learn from each other and encourage a search for best practice. These plans can be quite detailed. The annual National Action Plans under the Employment Strategy have, for example, covered over 20 guidelines grouped under four pillars: employability, entrepreneurship, adaptability and equal opportunities. Although the Commission produces assessments, much of the point of the arrangement is that it involves *multilateral surveillance*, so that each country is looking at the successes and failures of the others.

While there were obvious opportunities for window dressing, this process, labelled 'the Open Method of Coordination', appears to have worked. The key feature of the method was that it did not compel specific actions, but allowed each Member State, and indeed the regions within it, to respond to the challenges in the manner that best met its local conditions, institutions and structures. Given that the whole structure of social welfare varies across the EU, one can distinguish four different sorts of regime. For example, any given measure will have different outcomes in different Member States.[44] In a sense, this is an example of the operation of the subsidiarity principle.

6.3C.2.1 The Stability and Growth Pact and the Excessive Deficit Procedure

As argued above, the SGP and EDP had two features: a general orientation to ensure a policy that was sustainable over the longer term and a constraint on short-term actions – the excessive deficits – to ensure that the process was not derailed on the way. This general orientation was to achieve budgets that were 'in surplus or near balance', thereby reducing debt ratios year after year. While this was necessary anyway for Member States exceeding the 60 per cent limit, it was thought generally more desirable because of the expected strains on the system that were likely to occur with the ageing of the population. In any case, it made sense to have sufficient headroom to meet shocks. This headroom was required in two respects. First of all, given the structure of automatic stabilizers (how income taxes and welfare spending act to dampen fluctuations in real GDP), each Member State needed to be far enough away from the 3 per cent deficit ratio limit for the normal sorts of adverse economic shock not to drive them over that limit. If that threatened to happen, then the Member State would have needed to take fiscal action that contracted the economy when it was performing weakly.

The 2008 global financial crisis realized this problem in a major way with several Member States reaching the point at which they could not raise further debt because lenders did not believe they would be repaid (in full). The only solution then was a drastic reduction in government spending and a scramble to raise revenues just at the point when the economy was in recession. This has been labelled 'austerity', to highlight its gravity for much of the population. This is dealt with separately in Section 6.3C.2.3. The key point to note at this juncture is that this unacceptable situation has led to a major reformulation of the approach to fiscal policy co-ordination and a considerable increase in integration among the Eurozone countries (and a widening of the gap between them and those outside the area).

However, one of the reasons why this disastrous result was encountered was because of how the SGP had been run up until then. In 2003, the German authorities found that the combination of being too close to the limit and of lower-than-expected growth forced them a little over the

3 per cent limit. Needing to raise taxes and restrain expenditure proved politically difficult. At the same time, the French authorities also breached the SGP terms, although it is more arguable that this was deliberate rather than a result of incorrect forecasting. Consequently, the ECOFIN agreed to suspend the SGP rather than declare the two countries in breach of it, as recommended by the Commission. The Commission appealed this decision to the European Court of Justice (ECJ), which ruled that the ECOFIN could decide to take no action, but that it could not suspend the process. This provoked an intensive debate on how to improve the SGP in light of the difficulties, and a new agreement was reached in March 2005.

The extent to which a Member State needs to be inside the 3 per cent boundary to avoid an undue risk of a breach and to maintain a stance that is sustainable in the long run, depends on the extent of the automatic stabilizers and the distribution of expected shocks. Thus, a country like Finland, which has fairly large stabilizers and seems prone to above-average shocks, would need to run a small surplus if it is to avoid hitting the 3 per cent boundary in a downturn.

There is a danger that having the 3 per cent deficit boundary will have a deflationary longer-term bias on the EU if the Member States compete too strongly to have very strong stabilizers. However, theoretical considerations[45] might suggest that simply repaying debt should have no influence on longer-term growth. Because this would be tantamount to only having a higher tax burden today at the benefit of a lower burden in the future.

The SGP can be viewed as having two parts: a preventive part that tries to discourage the Member States from running imprudent and unsustainable fiscal policies, and a corrective part that requires them to return to prudence as soon as possible if a mistake has been made. The 2005 agreement eased both sides of this, allowing more latitude for problems before declaring a breach (an excessive deficit) and hence permitting a less onerous return to compliance. This was not the full extent of the changes, as the Member States also took the opportunity to improve the governance process of surveillance, tightening up the quality of statistics and accounting practices.

The general principles of the SGP remained unchanged. Attempts to correct underlying problems with it, such as the failure to take proper account of the economic cycle and to focus on the underlying problem of sustainable debt, were discussed extensively in the debate on revision, but ultimately not adopted despite pressure from the Commission. While the changes did not address the fundamental economic problems, they do represent a set of arrangements that are more likely to be adhered to. In practice, the idea that a country could ever be harshly penalized was ambitious. The penalties were intended as a deterrent. If naming and shaming did not work, then the SGP was always likely to change if a significant number of countries were affected. With the 2008 global financial crisis, the EDP has been applied to most Member States, but due to the severity of the recession there has been no thought of applying penalties. The impact of the crisis on the intentions of the SGP, as the fiscal consolidation achieved since its inception has been unwound in many of the Member States and the financial position of the most exposed – Cyprus, Greece, Ireland, Italy, Portugal and Spain – has become a cause for concern.

Various proposals were put forward for reforming the SGP, and indeed the Commission itself advanced proposals,[46] which were then taken into account in considering its reform. These can be classified under three main headings, but they all relate to means of easing the constraints somewhat without altering the overall principles. The first set of proposals relates to *symmetry*. The behaviour of the Member States is constrained when deficits are in danger of becoming too large. There is no such restraint on surpluses, but a switch from a 2 per cent surplus to balance can have just as much impact on aggregate demand as a switch from balance to a 2 per cent deficit. Hence countries that notch up major surpluses could destabilize the system somewhat simply by switching rapidly to a modest deficit well within the permissible limit. The Commission in particular suggested enhancing the ability to affect fiscal policy in 'good times' and this is reflected, albeit weakly, in the revised provisions shown in Box 6.2.

The second set of proposals sought to differentiate between the Member States according to whether they are well inside, near or above the 60 per cent limit for the debt ratio. Here, the argument was simply that countries with no sustainability problem should be allowed more licence in the short run over deficits. This line of argument, of course, runs against that in the first group, as such licence could easily result in much bigger swings in fiscal policy that will affect the overall level of inflationary pressure in the Eurozone if one is referring to larger countries.

The third group of suggestions related to measurement issues. In the traditional literature the concern is with 'cyclically adjusted' deficits. While measurement has indeed been improved, the idea of cyclical adjustment has not been followed. In the main, this is because what is trend and what is cycle can only be established after the event, which is incompatible with the pre-emptive rather than the corrective SGP orientation.

There was a fourth set of suggestions that looked for a more market-related solution to the question of fiscal discipline. One of the big advantages of the EMU has been that interest rates on sovereign debt in the previously more inflation-prone and more indebted parts of the Eurozone converged on those of the lowest. Credit ratings similarly increased. Although there was explicitly no agreement to bail out the Member States across the Eurozone, the market behaved as if there were. Or at least it behaved as if the excessive deficit procedure would restrain the Member States from running policies that would ever get them near default. This means that there was not so much pressure on marginal borrowing by those states that had debt or deficit ratio problems.

Box 6.2 Revisions to the Stability and Growth Pact agreed in March 2005

The revisions agreed by Council on the recommendation of the ECOFIN are quite detailed, but can be summarized as follows:

   (i) The basic precepts are unchanged both in terms of the 60 per cent debt ratio and the 3 per cent deficit ratio, and in terms of the sanctions to be applied if a Member State is determined to have an excessive deficit and has undertaken insufficient measures to end it.

  (ii) The adjustment processes required have been eased slightly, extending the time allowed by four months (to sixteen).

 (iii) The criteria under which there can be exceptions to the 3 per cent rule for an excessive deficit have been softened. A decline in GDP or an extended period of low growth below potential is now admissible, and 'all relevant factors' can be taken into account – although these are not specified in any detail.

 (iv) The medium-term adjustment to a sustainable fiscal position has been eased slightly, and the Member States' structural balance* should be 'close to balance or in surplus' (CTBOIS) and now allows a lower limit of a 1 per cent deficit.

  (v) While the Member States are still required to reduce their structural deficits to reach CTBOIS by 0.5 per cent of GDP per year, it is now admitted that they should do so faster in 'good times' and may do so more slowly in 'bad times' in the economic cycle.

 (vi) Temporary divergences can be allowed for the costs of structural reforms aimed at improving the longer-term position.

 (vii) If there are unforeseen events, the ECOFIN can issue changed deadlines and requirements.

(viii) Implicit liabilities such as those for the pension system from the ageing of the population should be taken into account.

In addition there is a set of requirements that should improve the governance and operation of GSP, which include stronger peer pressure, better national fiscal rules and institutions – such as greater scrutiny by parliaments – improved forecasting, and better statistics and standards.

  * Structural balance is defined as the cyclically adjusted deficit after removing the effect of temporary and one-off measures (as determined by the Commission).

This has all been completely changed by the 2008 global financial crisis. Interest rate spreads widened extensively and reflected lenders' concerns that some Member States might default. The extent of the market pressure was such that the EU and the International Monetary Fund (IMF) drew up a joint fund, with strong conditionality, that Greece could draw on if it proved impossible for it to raise new debt or roll over existing debt satisfactorily in the market. While initial support came from a European Financial Stabilisation Mechanism (EFSM), the mechanism had to be enlarged and extended to the Eurozone as a whole when the problem threated to spread to Ireland, Italy, Portugal and Spain. With resources of €440 million (plus any funding from the IMF) this European Financial Stability Facility (EFSF) was intended to restore confidence that all problems could be handled. By 2011, Greece, Ireland and Portugal were all drawing on the EFSF, with associated strong conditionality requiring determined efforts to bring the rising government debt under control. These facilities have been replaced by a more permanent arrangement called the European Stability Mechanism (ESM), established on 27 September 2012, with a maximum lending capacity of €600 billion. All new bailouts for any Eurozone Member State will now be covered by the ESM, while the EFSF and the EFSM will continue to handle money transfers and programme monitoring for the previously approved bailout loans to Ireland, Portugal and Greece. Spain and Cyprus have drawn on the ESM. In the case of Spain, the funding has gone to recapitalize the banking system. While the individual banks are liable for the repayment, if they fail to do so then the Spanish government has to reimburse the ESM.

The Eurozone has thus got itself to a position that it previously resisted. The Member States did not want to bail each other out, and the SGP and the TEU criteria were designed to make such a threat implausible. By admitting Member States with debt problems, albeit assisted in the Greek case by incorrect national accounts statistics, and by not having a stronger SGP, it has reached the point at which the weaker states can threaten the system. Much of the reason for the compromise was, however, that financial institutions in the other Member States had bought Greek government debt and hence stood to make major losses in the event of a default.

6.3C.2.3 *The response to the global financial crisis*

While it looked in 2007 as if the impact on Europe of the financial crisis in the US would be light, the picture all changed with the collapse of Lehman Brothers in September 2008. Initially the problem seemed to be restricted to a banking crisis, which hit the UK hard, and which resulted in the collapse of the banking system in Iceland and the need to seek an IMF bailout for Latvia. The most drastic impact in the Eurozone was on Ireland, in which the bailout cost was more than 30 per cent of GDP in 2009 alone. However, as the world economy turned down, it became evident that there were going to be fiscal problems for Italy, Portugal and Spain and, most of all, for Greece, in which the expected path of debt looked as if it would lead to default and possibly exit from the Eurozone. While the EU progressively addressed the immediate debt problem through the creation of the EFSF and the ESM, strict conditionality on joint lending with the IMF and the restructuring of privately held Greek government debt as described above, the EU also took a series of major steps towards correcting the weaknesses in the system of fiscal coordination that had led to it.[47]

There were three main steps, a set of six measures proposed in September 2010, colloquially labelled the 'Six Pack', a set of two further measures introduced in 2012 (the 'Two Pack') and a new treaty on Stability, Coordination and Governance (TSCG) that came into force at the beginning of 2013. Among them, these measures require the signatories to aim their budgets at a 0.5 per cent surplus, to embody the rules in national law, to have independent assessments of fiscal plans, to submit their budgets to the Commission for appraisal at the beginning of the year as part of the European Semester, before confirmation by national parliaments, to improve the statistical base, to strengthen the EDP and to introduce the new Excessive Imbalance Procedure.

This is an impressive list of measures, and it gives the Commission an unprecedented opportunity to control the prudence of the Member States' fiscal plans. Moreover the strengthening of the EDP entailed a change in how QMV was to apply to decisions. The Commission's recommendations would be implemented unless a qualified majority excluding the country in question voted against them. Previously, it was necessary to get a qualified majority in favour, which is a much more difficult proposition.

Getting this tough legislation passed through the Council and the European Parliament involved an innovation which extended the scope of the idea of a 'two-speed', or more accurately, a 'multiple geometry' Europe. Thereby, while the Eurozone Member States were bound by all of it, the remainder did not have to comply, particularly in the case of the TSCG, which the UK and the Czech Republic did not sign. In instituting the EIP, the EU takes an important further step in the EMU by insisting that the structure of the Eurozone economies should not get too out of line with each other and should not threaten instability for the whole area. These imbalances are measured by a set of indicators relating to financial pressures through credit growth, labour market pressures, balance of payments measures and product market problems. It is accompanied by the ability to impose sanctions should a participant refuse to comply.

Matching the changes in the framework for fiscal policy, the ECB rapidly eased monetary policy down to the bound of zero nominal interest rates by 2009 and expanded the range of collateral accepted so that banks could obtain adequate liquidity. The extent of these measures dwarfs the ESM. At their height in 2012, the NCBs of the troubled countries had built up balances at the ECB with respect to the other NCBs of over one trillion euro. This has been highly controversial because the ECB has been holding large balances of troubled Member State debt through its Target-2[48] settlement system, which some feel is the equivalent of the monetary financing of these regimes.[49] However, it reflects the fact that while political agreement on the treatment of the sovereign debt and fiscal problems may have been slow and difficult to achieve, the ECB has got on with the job of saving the Eurozone from crisis. The most striking contribution was the statement by the ECB president, Mario Draghi, on 12 July 2012, that the ECB would 'do whatever it takes to preserve the euro'. From that point, interest spreads for the troubled countries have fallen markedly, and all but Greece and Cyprus had been able to re-enter the market by early 2014 and raise debt on their own without the need to resort to the ESM.

The drama is not necessarily over. China and other hitherto strong emerging markets may face difficulties and halt the slow economic recovery of much of the EU. The move to recapitalize banks may be insufficient to prevent more failures and the structural changes in Greece may still turn out to be insufficient to halt the ever-rising debt. Furthermore, exiting from quantitative easing and the very easy monetary policy around the world may pose its own instabilities, including on the ECB's Target-2 balances

6.3C.2.4 *Policy coordination*

The type of policy coordination described thus far differs from that normally discussed in the literature, in which much of the point is the coordination of monetary and fiscal policy. The argument is that there are some choices that can be made over how much to use fiscal policy rather than monetary policy to smooth fluctuations in the real economy or maintain price stability. The set-up within the EMU rests upon a fairly simple economic model. One aspect of this model claims that monetary policy cannot be used effectively to achieve longer-term real objectives, except in two senses. The first is that having higher rates of inflation beyond levels near zero will tend to result in reductions in the overall rate of economic growth and indeed having falls in the price level may also be damaging. The second is that inept policy that does not generate credibility will also impose a cost on society.

In general, taking these together, the argument is in effect that monetary policy per se will not have adverse effects on the longer-term level of unemployment. Monetary policy can therefore be targeted appropriately at the stabilization of the price level rather than on objectives for the real economy. The scope for using monetary policy for smoothing real behaviour beyond that point is limited. In general, the impact of monetary policy on inflation variation and output gap variation should be regarded as one of complements rather than trade-offs.[50] A credible monetary policy aimed at restricting inflation to a fairly narrow range in a smooth manner should ipso facto also restrain the fluctuations in output around the sustainable path.

Similarly, in this simple paradigm, fiscal policy can affect the rate of growth in terms of how funds are raised and spent. For example, one can view this in terms of incentives. Moreover, as discussed above, for fiscal policy to be consistent with price stability over the medium term, it has to be sustainable (and believed to be as such by markets). But discretionary fiscal policy, beyond the automatic stabilizers, is unlikely to be of much value, except to help exit the deflationary spiral.[51] One of the main reasons for avoiding discretionary fiscal policy in addressing fluctuations in the economy is that policy operates with a lag, and there is a danger that by the time the problem is identified, the necessary measures have already been agreed by the legislature and implemented, and when the impact occurs, it may destabilize what is then going on.

In the event of a major adverse shock, such as the 2008 global financial crisis, the model is still not disturbed. The shock is so great that emergency action is warranted. Each Member State, acting in its own interests, nevertheless acts to stimulate joint demand and reduce the short-run impact (albeit at the expense of higher taxation in the future to pay for the surge in debt).

Under these circumstances, there is no need for much policy coordination between the monetary and fiscal authorities beyond transparency. The monetary authorities need to be able to make a reasonable assessment of the inflationary pressure likely to stem from fiscal policy, and the fiscal authorities need to know what to expect from monetary policy when setting their fiscal objectives. The potential conflict comes from the fact that, unlike fiscal policy, monetary policy can be changed quickly and substantially, and indeed with fairly limited transaction costs. In the EU's framework the coordination works because the monetary authorities are predictable. If they do react quickly, it is to specific crisis signals like the shock of 11 September 2001. Given the time lag for fiscal changes, the fiscal authorities need to be confident that their monetary counterparts will not do anything in the intervening period that will render their policy stance inappropriate.

Pinning the ECB down to a single objective helps achieve this predictability. In the same way, the SGP rules and macroeconomic coordination ensure that the ECB has plenty of warning about the way in which fiscal policy is likely to develop and hence is less likely to set inappropriate levels for interest rates. EMU coordination will not work if the Eurosystem believes that the fiscal authorities will always be too inflationary and/or if the ECOFIN believes that the Eurosystem will always set interest rates that are 'too high'. Under these circumstances, the problem will be self-fulfilling and monetary policy and fiscal policy will tend to push against each other at a real cost to the economy. Fiscal policy needs to be credible to the monetary authority and vice versa. There is a danger of paying too much attention to the rhetoric in this regard.

The final part of the simple model that underlies the coordination mechanism is the belief that it is structural policies that will change the underlying rate of economic growth. Hence these form a key part of the continuing annual policy discussion. Once fiscal policy is largely automatic with respect to shocks, the surveillance mechanisms can focus on sustainability and on whether the size of budgetary swings that the automatic processes deliver are appropriate. If there were little concern for fine-tuning, then having more than the current six-monthly informal dialogue laid down by the Cologne process would seem unnecessary.

63C.2.5 *Asymmetry*

Traditionally, the focus on the suitability and sustainability of the EMU has been on asymmetry in the sense of the differences between the Member States, as discussed above. However, a different asymmetry is also present in the Member States' behaviour, namely asymmetry over the cycle.[52]

The total deficit is much more responsive in the downward than the upward phase. While responsiveness over the cycle as a whole is of the order of 0.2 to 0.3 (a 1 per cent increase in real GDP lowers the deficit ratio by 0.2 per cent to 0.3 per cent) in the first year, it is five times as large in the downturn as the upturn. This bundles together all the influences: automatic stabilizers, discretionary policy changes, interest rate changes and any special factors. On unbundling, one can see that the automatic or cyclical part of the deficit behaves in a fairly symmetric manner. It is what governments choose to do with the structural part of the deficit that causes the asymmetry. What has happened is that governments increased the structural deficit in both downturns and upturns. Thus in good times governments tend to allow the system to ratchet up. The effect is split between revenues and expenditures, but the asymmetry is more prominent on the revenue side. Tax rates are cut in upturns so that the revenue-to-GDP ratios do not rise.

The SGP, EDP and the other components of macroeconomic coordination in the EMU would have to lean against this tendency for asymmetric behaviour to reduce the pressures it generates. In practice, the pressure is placed somewhat more on the downside: the area in which governments have themselves responded more effectively in the past. Tackling this asymmetry and 'pro-cyclicality in good times' was incorporated in general terms in the revised SGP. Whether this will have much effect is debatable, especially after the experience of the 2008 financial crisis.

6.3C.3 Completing EMU

It has to be said that the earlier discussion of coordination leaves a lot to the credibility of the process. Institutional credibility would be much greater if the degree of control over fiscal actions at the EU level were larger and there were some parallel institution to the ECB on the fiscal side. While this is now on the political agenda, but nowhere near adoption, its relevance would be much greater if one further plank, which characterizes most economic and monetary unions, were in place, namely, a significant revenue-raising and spending capability at the EU level. This does not have to take the form of a larger budget per se, as transfers from one region or Member State to another in a form of fiscal federalism would also suffice. Currently, stabilization takes place automatically *within* the Member States. It only takes place *between* them to the extent that their agreed and automatic actions spill over from one to another because of their economic interdependence. The actual size of such a budget (around 2.5 per cent to 7 per cent of the EU GDP) would be highly effective,[53] but is quite small compared to many existing federal states. It is, however, large compared to the structural funds and the current budgetary limit.

The EU enlargement has increased the need for fiscal federalism, although the current small economic size of the new Member States keeps the scale of any transfers needed down in the short term. The concern here is with cross-border fiscal flows to help balance out the effect of asymmetric shocks. Dealing with income inequality is a problem of a very different order. Nevertheless, given the persistence of shocks, particularly with respect to their impact on the labour market, if fiscal flows do not ease the pressure, then other changes will result to compensate. The most obvious would be an increase in migration. That is also not politically attractive at present. It remains to be seen whether some greater integration on the macroeconomic side of the EMU may not be preferred to increasing flexibility through cross-border migration. The relative attraction of stabilizing flows is that, according to their definition, they should be temporary. However, the shape of economic cycles does vary across the EU. Nevertheless, as economic and financial integration increases across the EU, so self-insurance increases with diversification of income and wealth generation across the EU as a whole, helping to smooth the asymmetric shocks hitting any particular region without recourse to fiscal transfers.[54]

6.3C.4 Eurozone enlargement

Before EMU moves further towards 'completion', it is likely to continue to expand through the inclusion of new members. Thus far, the six new Member States that have joined, Cyprus, Estonia, Latvia, Malta, Slovakia and Slovenia, are all small. Even if many of the new Member States were to join, the economic effect would be limited. Only Poland and to a lesser extent Romania are of any size. Their effect on the dynamics of decision-making would be much more dramatic, and indeed the Eurosystem may well invoke its ability to alter the voting arrangements on monetary policy in order to move the balance back in favour of the large original members. Adding Denmark and Sweden would make little difference to the structure of the Eurozone or the issues that have been raised in this section. If the UK were to join, the position would be different, as the country is large enough to alter the balance of the single monetary policy. Also, since the UK is somewhat different, both in its flexibility of response and its symmetry with the other Member States, the consequences could be measurable. Any of the Member States that join are likely to have a level of income per head well below the average of the existing members, as convergence in these real terms is not one of the criteria. This could alter the character of the Eurozone.

It has already been noted that in the run-up to membership, there was greater convergence of the Member States than there has been in the period afterwards. This was because they had to run their monetary and fiscal policies individually to converge to quite a narrow band. Once inside, the SGP, the Excessive Deficit procedure and the rest of the coordination under the Broad Economic Policy Guidelines apply, but the SMP is no longer related to the inflation concerns of each country, just the total, so more inflation and indeed growth variation is possible and feasible. This experience is likely to be even stronger for the new members, as they are generally expected to 'catch up' quite rapidly with the existing members in real terms. This means that they will have faster rates of growth, driven primarily by productivity, which may have implications for inflation and monetary policy. While the price of tradable goods and services may be reasonably similar across the EU, the same is not the case for non-tradable commodities. Large portions of non-tradable commodities are public and private services, in which their principal input is labour. As productivity grows in the tradable industries, so wages are likely to rise with it. In turn, in a competitive economy, this is likely to result in wage increases in the non-tradable sector. There, it will not be so easy to find productivity growth to offset it, and prices will tend to rise. Insofar as there are no offsets elsewhere, this will result in a rise in the general price level that is faster than in the rest of the Eurozone.

This process, known as the Balassa-Samuelson effect, will probably not be substantial by the time the new Member States join the Eurozone, perhaps of the order of 1 per cent a year.[55] Given that the new Member States, taken together, constitute only a fraction of the Eurozone GDP, this implies that the total effect on inflation would be of the order of 0.2 per cent a year. That may seem very small, but with a medium-term target of inflation below 2 per cent, it could represent an increase in the rate of interest. The actual impact is speculative, and could vary from the disastrous to the trivial. It would be disastrous if some countries cannot cope with the increase in the real exchange rate (relative price and cost levels) that this relative inflation might imply, as appears to be the case for those Member States that have faced a sovereign debt crisis since 2009. The problems of asymmetry that have worried some of the old Member States could be much larger for the new Member States, yet the drive for locking in credibility and buying lower interest rates by Eurozone membership may be sufficient to play down the worries about sustainability at the time of joining. Too rapid an expansion of the EMU could actually harm the prospects of the enterprise as a whole. It is therefore not surprising that the ECB has already blown relatively cold on some of the ideas implying early membership and has sought to toughen the interpretation of the convergence criteria.

Nevertheless, the experience of the Baltic States in the global financial crisis has shown that they can cope with the largest adverse shocks that are likely to hit them and bounce back sufficiently to meet the convergence criteria for joining the Eurozone. With a currency board, some of them have effectively been members of the Eurozone since its inception, but without a vote.

6.4 The survival of the EMU

Despite the turmoil in the Eurozone since the financial crisis, the EU has achieved the most demanding of international economic integration elements. But the design of the EU's EMU has been faulty since it lacks the 'economic' part of 'economic and monetary union'. Indeed it has been more like the 'European monetary union' that many think EMU stands for. This defective architecture has been clearly exposed since the 2008 global financial crisis. However, the EU has now agreed and is in the process of creating a 'banking union', which, if accomplished, will regulate and supervise banking activities across the Eurozone and other Member States if they choose to join.[56] Moreover, the fact that the remark by president of the ECB that he was ready to do whatever it takes to preserve the euro was sufficient to restore confidence in financial markets shows the underlying strength of the system. Nevertheless, for the EU's EMU to stand the test of time, fiscal integration in the Eurozone should be considered very seriously. Makeshift arrangements are fine, but the architecture must have a proper foundation.

Recommended Reading

Commission of the European Union (2008) *EMU@10 Successes and Challenges After 10 Years of Economic and Monetary Union*, DG ECOFIN, Brussels.
De Grauwe, Paul (2012) *The Economics of Monetary Union*, Oxford University Press, Oxford.

European Central Bank (2011) *The Monetary Policy of the ECB*, ECB, Frankfurt, available at http://www.ecb.europa.eu/pub/pdf/other/monetarypolicy2011en. pdf.

International Monetary Fund (2014) *From Fragmentation to Financial Integration in Europe*, IMF, Washington DC.

Issing, Ottmar (2008) *The Birth of the Euro*, Cambridge University Press, Cambridge.

7
The Importance of the EU

7.1 Introduction

It was established in Chapter 1 that the European Union (EU) is the most significant and influential of all schemes of international economic integration. This is due to several EU attributes. Because of its Single European Market (SEM), people, goods, services and capital (both money and the right of establishment) are free to move across the entire EU. It speaks with one voice in international trade negotiations through the Commissioner in charge of Trade. Eighteen of its twenty-eight Member States have the same currency (the euro), with the European Central Bank (ECB) in charge of the Eurozone monetary policy, and all the remaining Member States bar two (Denmark and the UK) must join the Eurozone when ready by meeting the Maastricht criteria. It has a system for monitoring and influencing fiscal policy, the Stability and Growth Pact. It has its own budget, financing a wide range of policies. It has a single president of the European Council who speaks on behalf of the entire EU for two and a half to five years. There is no more 'who to call when one wants to speak to Europe?' It has, as a member of the Commission, thus in office for five years, a Foreign Policy Chief (High Representative, HR) who deals with all foreign policy matters on behalf of the whole EU and controls a vast diplomatic corps. It has the European Financial Stability Facility (EFSF) as well as the European Stability Mechanism (ESM) with huge funds to assist Eurozone Member States in financial trouble, and it is in the process of creating a banking union. It is the largest single economy in the world, with five Member States in the top ten world economies. It is a voluntary association open to all European nations with elected governments and is very close to comprising the whole of Europe, and beyond, when the geographical limits of the Continent are loosely defined. And it has plans for more integration, including a banking union and in fiscal policy. No other scheme of international economic integration matches these attributes, and the schemes comprise practically the whole world, with some members belonging to more than one scheme.

Chapter 2 traces the journey that the EU took to arrive at its present level of integration. The trip commenced in 1951 when the Original Six created the European Coal and Steel Community (ECSC) by the Treaty of Paris. It finished with today's EU of 28 Member States, based on the Treaty of Lisbon that came into force on 1 December 2009. The journey revealed how the EU acquired the mentioned attributes and, vitally, examined the reasons for the drive to achieve them. The chapter shows that the trip was not always a smooth one, but that the Member States have consistently managed to emerge from adversity by adopting more and bolder acts of integration.

Chapters 3–6 respectively describe and discuss how the EU reaches its decisions, what policies it has adopted, how it finances them (i.e. its general budget), and its single currency. In other words, they reveal its true substance.

Thus, the introductory chapter and Chapters 1–6 are about the nature of the EU. What remains is to briefly discuss the importance of the EU, and to this we now turn, briefly, simply because the 'nature' of this organization has revealed many facets of the 'importance'.

7.2   The importance of the EU

The EU is important both for its own Member States, in other words, for itself, as well for the entire world. However, in many cases there is no clear distinction between 'for itself' and 'for the entire world', so there is no need to have separate subsections for the two categories. And since the EU is set to encompass the whole of Europe and go beyond it, 'Europe' can stand for 'EU'.

A Europe at peace. Since 1945, the EU Member States have been at peace with each other. This is a vast transformation for a continent that had caused two major world wars and more, with the loss of millions of its own and other peoples' lives and the continent's infrastructure completely destroyed. This peace is attributed to their working together in economic matters, instead of each looking after its own. As we saw in Chapter 2, the rationale for the creation of the ECSC in 1951 was to end the historic rivalry of France and Germany by making a war between the two nations not only unthinkable but also materially impossible. Indeed, the founding fathers of the EU dreamed of the creation of a United States of Europe because they believed that there was no other means of putting an end to the Continent's woeful history of conflict, bloodshed and suffering. They realized so soon after the Second World War that this was not possible, but that by working together in the economic field and getting to know each other well, a federal Europe would be possible. In other words, they saw unity as the only way to achieving eternal peace on a continent with a long history of deep divisions and devastating wars.

Some would argue that European economic integration has not been the main cause of peace in Europe. Rather, that it is the protection provided by the US through the North Atlantic Treaty Organization (NATO) that has propelled it, combined with the desire for war having been exhausted since 1945. Of course, Europe cannot have a monopoly claim on its peace, but there is no escaping the fact that European integration has enhanced peace in Europe by eliminating the factors that led to war: mistrust, opposing interests and competition for power and resources.[1] Indeed, this was recognized by the Nobel Committee when it awarded its Peace Prize for 2012 to the EU because *'for over six decades* [it] *contributed to the advancement of peace and reconciliation, democracy and human rights in Europe'* (emphasis in original). Sceptics would raise their arms in protest, shouting that the Nobel Peace Prize has on many occasions been awarded to controversial people,[2] organizations[3] and causes,[4] but although such complaints may be warranted, there is no justification whatsoever for claiming that they have peculiar pertinence in the case of the EU.

A Europe promoting democracy and protecting human rights. As stated in Chapter 2, any European country is entitled to apply for EU membership provided it meets the Copenhagen criteria, adopted in June 1993. These demand that a candidate country 'has achieved stability of institutions guaranteeing democracy, the rule of law, human rights, respect for and protection of minorities, the existence of a functioning market economy as well as the capacity to cope with competitive pressure and market forces within the Union'. EU membership presupposes the candidate country's ability to take on the obligations of membership, including adherence to the aims of political, economic and monetary union, and the *acquis communautaire*, which dictates that all EU legislation to date should be incorporated into national law. Indeed, even well before 1993, the European Community (EC) excluded Greece when it was taken over and run by a military junta during 1967–75 and did not consider Spain as a candidate until the death of General Francisco Franco y Bahamonde in 1975, who had ruled Spain from

1939 to 1975. In promoting democracy and protecting human rights, the EU is very important indeed.

A Europe with a single market. As explained in Chapter 4, the SEM programme is remarkable for its broad aims and ambitions, and the development of a clear approach to achieving them. It embraced measures as diverse as animal health controls and licensing of banks; public procurement; and standards for catalytic converters for car exhausts. It covered not just traditionally tradable services such as banking, insurance and transport but also the new areas of information, marketing and audio-visual services. With regard to transport, the agenda included the 'phasing out of all quantitative restrictions (quotas) on road haulage', and further liberalization of road, sea and air passenger services through the fostering of increased competition. The aim for audio-visual services was to create a single EC-wide broadcasting area.

Before the introduction of the SEM, three types of barriers segmented the EU: physical, fiscal and technical barriers. Physical barriers were checks at borders, considered necessary for controlling the movement of persons for immigration purposes; for customs purposes due to differences in indirect taxes for the protection of animal and plant health; and for checks on lorries and drivers for safety reasons and for enforcement of national restrictions on foreign hauliers. Fiscal barriers were imposed to check the goods crossing borders, due to differences in indirect taxes: VAT and excise duties on alcohol, tobacco and so forth, which provided the documents for remitting the taxes on exports and imposing them on imports. And technical barriers covered an enormous range of measures that affect trade. These barriers meant that considerable expense was incurred in the case of lorries crossing borders, in preparing the documentation needed, not to mention the delays at borders, which further increased the cost of inter-EU transport. Big businesses saw the segmentation of the EU into national markets as hampering their international competitiveness, by depriving them of the economies of scale afforded by larger markets. They were unable to get the long production runs necessary to keep costs down and to spread the costs of research and development (R&D).

The SEM, although not yet fully complete, especially in the case of services, has removed most of these barriers, enabling the EU to achieve savings equivalent to an increase in the rate of gross domestic product (GDP) growth of 2–3 per cent. That is not something to scoff at when a rate of growth of between 2 per cent and 4 per cent is regarded as a success story these days. It has also attracted substantial foreign direct investment (FDI), since locating within any EU Member State enables a foreign company to sell anywhere within the EU, provided it has met the 'origin' rules. Therefore, the SEM market has been very important for the EU and could not have been established without EU integration.

A Europe with a single currency. Although at present only 19 of the Member States belong to the Eurozone, as mentioned in Chapters 1, 2 and 6, except for Denmark and the UK for their 'opt-outs', every other Member State must join when it meets the Maastricht criteria. However, for the 18 Member States of the Eurozone, the single currency has realized at least some of the possible gains from the economic and monetary union (EMU) discussed in Chapter 6. First, transaction costs incurred when one currency is exchanged for another have been avoided. Second, competition in the SEM has been enhanced because of the greater transparency and certainty the euro provides: prices can be more easily compared across national borders, so competition has been intensified. Since exchange rate movements have been eliminated, differences in prices and costs between locations have become more apparent; therefore, at least some production has been shifted to where costs are lowest. Third, the stability of exchange rates has enhanced trade, through reduced price uncertainty, encouraged capital to move to where it is most productively rewarded, and provided incentives to labour to move to where the highest rewards prevail. Fourth, because the ECB sets the monetary policy for the entire Eurozone, there has been a clear interest rate gain for the smaller and previously high-inflation countries, since they are able to borrow at lower interest rates due to inflation expectations being reduced and to the greater efficiency of larger and deeper capital markets in the Eurozone. And, the CEB has been supporting all the countries that have suffered greatly from the 2008 financial crisis. Moreover, the adoption of the euro has transformed the currency into a major world medium that competes with the US dollar.

A Europe with a single Trade Commissioner. As explained in Chapters 1 and 2, the Commission has sole responsibility for acting on behalf of all the Member States in all matters concerning trade and related matters with the outside world. This has enabled it to negotiate on equal terms with the US in the General Agreement on Tariffs and Trade (GATT) rounds, producing successful results in reducing restrictions on international trade and investment (Table 1.2), as well as the inclusion of services, intellectual property rights and agriculture in the World Trade Organization (WTO) agenda. There is no doubt that without the EU, no single European nation would have been able to influence the governing of the international trading system and the conduct of trade and foreign investment or to achieve much for itself. In other words, it is vital for the Member States to delegate authority to negotiate international trade and investment deals to a single Commissioner, rather than for each to act alone. Otherwise, they would be at the mercy of the big actors, now not just the US but Japan, China and more. Thus the EU is of vital importance to its Member States.

A Europe with a single president. The 2009 Treaty of Lisbon introduced the office of resident of the EC, that is, of the EU. Before that, the presidency was for a rotating six months between the Member States in the Council (of Ministers) of the European Union, which was very unsatisfactory. This was not just because the ministers represented the limited interests of their own ministries (agriculture, transport, the environment and the like; see Chapter 3). It was also because six months was not long enough to produce significant results; some of the poorer Member Nations were not in a position to cope with its financial demands (not all the financing was provided by the EU); and, vitally, some ministers could not exert the necessary prestige needed on the world stage (some were not even known within the EU). Indeed, those were the reasons why Henry Kissinger, President Richard Nixon's National Security Advisor during 1969–73 and US secretary of state for Presidents Nixon and Gerald Ford during 1973–7 uttered his famous words regarding whom he should call when he needed to speak with the EU.

Having a single EU president for a period of up to five years has enabled the EU Council to carry out its main functions (setting the strategic agenda, managing crises, arbitrating as a final court and shaping the EU). Indeed, it is difficult to imagine how the EU could have eased the Eurozone crisis and continued to do so in its aftermath without Herman Van Rompuy's excellent ability to generate consensus amongst the 28 Heads of State and Government of the Member Nations. And in doing so, he has enhanced the EU's international image.

A Europe with a single foreign policy chief, the High Representative. No Member State acting single-handedly can have a substantial impact on serious world problems that have repercussions on Europe or are vital in their own right. How much can even Germany, France or the UK each by itself help ease the lamentable situation in Syria, let alone completely resolve it, and peacefully? Or eliminate the threat of the 'Islamic State' jihadists? Or entice Iran into serious discussions regarding its nuclear programme to confine it to only peaceful exploitation? Or assist the majority of Ukrainians in their pursuit of closer association with the EU? Or get the Israelis and Palestinians to seriously pursue peace in the most troubled part of the world? Indeed, it is precisely because the EU has a single foreign policy chief that it has been invited to participate on equal terms with the US and Russia on these and other serious issues.

A Europe for survival in a competitive new world order. Europe needs not only to continue to be united but also to become more intensively so, in order to face the challenges created by the emergence of China and India and a Russia determined to be a, if not the, dominant world actor.

As mentioned in the introductory chapter, the rise of China and India, with more than a third of total world population, and with China becoming the second-largest economy after the US, and which will be the first-largest by the time this book is published, is of course most welcome. Welcome, because both countries remain very poor nations in terms of per capita GNI (China, $5,720; India, $1,580; EU average, $33,510; US, $52,340), so hopefully they will continue to develop and do so quickly so that they can catch up with the advanced world. What is vital for the EU, however, is that the EU is now in a world in which a few nations loom large, with East Asia becoming more and more prominent not only because of China and India but also because of Japan, Indonesia and the like. Thus, most countries in the West must try their best to ensure that they get a share of the markets in the East as well as entice FDI from them. Indeed, that is precisely what the US has been doing since it has prioritized the region for its global attention, hence the ongoing negotiations on a Trans-Pacific Partnership (TPP). Given the US economic interests in the area combined with its military commitment to defend it against attack, notably to defend Japan through the US-Japan Security Treaty, one can rest assured that the US will continue to pay more attention to the region. Some would counter by stating that the US is also involved in ongoing negotiations with the EU for a Trans-Atlantic Trade and Investment Partnership (TTIP) and is committed to the defence of Europe through NATO. Of course, the US must protect its interests in both regions, but there is no denying its prioritizing Asia. Therefore, the EU must face the reality of having to do more for itself, especially when it has a very good chance of becoming one of the major forces in the world.

The implications of these developments for the EU are clear. Indeed, all the Member States should be well aware of them. This is due to the fact that on 29 June 1998, the European Council adopted a Communication from the Commission that asked that the EC *'develop a long-term relationship with China that reflects China's worldwide, as well as regional, economic and political influence'*. That is because *'relations with China are bound to be a cornerstone in Europe's external relations, both with Asia and globally'* (emphasis in original). It added that the EC 'needs an action-oriented, not a merely declaratory policy, to strengthen that relationship'. The rest of the Communication examined the specific concerns of the EC, especially how to enable EC enterprises to compete success-fully in the expanding Chinese market, and developed a detailed picture of all considerations, as well as articulated policy recommendations and actions on each.[5] On the basis of this, the EU-China Relationship Agreement was established.[6]

In other words, it would be futile for the Member States to pursue their individual interests in Asia; they have to act collectively. The EU is therefore important for the survival of the Member States in a world that is increasingly dominated by the US and the East. Sadly, that is precisely what the Member States have not been doing. Witness the uncoordi-nated dispatch to China of high-level officials and business people by Germany, the UK and others. Some would argue that a large group is not essential for survival in an increasingly hostile world, citing as exam-ples the cases of New Zealand, Norway and Switzerland. Leaving aside the question regarding why such countries are successful (Norway and oil; Switzerland and membership of the European Economic Area; New Zealand and its 'closeness' to the EU and Australia), do these countries have any impact on world affairs, hence on their long-term prospects?

And it is not just in the economic field that the EU is vital for its Member States in the new global order. As mentioned above, the EU has to have a single voice if it is to be an actor in the political, military and security fields. Even at the United Nations (UN), the EU nations, although they sometimes coordinate their stances on certain issues, on the whole act individually. They would be more assertive and successful if they acted as one. Of course, they would then stand to lose a perma-nent seat on the Security Council (a seat for the EU, instead of one each for France and the UK), but is that really more important that having one voice?

Within this last context, the threat of a Russia that is determined to become a global political leader along lines that are not generally shared by the West looms large. Witness how Russia managed to 'annex' the Crimea, how it is helping those in East Ukraine fight for independ-ence to follow in the footsteps of the Crimea, how it is undermining efforts by the West to deal with the tragic situation in Syria and how it has not acted constructively in the handling of the Iranian situation regarding nuclear energy and aiding Hamas in Palestine and Hezbollah in Lebanon. The EU failed to stop Russia's insurgence in Ukraine simply because its Member States could not agree on a common stance. If the EU is to succeed in this regard, the High Representative (above) should be empowered to act forcefully on behalf of a united EU. Unfortunately, the first occupier of the position, Britain's Catherine Ashton (Baroness

Ashton of Upholland), failed miserably in respect of Russia, although she acted admirably in the cases of Syria and Iran, but her failure was not due to her incompetence, rather to the disagreements of the Member States on what action to undertake. Hopefully, her successor since 1 November 2014, Federica Mogherini, will be able to secure the consensus amongst the Member States that is necessary for effective action. However, the main message should not go amiss: if each Member State acted alone, the EU would stand no chance in taming Russia.

7.3 The UK dilemma

What is the significance of the importance of the EU for the ongoing discussion in the UK regarding the renegotiation of the terms of its membership and the holding of a referendum in 2017 if the Conservative Party were to secure an outright win in the 2015 general election? The answer can be very brief since it is more than implicit in the importance of the EU given above as well as in the main chapters of the book.

As argued above, it is extremely important for the Member States to stick together and to integrate even more if they are to succeed individually and, vitally, to survive in a very different new world order. Thus those who wish to water down the EU treaties should be asked to think twice. This does not mean that no changes should be contemplated. After all, the EU is far from being perfect. To agree to limit the free movement of labour to those actually seeking work, rather than claiming social security (on 11 November 2014, the European Court of Justice [ECJ] ruled in favour of Germany's stating that Member States can deny certain payments to unemployed EU citizens who move to that country just to claim benefits), would not do much damage to the SEM, but would of course undermine the 'spirit' of free movement. But to ask for a 'repatriation' of some basic pillars of the club, would of course be more problematic, if not highly undesirable. The UK cannot pick and choose what it deems suitable, and it is about time it realized that the EU was never meant to be just for 'economic' purposes. Sadly, as revealed in Chapter 2, that has always been the UK's position: it refused to be 'at the table' at Messina when it realized that the Six wanted more than a 'free trade area' for the European Economic Community (EEC) in 1957. Indeed, as we have seen in Chapter 2, the UK applied for EC membership several times in the 1960s for no other reason than that the Six were registering high rates of economic growth, while it was suffering from the 'British disease'. Charles de Gaulle exercised his 'veto' against UK membership while he was president of France because he was adamant that the UK was not truly committed to the European venture. On 14 January 1963, in his New Year press conference, de Gaulle explained in detail the economic and political differences between the Six and the UK, and the danger of US influence on European politics through its 'British outpost', before declaring offhandedly,

> It is possible that one day England might manage to transform herself sufficiently to become part of the European community, without restriction, without reserve and preference for anything whatsoever; and in this case the Six would open the door to her and France would raise no obstacle.[7]

Has anything changed since 1963? The British attitude seems to have worsened. This is not just because of the ascendance of the UK Independent Party (UKIP), a party with the main manifesto agendum of UK withdrawal from the EU. It is also because, given the 'alleged' general scepticism of the British public towards the EU, the Labour Party may have to match the promise by the Conservative Party for a referendum if it is to stand a chance of competing on equal terms. And the Liberal Democratic Party, the only one committed to EU membership, is on the decline. It is therefore vital that we should strive to convince UK citizens of the true benefits of the EU and our membership of the club. The fact that a UK poll conducted by Ipsos Mori Political Monitor on 11–14 October 2014 found that 56 per cent support UK membership of the EU, while only 31 oppose it, with 8 per cent undecided, does not contradict the allegation unless the finding is repeated several times.

Given this general picture, had Scotland decided on 18 September 2014 to become independent of the UK, such an outcome would have impacted on both the UK and the EU. Of course, had Scotland decided to go its own way, this would have greatly impacted on the UK itself, but not for economic reasons: Scotland accounts for only 8.3 per cent of the UK's population and 8.1 per cent of UK's GDI (see the introductory chapter). What is important is that the break-up would have undermined the 'unity' that has served the UK well since 1707 both internally and externally. The internal, such as the stability of having one currency, is too obvious to mention; the external would have included whether the UK would have continued to be one of the most influential EU Member States. At present, the UK has roughly the same population as that of France and Italy, both 20 million short of Germany's, but without Scotland, it would have become a halfway house between them and Spain. A diminished UK could possibly also have lost its permanent seat on the UN's Security Council, impacting on its ability to exert vital influence on disturbing global developments. Since a 'powerful' UK is vital for both the EU itself and for the world as a whole, UK withdrawal would diminish the EU. That is why President Barack Obama has urged the UK to stay in the EU family, but, as we saw in Chapter 2, his position is not new: the US encouraged European unification well before the signing of the Treaty of Paris, which created the ECSC in 1951. However, all this may seem irrelevant now that Scotland has decided to stay in the UK, but developments since the 18 September 2014 referendum regarding what Scotland was promised by the three major UK parties in the case of a 'no' vote clearly indicate that Scottish independence has not dropped from the agenda 'for a generation' as Alex Salmond, the leader of the Scottish National Party during the referendum, has publicly stated, and so has his successor, Nicola Sturgeon.

7.4   A bleak future without a united Europe

The conclusion is simple. The EU is vital for its Member States because if each acted alone, it would stand no chance of coping in a world in which economic dominance continues to shift to the East, especially with the US being on a declining long-term trajectory. And the EU is even more crucial for Europe if it is to have a say in how the world political order should develop in a future with an increasingly assertive China and a Russia acting in alarming ways. In short, the EU is of the essence for its Member States in both economic and political terms since as individual countries their future would be bleak.

Recommended Reading

McCormick, John (2013) *Why Europe Matters: The Case for the European Union*, Palgrave Macmillan, Basingstoke, UK.

8
The Future of the EU

8.1 Introduction

The introductory chapter and Chapters 1–7 have together established the nature and importance of the European Union (EU). On the importance of the EU, it was argued in Chapter 7 that if each Member State decided to go it alone, it would stand no chance of coping well, if at all, in a dramatically changing world economic and political order. This implies that the future for the EU is in this respect already predetermined: the Member States need to stick together and to integrate even more in both the economic and political fields if they are to survive, let alone succeed. But has this message struck a sensitive chord amongst the EU political leaders? This final chapter is devoted to providing a somewhat brief answer to this question.

I should hasten to add, however, that by the future I do not mean the intermediate term, which would be concerned with how the EU should continue to deal with the aftermath of the 2008 global financial crisis, the problems concerning the Eurozone, budgetary deficits, the Turkish membership negotiations and the like since these are dealt with in the relevant chapters. Nor am I asking about how the EU economy will develop in the longer term because this question is connected to the importance of the EU. Therefore, to reiterate, the economic prospects would be bleak if the EU Member States did not stay together and integrate even more by finalizing the Single European Market (SEM) by fully extending it to the services and digital sectors, consolidating the European Monetary Union (EMU) by adding the necessary fiscal elements and so on. Concentration here is on a longer-term perspective regarding how the political leaders perceive the EU future should be since they are the ones who would make the decisions, albeit subject to referendums under certain circumstances.

Since concentration is on the political prospects, in order to offer a meaningful answer, one needs to take into consideration the views of all those who play influential roles in the drive behind European integration and set them against the vision of the founding fathers. It is, however, neither feasible nor desirable to provide a full and detailed chronological account, due to the need for brevity and that only major episodes that highlight the visions are of the essence.

8.2   The vision of the founding fathers

As fully documented in Chapter 2, the founding fathers dreamed of the creation of a United States of Europe. This was because they believed that there was no other means of putting an end to the Continent's woeful history of conflict, bloodshed and suffering. They saw unity as the only way to achieving eternal peace on a continent with a long history of deep divisions and devastating wars.

The switch of emphasis to economic integration came later, but in a reinforcing manner. There were two facets to it. In the early 1950s, with war wounds fresh in peoples' minds, it was felt that although political integration remained the ultimate objective, it was surely out of the question at that time. That is why, when calling for the creation of the European Economic Community (EEC), the Benelux countries reasoned that experience gained through working together in the economic field would pave the way for political unification later on: experience clearly borne out by the success of the 1952 European Coal and Steel Community (ECSC). Second, Europe then, and now, as shown in Chapter 7, stood no chance of being on a par with the US, China and Japan in terms of economic influence and excellence in world affairs without being united on both fronts. Thus, with economic unity being only a means to an end, until a single European nation became the reality, the energies of those dedicated to the dream of the founding fathers were/are still devoted to finding ways of realizing it; political unity was to be introduced through the backdoor of economic integration.

However, there are those who question the wisdom, in the modern age, of creating one nation for either the purpose of peace or for economic prosperity. With regard to peace, they argue that the ethnic-based struggles in Eastern Europe and the splitting of Czechoslovakia and Yugoslavia show that separation may be a more stable equilibrium, especially with Russia then being relatively weak and focusing on economic reform and industrial rebuilding.[1] They can appeal to reality to reinforce their argument by claiming that today there are not many of the founding fathers around and vehemently asserting that their dream is not shared by the new generation of Europeans, who have not experienced war. Add to this the resurgence of national sovereignty, with even Germany, the central protagonist of integration, prepared to assert its national interest. However, European integration has ebbed in the past, especially in difficult economic times, only to re-emerge with renewed vigour. For example, the loss of a decade of integration, following the first oil shock in the early 1970s, led to the establishment of the SEM, which has become the coveted prize of EU integration for the believers and non-believers alike (Chapters 2 and 4). And the recent events in Ukraine, especially in the Crimea, leading to its annexation to Russia, clearly demonstrate that Russia is no longer a non-threat to peace.

As to the benefit of size for economic excellence, some argue that the experience of smaller nations such as Switzerland, Singapore and New Zealand is ample proof that size does not matter. That may in economic terms be so, but as argued in Chapter 7, the destiny of successful individual small nations is highly vulnerable to the activities of the larger nations, now including China and soon India. Hence, in this context, size is of the essence as the rise of China's economy and political power clearly demonstrates.

There is therefore no need to dwell on this issue because the political vision of the founding fathers relates to the long term, the road to which is inevitably far from smooth. It is vital, however, to learn what the recent and present EU leaders think the EU's future will entail, since one wants to know whether their vision contradicts or lends support to that of the founding fathers.

8.3   The vision of contemporary politicians

Turning to the vision of contemporary political leaders, one needs to know their views regarding whether the SEM, EMU and the full implementation of the Treaty of Lisbon (TFEU) are ends in themselves or merely staging posts on the way to greater economic and political union. To concentrate attention and liven the debate, I shall consider interchanges between the leaders of the main driving forces behind EU integration: France, Germany and the European Commission (hereafter, Commission), as well as the largest reluctant partner, Britain. Due to space limitations, I shall concentrate on two examples of interchange, one between them before the adoption of the euro, the other relatively recent, but ongoing, since these should enlighten us about general trends as well as show us whether Britain is still out on a limb.[2]

8.3.1 The vision of political leaders: the 1980s and 1990s

The first example relates to the interchanges that took place between then-British prime minister Margaret Thatcher, the Commission president during the late 1980s, Jacques Delors, and Germany's chancellor, Helmut Kohl. During the summer of 1988, Delors, in a speech delivered to the European Parliament (EP), predicted that 'in ten years time 80 per cent of economic, and perhaps social and tax legislation would be of Community origin'. In early September of the same year, he followed this with a speech to the UK's Trade Union Congress (TUC) in which he spoke strongly of the 'social dimension' of the SEM and called for a 'platform of guaranteed social rights', including the proposal that every worker should be covered by a collective agreement with his or her employer: a proposal that is close to the hearts of most British trade unionists.

Later, during the same month, Thatcher responded in very strong terms: 'We have not rolled back the frontiers of the state in Britain only to see them re-imposed at a European level, with a European superstate exercising a new dominance from Brussels'. Subsequently, she repeated similar phrases regarding the 'nightmare of an EC government' on many occasions. Nor did she confine her attacks to broad policy issues. She also attacked every single practical measure by which her fellow EU leaders sought to achieve progress within the EU. She told a somewhat bemused Italian prime minister (Ciriaco De Mita), 'I neither want nor expect to see a European central bank or a European currency in my lifetime or…for a long time afterwards'. A few years later, she declared her regret at having endorsed the EMU during the 1989 Madrid Summit, and backed William Hague for the leadership of the Conservative Party to succeed her immediate replacement (John Major) simply because Hague had vehemently announced that qualification for membership in his shadow cabinet would require unwavering commitment to ensuring that the euro would have no place in Britain. Hague's choice of Michael Portillo as Shadow Chancellor soon after the latter's return to politics was consistent with that stance since Portillo was, and continues to be, a vehement opponent of the UK's adopting the euro, and actually believes in its imminent demise on the grounds that no single European currency has ever succeeded (see Chapter 6).

The first rebuttals of Thatcher's vehement utterances came not from the 'socialist' leaders of the other European Community (EC) Member

Nations,[3] but from the more right wing.[4] The most outspoken was Chancellor Kohl, hitherto Thatcher's closest ally. He declared flatly in Brussels in November 1988 that

1. all internal frontiers within the EC must disappear by 1992;
2. tax harmonization is indispensable;
3. a European police force is the answer to crime and terrorism;
4. by pooling sovereignty, the EC states will gain and not lose; and
5. the EC must have (in alliance with the US) a common defence policy, leading to a European army.

He did not mention Thatcher by name, but every point he emphasized was one on which she was on record as taking the opposite view.

It should be stressed that Thatcher's stance on these matters suggested that she believed that the EU was predominantly a zero-sum game: every increase in EU sovereignty was at the expense of that of the Member Nations, especially the UK's. However, most of the other EU leaders had fewer illusions about what the medium-sized EU Member States could achieve by themselves: very little indeed. They reckoned that by 'pooling sovereignty', they would increase the range of possibilities for the EU as a whole and thus for their own countries as well.

In short, it could be claimed that the other European Community (EC) leaders saw Thatcher following the example of Charles de Gaulle, whose anti-EC policies in the 1960s held back the EC development, ironically including UK admission. The comparison may have been one which Thatcher herself found flattering; would she have realized, however, that de Gaulle's intransigence eventually did much to undermine French influence for a long time both within the EC and outside it? Yet, despite all this, one should not forget what de Gaulle stood for. In 1967, he said, 'if a united Europe is to be built by itself and for itself without being subjected to an economic, monetary or political system that is foreign to it, if Europe is to counterbalance the immense power of the United States, then the ties and rules that hold the community together must be strengthened, not weakened'.[5]

So what is the message behind this interchange in terms of the vision of the EU leaders in the 1980s regarding the future of the EU? The answer is that, during that period, Germany and the Commission president, as well as the silent majority of the EU nations, saw the EU as evolving beyond the commitments entered into then. In short, they envisaged the EU would become more than an EMU with a common currency and coordinated policies on foreign affairs, defence and justice and home security. Britain took a different view and was supported by Denmark, her closest ally since well before the creation of the European Free Trade Association (EFTA) in 1960, after it became clear that Britain could not go along with what the original Six aspired to. However, since Britain had always seen a different role for itself from that envisaged by the 'Continent', one can claim that the countries most involved with EU integration acted in a manner that suggested that the future would bring about deeper integration. Although this was not expressed in the form of concrete political unity, what is pertinent is that their vision for the next steps to be taken for further EU integration was on the whole consistent with the dream of the founding fathers.

8.3.2 The vision of more recent political leaders

We now turn to the second example of interchange by considering what more recent EU leaders think of how the future should be shaped for EU.

8.3.2.1 The post-Maastricht leaders

Following the Thatcher-Kohl exchange, without a shadow of doubt the debate was opened by Joschka Fischer, the German foreign minister, on 12 May 2000, in a speech delivered at Humboldt University. He began by asking his audience to allow him to cast aside the mantle of Minister and to speak, in a purely personal capacity. He said that

in the coming decade, we will have to enlarge ... the EU to the east and south-east, and this will, in the end, mean a doubling in the number of members. And at the same time, if we are to be able to meet this historic challenge and integrate the new member states without substantially denting ... [the] EU's capacity for action, we must put into place the last brick in the building of European integration, namely political integration'.[6]

He added that this 'finalité politique' would be preceded by the formation of a 'centre of gravity' within the Union: an 'avant garde', the driving force for the completion of political integration. With regard to the institutional arrangement, he asked for

a constitutional treaty centred around basic human and civil rights; shared sovereignty and a clear definition of competences between European and nation-state levels of governance; a division of powers among the European institutions, including a European Parliament with two chambers, a European government and, possibly, a directly elected president, with broadly administrative powers.

With this 'division of sovereignty' between the EU institutions and the nation states, he thus distanced himself from a European superstate transcending and replacing the national democracies.

The speech attracted a great deal of criticism and generated open hostility in some quarters in which the word federation is not in the dictionary of European integration. Also, scholarly reactions have ranged from criticism of Fischer's logical inconsistency in wanting a federation in which the member states remain sovereign, to the fact that he had not worked out the path to be taken to the ultimate objective. With regard to inconsistency, Leben[7] argues that classical constitutional theory recognizes only confederate and federal states, and hence wonders if there can be a third type: 'a federation but not a federal state, as ... Fischer's speech seems to suggest?' However, our concern here is with what political leaders, not academics, think.[8]

A year later, on 30 April 2001, German chancellor Gerhard Schröder added to Fischer's framework in the publication for the November congress for his Social Democrat party. He called for the restructuring of the EU institutions, including the building of the Commission into a strong executive, the transformation of the Council of the European Union into a chamber of European states and the drafting of a constitution for the EU. Singling out the weaknesses of the common agricultural and regional policies, he laid stress on greater transparency by insisting that the Member States should themselves assume responsibility for the tasks that they can carry out more effectively than through a central administration, which is consistent with the subsidiarity principle, incorporated in the Amsterdam Treaty (see Chapter 2).

On 27 June 2000, French president Jacques Chirac, in a speech delivered to the German Parliament in Berlin, called for the formation of an 'inner core of EU members' willing to push more rapidly towards further integration, thus echoing Fischer's appeal for a centre of gravity, which some would rather call a two-speed Europe. Also, he endorsed the idea of a future constitution for the EU. Some analysts saw this as support for Germany's call for EU federalism, while others saw it as politically calculated rhetoric lacking in substance. He stressed, however, that neither France nor Germany envisaged the creation of a 'European superstate that would take the place of our nation states', that is, he was advocating 'not a United States of Europe, but a Europe of united states'.

On 28 May 2001, Lionel Jospin, while still the French premier, spelled out his vision for the EU as a 'federation of nation states', but rejected the German views of federalism and distanced himself from President Chirac's idea of a 'pioneer group' to forge ahead with integration. Noting that 'federation' might appear to be a simple and coherent word, but that it was subject to several interpretations (above), he went on to reject any model based on the German federal system. He added that 'if federation means a gradual, controlled process of sharing competences, or transferring competences to the union level, then this refers to the federation of nation states coined by [ex-EU Commission President] Jacques Delors and is a concept which I fully support'. Being a dedicated socialist, he reinforced his previous suggestions that the EU should enhance its social legislation with the adoption of a social treaty, the firming up of tax harmonization, and a tighter legal framework to enshrine the role of public services in the EU.

Of the EU Member States considered here, this leaves the British government. Tony Blair, the leader of the reformed Labour Party (some argue it is the old Conservative Party in a pleasant disguise) had been at the British helm for a decade and seemed warm towards the EU, hence out of step with the late Baroness Thatcher.[9] After assuming office in 1997, he was sympathetic towards the EU. In a speech (in Ghent, near Bruges, where Thatcher delivered hers) on 23 February 2000, he said that he believed that, by winning the argument for economic reform in Europe, he could mould the EU agenda and in doing so simultaneously defuse much of the resentment Britons felt towards the EU. In short, he wanted the UK to act from within the EU to the betterment of the EU itself and to make it attractive to Britons, adding that British ties with the US had been undermined by the failure of the UK to play an active role within the EU. Later, he committed his government to the adoption of the euro, provided that Britain passed his chancellor's economic tests and on the condition that the UK citizens endorsed adoption in a referendum. However, he remained adamant that he did not see the EU going beyond the economic and that the alliance with the US would be strengthened. The events leading to the 2003 US-British (and alliances) war with Iraq clearly demonstrated that.

On 6 October 2000, in his speech to the Polish Stock Exchange in Warsaw, Blair came up with his proposals for EU political reform, which, given its date, were obviously his response to Fischer and submission to the Convention of the Future of Europe. First, he wanted only the European Council to set the EU integration agenda, rather than merely offering blueprints which the Commission would develop into concrete proposals, but with the Commission president playing a part in drawing up the agenda, the Commission continuing as the guardian of the treaties, and the Council having term presidencies with greater continuity. Second, he did not want to see a single document called the EU Constitution, opting instead for continuation of the prevailing system of treaties, laws and precedents, that is, to retain the British style of an unwritten constitution and to decide on what was to be done and not done at the EU level: thus be more specific about subsidiarity. Third, he wanted to have a second chamber for the European Parliament whose most important function would be to review the EU's work. Fourth, he wanted to streamline the Commission, since with enlargement it would have 30 members and would become unworkable, but he indicated that there was no need to discuss this at that time. In short, he wanted to see the EU as a 'superpower, but not a superstate...an economic powerhouse through the completion of the world's biggest single market [the SEM], the extension of competition, an adaptable and well educated workforce, the support for businesses large and small', all of which amounted to saying 'no thank you' to Fischer. Although he wanted to stress his positive commitment to the EU, this went only so far as a slightly strengthened EU.

It is interesting to note that in his speech to the European Parliament on 23 June 2005, Blair said that the EU 'is a union of values, of solidarity between nations and people...not just a common market in which we trade but a common political space in which we live as citizens'. He added, 'I believe in Europe as a political project. I believe in Europe with a strong and caring social dimension'. And he rejected the 'division between the Europe necessary to succeed economically and social Europe' and stressed that 'Political Europe and economic Europe do not live in separate rooms'.

To complete the picture, one must consider the position of the then-Commission president, Romano Prodi, who was the Italian Prime Minister from 1996 to 1998 and 2006 to 2008. His opinions are clearly shown in a speech delivered to the French National Assembly on 12 March 2003. He asked, 'What Europe do we want? What common projects are we aiming for? Just a "supermarket" or a political area that allows us to defend convictions on the world stage?' and 'a Union that can "exercise the responsibilities of a world power"', and suggested that current disagreements between EU leaders about the war in Iraq 'will eventually help defend the idea on which European integration was founded' and 'when a political Union emerges, it will reap the benefit' of this approach.

Thus practically all the major players were not only still envisaging the EU's going beyond its commitments then but also evolving into some sort of a closer political union. The debate on whether this should be a 'United States of Europe' or a 'Europe of united states' does not undermine this, since, to reiterate, a federation can take different forms. Hence the vision of most of the former major EU political leaders was consistent with the substance of the dream of the founding fathers.

Before turning to the current leaders, some further consideration of federation is warranted. According to constitutional theorists, federalism fulfils two major functions. The first is a vertical separation of powers by assigning separate responsibilities to two government levels. The components and the federation are usually geographically defined, 'although "societal federalism" considers non-territorial units as components of a federation'. The second is the integration of heterogeneous societies, but without destroying their cultural and/or political autonomy.[10] Implicit in both functions is that the components and the federation have autonomous decision powers that they can exercise independently; thus, sovereignty is shared or divided, rather than being exclusively located at one level. Even without the legitimate monopoly of coercive force, the EU has acquired some fundamental federal qualities. As witnessed by this book, it possesses sovereignty rights in a wide variety of policy sectors. These range from exclusive jurisdiction in the area of EMU to far-reaching regulatory competences in sectors such as consumer protection, energy, the environment, health and social security and transport. Also, the EU is 'increasingly penetrating even the core of traditional state responsibilities such as internal security (Schengen, Europol)'.[11] In most policy areas, EU law is not only superior to national law but it can also deploy direct effect, giving citizens the right to litigate against their states for violating the EU laws conferred on them.[12] This is part of a second development, which has been addressed more recently.

> The EU is transforming itself into a political community within a defined territory and with its own citizens, who are granted (some) fundamental rights by the European Treaties and the jurisdiction of the European Court of Justice .... With the Treaties of Maastricht and Amsterdam, however, the [SEM] has been embedded in a political union with emerging external boundaries [Article 11 of the Union treaty refers to the protection of the integrity of the Union and its external boundaries] and proper citizenship.[13]

Not only has the EU developed into a political community with comprehensive regulatory powers and a proper mechanism of territorially defined exclusion and inclusion (EU citizenship) but it also shares most features of what defines a federation. First, the EU is a system of governance that has at least two orders of government, each existing in its own right and exercising direct influence on the people. Second, the EU treaties allocate jurisdiction and resources to these two main orders of government. Third, there are provisions for 'shared government' in areas in which the jurisdiction of the EU and Member States overlap. Fourth, EU law enjoys supremacy over national law: it is the law of the land. Fifth, the composition and procedures of the EU institutions are based not solely on principles of majority representation, but guarantee the representation of 'minority' views. Sixth, the European Court of Justice (ECJ) serves as an arbitrator to adjudicate on conflicts between the EU institutions and the Member States. Finally, the EU has a directly elected parliament.

The EU only lacks two significant features of a federation. One is that the Member States remain the 'masters' of the treaties, that is, they have the exclusive power to amend or change the constitutive treaties of the EU. The other is that the EU has no real 'tax and spend' capacity, that is, it has no fiscal federalism. 'Otherwise...the EU today looks like a federal system, it works in a similar manner to a federal system, so why not call it an emerging federation?'[14] In short, one wonders why the word federalism frightens some EU nations and citizens so much.

One obvious reaction to the position of these political leaders would be that their statements summarized above should not be taken seriously since they were meant merely to set the scene for the Convention for the Future of Europe (see Chapter 2). In other words, given past experience, these positions would have to be greatly watered down if consensus were to materialize, and consensus would be needed since a new treaty would require unanimity. This was especially so when it was being claimed that the Convention was to be a historic moment for the EU, just as the Philadelphia convention was for America, since it would give the EU a single legal personality and provide all its institutions with a constitutional basis for their powers, as well as transfer sovereignties over internal affairs (immigration, cross-border crime, drug trafficking) to the EU institutions. One should add, however, that Peter Hain, British prime minster Blair's representative on the Convention, insisted that it would be much less important than the Maastricht Treaty.

It is therefore pertinent to refer to the draft constitution, submitted on 6 February 2003, to find out what light it sheds on the matter, and to follow this by considering the Treaty of Lisbon since doing so will help shed light on the above-mentioned 'watering down' during negotiations. There is, however, no need to examine the final draft, adopted in the Thessaloniki Greek summit on 20 June 2003, and signed in Brussels in the intergovernmental conference in June 2004 because it is the adopted treaty that is of the essence.

Consider the first articles of the 2003 draft constitution, largely attributed to Valéry Giscard d'Estaing, chairman of the Convention and former French president, and his 12-member 'inner praesidium'.[15] It envisaged a major role for the EU in the economy, foreign policy and even space exploration. Sixteen of its forty-six articles dealt with the EU aims, values and powers. Article 1, on establishing an entity for the EU, stated that it should be 'A Union of European States which, while retaining their national identities, closely coordinate their policies at the European level, and *administer certain common competences on a federal basis*' (italics added). Article 3, on the EU objectives, called for, inter alia, the 'development of a common foreign and security policy, and a common defence policy, to defend and promote the Union's values in the wider world'. Indeed, 'the tone of the document is more federalist than expected', and in particular the 'Commission was pleased with the clause to allow national governments and the European Parliament to give ... the EU more powers' (*Financial Times*, 7 February 2003), if needed for the attainment of the objectives set by the Constitution.

These were labelled surprising proposals, given that the Convention had been entrusted with proposing a framework and structures for the EU that were geared to changes in the world situation, the needs of the EU citizens and the future development of the union. In other words, according to Amato, one of the two vice chairmen of the Convention, the Convention was largely meant to simplify and restructure the EU basic treaties.[16] No wonder Britain immediately labelled the draft 'unacceptable', claiming it went further than expected towards creating a federal Europe (*Financial Times*, 7 February 2003). However, Amato responded in the same article by arguing that the 'institutional structure ... should also reflect and help develop Europe's broader aspirations. Europe must be more than a vehicle of economic integration'. What was even more interesting was that Giscard d'Estaing proposed the streamlining of the EU foreign policy apparatus by the creation of a single post of a EU foreign minister (to replace the two roles then held by Javier Solana, the EU foreign policy chief and Christopher Patten, the Commissioner in charge of external relations) as well as scrapping the rotating six-monthly presidency of the European Council (*Financial Times*, 16 April 2003).

That was the draft, but how does it compare with Lisbon Treaty? Since this is detailed in Chapter 2, there is no need to dwell on it. A glance at the relevant sections of Chapter 2 and the treaty should reveal that the changes have been minimal. That is why many have claimed that the Lisbon treaty is the constitutional treaty in disguise. Thus, it would seem that the pre-Convention utterances were not mere political gesturing; hence, they should be taken seriously.

8.4   The current leaders

Turning to the current leaders, there have been changes in all the major actors who have so far been considered. Angela Merkel has been German chancellor since 2005. Nicolas Sarkozy assumed the French presidency in 2007, but was succeeded by François Hollande in 2012. David Cameron became the UK prime minister in 2010 in a Conservative/Liberal Democratic Party coalition. José Manuel Barroso, ex-prime minister of Portugal, assumed the presidency of the Commission in 2004 and again in 2009, and so stepped down in 2014 to be replaced by Jean-Claude Juncker. Romano Prodi was replaced as Italy's prime minister by Silvio Berlusconi in 2008, but Berlusconi has been followed by three prime ministers since then: Mario Monti in 2011, Enrico Letta in 2013 and Matteo Renzi in 2014.

Following the rejection of the constitutional treaty by France and the Netherlands in 2005, Merkel asserted that the failed Constitution must be revived, stressing that clearing the EU institutional mess must be a priority over economic reform. Sarkozy went along with her and so did Barroso. And although there were some differences between the EU political leaders, the Lisbon Treaty became a reality in 2009. Since the Lisbon Treaty is more or less the same as the constitutional treaty – indeed, as we have seen, many analysts claim it is the latter in disguise (above) – it follows that the current vision of several of the main actors is consistent with those of their immediate predecessors. This is specially so since Hollande has so far not expressed any differences between him and Sarkozy in this respect. The two recent successors of Prodi have not been in office long enough to express where they stand, but there is no reason to believe that they hold different views, despite Italy's complaints about the German attitude on bailing out the Eurozone Member States in crisis. Monti is a deeply committed Europeanist who served the Commission well when he was in charge of the Competition directorate. This leaves the UK.

Cameron has been UK prime minister since 11 May 2010, and Hague was his foreign minister until 14 July 2014, who continued to stick to his guns on the EU. Although Cameron has stated that Britain will play 'a positive, active [and] engaged' role in Europe, he added that 'We're not a member of the euro, nor are we going to become a member of the euro'. He also stressed that he would 'stoutly defend British red lines', warning that he was 'only willing to back proposals that left UK powers untouched'. Moreover, he declared after the 2010 summit that 'of course there are those ... who want to press for greater integration or still seek treaty changes to bring that about' so 'You've got to be on your guard'. He was also absent from the pre-summit meeting of EU leaders from the centre-right European Peoples Party (EEP, see Chapter 3), which included Merkel, Sarkozy and Berlusconi, but this was consistent with his controversial decision in 2009 to pull the Tory Members of the European Parliament (MEPs) out of the EPP to form a new Eurosceptic group, the European Conservatives and Reformist group (ECR). Moreover, at the 2011 summit, he used his veto to block a vital new EU treaty, leaving practically all the other Member States to forge a pact to salvage the single currency. He did so, much to the surprise of Nick Clegg, his deputy prime minister and the leader of the Liberal Democratic Party, a party fully committed to continuing UK EU membership. All are agreed that Cameron exercised his veto in order to please his Eurosceptic Conservative members of the Westminster Parliament, who are scared of the growing popularity of the UK Independent Party (UKIP), the main concern of which is the withdrawal of the UK from the EU. Furthermore, as we have seen in Chapter 7, Cameron has declared that he wants to 'repatriate' a number of EU competences back to the UK and has decided that if his Conservative Party wins the general elections in 2015 and he fails to secure the repatriation, he will offer the UK a yes/no referendum on EU membership in 2017.

After a very long silence, on 16 March 2014,[17] Cameron at last revealed his key priorities for change in the UK's relationship with the EU in a seven-point plan. These points are that (a) powers should flow away from Brussels, not always to it; (b) national parliaments should be able to work together to block unwanted EU legislation; (c) businesses should be liberated from EU red tape to enable them to benefit from the strength of the EU's own SEM and from freer trade with North America and Asia; (d) the UK's police forces and justice systems should be able to protect British citizens, unencumbered by unnecessary interference from the EU institutions, including the European Court of Human Rights; (e) the freedom of movement in the EU should be limited to people who want to take up work, not to claim free social benefits; (f) the continued enlargement of the EU should be encouraged, but with new mechanisms put in place to prevent vast migrations across the EU; and (g) the UK will no longer be subject to the 'ever closer union' that is enshrined in the EU treaties. He added that some of these points would require changes in the EU treaties, while others could be achieved by 'different means', but without specifying what these means would be.

Anyone who has read this book, especially Chapters 2 and 3, would know the significance or otherwise of Cameron's points. Here is just a short reminder. On the first point, as mentioned in Chapter 2, the EU treaties contain the principles of subsidiarity and proportionality; hence, nothing would be done at the EU level unless there is a compelling reason for doing so.[18] Therefore, that cannot be what Cameron means. Nor can he have in mind that the other Member States, especially those in the Eurozone, should not adopt further integrative actions they deem necessary to protect the euro since the UK has an opt-out of the euro enshrined in the treaties so there is nothing to repatriate. However, if he is demanding that the EU should never contemplate any changes in the treaties, then that would be out of the question.

The second point is already catered for in the 2009 Treaty of Lisbon. It is stated in the conclusion to Chapter 3 that national parliaments may submit a 'reasoned opinion' within eight weeks to the institution proposing a draft legislative act, usually the Commission, outlining why the proposal does not comply with the principles of subsidiarity and proportionality. If a third or more of the EU national parliaments submit reasoned opinions (the threshold drops to a quarter for legislation in the field of cooperation in criminal matters), the originating institution is usually bound to review its proposal with a view to maintaining, amending or withdrawing it. So, again, Cameron's point is already catered for in the EU treaties.

Also, there is nothing novel about the third point. The Single European Act (SEA) is doing precisely what Cameron wants (see Chapters 3 and 4). Moreover, as mentioned in Chapters 2 and 4, the EU is in the process of negotiating a transatlantic free trade and investment agreement (TTIP) to open up the American market to EU businesses and citizens. And the EU has a vast web of trade and investment agreements with practically the whole world, including many in Asia, especially with China, the spaghetti bowl depiction in Chapter 2.

The fourth point is left to the end, but the fifth point is one that Cameron may be able to negotiate since several of the EU's richer nations, including Germany, are demanding the same. Indeed, on 11 November 2014, the ECJ ruled, in the Dano case, in favour of Germany, stating that economically inactive EU citizens who go to another Member State solely in order to obtain social assistance may be excluded from certain social benefits.[19] The sixth point is out of the question since it would undermine the SEM that ensures the complete free movement for citizens of the EU. Recall that the SEM was introduced at the behest of the UK during the Thatcher years, so to try to undermine it, especially when Cameron continues to declare that the SEM is what he values most about the EU, beggers belief. The final point is also not new since as we have seen in Chapter 2, all UK governments over decades have wanted nothing from the EU other than pure economic benefits. Nor do the rest of the Member States believe that the UK has the 'ever closer union' close to heart.

However, it should be added that on 28 November 2014, Cameron delivered a speech in a factory in the West Midland in which he proposed the final version of his demands. These are to (a) stop EU migrants from claiming in-work benefits, such as tax credits, and getting access to social housing for four years; (b) stop migrants from claiming child benefit for dependents living outside the UK; (c) remove migrants from the UK after six months if they have not found work; (d) restrict the right of migrants to bring non-EU family members into the UK; (e) stop EU jobseekers claiming Universal Credit; (f) speed up deportation of convicted criminals; (g) introduce longer re-entry bans for beggars and remove fraudsters from the UK; and (h) stop citizens from new EU entrants working in the UK until their economies have converged more closely. He must have woken up to what is stated above, which was written more than six months earlier. Most of these are negotiable, but one has to await the reaction of his party's Eurosceptics.

This takes us to the fourth point. Although the Court of Human Rights is not in the EU lexicon, it should nevertheless be discussed. The reader would be aware that it is about the problem posed by the Abu Qatada case. He is a Palestinian Muslim with Jordanian citizenship and is under worldwide embargo by the United Nations Security Council Committee 1267 for his alleged affiliation with al-Qaeda. The UK repeatedly imprisoned and released him after he was first detained under anti-terrorism laws in 2002, but was not prosecuted for any crime. The UK tried several times to deport him to Jordan, but on 12 November 2012, the Special Immigration Appeals Commission (SIAC) upheld his appeal against deportation and released him on restrictive bail conditions. After several more attempts to deport him, he appealed to the European Court of Human Rights (ECHR), and it ruled on his right to stay in Britain on the grounds that he might be prosecuted unfairly in Jordan. However, finally, in May 2012, the ECHR denied him leave to appeal against deportation without specifying a reason. Consequently, he was deported to Jordan on 7 July 2013, after the UK and Jordanian governments agreed and ratified a treaty satisfying the need for clarification that evidence gained through torture would not be used against him in his trial. Thus, Cameron's fourth point is about ensuring that in the future, the UK would be able to deport such a person without that person's being able to appeal to the ECHR. The upshot of this is that Cameron believes that the ECHR makes it difficult, if not impossible, for the UK to carry out proper security and justice. But to secure this demand would not entail a change in the EU treaties since the ECHR is an institution independent of the EU. This leaves one wondering what EU institutions make it difficult for the UK to carry out policing and justice.

But what is of the essence for the future of the EU is that the leader of the UK Conservative Party does not want to see the EU to be anything other than a SEM. Even here, he has reservations, given his demands on labour movement within the EU and an extensive period of no migration from any country joining the EU in the future. In short, he wants either a diminished EU or a UK only as a satellite.

This leaves us with the leader of the UK Labour Party, Ed Miliband. He has declared that he will not offer a referendum on EU membership unless the EU asks for treaty changes that require the surrender of British sovereignty. Since he has not added anything on the euro membership for the UK, this means that he wants to keep the status quo. However, it does not mean that he does not envisage some new developments, only that they should not require changes to existing EU treaties. In other words, he does not see the EU adopting fundamental leaps in its integrative efforts.

8.5 The dream lives on

In short, excepting Britain's, the majority of European political leaders who really matter envisage a long-term future for the EU that is not limited to what it has achieved to date. Those who share the dream of the founding fathers would stress that this is tantamount to being on the road leading to the creation of a United States of Europe. They would, however, differ with regard to how soon they will arrive at the destination, and what precise form they want it to take. On the other hand, both the Eurosceptics and those who have no memory of past wars or have not at all experienced them would argue that all that is likely to happen is to simply concretize and fine-tune the economic achievements to date.

Recommended Reading

Marquand, David (2011) *The End of the West: The Once and Future Europe*, Princeton University Press, Princeton and Oxford.
Tsoukalis, Loukas (2005) *What Kind of Europe?* Oxford, Oxford University Press.

Appendix: The Causes of the 2008 Financial Crisis

The world has been gripped by the severest global financial (and economic) crisis since the Great Depression of the 1930s. How did it come about? What is being done to dampen its consequences? And, vitally, what measures should be undertaken to insure against its recurrence? These are questions that must be addressed.

However, preventing 'financial crises' from ever happening again is completely out of the question. This is because they are inherent to the economic system. Within this context, on 5 November 2008, during a visit to the London School of Economics and Political Science (LSE), Her Majesty Queen Elizabeth II asked why economists had not foreseen the coming of the financial crisis. In a letter in the *Financial* Times,[1] and later another in the Royal Economic Society's *Newsletter*,[2] I provided the answer with which most economists would agree. I likened financial crises to earthquakes. This is because, no matter how sophisticated the science of seismology becomes, it will never be able to predict earthquakes precisely; it can only warn where they may be imminent. All that can be done is to be prepared so that their impact can be lessened. Hence, what is at issue is what can be done about financial crises, especially those of the 'severest' kind, and this requires understanding their causes. Fortunately, a vast literature has been accumulating on the explanations of the 2008 crisis, so the intention here is not to add to it and reinforce the perception that economists will offer more opinions on a single issue than the total membership of any assembled group thereof. Hence, this appendix is confined to a consideration of the most convincing explanations. Due to space limitations, I shall not examine the recommendations for future action in all the mentioned areas, but will do so for what is being offered to cater for the capital adequacy and pro-cyclicality considerations since they are of the essence and involve many players. Those interested in a detailed exposition are advised to turn to Martin Wolf, The *Financial Times'* chief economics commentator has written a book that not only explains the malaise in which the world, especially the Eurozone, has been mired since 2008 but also, and depressingly, provides a convincing analysis of why the situation is likely to remain so.[3]

Explanations for the financial crisis have been forthcoming from a growing number of analysts. Credit must however go to Turner[4] for being the first to offer a comprehensive rationale for it in January 2009. He did so in a public lecture, based on the definitive and detailed exposition made available in March of the same year.[5] Indeed, the excellent analysis by de Larosière et al.[6] in February 2009 in their report to the European Commission acknowledges this by their explicit reference to Turner's lecture (p. 17). It therefore suffices to confine the exposition to only these two.[7]

Turner begins by cautioning that it is only with hindsight that a fairly compelling and broadly agreed explanation of the crisis can be set out. He then states that the crisis arose from a combination of macro-imbalances and financial market developments and innovations. The first have grown rapidly in the past decade. The second have been in progress over three decades, but accelerated over the past ten to fifteen years, partly under the stimulus of macro-imbalances. And de Larosière et al. reinforce this by arguing that the crisis is the outcome of a 'complex interaction of market failures, global financial and monetary imbalances, inappropriate regulation, weak supervision and poor macro-prudential oversight'.[8]

They earlier elaborate that ample liquidity and low interest rates were the main culprits in the present crisis, but that financial innovation intensified and accelerated the outcomes of excess liquidity and rapid credit expansion. Strong macro-economic growth since the mid-1990s created an illusion that permanent and sustainable high levels of growth were not only possible but also likely. Due to both inflation and interest rates being low, the volume of credit accelerated, and central banks, especially the US Federal Reserve, did not see a need for tightening monetary policy. Instead of raising the prices of goods and services, excess liquidity led to soaring asset prices. Such monetary policies then led to increasing imbalances in global financial and commodity markets.

It seemed natural to surmise that the very low US interest rates must have contributed to the creation of the widespread housing bubble. Both Turner and de Larosière et al. are of the opinion that the bubble was fuelled by unregulated, or insufficiently regulated, mortgage lending and by complex securitization financing techniques. Insufficient oversight over US government-sponsored entities (such as Fannie Mae and Freddie Mac) and strong political pressure on them to promote home ownership for low-income households aggravated the situation. Both recognize that within Europe, where there are different housing finance models, a number of European Union (EU) Member States experienced unsustainable increases in house prices, but in some they grew more moderately and, in general, mortgage lending was more responsible.

De Larosière et al. then provide statistical information, and Turner offers an array of figures, tables and diagrams in support of their explanations. These clearly indicate that in the US personal savings fell from 7 per cent as a percentage of disposable income in 1990 to below zero in 2005 and 2006. Hence, it is not surprising that consumer credit and mortgages expanded rapidly. In particular, the subprime mortgage lending in the US rose significantly from $180 billion in 2001 to $625 billion in 2005. This was accompanied by the accumulation of huge global imbalances. The credit expansion in the US, depicted by a current account deficit of above 5 per cent of GDP (or $700 billion a year) over a number of years, was financed by massive capital inflows from the major emerging countries and oil producers with external surpluses, notably China and Saudi Arabia. By pegging their currencies to the dollar, these countries in practice imported the loose US monetary policy, thus allowing global imbalances to build up. Turner stresses that since China and other surplus countries are committed to fixed or significantly managed exchange rates, their excess savings take the form of central bank reserves, which are typically invested not in a wide array of equity, property or fixed-income assets, but almost exclusively in apparently risk-free or close to risk-free government bonds or government guaranteed bonds. The current account surpluses in these countries were therefore recycled into US government securities and other lower-risk assets, depressing their yields and encouraging other investors to search for higher yields from more risky assets.

In 2013, Yifu Lin challenged this viewpoint, but his explanation is far from convincing.[9]

Turner and de Larosière et al. are also agreed that in this environment of plentiful liquidity and low returns, investors actively sought higher yields and went searching for opportunities. Consequently, risk became undervalued, enticing the originators of investment products to develop more and more innovative and complex instruments designed to offer improved yields, often combined with increased leverage. In particular, financial institutions converted their loans into mortgage- or asset-backed securities (ABS), which were subsequently turned into collateralized debt obligations (CDOs), often via off-balance special purpose vehicles (SPVs) and structured investment vehicles (SIVs), generating a dramatic expansion of leverage within the financial system as a whole.

For example, the issuance of US ABS increased from $337 billion in 2000 to over $1.25 trillion in 2006, about a fourfold increase. Also, non-agency US mortgage-backed securities (MBS) rose from about $100 billion in 2000 to $773 billion in 2006. De Larosière et al. argue that, although securitization is in principle a desirable economic model, it was accompanied by opacity, which camouflaged the poor quality of the underlying assets, thus contributing to credit expansion and the belief that risks were spread.

In turn, this led to increases in leverage and even more risky financial products. Given the macroeconomic conditions preceding the crisis just mentioned, high levels of liquidity resulted finally in risk premiums falling to historically low levels. Exceptionally low interest rates, combined with fierce competition, pushed most market participants (both banks and investors) to search for higher returns, whether through an increase in leverage or investment in more risky financial products. Greater risks were taken, but not properly priced, as shown by the historically very low spreads. Financial institutions engaged in very high leverage (on and off balance sheet), with many financial institutions having a leverage ratio of beyond 30, sometimes as high as 60, making them exceedingly vulnerable to even a modest fall in asset values.

They stress that these problems developed dynamically. The rapid recognition of profits which accounting rules allowed led both to a view that risks were falling and to increases in financial results. This combination, when accompanied by constant capital ratios, resulted in a fast expansion of balance sheets and made institutions vulnerable to changes in valuation as economic circumstances deteriorated.

This raises the question of why investors acted as just described when spreads were very low. El-Arian[10] offers a very convincing answer. He claims that the biggest puzzle of all centred on the reaction of investors, particularly the ability *and* willingness of the financial system to overconsume and overproduce risky products in the context of such large systemic uncertainty. Like others, El-Arian was struck by how two phenomena that one would expect to be negatively correlated ended up being positively correlated for so long – namely, the significant fall in the premiums which investors were paid to assume risk and the investors' desire to assume more risk. He believes that the dynamics behind this positive correlation went something like this. Some investors were hesitant to accept the lower expected returns associated with the generalized decline in risk premiums. Accordingly, they tried hard to squeeze out additional returns. Leverage served as the best way to do so: by borrowing, they could put more money to work in their best investment idea, and this seemingly made sense as long as the expected return was higher than the cost of borrowing. In turn, the leveraged positions pushed risk premiums even lower, encouraging another round of leverage.

Risk management

Since risk management lies at the very heart of the problem, it warrants special consideration. Here, again, there is complete agreement between Turner and de Larosière et al. that there had been quite fundamental failures in the assessment of risk, both by financial firms and by those who regulated and supervised them. They point out that there were many manifestations of this, with a misunderstanding of the interaction between credit and liquidity, and a failure to verify fully the leverage of institutions being amongst the most important. The cumulative effect of these failures was an overestimation of the ability of financial firms as a whole to manage their risks, and a corresponding underestimation of the capital they should hold.

De Larosière et al. elaborate on this by stating that the extreme complexity of structured financial products, sometimes involving several layers of CDOs, made proper risk assessment challenging for even the most sophisticated individuals in the market. Moreover, model-based risk assessments underestimated the exposure to common shocks and tail risks, and thereby the overall risk exposure. Stress testing too often was based on mild or even wrong assumptions. Clearly, no bank expected a total freezing of the interbank or commercial paper markets.

They believe that this was aggravated further by a lack of transparency in important segments of the financial markets, even within financial institutions, and the build up of a 'shadow' banking system. There was little knowledge of either the size or location of credit risks. While securitized instruments were meant to spread risk more evenly across the financial system, the nature of the system made it impossible to verify whether risk had actually been spread or simply reconcentrated in less visible parts of the system. This contributed to uncertainty on the credit quality of counterparties, a breakdown in confidence and, in turn, the spreading of tensions to other parts of the financial sector.

They draw attention to two aspects that are important in this respect. The first is that the Basel 1 framework did not cater adequately for, in fact encouraged, pushing risk-taking off balance sheets. They note that this has, however, been partly corrected by the Basel 2 framework. The second is the explosive growth of the 'over-the-counter' credit derivatives markets, which were supposed to mitigate risk, but in fact compounded it.

They add that as the 'originate-to-distribute' model developed, it created perverse incentives. This is because it blurred the relationship between borrower and lender as well as diverted attention away from the ability of the borrower to pay towards lending, often without recourse against collateral. Indeed, a mortgage lender who knew that his/her clients could transfer (sell) their entire default risks through MBS or CDOs had no incentive to ensure high lending standards. The lack of regulation, especially on the US mortgage market, worsened the situation. De Larosière et al. believe that empirical evidence suggests that there was a drastic deterioration in mortgage lending standards in the US during 2005–7 with default rates increasing.

They point out that this was compounded by the substantial underestimation of liquidity risk by the financial institutions and supervisors. This is because many financial institutions did not manage the maturity transformation process with sufficient care. What looked like an attractive business model in the context of liquid money markets and positively sloped yield curves (borrowing short and lending long) turned out to be a dangerous trap once liquidity in credit markets dried up and the yield curve got flattened.

They are also certain that the Credit Rating Agencies (CRAs) aggravated the problem by lowering the perception of credit risk by awarding AAA-ratings to the senior tranches of structured financial products, such as CDOs, the same rating they extended to standard government and corporate bonds. The major underestimation by CRAs of the credit default risks of instruments collateralized by subprime mortgages resulted largely from flaws in their methodologies for rating (below). The lack of sufficient historical data relating to the US subprime market, the underestimation of correlations in the defaults that would occur during a downturn and the inability to take into account the severe weakening of underwriting standards by certain originators contributed to poor rating performances of structured products between 2004 and 2007.

They add that the conflicts of interests in CRAs made matters worse. The 'issuer-pays' model, as it had developed, has had particularly damaging effects in the area of structured finance. Since structured products are designed to take advantage of different investor risk appetites, they are structured for each tranche to achieve a particular rating. Conflicts of interest became more acute as the rating implications of different structures were discussed between the originator and the CRA. Issuers shopped around to ensure they could get an AAA-rating for their products. Furthermore, the fact that regulators required certain regulated investors to only invest in AAA-rated products also increased demand for such financial assets.

Failures in risk assessment and risk management were aggravated by the fact that the checks and balances of corporate governance also failed. De Larosière et al. claim that many boards and senior managements of financial firms did not understand the characteristics of the new, highly complex financial products with which they were dealing. On top of that, they were oblivious to the aggregate exposure of their companies, thus seriously underestimating the risks they were running. They add that many board members did not provide the necessary oversight or control of management and that the shareholders, the owners, were complicit in this. Moreover, the remuneration and incentive schemes within financial institutions contributed to excessive risk-taking by rewarding short-term expansion of the volume of (risky) trades rather than the long-term profitability of investments. And, the pressure exerted by shareholders on management to deliver higher share prices and dividends meant that exceeding expected quarterly earnings became the benchmark for the performance of many companies.

Regulatory, supervisory and crisis management failures

There is also broad agreement between Turner and de Larosière et al. that these pressures were not contained by regulatory or supervisory policy or practice. They believe that some long-standing policies, such as the definition of capital requirements for banks, placed too much reliance on both the risk management capabilities of the banks themselves and on the adequacy of ratings. In their opinion, it was in fact the regulated financial institutions that turned out to be the largest source of problems. For instance, capital requirements were particularly light on proprietary trading transactions, while (as events showed later) the risks involved in these transactions proved to be much higher than the internal models had expected.

Both Turner and de Larosière et al. point out that one of the mistakes made was that insufficient attention was given to the liquidity of markets. In addition, too much attention was paid to each individual firm and too little to the impact of general developments on sectors or markets as a whole (more on this below): regulators were too focused on the institution-by-institution supervision of idiosyncratic risk, and central banks were too focused on monetary policy tightly defined, meeting inflation targets. And reports which did look at the overall picture, for instance the International Monetary Fund's (IMF's) *Global Financial Stability Report*, sometimes simply got it wrong, and when they did get it right, for instance in their warnings about over rapid credit growth in the UK and the US, they were largely ignored. They stress that these problems occurred in very many markets and countries, and aggregated together contributed substantially to the developing problems. Once problems escalated into specific crises, there were real problems of information exchange and collective decision-making involving central banks, supervisors and finance ministries.

Both Turner and de Larosière et al. add that derivatives markets rapidly expanded (especially credit derivatives markets) and off-balance sheet vehicles were allowed to proliferate, with credit derivatives playing a significant role in triggering the crisis. While the US supervisors should have been able to identify (and prevent) the marked deterioration in mortgage lending standards and intervene accordingly, the EU supervisors had a more difficult task in assessing the extent to which exposure to subprime risk had seeped into EU-based financial institutions. Nevertheless, they failed to spot the degree to which a number of EU financial institutions had accumulated (often in off balance-sheet constructions) exceptionally high exposure to highly complex, later to become illiquid, financial assets. Taken together, these developments led over time to opacity and a lack of transparency.

De Larosière et al. conclude that this pointed to serious limitations in the existing supervisory framework globally, both in a national and a cross-border context. It suggested that financial supervisors frequently did not have, and in some cases did not insist on getting, or received too late, all the relevant information on the global magnitude of the excess leveraging; that they did not fully understand or evaluate the size of the risks; that they did not seem to share their information properly with their counterparts in other EU Member States or with the US; and that, in fact, the business model of the US-type investment banks and the way they expanded was not really challenged by supervisors and standard setters. Insufficient supervisory and regulatory resources, combined with an inadequate mix of skills, as well as different national systems of supervision made the situation worse.

Regulators and supervisors focused on the micro-prudential supervision of individual financial institutions and not sufficiently on the macro-systemic risks of a contagion of correlated horizontal shocks. Strong international competition among financial centres also contributed to the reluctance of national regulators and supervisors to take unilateral action.

Whilst the building up of imbalances and risks was widely acknowledged and commented upon, there was little consensus among policymakers or regulators at the highest level on the seriousness of the problem, or on the measures to be taken. There was little impact of early warning in terms of action, and most early warnings were feeble anyway.

Multilateral surveillance (by the IMF) did not function efficiently as it did not lead to a timely correction of macroeconomic imbalances and exchange rate misalignments. Nor did concerns about the stability of the international financial system lead to sufficient coordinated action, for example through the IMF, the Financial Stability Forum (FSF), the Group of Eight (G8) or anywhere else.[11]

Recommended Reading

International Monetary Fund (2014) *From Fragmentation to Financial Integration in Europe*, IMF, Washington DC.

Legrain, P. (2014) *European Spring: Why our Economies and Politics are in a Mess and How to Put them Right?* Philippe Legrain.

Wolf, Martin (2014) *The Shifts and the Shocks: What We've Learned – and Have Still to Learn – from the Financial Crisis*, Allen Lane, London.

Notes

Introduction

1. Germany's Chancellor Angela Merkel, together with the European Commission and the European Central Bank, threatened to deprive Greeks of the use of their own currency, the euro, unless their government accepted punitive conditions. Greeks have been forced to accept brutal austerity measures in order to continue to service an unbearable debt burden, thereby limiting losses for French and German banks and for Eurozone taxpayers whose loans to Greece bailed out those banks; see, inter alia, Legrain at http://www.project-syndicate.org/commentary/philippe-legrain-lays-the-blame-for-the-disastrous-outcome-of-the-european-parliament-election-at-germany-s-feet and his 2014 book.
2. See, inter alia, De Grauwe (2012b).
3. In mid-November 2011, both the prime minister of Greece, George Papandreou, and Italy, Silvio Berlusconi, had to resign and be replaced by technocrats, respectively, Lucas Papademos and Mario Monti as a condition for bail-out measures.
4. On 15 November 2004, Greece admitted that the budget figures it used to gain entry to the euro three years previously were fudged; the Finance Minister, George Alogoskoufis, said that the true scale of Greece's budget deficit was massively understated, enabling Athens to meet the Maastricht criteria, spelt out in chapter 6, for euro membership.
5. See, inter alia, Dustmann and Frattini (2014).
6. See chapter 8, p. 350.
7. On 18 September 2014, those resident in Scotland, including for the first time 16- and 17-year-olds, voted by 2,001,926 (55 per cent) to 1,617,989 (45 per cent) against independence, with a voter turn out of 85 per cent and a voting registration rate of over 95 per cent.
8. Four centuries, really, as the two countries had had the same monarch since 1603, when James VI of Scotland became James I of England.
9. As happened on 1 January 2006, when Russia cut off gas supplies to the EU which passed through Ukrainian territories.

1 The EU within Regional Integration Worldwide

1. By setting production quotas, and hence determining prices.
2. By Kuwait, Libya and Saudi Arabia, and joined in May 1970 by Algeria and the four Arab Gulf Emirates (Abu Dhabi, Bahrain, Dubai and Qatar). In March 1972, Iraq and Syria became members, and Egypt followed them in 1973. Tunisia joined in 1982, but withdrew in 1986. OAPEC was temporarily liquidated in June 1971.
3. Machlup (1977).

4. Tinbergen (1954).
5. The International Trade Organization (ITO) was successfully negotiated soon after the creation of the World Bank (WB) and the International Monetary Fund (IMF), the so-called Bretton Woods institutions dedicated to international economic cooperation. The ITO was to be a United Nations specialized agency and would address not only trade barriers but other issues indirectly related to trade, including employment, investment, restrictive business practices, and commodity agreements. But the ITO treaty was not approved by the United States and a few other signatories and never went into effect.
6. GATT (1986, p. 42), now under the WTO at http://www.wto.org/english/res_E/booksp_E/analytic_index_E/gatt1994_09_E.htm.
7. Inter alia, Dam (1970).
8. See El-Agraa (1999) for the arguments for and against.
9. See El-Agraa (1997) for full and detailed coverage, and the WTO's website for the latest information.
10. Haberler (1964).
11. Adedeji (2002, p. 6).
12. See El-Agraa (2003).
13. Robson (1997).
14. Active participation suspended in June 2012.
15. Arndt and Garnaut (1979).
16. Inter alia, El-Agraa (2010ab).
17. El-Agraa (1988a).
18. There were and continue to be four such bodies: the Pacific Economic Cooperation Conference (PECC), which is a tripartite-structured organization with representatives from governments, business and academic circles and with the secretariat work being handled between general meetings by the country next hosting a meeting; the Pacific Trade and Development Centre (PAFTAD), which is an academically oriented organization; the Pacific Basin Economic Council (PBEC), which is a private-sector business organization for regional cooperation; and the Pacific Telecommunications Conference (PTC), which is a specialized organization for regional cooperation in this particular field.
19. See Smith (1977).
20. El-Agraa (1988b).
21. Except Slovenia.
22. Plus the autonomous territories of the Faroe Islands, Greenland and Åland.
23. Cuba became the seventy-ninth member in 2000, but has not participated in the agreements.
24. Inter alia, El-Agraa (2011a).
25. The concepts of trade creation and trade diversion were pioneered by Viner (1950).
26. UTR was pioneered by Cooper and Massell (1965).
27. Pioneered by Viner (1950).

2 The Passage to the EU

1. The writer Victor Hugo is noted for being the first to use the term 'United States of Europe'; he did so in 1849 (Luuk van Middelaar, 2013, p. 3).
2. His most noted books are Coudehove-Kalergi (1926, 1938, 1943 and 1953).

3. Greece and Turkey joined NATO in 1952, West Germany became a member in 1955 (more below), and Spain was added in 1982, after the disappearance of General Franco from the political scene. Following the collapse of communism in Eastern Europe, the Czech Republic, Hungary and Poland joined in 1999; Bulgaria, Estonia, Latvia, Lithuania, Romania, Slovakia and Slovenia in 2004; and Albania and Croatia in 2009 to give NATO 28 members, and, vitally, NATO and Russia signed the *Act on Mutual Relations, Cooperation and Security*.

4. See Young (1998) for an excellent exposition of the British attitude towards European unification. Also, see Liddle (2014) for an insider's view.

5. Having reached the conclusion that the key to policy on Germany lay in Paris, US secretary of state Dean Acheson, in a letter to his ambassadors in Europe on 19 October 1949, advocated the founding by Europeans of 'supra-national institutions, operating on a less than unanimity basis for dealing with specific economic, social and perhaps other problems' (see Milward, 1984, p. 391; van Middelaar, 2013, p. 141).

6. See Winston Churchill (1949), pp. 182–3.

7. For a detailed exposition, see Young (1998).

8. The GSP is a system of exemption from the most-favoured-nation (MFN; see chapter 1) clause that obliges the WTO member countries to treat the imports of all other WTO member nations no worse than they treat the imports of their most-favoured trading partner. The GSP exempts the WTO member countries from MFN for the purposes of lowering tariffs from the least developed nations, without also lowering them for the advanced nations.

9. As mentioned, two of the major aims were the creation of the customs union (CU) and the common market (CM). The basic elements of the CU, i.e. the removal of the internal tariffs, the elimination of import quota restrictions and the creation of the CETs, were established a year and a half ahead of schedule (Appendix A2.1 and A2.2 provide their evolution).

As to the CM elements, initial steps were undertaken and measures proposed to tackle the many NTBs to the free movement of goods, services and factors of production. However, laying down the rules for mobility was no guarantee of its taking place, especially in the case of labour since Europeans had a strong tendency to stay close to their birthplace and still largely do (see Chapter 7). Given this proviso, one can say that by 1969 a recognizable CM existed.

Recall that the aims also included the creation of common policies. Because of French demands, sometimes bordering on threats, the CAP was almost fully operational by 1969. However, the CTP was slow to evolve. But transport was not just an industry, rather, it was and is largely a provider of services and publicly owned, and thus not easy to tackle (witness the havoc created by privatization in some EU nations, especially the UK). Moreover, the ESF and the EIB were duly established and were fully operational at an early stage, with the EIB given a treble-A rating: the highest award. Furthermore, steps were taken to create a Common Commercial Policy (CCP), and the Six undertook appropriate trade and aid arrangements in respect of their colonial and ex-colonial dependencies. Also, a rudimentary system of macroeconomic policy coordination was devised. Thus, there was complete success in the case of the CU, and variable and steady success with regard to the CM aspects, although, given their nature, that was hardly surprising.

There is no need to evaluate Euratom since it then involved only France.

10. CEU (1970).
11. El-Agraa (2011a), chapters 19 and 21.
12. Ibid., chapters 23 and 24.
13. EEA membership smoothed negotiations, and Austria, Finland and Sweden joined the EU in 1995 (chapter 1).
14. CEU (1997a).
15. The missing seven were the Foreign Ministers of the Czech Republic, Denmark, France, the Netherlands, Poland, Sweden and the UK.
16. In November 2008, Klaus said in an interview with Czech television: 'I can only repeat aloud one of my verdicts. If indeed all agree that the Lisbon Treaty is a "golden nut" for Europe that must be, and that there is only one single person who would block it, and that person is the Czech president, so this is what I will not do. This is all'.

    As to 'accommodation', while in exile during 1940–5, the Czechoslovak government ordered that all German speakers in the Sudetenland region of Czechoslovakia should be deported and their property seized. Klaus claimed that the EU Charter of Fundamental Rights, incorporated into the Lisbon Treaty, might become the basis for property restitution lawsuits by descendants of those German speakers. He demanded a clause in the treaty guaranteeing that the order will never be invalidated.

3   Decision-making in the EU

1. The Court of Auditors was established in 1975 by the Treaty of Brussels and became operative in 1977 when the EC budgetary arrangements were revised. It is located in Luxembourg.

    The main function of the court is to ensure that the EU budget is properly implemented, i.e. it is entrusted with the external monitoring of EU revenues and expenditures. In exercising this function, it also tries to secure sound financial management and to enhance the effectiveness and transparency of the whole system. It has no legal enforcement powers, so it informs the European Anti-Fraud Office when it detects any irregularities.

    To carry out these responsibilities, the court needs to be independent, and indeed it is. However, the court does communicate and collaborate with other institutions. It assists the EP and the Council, the joint budgetary authority, by presenting them each year with observations on the execution of the budget for the previous year. These observations are taken seriously by the EP and influence its decision on the granting or otherwise of the implementation of the budget. It also submits to them statements of assurance regarding the proper use of EU revenues. Moreover, it gives its opinion on the adoption of financial regulations; it can submit observations on specific issues and responds with opinions to any request from any EU institution. Furthermore, in the reports issued by the court, based on its investigation of documents and where necessary of organizations managing revenues and expenditures on behalf of the EU, it draws the attention of both the Commission and Member States to any outstanding problems.

    The court consists of twenty-eight members, one from each Member State, appointed by the Council, but consulting the EP, and it must decide by unanimous agreement. The appointees are chosen from those who have worked for auditing institutions in their Member States or are specifically qualified for the job, and must meet the requirements of independence and full-time work. They have six-year renewable terms, they elect one of them to be President for three years and they have the option of operating in chambers. The court has a staff of about 900 most, of whom are qualified auditors, divided into 'audit groups' according to the nature of their work, and they prepare reports for the court to help it reach its decisions.

2. The EIB was set up in 1958 in Luxembourg to fund both private and public investment projects that enhance economic integration, and to this the TEU was later added, to promote the balanced development and economic and social cohesion of the Member States. In global terms, the EIB meets the financial obligations of the EU agreements on development aid and cooperation policies. The EIB capital is provided by the Member States, each contributing according to its relative GNP standing within the league of all the Member States, and it is empowered to make its own decisions on the projects to finance.

The EIB has a board of governors, a board of directors, a management committee and an audit committee. The board of governors, consisting of ministers appointed by the Member States, usually the finance ministers, defines the general guidelines for lending, approves the balance sheet and annual report, decides on the funding of projects outside the EU (see below) and further capital generation, and appoints the members of the other three boards. The board of directors, comprising 29 members on five-year terms, one nominated by each Member State and one by the Commission, and headed by the EIB's President, has sole responsibility for decisions on loans, guarantees and borrowings, and ensures that the EIB is run properly and in accordance with the EU treaties. The board also has 18 alternates, necessitating sharing between the Member States, and can co-opt up to six non-voting experts (three members and three alternates) for their advice. Since 1 May 2004, it has been deciding by a majority of those eligible to vote, but who must constitute a minimum of 50 per cent of the subscribed capital. The management committee is the full-time executive and consists of the EIB president and eight vice presidents, appointed for six-year renewable terms. The audit committee, comprising three members and three observers on three-year terms, not only oversees the proper management of the EIB operations and financial resources but also cooperates with the Court of Auditors for the EIB's external auditing.

The EIB is usually invited by the EP to participate in the committees concerned with EIB operations. It also has an input in preparing the work of the Council – hence the EIB president may be asked to attend some meetings of the Council – and the EIB cooperates with other institutions concerned with its activities.

The EIB finances its activities by borrowing on the financial markets; thus, it does not receive any EU budgetary contribution, and is run as a non-profit-making entity. It is, however, different from traditional banks since it does not offer current and savings accounts. It follows three criteria in deciding which investment projects it should fund. First, the investment must be instrumental in enticing other sources of funding; second, it must be in specified fields; third, it must be in the most disadvantaged regions. The EIB has steadily grown in stature and is now ranked AAA, the highest credit rating on the capital markets, and this enables it to raise funds on the most competitive of terms. It is also a majority shareholder in the European Investment Fund (EIF), created in 1994 and located in Luxembourg, to assist with the financing of investments in the SMEs. The EIB deals directly with those promoting large-scale projects, worth at least €25 million, but cooperates with about 180 banks and specialist European financial intermediaries in the case of the SMEs and local authorities.

The EIB activities promote EU integration in a wider sense. This is because about 10 per cent of its funding goes to projects in applicant countries, Mediterranean nations and the ACP countries as well as to some Asian and Latin American nations for ventures of common interest.

3. Following the TEU call for the establishment of a European Ombudsman to deal with complaints raised by EU citizens, the post was created in 1995. The appointment, which is for five renewable years, is the prerogative of each new EP; hence, it coincides with each EP's life. The office is located in Strasbourg, where there is a secretariat whose principal administrator is appointed by the Ombudsman.

Being authorized to act independently as a full-time intermediary between EU citizens, including foreigners residing or having registered offices in the EU, and authorities (only the ECJ and General Court, in their judicial roles, do not come under Ombudsman jurisdiction), the Ombudsman uncovers malpractices in the EU institutions and bodies and makes recommendations for their elimination. The Ombudsman can also investigate on its own initiative. The Ombudsman's findings are referred to the EP to act on. The Ombudsman also presents an annual report on his/her activities to the EP.

Complaints to the Ombudsman must be submitted within two years of their being brought to the attention of the offending party, provided that the administrative procedures have already been undertaken and no legal proceedings have been initiated. When the Ombudsman has lodged comments on an issue with the institution or body concerned, it can respond to them, and it is also obliged to provide the Ombudsman with any solicited information or access to relevant files, except where there are justifiable confidentiality grounds. If a case of malpractice is established, the Ombudsman notifies the institution or body involved, and the latter must respond within three months with a detailed opinion. The Ombudsman then lodges a report with both the EP and the institution or body involved, and notifies the complainant of the outcome of the investigations.

4. The call for this goes back to Article 286 of the EEC Treaty, but it was Council/EP regulation 45/2001 (of 18 December 2000) which enacted the protection of individuals with regard to the processing of personal data by EU institutions and bodies and on the free circulation of such data, and the appointment of the first five-year term supervisor, who has a deputy, was made in 2004, following a public call for candidates.

5. Herman Van Rompuy, prime minister of Belgium from 30 February 2008 to 25 November 2009, became the first EU President and served for two terms, from 1 December 2009 to 30 November 2014. His successor is Donald Tusk, prime minister of Poland during 2007–14.

6. Baroness Catherine Ashton of Upholland, a British Labour Party politician, became the first HR and served two terms, from 1 December 2009 to 1 November 2014. Her successor is Federica Mogherini, a successful Italian diplomat and politician.

7. Van Middelaar (2013, p. 23). Liddle (2014, chapter 7) attributes the making of the European Council into the EU's top decision-making body to Tony Blair when he was the UK prime minister. He claims that for Blair, the key to the EU's democratic legitimacy was that the overall direction of the EU should be in the hands of its Member States; they should remain as the centre of EU governance. Liddle also claims that Blair's big achievement in the reform of the EU was to be the formalization and the strengthening of the role of the European Council (p. 105).

8. Although not usually in the large Member States.

9. Vaubel (2009).

10. In his *Mission Letters* to the 2014 Commissioners, an example of which can be found at http://ec.europa.eu/commission/2014-2019_en.

11. In his *Mission Letters*, another example of which can be seen at http://ec.europa.eu/about/juncker-commission/docs/pg_en.pdf. There, he tells the new Commissioners that he had decided to organize the Commission differently from its predecessors by entrusting a number of well-defined priority projects to vice presidents and asking them to steer and coordinate work across the Commission in key areas of the 'Political Guidelines' (PGs) that he had presented to the Commission and EP on 15 July 2014. The PGs comprise ten points: a new boost for jobs, growth and investment; a connected digital SEM; a resilient energy Union with forward-looking climate change policy; a deeper and fairer SEM with a strengthened industrial base; a deeper and fairer EMU; a reasonable and balanced free trade agreement with the US; an area of justice and fundamental rights based on mutual trust; a movement towards a new policy on migration; a transformation of the EU into a stronger global actor; and the making of the EU into a union of democratic change.

   To empower the Commissioners to deliver on their priority projects, he asks the vice presidents to act on his behalf to help him exercise his rights and prerogatives in their area of responsibility. To this end, the vice presidents are put in charge of steering and coordinating work in their area of responsibility, which involves bringing together several Commissioners and different parts of the Commission to shape coherent policies and deliver results; and assessing how and whether the proposed new initiatives fit with the focus of his PGs, categorically stating that he will not include a new initiative in the Commission Work Programme or place it on the agenda unless it is recommended to him by one of the vice presidents 'on the basis of sound arguments and a clear narrative that is coherent with the priority projects of the [PGs]'; assessing how and whether proposed new initiatives fit with the focus of his PGs, adding that he will not include a new initiative or place it on the agenda 'unless it is recommended to me by one of the Vice-Presidents on the basis of sound arguments and a clear narrative that is coherent with the priority projects of the [PGs]'; and promoting a proactive and coordinated approach to the follow-up, implementation and communication of the priority projects across the EU and internationally. He also asks the vice presidents to manage and organize the representation of the Commission in their area of responsibility in the EP, the Council, the national Parliaments and other institutional settings, as well as at the international level.

12. Most of the 23,000 staff is in Brussels, but nearly 4,000 are in Luxembourg. There are representatives in every EU Member State, and Commission agencies are spread across the EU, as well as in Delegations in almost all other countries. Although the number of people working for the Commission may seem excessive, it is actually fewer than those employed by a medium-sized EU city council (CEU, 2010a).

13. See the Prologue to van Middelaar (2013) for an interesting look on how COREPER came to be.

14. Inter alia, Gillingham (2003).

15. Inter alia, Vaubel (2009).

16. See El-Agraa (2011a, chapter 4) for details, including who are in them and for all that follows in this section.

17. CEU (2012).

4   EU Policies

1. El-Agraa (2011a).
2. Monti (2010, p. 20).
3. CEU (1985).
4. At the beginning of 2014, the average transposition rate for the EU was 0.7 per cent, i.e. only 7 directives were not implemented. But for individual Member States, there was a big variation. Croatia did best (0.1 per cent), and was followed by Denmark, Estonia, Greece and Malta (0.2 per cent). Then: Finland and the UK (0.3 per cent); Lithuania, the Netherlands and Sweden (0.4 per cent); the Czech Republic (0.5 per cent); Bulgaria, France, Hungary, Ireland, Latvia and Slovakia (0.6 per cent). Italy and Spain were on average (0.7 per cent). The rest were above average: Germany and Portugal (0.8 per cent); Luxembourg and Poland (1 per cent); Romania (1.1 per cent); Belgium and Cyprus (1.3 per cent); Slovenia (1.4 per cent); and Austria (1.5 per cent).
5. CEU (2013, p. 9).
6. CEU (2004a).
7. European Council (1997a).
8. CEU (2006a).
9. CEU (1988a).
10. Monti (2010).
11. Kyla et al. (2009).
12. See El-Agraa (2011a, chapter 8).
13. Straathof et al. (2008).
14. See CEU (1988a); Emerson et al. (1988).
15. CEU (1996f).
16. CEU (2002q).
17. Salgado (2002), Nataro (2002) and Ilkovitz et al. (2007).
18. Straathof et al. (2008).
19. The original was Robert Solow's 1987 remark that 'you can see the computer age everywhere but in the productivity statistics'.

20. El-Agraa (2011a, chapter 14).
21. European Council (2000a).
22. European Council (1998).
23. European Council (1999b).
24. European Council (2000).
25. European Council (2000).
26. Kok (2004, p. 16).
27. CEU (2005a).
28. European Council (2005).
29. CEU (2010b).
30. 20- to 64-year-olds.
31. Under the destination principle, tax revenue would be attributable to the country of final purchase. For example, if the UK levies VAT at 8 per cent and France at 16 per cent, a commodity exported from the UK to France would be exempt from the UK tax, but would be subjected to the tax in France. Hence, France would collect the tax revenue, and the UK's exports would compete on equal terms with French products in the French market. Under the origin principle, tax revenue would be distributed according to the value added in each country. Hence, a commodity exported by the UK to France would pay the UK tax (8 per cent), and in France additional tax would be levied to bring the overall tax on the commodity to 16 per cent. Under strict conditions, equivalence would apply: tax revenue and its distribution would be the same under the destination and origin principles. These conditions are that the tax systems in both countries must be exactly the same in terms of base, rules and rates, and trade should be balanced. In this situation the tax collected from foreign countries on exports would be the same as the tax paid to foreign countries on imports. In the absence of these conditions, the destination and origin principles will lead to an uneven distribution of the tax burden between countries. The destination principle requires border tax adjustments, so it was argued that a borderless EU needed a shift to the origin principle. In the absence of the equivalence conditions, both systems involve potential jurisdiction and distortion problems, so it is practical issues that will decide the choice of system.
32. CEU (1985).
33. Part of the justification for high vehicle taxes is to reduce emissions for environmental reasons. The Commission's proposal for a carbon tax was not approved, but some Member States have introduced carbon taxes (see chapter 18).
34. CEU (2003a).
35. The problem of tax avoidance on interest by the use of accounts in another EU country has been dealt with by an agreement to exchange information on such accounts (CEU, 2003b).
36. This of course could constrain government expenditure considered desirable by the population.
37. In order to reduce EU dependence on imports of energy, the EU Member States are in agreement on increasing the share of renewable energy in the EU. The European Council decided on 23/24 October 2014 to set a target of at least 27 per cent for the share of renewable energy consumed in the EU in 2030.

38. European Council (1997b, Article 1.2).
39. This is not the same as Best Available Technology, which is limited by costs.
40. In its 23/24 October 2014 conclusions, the European Council endorsed a binding EU target of at least 40 per cent domestic reduction in greenhouse gas emissions by 2030 relative to 1990. The target is to be delivered collectively by the EU in the most cost-effective manner possible, with reductions in the ETS and non-ETS sectors amounting to 43 per cent and 30 per cent respectively by 2030 relative to 2005. With regard to the ETS, the annual factor to reduce the cap on the maximum permitted emissions will be changed from 1.74 per cent to 2.2 per cent from 2021 onwards. As to the non-ETS sectors, all the Member States will contribute to the overall reduction in 2030, with the targets ranging from zero per cent to minus 40 per cent relative to 2005.
41. CEU (1997).
42. Armstrong (1978, 1985).
43. CEU (1989).
44. CEU (1996bc).
45. CEU (2000).
46. CEU (2006b, c, d).
47. Social exclusion policies aim to reduce the extent to which certain groups are unable to participate fully in society.
48. Which includes discrimination on the grounds of nationality and social security coordination.
49. The EU policy involvement in these areas, however, still varies substantially.
50. A number of studies have analysed the different elements of the EU's relations with DCs, which have provided a better understanding of the dynamics behind these relationships (Cosgrove-Sacks and Scapucci, 1999; Van Dijck and Faber, 2000; Arts and Dickson, 2004; Stokke and Hoebink, 2005).

5   The EU General Budget

1. EU general budget excludes the European Development Fund (see Chapter 4).
2. Moral hazard is the problem that, if the government guarantees the financial viability of banks in a crisis, this may encourage greater risk-taking by banks, which in turn could lead to a crisis.
3. Where the proportion of income paid in tax increases as income rises.
4. There is again a moral hazard problem here: if the government provided adequate pensions, this would reduce the incentives, particularly among the less well off, to purchase private pensions.
5. In practice, responsibility for many services is shared between different levels of government. This may allow some of the benefits of centralization and decentralization to be achieved. It may also blur responsibilities and be associated with problems of administration.
6. It would be difficult to justify such variation for policies funded from national taxation; the call is usually for equality of provision.
7. Oates (1977).

8. Externalities and economies of scale do not necessarily require central government provision; cooperation among local governments may be sufficient, but this can be problematic (Berglöf et al., 2003, p. 9).
9. CEU (1977); Padoa-Schioppa et al. (1987); and CEU (1993a).
10. CEU (1993a).
11. Comparisons of income are probably made within rather than between countries, even with Eurozone.
12. For a different view, see Berglöf et al. (2003).
13. CEU (2009, p. 10).
14. For a discussion of the EU's stabilization role, see Chapter 6.
15. Sapir et al. (2003a).
16. Deficits would be carried over as expenditure, but surpluses are normal because planned expenditure (commitment appropriations) is usually underspent, so actual expenditure (payment appropriations) is usually lower.
17. It also guarantees loans.
18. Treaty amending Certain Financial Provisions of the Treaties establishing the European Communities, *OJ* L, 2, 2 January 1971.
19. If the budget is not approved, the EU works with the previous year's budget.
20. CEU (2013).
21. The same principles should apply to benefit systems.
22. The Netherlands also seemed to be making excessive contributions, but this was largely because of the Rotterdam problem.
23. It was reduced to 1 per cent in 1988, 0.5 per cent in 2002 and 0.3 per cent in 2007. For 2007–13, lower VAT rates applied to Austria, Germany, the Netherlands and Sweden.
24. European Council (1999).
25. For 2007–13, the Netherlands and Sweden benefited from a reduction in their GNI contribution.
26. Shown by the fact that countries are near or on the 45 per cent line, indicating that their income relative to EU average is the same as their contribution.
27. Not all expenditure can be allocated to individual Member States. The categories not allocated are administration for the reasons given above, external action and pre-accession aid – 9.9 per cent of expenditure in 2008.
28. There are in addition methodological problems with the measurement of net contributions (CEU, 2004h, annex II).
29. CEU (2004gh).
30. Further adjustments are made for the capping of VAT and the increase in 'own resource' collection costs for the Member States from 2001. From 2009, the additional expenditure due to the 2004 and 2007 enlargements was eliminated from the calculation.
31. The UK's 2004 net contribution without the rebate would have been 0.57 per cent and that of the Netherlands 0.65 per cent of GNI.
32. The difficulties caused by the UK budgetary situation after the first enlargement, indicate the necessity of accommodating the needs of new Member States.
33. European Council (2002b).
34. CEU (2004e).
35. CEU (2004i, p. 70).
36. European Council (2005b).
37. CEU (2009d).

6 Economic and Monetary Union

1. See Corden (1972).
2. Frankel and Rose (2002).
3. Seignorage is the difference between the return the central bank can earn on providing its currency to the financial system and the costs of printing and distributing it to them. The more a currency is used outside the country, the greater the seignorage.
4. Pioneered by Mundell (1961), with immediate contributions coming from McKinnon (1963) and Kenen (1969), and followed by, inter alia, Mundell (1973a, b) himself and, within the context of the UK and the euro, Buiter (2000) and Barrell (2002).
5. Those interested in a more comprehensive coverage should consult de Grauwe (2012a).
6. These are referred to as the Mundell-McKinnon-Kenen criteria (respectively, 1961, 1963 and 1969).
7. Note, however, that the maximum percentages for both exports to and imports from each other for most Member States occurred in 2004. One can be confident in stating that the declines since 2004 have been due to the 2008 financial crisis, which depressed the economies of the Member States, thus reducing their imports from each other.
8. Corden (1972).
9. Bayoumi and Eichengreen (1996).
10. Capie and Wood in El-Agraa (2002b).
11. Issing (2008, p. 50).
12. Mayes and Suvanto (2002).
13. See El-Agraa (1988a, chapter 8).
14. Sala-i-Martin and Sachs (1992).
15. Fatás (1998); Asdrubali et al. (2002).
16. It is national economies that are important here, because the persistence of large national budgets means that interregional transfers can continue within nation states, albeit constrained by the requirement of the Stability and Growth Pact.
17. There are potential problems such as crowding out and government borrowing reducing private borrowing and investment. Expanding the money supply to finance the government debt servicing can be inflationary or hyperinflationary. This places constraints on governments' use of such financing.
18. Debt markets should have constrained Eurozone government borrowing by requiring much higher rates of interest from governments with high levels of debt. This did not happen until the recent recession made obvious the problems of these countries.
19. OJC (1971).
20. However, avoiding structural and regional imbalances without some form of positive policy is unrealistic. Indeed, this is where the European Regional Development Fund and the cohesions Funds came from.
21. *Bulletin of the European Communities*, no. 6, 1978, pp. 20–1.
22. These revisions ended in 1989 when Portugal and Spain were added, and the same weight continued until the ECU was replaced by the euro. Thus, when Austria, Finland and Sweden joined the EU in 1995, their currencies did not

become components of the ECU, even though the first two later joined the ERM.
23. Ungerer et al. (1986).
24. Denmark was constitutionally required to hold a referendum on the Treaty changes for the EMU. The proposal was narrowly rejected. The EU therefore had to change some of the provisions to make it more attractive to Danish voters. The changes led to approval in a second referendum.
25. Buiter et al. (1993)
26. EMI (1998).
27. CEU (1998e, p. 33).
28. Cobham (1996) provides a helpful exposition of the different possible explanations of the crisis.
29. Austria, Finland and Sweden joined the EU on 1 January 1995.
30. Lithuania failed by 0.1 per cent on the inflation criterion, and since two of the three countries with the lowest inflation rates at the time (Finland, Poland and Sweden) were outside the Eurozone, the decision seemed harsh.
31. Most people are familiar with the *nominal exchange rate,* the price of one currency in terms of another. It is usually expressed as the domestic price of the foreign currency: if it costs a US dollar holder $1.36 to buy one €, from a €-holder's perspective, the nominal rate would be 0.735. But the nominal exchange rate is not the whole story. The person or company that purchases another currency would be interested in what can be bought with it. Are they better off with $s or with €'s? That is where the *real exchange rate* comes in: it seeks to measure the value of a country's goods against those of another country, a group of countries, or the rest of the world, at the prevailing *nominal* exchange rate.
32. Other countries that are currently outside the EU but are hoping to join, such as Albania, also experience constraints through substantial euroization, as did Croatia before it joined in 2013. Bosnia-Herzegovina has a currency board backed by the euro, and Montenegro and Kosovo use the euro and do not have their own currencies. Thus several of those wanting to adopt the euro at an early stage may also be those that are a long way off real convergence.
33. See Liddle (2014) for a detailed account of Prime Minister Tony Blair's enthusiasm for UK membership of the euro and Gordon Brown's resistance, hence the added proviso on his 'tests'.
34. See, inter alia, Barrell (2002), and the various papers in the 2,000 pages that accompanied the Treasury assessment (UK Treasury, 2003).
35. ECB (2001) is one of the most comprehensive and straightforward of the many available descriptions of the institutional arrangements; see also Chapter 3.
36. The Eurosystem has also made arrangements to move to a system in which only some of the Governors have a vote (by rotation). However, it will still be the case that the number of voting Governors will substantially exceed the number of Executive Board members.
37. Sometimes more than one.
38. Monetary policy is set by consensus, so a transcript would be required to judge individual opinions. It has recently been suggested that the Governing Council may soon publish some form of minutes.
39. The frequency at which one unit of a currency, be it the dollar, euro or whichever, is used to purchase domestically produced goods and services per

unit of time. If the velocity of money is increasing (decreasing), more (less) transactions will be taking place between individuals in an economy. In the past, it was believed that the velocity of circulation had a constant value, due to the institutionalized behaviour of societies regarding how money is spent, but recently it has become accepted that the value will change over time and is influenced by a variety of factors.

40. Mayes and Virén (2000, 2002c).
41. The European Council, meeting in Cardiff in June 1998, stressed the importance of sustained and durable growth in promoting job creation. To make the most of growth, it decided to put in place an improved macroeconomic dialogue on economic reforms, with a view to unleashing a more dynamic economic performance.
42. See Hodson and Maher (2004) for a clear exposition of the processes and their role in policymaking. These various processes are brought together under the 'Helsinki process'.
43. It was amended at the end of 2002, at the Laeken Council, by the addition of a social policy strategy, which follows the same form of process as for the labour market.
44. Mayes et al. (2001).
45. What economists call Ricardian equivalence.
46. Buti et al. (2002); and CEU (2002a).
47. The EU was widely criticized for its obviously reluctant approach to solving the debt problem progressively over a couple of years rather than offering a major fund upfront to restore confidence, as had been done in the US.
48. Target-2 refers to an interbank payment system for the real-time processing of cross-border transfers across the entire EU. This replaced TARGET (the Trans-European Automated Real-time Gross Settlement Transfer System) in November 2007. Target-2 must be used for all payments concerning the Eurosystem, together with the settlement of the operations of all large-value net settlement systems and securities systems handing the euro. The business relationships are established between the Target-2 users and their national central banks, which then settle with the ECB.
49. Sinn (2014) for example.
50. Thornton (2002).
51. Keynes identified this in his seminal 1936 book; Feldstein (2002) offers a clear exposition of this view.
52. The study uses annual data for the period 1960–99 for the 2002 EU Member States, excluding Luxembourg, and treats them as a panel. The structural deficits are as defined by Commission.
53. MacDougall Report (1977); Mayes et al. (1992).
54. Mundell (1973b).
55. Björksten (1999).
56. Banking Union, including all the measures to enable the resolution of large banks without the need to resort to taxpayer funds, is only part of an extensive programme to improve the capitalization, liquidity and prudent operation of the EU financial system, including the creation of the European Systemic Risk Board (ESRB), the European banking Authority (EBA), the European Securities Markets Authority (ESMA) and the European Insurance an Occupational Pensions Authority (EIOPA).

7 The Importance of the EU

1. McCormick (2013, chapter 2, p. 165).
2. For example, US president Barack Obama in 2009 for his '"extraordinary efforts" to strengthen international diplomacy and cooperation between peoples' so soon after he assumed the US presidency in 2008.
3. For example, the UN and its Secretary-General, Kofi Annan, in 2001 for 'their work for a better organized and more peaceful world'.
4. For example, Wangari Maathai in 2004 for 'her contribution to sustainable development, democracy and peace'; the award was widely praised as a recognition of a woman (African) creating social change. And Al Gore and the IPCC in 2007 'for their efforts to build up and disseminate greater knowledge about man-made climate change, and to lay the foundations for the measures that are needed to counteract such change'. The award received criticism on the grounds of political motivation and because the winners' work was not directly related to ending conflict.
5. The conclusions drawn by the Council on the basis of the Communication set the aims of the EC-China relationship to be (a) to engage China further, through upgraded political dialogue, in the international community; (b) to support China's transition to an open society based upon the rule of law and the respect of human rights; (c) to integrate China further into the world economy by bringing it more fully into the world trading system and by supporting the process of economic and social reform underway in the country, including in the context of sustainable development; (d) to make better use of existing EC resources; and (e) to raise the EC's profile in China. All the essential elements in the Communication were formally adopted by the Commission on 25 March 1998 in its 'Building a Comprehensive Relationship with China' and endorsed by the Council on 29 June 1998.
6. See El-Agraa (2007).
7. De Gaulle, *Mémoires d'espoir*, p. 839, translated at http://aei.pitt.edu/5777/1/5777.

8 The Future of the EU

1. See, inter alia, Feldstein (1997, pp. 24–6).
2. See Young (1998) for excellent documentation and analysis, and Liddle (2014) for an insider's narrative on the British attitude to the EU.
3. Such as France's François Mitterrand, Spain's Felipe Gonzalez and Greece's Andreas Papandreou.
4. Such as Germany's Helmut Kohl, Italy's Ciriaco De Mita, Holland's Ruud Lubbers and Belgium's Wilfred Martens.
5. De Gaulle, *Mémoires d'espoir*, translated at http://aei.pitt.edu/5777/1/5777, and van Middelaar (2013).
6. Translated into English in Joerges et al. (2000).
7. In Joerges et al. (2000, p. 101).
8. Those interested in a purely academic discussion should turn to the excellent collection in Joerges et al. (2000)
9. See Liddle (2014) for a detailed description of Blair's position on the EU, particularly on UK membership of the euro.

10. Börzel and Risse (2000).
11. Ibid.
12. See Maher, in El-Agraa (2011, chapter 4).
13. Börzel and Risse (2000).
14. Ibid.
15. Easily accessible from the EU website at http://european-convention.eu.int.
16. Giuliano Amato, one of the two vice chairmen of the Convention and ex-prime minister of Italy, Project Syndicate/Institute for Human Science (2002).
17. The Sunday Telegraph.
18. An alternative understanding of this demand is that there is too much law coming from the EU. This is because shortly after promising his EU referendum, Cameron, in mid-2012, set up a review of the balance of competences between the EU and the UK. This led to a 32-volume report and 3,000 pages of evidence in 2014 (https://www.gov.uk/review-of-the-balance-of-competences) which, much to the surprise of all concerned, has been completely ignored by Cameron. This mystery is solved in a book edited by Emerson (2015) which reveals that the conclusions that can be drawn from the evidence is that in almost all respects the balance between Brussels and the national governments is broadly sensible.
19. http://curia.europa.eu/jcms/upload/docs/application/pdf/2014-11/cp140146en.pdf

Appendix: The Causes of the 2008 Financial Crisis

1. *Financial Times*, 31 July 2009.
2. El-Agraa (2010c).
3. See, inter alia, Joseph Stiglitz's review of the book in the *Financial Times* of 29 August 2014.
4. Turner (2009, January).
5. In March, in two publications by the UK Financial Services Authority (FSA), of which he was chairman: the *Turner Review* (UK Financial Services Authority, 2009a) and *Discussion Paper* (UK Financial Services Authority, 2009b).
6. De Larosière et al. (February 2009).
7. See El-Agraa (2011b) for a comprehensive summary.
8. De Larosière et al. (2009, p. 13).
9. Justin Yifu Lin (2013).
10. El-Arian (2008, pp. 20–1).
11. De Larosière et al. (2009, pp. 10–11).

References

Adedeji, A. (2002) 'History and Prospects for Regional Integration in Africa', paper presented on 5 March at the African Development Forum III, held in Addis Ababa, Ethiopia.

Armstrong, H. W. (1978) 'European Economic Community Regional Policy: A Survey and Critique', *Regional Studies*, 12 (5), 67–89.

—— (1985) 'The Reform of European Community Regional Policy', *Journal of Common Market Studies*, 23 (4).

Arndt, H. W. and Garnaut, R. (1979) 'ASEAN and the Industrialisation of East Asia', *Journal of Common Market Studies*, 17 (3).

Arts, K. and Dickson. A. (eds) (2004) *EU Development Cooperation: From Model to Symbol*, Manchester University Press, Manchester.

Asdrubali, P., Sorensen, B. and Yosha, O. (2002) 'Channels of Interstate Risk Sharing: United States 1963–1990', *Quarterly Journal of Economics*, 111.

Baldwin, R. (1989) 'The Growth Effect of 1992', *Economic Policy*, no. 9.

Baldwin, R. E. (1971) *Non-tariff Distortions of International Trade*, Allen and Unwin, London.

Barnes, P. and Barnes, I. (1999) *Environmental Policy in the European Union*, Edward Elgar, Cheltenham.

Barrell, R. (2002) 'The UK and EMU: Choosing the Regime', *National Institute Economic Review*, no. 180, April.

Bayoumi, T. and Eichengreen, B. (1996) 'Operationalising the Theory of Optimum Currency Areas', Discussion Paper no. 1484, Centre for Economic Policy Research, London.

Berglöf, E., Eichengreen, B., Roland, G., Tabellin, G. and Wyplosz, C. (2003) *Built to Last: A Political Architecture for Europe*, CEPR, London.

Björksten, N. (1999) 'How Important Are Differences between Euro Area Economies?' *Bulletin*, Bank of Finland, Helsinki.

Börzel, T. A. and Risse, T. (2000) 'Who Is Afraid of European Federation? How to Constitutionalise a Multi-Level Governance System', in C. Joerges, Y. Mény and J. H. H. Weiler (eds), *What Kind of Constitution for What Kind of Policy? Responses to Joschka Fischer*, Robert Schuman Centre for Advanced Studies, European University Institute and Harvard University. http://cadmus.eui.eu/bitstream/handle/1814/17255/ResponsesToJ.FISCHER_2000.pdf?sequence=1

Buiter, W. H. (2000) 'Optimal Currency Areas: Why Does the Exchange Rate Regime Matter? With an Application to UK membership in EMU', *Scottish Journal of Political Economy*, 47 (3).

Buiter, W. H., Corsetti, G. and Roubini, N. (1993) 'Excessive Deficits: Sense and Nonsense in the Treaty of Maastricht', *Economic Policy*, 16.

Buti, M., Eijffinger, S. and Franco, D. (2002) 'Revisiting the Stability and Growth Pact: Grand Design or Internal Adjustment?' mimeo, November, Centre for Economic Research, University of Tilburg, The Netherlands.

Cecchini, P. (1988) *The European Challenge 1992: The Benefits of a Single Market*, Gower, Aldershot.

CEU (Commission of the European Union) (1970) 'Report to the Council and the Commission on the Realisation by Stages of Economic and Monetary Union in the Community', *EU Bulletin,* Supplement no. 11 (the Werner Report).

—— (1977) *Report of the Study Group on the Role of Public Finance in European Integration,* 2 vols. (the MacDougall Report).

—— (1985) *Completing the Internal Market* (White Paper from the EC Commission to the EC Council), COM (85) 310.

—— (1987) 'The Single European Act', *OJ L,* 169, 29 June.

—— (1988) *Research on the Cost of Non-Europe: Basic Findings,* 16 vols. (the Cecchini Report).

—— (1989) *Guide to the Reform of the Community's Structural Funds.*

—— (1990) 'One market, One Money: An Evaluation of the Potential Benefits and Costs of Forming an Economic and Monetary Union', *European Economy.* http://ec.europa.eu/economy_finance/publications/publication7454_en.pdf

—— (1992) *A Community Strategy to Limit Carbon Dioxide Emissions and to Improve Energy Efficiency,* COM (92) 246 final.

—— (1993a) 'Stable Money: Sound Finances', *European Economy,* no. 53.

—— (1993b) 'Growth, Competitiveness, Employment: The Challenges and Ways Forward into the 21st Century', *White Paper,* COM (93) 700.

—— (1996a) 'The 1996 Single Market Review', *Commission Staff Working Paper,* SEC (96), 2378.

—— (1996b) *First Report on Economic and Social Cohesion.*

—— (1996c) *First Cohesion Report,* COM (96) final.

—— (1996d) *Energy for the Future. Renewable Sources of Energy – Green Paper for a Community Strategy,* COM (96) 576.

—— (1997a) *Agenda 2000: For A Stronger and Wider Union.*

—— (1997b) 'Regulation 1310/97 Amending Regulation 4064/89 on the Control of Concentrations between Undertakings', *OJ L,* 40.

—— (1997c) 'Treaty of Amsterdam', *OJ C* 340.

—— (1998a) *Proposed Regulations and Explanatory Memorandum Covering the Reform of the Structural Funds 2000–2006,* DG XVI.

—— (1998b) 'Financing the European Union: Commission Report on the operation of the Own Resources system', DG Budget, www.europa.eu.int/comm/budget/agenda2000reports_en.htm.

—— (1998c) 'Convergence report 1998', *European Economy,* no. 65.

—— (1999) *The Amsterdam Treaty: A Comprehensive Guide.*

—— (2000) *Agenda 2000 – Setting the Scene for Reform,* 2 vols., www.europa.eu.int/comm/agriculture/publi/review 98/08_09_en.pdf.

—— (2002a) 'Communication from the Commission to the Council and European Parliament', ECFIN/581/02-EN rev. 3, 21 November.

—— (2002b) 'Consolidated Version of the Treaty establishing the European Community', *OJ C,* 325, 24 December 2002, pp. 33–184.

—— (2002c) 'Taking Stock of Five Years of the European Employment Strategy', COM (2002) 416.

—— (2002d) 'The Internal Market – 10 Years without Internal Frontiers', Commission working document, http://ec.europa.eu/internal_market/10years/docs/workingdoc/workingdoc_en.pdf.

—— (2003a) 'External Costs: Research Results on Socio-Environmental Damages due to Electricity and Transport', DG Research, EUR 20198.

—— (2003b) 'Proposal for a Council regulation on the Control of Concentrations between Undertakings', *OJ L*, 20, 28 January 2003, pp. 4–57.

—— (2004a) 'Proposal for a Directive on Services in the Internal Market', COM (2004) 2.

—— (2004b) 'Proposal for a System of the ECs' Own Resources', COM (2004) 501 final.

—— (2004c) 'Building Our Common Future – Policy Challenges and Budgetary Means of the Enlarged Union 2007–2013', COM (2004) 101 final.

—— (2004d) 'Financial Perspectives 2007–2013', COM (2004) 487 final.

—— (2004e) 'Financing the EU: Commission Report on the Operation of the Own Resources System', COM (2004) 505 final, vol. I and II.

—— (2005a) *Third Progress Report on Cohesion: Towards a New Partnership for Growth, Jobs and Cohesion*, Communication from the Commission COM (2005) 192 final.

—— (2005b) 'Second Implementation Report of the Internal Market Strategy 2003–2006', COM (2005) 11.

—— (2005c) *White Paper on Financial Services 2005–10*.

—— (2005d) 'Working Together for Growth and Jobs: A New Start for the Lisbon Strategy', COM (2005) 24.

—— (2006a) 'Directive of the European Parliament and of the Council on Services in the Internal Market', COM (2006) 160.

—— (2006b) 'Implementing the Community Lisbon Programme: Progress to Date and the Next Steps towards a Common Consolidated Corporate Tax Base (CCCTB), COM (2006) 157.

—— (2006c) *A Reformed Cohesion Policy for a Changing Europe: Regions, Cities and Border Areas for Growth and Jobs,* Inforegio Factsheet.

—— (2006d) *The Growth and Jobs Strategy and the Reform of European Cohesion Policy: Fourth Progress Report on Cohesion*, Communication from the Commission COM (2006) 281.

—— (2006e) *The Community Strategic Guidelines on Cohesion 2007–2013*, Commission Communication COM (2006) 386.

—— (2006f) 'Global Europe: Competing in the World', Commission Staff Working Document, Brussels, 4 October 2006, SEC(2006) 1230.

—— (2006g) *Green Paper: A European Strategy for Sustainable, Competitive and Secure Energy*, COM (2006) 105 final, downloaded 22 October 2006 from URL http://ec.europa.eu/energy/green-paper-energy/doc/2006_03_08_gp_document_en.pdf.

—— (2007) A Single Market for 21st Century Europe, COM (2007) 724.

—— (2009a) 'Third Strategic Review of Better Regulation in the European Union', Brussels, 28.1.2009, COM(2009) 15 final.

—— (2009b) *EU Budget 2008 Financial Report*, Luxembourg.

—— (2010a) 'Europe 2020: A Strategy for Smart, Sustainable and Inclusive Growth', COM (2010) 2020.

—— (2010b) 'Ex-Post Evaluation of Cohesion Programmes 2000–2006 Co-Financed by the ERDF: Synthesis Report, DG Regional Policy.

—— (2010c) The Internal Market Scoreboard No20, December 2009, http://ec.europa.eu/internal_market/score/docs/score20_en.pdf.

—— (2010d) 'EU Budget 2009: Financial Report', Luxembourg: OOPEC.

—— (2010e) *Staff Figures*, http://ec.europa.eu/civil_service/about/figures/index_en.htm

—— (2010f) Regulating Financial Services for Growth, COM (2010) 301.

—— (2013a) The Internal Market Scoreboard No. 26, December 2013.

—— (2013b) '20 years of the Single European Market', at http://ec.europa.eu/internal_market/publications/docs/20years/achievements-web_en.pdf.

Coase, R. (1937) 'The Nature of the Firm', *Economica*, 16.

—— (1960) 'The problem of Social Costs', *Journal of Law and Economics*, 3 (1).

Cobham, D. (1996) 'Causes and Effects of the European Monetary Crises of 1992–93', *Journal of Common Market Studies*, 34.

Cockfield, Lord (1994) *The European Union: Creating the Single Market*, Wiley Chancery Law, London.

Cooper, C. A. and Massell, B. F. (1965) 'A New Look at Customs Union Theory', *Economic Journal*, 75.

Corden, W. M. (1972) 'Monetary Integration', *Essays in International Finance*, no. 93, Princeton University, Princeton, NJ.

Cosgrove-Sacks, C. and Scappuci, G. (1999) *The European Union and Developing Countries: The Challenges of Globalisation*, Macmillan, Basingstoke.

Coudehove-Kalergi, Count Richard Graf Nicolas (1926) *Pan-Europa*, Putnam, New York.

—— (1938) *The Totalitarian State against Man*, F. Fuller Ltd, London.

—— (1943) *Crusade for Pan-Europe*, Putnam, New York.

—— (1953) *An Idea Conquers the World*, Hutchinson, London.

Dam, K. W. (1970) *The GATT: Law and International Economic Organization*, University of Chicago Press, Chicago.

De Grauwe, P. (2012a) *Economics of Monetary Union*, Oxford University Press, Oxford.

—— (2012b) 'In Search of Symmetry in the Eurozone', *Policy Brief* No. 268, Centre for European Policy Studies (CEPS), Brussels.

De Larosière, Jacques, Balcerowicz, Laszek, Issing, Otmar, Masera, Rainer, McCarthy, Callum, Nyberg, Lars, Pérez, José and Ruding, Onno (2009) *The High-Level Group on Financial Supervision in the EU*, European Commission, Brussels 25 February. http://ec.europa.eu/internal_market/finances/docs/de_larosiere_report_en.pdf.

Dustmann, B. and Frattini, T (2014) 'The Fiscal Effects of Immigration to the UK', *Economic Journal*, 124 (580).

ECB (2001) *The Monetary Policy of the ECB*, Frankfurt, August.

—— (2003) 'Recommendation on an Amendment to Article 10.2 of the Statute of the ECB', Frankfurt, 3 February.

—— (2006) *Convergence Report 2006*, Frankfurt, May.

El-Agraa, A. M. (ed.) (1983) *Britain within the European Community: The Way Forward*, Macmillan, Basingstoke.

—— (1984) 'Is Membership of the EEC a Disaster for the UK?' *Applied Economics*, 17 (1).

—— (1988a) *Japan's Trade Frictions: Realities or Misconceptions?* Macmillan and St. Martin's, New York.

—— (ed.) (1988b) *International Economic Integration*, 2nd edn, Macmillan and St. Martin's, New York.

—— (1997) *Economic Integration Worldwide*, Macmillan and St. Martin's, New York.

—— (1999) *Regional Integration: Experience, Theory and Measurement*, Macmillan, London; Barnes and Noble, New York.

—— (ed.) (2002) *The Euro and Britain: Implications of Moving into the EMU*, Pearson Education, Harlow.

—— (2004) 'The Enigma of African integration', *Journal of Economic Integration*, 19 (1). A simpler version can be found in 'La integración regional en Africa: un intendo de análisis' (Understanding African integration), *Tiempo De Paz*, 67, November 2002.

—— (2007) 'The EU/China Relationship: Not Seeing Eye to Eye?', *The Asia Europe Journal*, 5 (2).

—— (2008) 'EU "Economic and Human Rights" Examined within the Context of Regional Integration Worldwide', *The Asia Europe Journal*, 6 (3/4), November.

—— (2009a) 'Economic Rights and Regional Integration: Considering the EU and ASEAN Charters within the Perspective of Global Regional Integration', *Journal of Economic Integration*, 24 (4).

—— (2009b) 'Financial Crises are Like Earthquakes', *Financial Times*, 31 July. Also, see related letter in *Newsletter* no. 148, January 2010, p. 16, Royal Economic Society.

—— (2010a) 'On the East and Northeast Asian Communities', *Journal of Global Issues and Solutions*, 10 (3), May–June.

—— (2010b) 'The East Asian Community and the EU: A Mismatch?' *Journal Global Issues and Solutions*, 10 (3), July–August.

—— (2010c) 'Correspondence', *Newsletter* no. 148, January 2010, p. 16, Royal Economic Society.

—— (2011a) *The European Union: Economics and Policies*, Cambridge University Press, Cambridge.

—— (2011b) 'The Causes of the Global Financial Crisis: With Emphasis on Capital Adequacy and Pro-cyclicality', in Jonathan A. Batten and Peter G. Szilagyi (eds), *Contemporary Studies in Economics and Financial Analysis: The Impact of the Global Financial Crisis on Emerging Financial Markets*, Emerald, Hong Kong.

El-Arian, Mohammed A. (2008) *When Markets Collide: Investment Strategies for the Age of Global Economic Change*, McGraw Hill, New York.

Emerson, M. (ed.) (2015) *Britain's Future in Europe: Reform, Renegotiation, Repatriation or Secession?* Rowan and Littlefield International, London and Centre for European Policy Studies (CEPS), Brussels.

Emerson, M., Anjean, M., Catinat, M., Goybet, P. and Jacquemin, A. (1988) *The Economics of 1992: The EC Commission's Assessment of the Economic Effects of Completing the Internal Market*, Oxford University Press, Oxford.

EMI (1998) *Convergence Report*, Frankfurt, March.

European Council (1988) 'Brussels European Council', *Bulletin of the European Communities*, no. 2.

—— (1997a) 'Special Luxembourg European Council on Employment', *Bulletin of the European Union*, no. 11.

—— (1997b) 'The Treaty of Amsterdam', *Official Journal C*, 340.

—— (1998) 'Cardiff European Council', *Bulletin of the European Union*, no. 6.

—— (1999b) 'Cologne European Council', *Bulletin of the European Union*, no. 6.

—— (2000a) 'Presidency Conclusions: Lisbon European Council 23 and 24 March 2000', *Bulletin of the European Union*, no. 3.

—— (2005a) 'Brussels European Council, 20–21 March', *Bulletin of the European Union*, no. 3.

—— (2005b) 'Financial Perspective, 2007–13, CADREFIN 238', 15915/05.

—— (2010a) 'The Treaty of Lisbon', *Official Journal of the EU C*, 306.

—— (2010b) 'Conclusion of European Council 17 June', EUCO 13/10, http://www.european-council.europa.eu/council-meetings/conclusions.aspx?lang=en.

Eurostat (2010a) *Taxation Trends in the European Union 2010*, Luxembourg, EUPublications Office, http://epp.eurostat.ec.europa.eu/cache/ITY_OFFPUB/KS-QA-09–029/EN/KS-QA-09–029-EN.PDF.

Fatás, A. (1998) 'Does EMU Need a Fiscal Federation?' *Economic Policy*, 26, April.

Feldstein, M. B. (1997) 'The Political Economy of the European Economic and Monetary Union: Political Sources of an Economic Liability', *Journal of Economic Perspectives*, 11.

Frankel, J. A. and Rose, A. K. (2002) 'An Estimate of the Effect of Common Currencies on Trade and Income', *Quarterly Journal of Economics*, 117 (2).

GATT (1986) *The Text of the General Agreement on Tariffs and Trade*, Geneva: GATT, http://www.wto.org/english/docs_e/legal_e/gatt47_e.pdf.

—— (1994) *Market Access for Goods and Services: Overview of the Results*, Geneva.

Gillingham, J. (2003) *European Integration, 1950–2003: Superstate or New Market Economy?* Cambridge University Press, Cambridge.

Haberler, G. (1964) 'Integration and Growth in the World Economy in Historical Perspective', *American Economic Review*, 54.

Hodson, D. and Maher, I. (2001) 'The Open Method as a New Mode of Governance: The Cases of Soft Economics Policy Co-ordination', *Journal of Common Market Studies*, 39 (4).

—— (2004) 'Soft Law and Sanctions: Economic Policy Coordination and the Reform of the Stability and Growth Pact', *Journal of European Economic Policy*, 11 (5).

International Monetary Fund (2014) *From Fragmentation to Financial Integration in Europe*, IMF, Washington, DC.

Issing, O. (2008) *The Birth of the Euro*, Cambridge University Press, Cambridge.

Kenen, P. (1969) 'The Theory of Optimum Currency Areas: An Eclectic View', in R. A. Mundell and A. K. Swoboda (eds), *Monetary Problems of the International Economy*, MIT Press, Cambridge, Mass.

Keynes, J. M. (1936) *The General Theory of Employment, Interest and Money*, Macmillan, Basingstoke.

Kok, W. (2004) *Facing the Challenge: The Lisbon Strategy for Growth and Employment'*, report of the High Level Group chaired by Wim Kok, OOPEC, Luxembourg.

Krugman, P. R. (1990) 'Policy Problems of a Monetary Union', in P. de Grauwe and L. Papademos (eds), *The European Monetary System in the 1990s*, Longman, Harlow.

Kyla, L., Tilden, M. and Wilsdon, T. (2009) *Evaluation of the Economic Impacts of the Financial Services Action Programme*, CRA International, Report for DG Internal Market, http://ec.europa.eu/internal_market/finances/docs/actionplan/index/090707_economic_impact_en.pdf.

Legrain, P. (2014) *European Spring: Why our Economies and Politics are in a Mess and How to Put them Right?* Philippe Legrain.

Liddle, R. (2014) *The Europe Dilemma: Britain and the Drama of EU Integration*, I. B.Tauris, London and New York.

Lipgens, W. (1982) *A History of European Integration, vol. I: 1945–47: The Formation of the European Unity Movement*, Clarendon Press, Oxford.

MacDougall Report (1977) *see* Commission of the European Communities (1977a).

Machlup, F. (1977) *A History of Thought on Economic Integration*, Macmillan, Basingstoke.

McCormick, J. (2013) *Why Europe Matters: The Case for the European Union*, Palgrave Macmillan, Basingstoke, UK.

McKinnon, R. I. (1963) 'Optimum Currency Areas', *American Economic Review*, 53 (4).

Marquand, David (2011) *The End of the West: The Once and Future Europe*, Princeton University Press, Princeton and Oxford.

Mayes, D. G. (1978) 'The Effects of Economic Integration on Trade', *Journal of Common Market Studies*, 17 (1).

—— (1983) 'EC Trade Effects and Factor Mobility', in El-Agraa (1983a), chapter 6.

—— (1988) Chapter 3, in A. Bollard and M. A. Thompson (eds), *Trans-Tasman Trade and Investment*, Institute for Policy Studies, Wellington, New Zealand.

—— (1993) *The External Implications of European Integration*, Harvester Wheatsheaf, London.

—— (1996) 'The Role of Foreign Direct Investment in Structural Change: The Lessons from the New Zealand Experience', in G. Csaki, G. Foti and D. G. Mayes (eds), *Foreign Direct Investment and Transition: The Case of the Viseg.rad Countries*, Trends in World Economy, no. 78, Institute for World Economics, Budapest.

—— (1997a) 'Competition and Cohesion: Lessons from New Zealand', in M. Fritsch and H. Hansen (eds), *Rules of Competition and East-West Integration*, Kluwer, Dordrecht.

—— (1997b) *The Evolution of the Single European Market*, Edward Elgar, Cheltenham.

—— (1997c) 'The New Zealand Experiment: Using Economic Theory to Drive Policy', *Policy Options*, 18 (7).

—— (1997d) 'The Problems of the Quantitative Estimation of Integration Effects', in A. M. El-Agraa (ed.), *Economic Integration Worldwide*, Macmillan and St. Martin's, New York.

—— (2004) 'Finland the Nordic Insider', *Cooperation and Conflict*, 39 (2).

Mayes, D. G. and Begg, I. with Levitt, M. and Shipman, A. (1992) *A New Strategy for Economic and Social Cohesion after 1992*, European Parliament, Luxembourg.

Mayes, D. G. and Suvanto, A. (2002) 'Beyond the Fringe: Finland and the Choice of Currency', *Journal of Public Policy*, 22 (2).

Mayes, D. G. and Virén, M. (2000) 'The Exchange Rate and Monetary Conditions in the euro Area', *Weltwirtschaftliches Archiv*, 136 (2).

—— (2002a) 'Macroeconomic Factors, Policies and the Development of Social Exclusion', in R. Muffels, P. Tsakloglou and D. G. Mayes (eds), *Social Exclusion in European Welfare States*, Edward Elgar, Cheltenham.

—— (2002b) 'Policy Coordination and Economic Adjustment in EMU: Will It Work?' in Ali M. El-Agraa (ed.), *The Euro and Britain: Implications of Moving into the EMU*, Pearson Education, Harlow.

—— (2002c) 'Asymmetry and the Problem of Aggregation in the Euro Area', *Empirica*, 29.

—— (2002d) 'The Exchange Rate and Monetary Conditions in the Euro Area', *Empirica*, 29.

Mayes, D. G., Bergman, J. and Salais, R. (2001) *Social Exclusion and European Policy*, Edward Elgar, Cheltenham.

Mayes, D. G., Hager, W., Knight, A. and Streeck, W. (1993) *Public Interest and Market Pressures: Problems Posed by Europe 1992*, Macmillan, London.

Milward, A. (1984) *The Reconstruction of Western Europe, 1945–1951*, University of California Press.

Monti, M. (1996) *The Single Market and Tomorrow's Europe: A Progress Report from the European Commission*, Office for Official Publications of the European Communities, Luxembourg; Kogan Page, London.

—— (2001) *The Future of Competition Policy*, Merchant Taylor's Hall, 9 July, Speech/01/340, http://europa.eu/rapid/pressReleasesAction.do?reference=SPEE CH/01/340&format=HTML&aged=0&language=EN&guiLanguage=en.

—— (2010) A New Strategy for the Single Market: At the Service of Europe's Economy and Society, Report to the President of the Commission, J. M. Barroso, http://ec.europa.eu/bepa/pdf/monti_report_final_10_05_2010_en.pdf.

Mundell, R. A. (1961) 'A Theory of Optimum Currency Areas', *American Economic Review*, 51.

—— (1973a) 'A Plan for a European Currency', in H. G. Johnson and A. K. Swoboda (eds), *The Economics of Common Currencies*, Allen and Unwin, London.

—— (1973b) 'Uncommon Arguments for Common Currencies', in H. G. Johnson and A. K. Swoboda (eds), *The Economics of Common Currencies*, Allen and Unwin, London.

Nataro, G. (2002) 'European Integration and Productivity: Exploring the Gains of the Single Market', London Economics Working Paper.

Oates, W. E. (ed.) (1977) *The Political Economy of Fiscal Federalism*, Lexington Books, Toronto.

—— (1999) 'An Essay in Fiscal Federalism', *Journal of Economic Literature*, 37 (3).

Obstfeld, M. and Peri, G. (1998a) 'Regional Non-Adjustment and Fiscal Policy', *Economic Policy*, 26, April.

—— (1998b) 'Asymmetric Shocks: Regional Non-Adjustment and Fiscal Policy', *Economic Policy*, 28.

Padoa-Schioppa, T., Emerson, M., King, M. et al. (1987) *Efficiency, Stability and Equity: A Strategy for the Evolution of the Economic System of the European Community*, Oxford University Press, Oxford.

Robson, P. (1997) 'Integration in Sub-Saharan Africa', in Ali M. El-Agraa (ed.), *Economic Integration Worldwide*, Macmillan and St. Martin's Press, New York.

Sala-i-Martin, X. and Sachs, J. D. (1992) 'Fiscal Federalism and Optimum Currency Areas: Evidence from Europe and the United States', in M. Canzoneri, V. Grilli and P. Masson (eds), *Establishing a Central Bank: Issues in Europe and Lessons from the US*, Cambridge University Press, Cambridge.

Sapir, A., Aghion, P., Bertola, G. et al. (2003a) *An Agenda for a Growing Europe: Making the EU Economic System Deliver*, report of an Independent High-Level Study Group Established on the Initiative of the President of the European Commission, Brussels.

—— (2003b) *An Agenda for a Growing Europe: The Sapir Report*, Oxford University Press, Oxford.

Selgado, R. (2002) 'Impact of Structural Reforms on Productivity and Growth in Industrial Countries', IMF Working Paper, January.

Sinn, H.-W. (2014) 'Responsibility of States and Central Banks in the Euro Crisis', *CESifo Forum*, 15(1).

Stokke, O. and Hoebink, P. (2005) *Perspectives on European Development Cooperation*, Routledge, London.

Straathof, B., Linders, G-J., Lejour, A. and Möhlmann, J. (2008) 'The Internal Market and the Dutch Economy: Implications for Trade and Economic Growth', CPB Document 168, CPB Netherlands Bureau for Economic Policy Analysis, http://www.cpb.nl/eng/pub/cpbreeksen/document/168/doc168.pdf.

Teasdale, A. and Bainbridge, T. (2012) *The Penguin Companion to the European Union*, Penguin Books, London.

Thornton, D. L. (2002) 'Monetary Policy Transparency: Transparent about What?' Federal Reserve Bank of St. Louis Working Paper 2002–028A, November.

Tinbergen, J. (1954) *International Economic Integration*, Elsevier, Amsterdam.

Tsoukalis, Loukas (2005) *What Kind of Europe?* Oxford, Oxford University Press.

Turner, Adair (2009) 'The Financial Crisis and the Future of Financial Regulation', *The Economist*'s Inaugural City Lecture, 21 January, http://www.fsa.gov.uk/pages/Library/Communications/Speeches/2009/0121_at.shtml.

UK Financial Services Authority (FSA) (2008) *Strengthening Liquidity Standards*, December. Access from the FSA's website: http://www.fsa.gov.uk/.

UK Financial Services Authority (FSA) (2009a) *The Turner Review: A Regulatory Response to the Global Banking Crisis*, March. Access from the FSA's website: http://www.fsa.gov.uk/

UK Financial Services Authority (FSA) (2009b) *A Regulatory Response to the Global Banking Crisis*, a Discussion Paper, March. Access from the FSA's website: http://www.fsa.gov.uk/.

UK Treasury (2003) *UK Membership of the Single Currency: An Assessment of the Five Economic Tests*. http://assessment.treasury.gov.uk.

Ungerer, H., Evans, D. and Nyberg, P. (1986) 'The European Monetary System – Recent Developments', *Occasional Papers*, no. 48, IMF.

Van Dijck, P. and Faber, G. (eds) (2000) *The External Economic Dimension of the European Union*, Kluwer Law International, Dordrecht.

Van Middelaar, L. (2013) *The Passage to Europe: How a Continent Became a Union*, Yale University Press, New Haven and London.

Vaubel, R. (2009) *The European Institutions as an Interest Group*, The Institute of Economic Affairs, London.

Viner, J. (1950) *The Customs Union Issue*, Carnegie Endowment for International Peace, New York.

Winston S. Churchill (1949) *The Second World War, vol. II: The Finest Hour*, Cassell & Co. Ltd, London.

Wolf, M. (2014) *The Shifts and the Shocks: What We've Learned – and Have Still to Learn – from the Financial Crisis*, Allen Lane, London.

WTOathttp://www.wto.org/english/res_e/booksp_e/analytic_index_e/gatt1994_09_e.htm.

Young, H. (1998) *This Blessed Plot: Britain and Europe from Churchill to Blair*, Macmillan, Basingstoke.

Yifu Lin, J. (2013) *Against the Consensus: Reflections on the Great Recession*, Cambridge University Press, Cambridge and New York.

Author Index

Subject Index

Page numbers in *italics* indicate tables or figures

CPSIA information can be obtained at www.ICGtesting.com
Printed in the USA
LVOW04s1827080515

437791LV00011B/190/P

9 781137 533647